CRITICAL
INSIGHTS

F. Scott Fitzgerald

CRITICAL INSIGHTS

F. Scott Fitzgerald

Editor
Don Noble
University of Alabama

Salem Press
Pasadena, California   Hackensack, New Jersey

Cover photo: Hulton Archive/Getty Images

Published by Salem Press

© 2011 by EBSCO Publishing
Editor's text © 2011 by Don Noble
"The *Paris Review* Perspective" © 2011 by Elizabeth Gumport for *The Paris Review*

∞ The paper used in these volumes conforms to the American National Standard for Permanence of Paper for Printed Library Materials, Z39.48-1992 (R1997).

Library of Congress Cataloging-in-Publication Data
F. Scott Fitzgerald / editor, Don Noble.
    p. cm. — (Critical insights)
Includes bibliographical references and index.
ISBN 978-1-58765-693-4 (alk. paper)
    1. Fitzgerald, F. Scott (Francis Scott), 1896-1940—Criticism and interpretation. I. Noble, Donald R.
PS3511.I9Z61376 2010
813'.52—dc22

2010029151

PRINTED IN CANADA

Contents_____

Career, Life, and Influence_____

Critical Contexts_____

Critical Readings_____

Resources

About This Volume

Don Noble

The status of F. Scott Fitzgerald in the American literary canon now seems secure. In the decades since the Fitzgerald revival of the late 1940s and 1950s, *The Great Gatsby* has risen to be regarded as the quintessential classic American novel, and the reputation of *Tender Is the Night* has grown steadily. Several of Fitzgerald's stories, such as "The Rich Boy" and "Babylon Revisited," have long been regarded as permanent, and now there is more respect being shown even for the author's once lightly regarded magazine work, such as the Pat Hobby stories.

Fitzgerald, along with his contemporaries William Faulkner, Ernest Hemingway, and John Steinbeck, is among the most written-about authors in the American canon. The Annual PMLA Bibliography usually shows Fitzgerald to be the third-most-discussed American author, after Nobel laureates Faulkner and Hemingway but ahead of laureate Steinbeck. This volume, then, makes perhaps its strongest contribution with its original essays, but it also presents a rich selection of previously published essays on many different aspects of Fitzgerald's work as well as his relationship to the American culture of the first half of the twentieth century.

Following an introductory essay and a brief biographical essay on Fitzgerald, Elizabeth Gumport, writing for *The Paris Review*, closes out the first section of this collection with a brief "perspective." Fitzgerald, she reminds us, may be associated in the popular mind with the 1920s, but today his work feels "more contemporary than ever." We are still a nation of dreamers, still believing that our financial and emotional resources are inexhaustible even in the face of bankruptcy, both personal and economic.

Critical Contexts

This section of new essays begins at the heart of the matter. As Jennifer Banach reminds readers early on, the American Dream is probably Fitzgerald's "signature theme." This idea, this concept, so important to Fitzgerald and, indeed, to most Americans, is widespread, one might even say ubiquitous, in Fitzgerald's novels and short stories as well as in his nonfiction, especially his once very controversial *Esquire* essays known collectively as *The Crack-Up*.

Fitzgerald may have written many times on this theme, but all his work is in the nature of exploration, not explication, for his attitudes were contradictory and shifting. On one hand, Fitzgerald, along with many of his characters, sought fame, wealth, and upward social mobility. One would be hard-pressed to be against these desires. Traditionally, in the mode of Benjamin Franklin or a Horatio Alger hero, an individual rises through the application of industry, sobriety, and thrift. But few Fitzgerald characters, like their creator, show much interest in these virtues.

Banach also suggests that Fitzgerald sounds a warning about the dangers inherent in placing too much faith in the American Dream, especially with *The Great Gatsby*. Gatsby presumes that his wealth will give him social status, enable him to reunite with the rich girl, Daisy, and grant him perfect happiness and fulfillment—a heaven on earth. Faith in wealth, Banach suggests, becomes a kind of religion that replaces the traditional faith that was mostly lost in the American 1920s. Alas, man cannot achieve bliss through money alone.

Suzanne del Gizzo's essay, "Within and Without: F. Scott Fitzgerald and American Consumer Culture," picks up some of these same themes. Again, Fitzgerald's attitude toward the American Dream is shown to be complex. Money is "enchanting" but also "dangerous." Wealth is "empowering" and "corrupting." His characters yearn to join the upper classes but have a poor sense of the ethical costs of obsessively accumulating wealth.

The 1920s were special, del Gizzo argues, in that wealth could be accumulated quickly and society's values were shifting from a culture of production to a culture of consumption. People were judged less by what Victorians might call "character" and more by what we know as "personality." And personality, a person's public image, is, of course, bolstered and reinforced by objects such as homes, cars, and clothes.

Again, inevitably in Fitzgerald, the issue of class intrudes. Can conspicuous consumption and pecuniary emulation, to use Thorstein Veblen's terms, admit one to the upper class? For Fitzgerald, the answer is no, especially when the newly rich fail to get the details quite right. Gatsby's mansion, a replica of a French city hall, is grotesquely oversized, his parties too large and loud, his suit too pink, and his Britishisms—such as "Old Sport"—fail to ring true. Tom Buchanan, on the other hand, though morally reprehensible and even despicable, really is of the upper class, complete with polo ponies.

Del Gizzo, like Banach, reminds the reader of Fitzgerald's own upper-middle-class background. His father, a distant relative of Francis Scott Key, who wrote the words to the song that became the American national anthem, was of an old, solid, respectable Maryland family, while his mother's family had the money, earned in St. Paul, Minnesota, through a wholesale grocery business. Fitzgerald, at the Newman School in New Jersey and later at Princeton University, found himself among old money and the upper classes but not of them.

Del Gizzo also spends some time discussing the plight of Dr. Dick Diver in *Tender Is the Night*. Having married the incredibly wealthy Nicole Warren, Diver tries, with no success, to maintain his integrity by keeping his finances separate from his wife's and to avoid being swamped by the Warren family fortune. It can't be done. Money is powerful and, like floodwaters, hard to hold back.

It is ironic, as all commentators on Fitzgerald's relationship to wealth have remarked in some degree, that *Tender* received only a disappointing, lukewarm critical reception. In part, this was because, then in the midst of a worldwide depression, critics found Fitzgerald's story of rich American expatriates on the French Riviera frivolous; to them, it was not empathetic to the miseries of the masses, nor was it Marxist or politically sensitive enough. However, Fitzgerald's own attitudes toward capitalism and wealth were too ambivalent for the novel to merit this reception, and there is still more work to be done in this area.

Cathy W. Barks, as bibliographer of the F. Scott Fitzgerald Society, is just the right person to comment on the critical reception of Fitzgerald. It is an interesting and sometimes ironic story, as in the case of *Tender*. Fitzgerald labored for nine years on that novel, and not only were the economic times against him but also, as Barks observes, Fitzgerald's reputation as a hard-drinking, dissolute partygoer was no longer considered admirable or cute. Barks reminds us, however, that over time opinion on *Tender* has shifted, and most readers, no longer affected by the economic conditions of the Great Depression or by Fitzgerald's public persona, place *Tender* on the top shelf right next to *Gatsby*.

Likewise, the essays gathered in *The Crack-Up*, which were received with dismay by many and with horror by Fitzgerald's friend Hemingway, are now held in high regard. The painful, honest, confessional mode they employ was unknown in Fitzgerald's time, but it has since become a commonplace with the work of Robert Lowell and other confessional poets, the interchapters of Norman Mailer's *Advertisements for Myself*, and, more recently, the advent of the tell-all (and more) memoir.

With his first two novels and with the stories of the 1920s, however, Fitzgerald had been wholly in synch with American culture. As Barks reminds us, Fitzgerald was thought to have captured the period's zeitgeist perfectly with his depictions of the "rhythms, fads, and beliefs of a new generation who were different in every way from their parents." And for this he was rewarded with huge sales, mostly great reviews, and national celebrity. Reviewers got it dead right about *Gatsby* as well, recognizing the novel as a masterpiece from the start. Fitzgerald's fellow fiction writers especially "got it," and Conrad Aiken in particular wrote of the tragic nature of Jay Gatsby.

Of the story collections, Barks reminds us, the reviewers said what reviewers always say about story collections. The contents were of a "mixed" nature, "uneven in quality." The critical judgments were none too bad, however. As Barks tells us, from *Flappers and Philosophers*, critics praised "The Ice Palace" and "Bernice Bobs Her Hair," while in the collection *All the Sad Young Men* they praised "The Rich Boy" and "Winter Dreams."

The Last Tycoon, the unfinished Hollywood novel, is a fascinating enigma to Barks, as it is to us all. Fitzgerald was on the wagon when he began it and returning to form. Would this have been his best work ever, the best Hollywood novel ever? If Fitzgerald had lived would he have joined his peers as a recipient of the Nobel Prize in Literature? Or do we overvalue *The Last Tycoon* because it ends suddenly, shockingly early and still full of promise, as Fitzgerald himself did?

In any case, Fitzgerald did die in 1940, at the nadir of his career and in relative obscurity, with little in print and even those works selling poorly. Then came the amazing "revival," which Barks, like all commentators, describes ecstatically. Fitzgerald's Princeton friend Edmund Wilson edited and published the *Esquire* essays in *The Crack-Up* and edited *The Last Tycoon* in the 1940s while Dorothy Parker edited Viking's *Portable F. Scott Fitzgerald*. In the 1950s Malcolm Cowley edited the stories, and Alfred Kazin put together his collection of essays. The resurrection was achieved when Arthur Mizener in 1951 and then Andrew Turnbull in 1962 published biographical studies

Following this period, we have had an avalanche of criticism and biographies, much of it by Matthew J. Bruccoli. Fitzgerald's fiction and nonfiction works have been collected and published, and we now have good bibliographies and collections of letters in various arrangements. Most recently there have been studies of Fitzgerald and gender, consumer culture, celebrity, youth culture, popular culture, and, most interesting perhaps, Fitzgerald and the intellectual currents of the 1920s. Fitzgerald—who was no honor student at Princeton, to say the least— turns out to have more intellectual gravitas than anyone had suspected.

The Fitzgerald revival, however extensive, did not shine any light on the short story "The Curious Case of Benjamin Button." It took a Hollywood film to do that. Matthew J. Bolton's essay on the adaptation of the Fitzgerald story to the big screen might have followed the very conventional line of pointing out the ways in which the screenplay remains "faithful" to the original and the ways in which it diverges. Happily, Bolton does much more. Referencing Jorge Luis Borges, Bolton reminds us that translation from one language to another—or, in this case, from one artistic medium to another—requires that the work be, in fact, "reinvented." As Bolton explains, the adaptation created by director David Fincher and screenwriter Eric Roth changes "Benjamin Button" from satirical fantasy to sentimental romance. Critics have noted that Roth's screenplay for "Button" is similar to the screenplay he wrote for the novel *Forrest Gump*, and of course the resemblances spring from the material as well as from the screenwriter's mind. Both fictions are fantastic, picaresque, and episodic, and the screenwriter, like any other writer, has a style and repeats the techniques that have been successful for him in the past.

Roth and Fincher started, of course, with the story, which is not typical of Fitzgerald. "Button," like "The Diamond as Big as the Ritz," is not a flapper story, and it did not appear in the *Saturday Evening Post.* It was a story Fitzgerald wrote because his muse, not his finances, required it. The story's plot, the protagonist, and the premise are all retained in Roth's adaptation: Button is born with the body of a seventy-year-old man, and as he ages he grows physically younger. But whereas in the story he is born the size of a man, in the movie he is born the size of a baby; another divergence is that in the story, his attitudes and behavior are controlled by the age of his body, but in the movie, Button learns from and is formed by experience. Whereas in the story Button simply loses interest in his wife as she grows older and he grows younger, in the film Button, sadly, feels he must exile himself from his wife, Daisy, and the daughter he loves. His "youthing" is melancholy, even tragic, not a humorous subject as it is in the story.

Of course, on the screen, special effects are required, and Bolton does a fine job of explaining how Roth decided to use the techniques of "magical realism," as, for instance, Gabriel García Márquez does in *One Hundred Years of Solitude*, to portray the fantastic as if it were an everyday occurrence. These techniques were not commonplace in Fitzgerald's day, but they work smoothly now because audiences have since become familiar with them.

Critical Readings

This volume's section of critical readings, chosen from a wide variety of sources, old and new, ranges widely over the vast territory of Fitzgerald studies, arranged roughly in the order of publication of the Fitzgerald works discussed. We begin with Kirk Curnutt's discussion of Fitzgerald's first two novels, *This Side of Paradise* and *The Beautiful and Damned*, and what Curnutt calls "the spectacle of waste." Traditionally, youth is temporary, only a phase, a stage, before one grows up and into adult responsibilities. But in these two hugely successful books, Fitzgerald's youths are golden and idealized, and his heroes are less definite as they navigate their entrance into adulthood. Like all youths, they have little power, except to discomfit their elders with rebellion. They have the power of "display" and can dramatize their discontent with shocking behavior.

In *This Side of Paradise*, Amory Blaine and his friends fear growing up, with its attendant corruption and loss of idealism. But grow up one must, and since youth will be lost, it must first be used. Curnutt argues that "wasted youth" is a genuine contradiction, for only by "wasting" it in pleasure and excess can one use it to its fullest, thus demonstrating how valuable an asset it truly is. But where Amory fears growing up, Curnutt argues, the Patches in *The Beautiful and Damned* dread growing old. They "ravage themselves" in dissipation because they feel it is the only victory possible over the inevitable ravages of time. As Curnutt writes, the book "elaborates upon Fitzgerald's belief that, given the temporal fixity of youth, its only practical value is the brief pleasure offered by its consumption." Sadly, dissipation does not prolong youth, and Gloria, at twenty-nine, looks too old to play the vamp in a film—"'Oh, my pretty face,'" she cries upon her discovery of this reality, "'Oh, I don't want to live without my pretty face'"—and Anthony, at thirty-three, looks forty.

Ruth Prigozy, in her essay "F. Scott and Zelda Fitzgerald in American Popular Culture," writes of when the Fitzgeralds were definitely not yet aged. The young, beautiful, glamorous couple were in fact the darlings of American popular culture for a number of years as they appeared on the covers of magazines and were written up in the papers. How did this happen? Prigozy suggests that, at least in part, they made it happen. They courted the media and gave outrageous interviews in which Scott all but bragged about his drinking and Zelda spoke of her wild spending. They rode on the roofs of taxicabs and jumped into public fountains. They made good "copy," to say the least, and, perhaps, originated the role of the glamorous celebrity couple in American popular culture. Like the roaring twenties they chronicled and even helped create, the Fitzgeralds went silent after the crash. When the Fitzgerald revival got under way in the late 1940s, along with reevaluations of the actual works, the Fitzgeralds became objects in a cautionary tale of the dangers of drink and the tragedy of madness and went from being glamorous icons to tragic examples of the dangers of wretched excess. What will the future hold? Prigozy is optimistic that balance will be achieved and that, once the biographers stop emphasizing the alcohol and the madness, we will again see the Fitzgeralds and their literary achievements clear and whole.

Scott Donaldson, a Fitzgerald biographer and critic, takes as his subject Fitzgerald and the South. Since we all know that Fitzgerald was a son of St. Paul and, like his narrator in *Gatsby*, one who came east, Fitzgerald's deep and abiding concern with southernness may seem odd, but Donaldson finds two major reasons for it. First was his father, Edward, a man Scott deeply respected. He felt his father possessed good judgment and fundamental decency along with good manners, respect for one's elders, and a sense of tradition. Edward Fitzgerald was from a respectable, even distinguished, Maryland family, and his great-great-grandfather was the brother of Francis Scott Key. As Donaldson shows, Fitzgerald often thought in terms of what his father would think or do, and he gave Dick Diver very similar thoughts. Scott also very much liked the four years he and Zelda lived in and around Baltimore, as he felt the city to be, in some way, home.

Second, as crucial, was that Scott met Zelda Sayre, the daughter of an Alabama Supreme Court justice, at a country-club dance while he was stationed at Camp Sheridan, outside Montgomery. The southern girl became an important and recurring character in Fitzgerald's fiction, at first as the dream girl incarnate, though her image was slowly tarnished as, Donaldson writes, Scott's "disillusionment" was "spun out in half a dozen stories" of the 1920s.

"The Ice Palace" is the most balanced of these southern girl stories, as southern warmth and gentle manners are compared to cold Yankee brusqueness and energy. Sally Carrol Happer is the narrator and a sympathetic character. In "Gretchen's Forty Winks" and "'The Sensible Thing,'" however, the southern girl is much less sympathetic. In each case, the girl wants the ease and affluence her husband's success will bring but has no patience for the time and work necessary to achieve that affluence. These girls are not "helpmeets" in any sense.

The harshest rejection of the southern girl, however, can be found in "The Last of the Belles." In this story, the belle, Ailie Calhoun, whom Donaldson calls a "heartless coquette," is so self-centered she cannot even feel grief at the suicide of a rejected lover. Instead, she only worries about what people will think. The northern boy, Andy, has his epiphany and that dream is over.

Although Fitzgerald would continue to write magazine stories throughout the rest of his life, the centerpiece of his work in the 1930s was *Tender Is the Night*. Edwin S. Fussell, Michael K. Glenday, and

James H. Meredith all write on different aspects of this novel, which, through critical reappraisal, has grown in stature over the past decade.

Edwin Fussell, a historian, warns of the dangers of repudiating history, tradition, historical necessity, and moral accountability. In his essay he asserts that Fitzgerald means to equate Jay Gatsby and his fate with America in general. A flight from reality, time, fate, death, and limits, in which one makes youth, wealth, and beauty into objects of worship, Fussell says, is the road to disaster, the road Gatsby and America follow. It is simply not true that all the magic of the world can be had for money, or that enough wealth can enable one to set back the clock.

In *Tender Is the Night,* Fussell writes, Fitzgerald "at once restates the essential theme and complicates it." The protagonist, Dr. Dick Diver, is, like Gatsby, caught up in "romantic wonder," and, like a kind of Riviera magus, is even able to dispense it to others. He leads a glamorous life while at the same time striving to keep himself financially independent of his wife's wealth. The Warrens are the quintessential American capitalist family; countless workers around the globe toil so the Warrens can spend freely. The injustice and the waste are enormous and obvious, but Fitzgerald goes further, Fussell points out. Nicole's father is not merely a heartless capitalist but an incestuous father as well, driving his own daughter to psychosis. Throughout his discussions of both novels, Fussell points out Fitzgerald's consistent use of religious imagery to make faith in the power of money a new religion.

Michael Glenday takes up *Tender* from a different angle. There once was, for a brief, shining moment, a nearly perfect place, an Eden on earth, he writes, and it was on the Riviera, at Gerald and Sara Murphy's Villa America, in the 1920s. It was this villa and this family, of course, that Fitzgerald used as the setting and models for the Villa Diana and Dick and Nicole Diver at the beginning of the novel. The expatriate Murphys had money and leisure and, most important, the proper attitude. The thing that counted was, as Gerald Murphy put it, not their leisure and wealth but what they did with their minds. The "invented" part of life—imagination, thoughtfulness, creativity—counted.

Reality—in the form of disease, death, misfortune—would come, could not be controlled, and was, finally, inevitable. Even this Arcadia could not be forever protected from the intrusion of crassness and reality. In real life, the Depression took much of the Murphys' money, and two of their three children died. Hordes of vulgar tourists, not artists, came to despoil the Riviera. In the novel, the beach that Dick Diver so lovingly created, nearly with his own hands, by cleaning the sand of rock and waste, has become virtually an amusement park. The Divers' marriage collapses and Dick—in a geographic irony, one might say— exiles himself to upstate New York.

James Meredith writes about *Tender* from yet another angle, insisting, convincingly, that it is a war novel, though not, however, a combat novel. The dehumanization of soldiers in World War I, in which they were just another "asset" and few saw the enemy, their killers, or the men they killed, extended beyond the combatants and into Western civilization. The no-man's-land of battle, the expanses of mud and corpses, led directly to the postwar wasteland of the twenties, and the repudiation of traditional faiths, values, and widespread disillusionment led to a world in which, as in *Tender*, father and daughter could be lovers, and psychiatrist and patient could be man and wife.

Meredith, an expert on the literature of war, contrasts *Tender* with novels by Stendhal and William Makepeace Thackeray, demonstrating one huge difference between the works: in the earlier novels noncombatants were not much affected by war, but in novels written after World War I, the psychological landscape of the West is changed as noncombatants and, indeed, Western civilization itself are traumatized, resulting in widespread insomnia, depression, personality disorders, regressive self-absorption, and self-medication with alcohol. This last is, indeed, Dick Diver's exact condition.

The American modernist novelist most associated with war fiction is, of course, Fitzgerald's friend Hemingway. Michael Reynolds takes up the ways in which these two men were both injured by the war and the modern world and the different ways in which they dealt with those wounds. As background, Reynolds reminds us that during Fitzgerald's and Hemingway's childhood years medievalism loomed large in American school curricula. Both authors read and knew the stories of knights and chivalry, and both allude extensively to medievalism in their own writings. Reynolds suggests that both men, unable to find guides for living in the postwar world, may have sought answers and values in the world of chivalry and especially in its stories, such as in the Knight's Tale of Geoffrey Chaucer's *Canterbury Tales*. Like all men, Chaucer's knight and the squire are on a journey. The older, scarred, and experienced knight was Hemingway's model, Reynolds suggests, a man who has learned how to live and die alone and do his duty. Fitzgerald, on the other hand, models himself after the squire, desiring to learn how to court the girl, the love object, even if she should prove to be unworthy. Both men were searching for absolutes in a modern world that no longer provided absolutes, and in both cases, Reynolds says, the lesson learned was not how to prevail but how to lose with dignity.

Partly because of the disappointing sales of *Tender Is the Night*, and partly because of the expenses of Zelda's poor mental health and of his daughter's enrollment at exclusive schools, by the late 1930s Fitzgerald was in financial distress. His stories of flappers were no longer needed at the *Saturday Evening Post*, but, now in Hollywood to learn the screenwriting trade and earn a living, he did have good material at hand in the movie business.

He wrote the Pat Hobby stories for money, yes. He needed it. But he also brought to them a lifetime of artistic prowess. He revised and re-revised the stories as they were published monthly from January 1940 to May 1941 and took great care in arranging them when they were published as a volume.

Milton R. Stern, in a lengthy examination of these stories, their construction, and their critical reception, believes they are better than most critics first thought, but he warns against a sentimental overevaluation. Fitzgerald critics, he warns, must be careful here. Just because it is a Fitzgerald story does not mean it is necessarily a great story. Of the protagonist, Pat himself, all are in agreement. Hobby is a plagiarist, a liar, a blackmailer, a thief, and a rummy; he is unimaginative, stupid, talentless, and abysmally fatuous. In short, as a fictional character, he is wonderful.

Stern reviews the criticism of the stories, which started off slow but has picked up in recent years. He warns that the stories were never meant to be a novel in story form and notes that they suffer from comparison to a book such as Sherwood Anderson's *Winesburg, Ohio*. They are, moreover, modern stories, not driven by plot twists like O. Henry stories but nonlinear, episodic, and epiphanic, like James Joyce stories or, more precisely, like Hemingway stories. Having much in common with Hemingway's *In Our Time*, these stories are less lyrical and generally tougher in tone than the average Fitzgerald story.

Lionel Trilling, one of the most influential American critics of the post-World War II era, used the publication of *The Crack-Up* essays to write his summary of Fitzgerald and his work. This essay as much as any other propelled the Fitzgerald revival. What Trilling saw in Fitzgerald was a writer who had, admittedly, not taken good care of his talent, and in this Trilling compares him to Milton's Samson, who also misused his powers. But, Trilling insists, Fitzgerald's work is still heroic, and it finds its power not in aggression but in warmth and love. Trilling praises Fitzgerald for his tone of "gentleness without softness," something that Fitzgerald's more hard-boiled friend Hemingway never understood.

Although during the 1930s most thinkers blamed the "social order" for all the world's disasters, Fitzgerald continued to insist on a sense of personal responsibility. More closely associated with the excesses of the Jazz Age than any other writer, he nevertheless wrote fictions that were almost entirely innocent of mere "sex." His heroes' senses of personal honor are maintained with an almost "masochistic scrupulousness."

Trilling places Fitzgerald among the "greats" and compares him, in differing ways, to Johann Wolfgang von Goethe, William Butler Yeats, and Henry James. Trilling has high praise for *The Great Gatsby* and understands it in a way that has influenced all further readings of the novel. Jay Gatsby is America, and Gatsby's dream, Trilling insists, is America's dream. Fitzgerald, like his heroes, lacked "prudence" but had "an extraordinary gift for hope, a romantic readiness."

Morris Dickstein, writing from the perspective of Fitzgerald's centennial, gives a sympathetic summary of the life and work. After the gaiety of the 1920s, Fitzgerald, like America, went into a depression in the 1930s and became "an emblem of failure." The nadir of his public image may have been reached with his disastrous interview in Asheville, North Carolina, with Michael Mok of the *New York Post* and in the publication of the *Esquire* articles chronicling his disappointments and mental decline. But, Dickstein tells us, there had always been in Fitzgerald's work "a kernel of tragedy, a dose of melancholy." In "Winter Dreams," the protagonist Dexter Green is crushed when he learns that the love of his life, Judy Jones, is no longer ravishing but only "commonplace," merely a pretty girl, and that her husband abuses her. The stories "One Trip Abroad" (1930) and "The Rough Crossing" (1929) show marriages in trouble, and "Babylon Revisited" (1931) is the harshest of all. It shows painfully how actions have far-reaching consequences; not only can the past not be relived, but it also cannot be left behind. Dick Diver, Dickstein reminds us, is one of Fitzgerald's most famous failures, as is, later in the decade, Pat Hobby.

It is true that Fitzgerald knew disappointment, pain, and failure, but what is so remarkable is that he learned from them and used them in his fiction. He acquired a sense of limits and the knowledge that not everything is possible. Even New York City, his magical Gotham, viewed from the top of the Empire State Building in "My Lost City" (1932), was seen to have limits. Dickstein shows that "the lyrical dreamer gave way to the disillusioned realist with his chastened sense of maturity," but the work stayed just as fine, or became even better.

This volume closes with a reminiscence by the novelist and screenwriter Budd Schulberg, who came to know Fitzgerald in Hollywood during the 1930s when the producer Walter Wanger teamed them up to write a screenplay for a film called *Winter Carnival*, which was to be at Dartmouth, Schulberg's alma mater. Since Fitzgerald died some eighty years ago, these firsthand accounts are increasingly rare and to be treasured. Schulberg writes of his collaboration with Scott, their flight east, Fitzgerald's drunken spree in Manhattan, then the comical catastrophe at Dartmouth, with Fitzgerald brilliant but hopeless and Wanger purely furious. Schulberg tells the story well, indeed has told it in fictionalized form in his novel *The Disenchanted*, and the story can only be diminished by summary. The most striking element in Schulberg's memoir, as it is in the memoir of Fitzgerald's last private secretary, Frances Kroll Ring, is how fond Schulberg was of Fitzgerald. Like so many who knew Fitzgerald, he cannot say enough about how Fitzgerald was generous, kind, and altogether a very, very nice man.

CAREER, LIFE, AND INFLUENCE

On F. Scott Fitzgerald

Don Noble

F. Scott Fitzgerald is now safely and securely in the pantheon of American writers. *The Great Gatsby* may be the most taught undergraduate text in the country; there is what seems to be an endless stream of articles, books, and popular magazine references to Scott and Zelda; and new biographies continue to appear, as one author after another is inspired to examine Fitzgerald's life and works.

Now, more than fifty years after his last, unfinished novel was published, the question that presents itself is, Why is all this happening? Why Fitzgerald? What is so beguiling about this man who married only once, who neither hunted lions like his friend Ernest Hemingway nor told gothic tales of the Old South like his contemporary William Faulkner? This volume will be the newest collection of essays explaining and examining Fitzgerald's work, but not the last. What is it about him and his work that generates this amount of attention?

The answer, I think, comes in parts. First, Fitzgerald lasts because he is a beautiful writer, a beautiful stylist. He was well read in the traditional literature of England and the United States. The Newman School in New Jersey and Princeton University may not have made a scholar out of young Scott, but he did leave with a thorough grounding in and appreciation for the masterworks of English literature and especially the strengths of the English Romantic poets, especially his favorite, John Keats. Fitzgerald had a distinctive style right from the start, and it was a poetic style. Without even knowing why, readers are taken and held by memorable passages in his novels and stories. I think of the scene in *Gatsby* in which Jay spends his first moments reunited with Daisy: it all ought to have been perfect, and yet Fitzgerald's narrator, Nick Carraway, remarks, "There must have been moments even that afternoon when Daisy tumbled short of his dreams—not through her own fault, but because of the colossal vitality of his illusion. . . . No amount of fire or freshness can challenge what a man will store up in his ghostly heart." Or one remembers the end of "Babylon Revisited," perhaps his best story, when Charlie Wales realizes he has failed to convince his sister-in-law to give him custody of his daughter, Honoria: "He would come back some day; they couldn't make him pay forever. . . . He wasn't young any more, with a lot of nice thoughts and dreams to have by himself. He was absolutely sure Helen wouldn't have wanted him to be so alone."

Fitzgerald not only wrote beautifully but also wrote about concerns central to the American consciousness. It seems a little tired to say so again, but we Americans are in fact consumed by what we, in short-hand, call the American Dream. We do wish to prosper, to rise in the world economically and socially. We want each generation to do better, to live more comfortably than the ones before it. And we worry about the cost. What will this chasing after material goods, this getting and spending, cost in human terms? For Gatsby, it costs everything.

And like everyone, everywhere in the West, since the concept was invented in Old Provence, we care intensely about romantic love. No one in serious, literary fiction does a better job with boy-meets-girl, boy-loses-girl, and boy-gets-girl-back—and, sometimes, boy-loses-girl-again-for-good—than F. Scott Fitzgerald. His stories of romance in all its ecstatic and frustrating forms are as fresh today as they ever were. We may have texting and cell phones now, but the young human heart is not much different from that of a hundred years ago. Fitzgerald's distinctive, poetic style, let us remind ourselves, is as appropriate for talking about love as Hemingway's terse declarative sentences are for describing an existential universe in which, after duty is done, we must all die, or Faulkner's filigreed style is for conveying the Deep South's complex tangles of race and blood.

Whether we are eager to admit it or not, Fitzgerald wrote about a subject of major concern to all of us: youth. He wrote of the joy, freshness, and exuberance of youth and the intrinsic fear that settles on almost all Americans as we contemplate losing our youth. Who can say what percentage of the gross national product is spent in attempting to preserve what cannot be saved, only savored, and is, finally, spent or misspent. In story after story, the age of thirty looms as a terrifying frontier, the end of the good times, and yet, generally speaking, we must live on, another forty or more years. How shall we use those years?

Sometimes, in rereading an author's corpus, we find that fewer of the works than we expected hold up. With Fitzgerald, however, the trend seems to be the reverse. The general opinion of *Tender Is the Night* has risen until the novel is nearly on a par with *Gatsby*. Critics find one story after the next has been undervalued, and the number of "stories by which he will be remembered" is growing, not shrinking, as whole volumes are dedicated to studies of Fitzgerald's "neglected" stories. The once-ignored Pat Hobby tales are now seen as worthy of extended discussion, and even the once thoroughly forgotten "The Curious Case of Benjamin Button" is in the news.

It is not just interest in the writings of Fitzgerald, however, that seems to last and even grow. We are more and more interested in Fitzgerald the man and in his lovely wife, Zelda. Why? First of all, they were indisputably beautiful people. Just as contemporary Americans cannot seem to get enough photographs and articles about the celebrity couples of Hollywood, so it was with Scott and Zelda in the 1920s and, to an amazing degree, even now. They were glamorous, full of panache and style, and bright and sassy; they danced the newest dances, wore the right clothes, and in some cases their clothes became the right clothes just because they wore them.

They were also lovers, and all the world loves lovers, even tragic ones, as they turned out to be. Their story joined the classic love stories, like that of Anthony and Cleopatra, as its theme shifted from bliss to "The World Well Lost" and "All for Love." In their marriage, as in so many of Fitzgerald's stories, what began in splendor ended in tragedy as Zelda's mental health and Scott's physical health collapsed. But, despite their travails, they were a couple in love, and each married only once. Zelda was probably unfaithful, once, with the now-famous

French aviator Edouard Jozan. Scott was probably a faithful husband, surely more faithful than his two peers, Hemingway and Faulkner, until Zelda was permanently institutionalized, and he took some comfort in a loving relationship with Sheilah Graham in Hollywood.

As much as Americans love a love story, and especially a love story with a tragic ending, we love a comeback story even more, and Fitzgerald is surely the number one literary "comeback kid" of all time. His reputation could hardly have been lower than it was in the late 1930s. His books were not selling, and, with no one recognizing him, Fitzgerald could eat lunch anywhere without being bothered by fans. But from the nearly total obscurity in which he died, his reputation soared to reach superstardom by 1960.

It is of no real use to say so, but I believe Fitzgerald, had he lived, would have finished *The Last Tycoon*; written a great many more fictions long and short; mastered the art of the screenplay, in which he was sincerely interested; and become a revered master of American letters in his own lifetime. I do not think it is too much to say that he would have joined his contemporaries Faulkner, Hemingway, and Steinbeck as a winner of the Nobel Prize in Literature. If the committee could award the prize posthumously, he would already have it.

Biography of F. Scott Fitzgerald_____

Jill B. Gidmark

Along with Ernest Hemingway and William Faulkner, Francis Scott Key Fitzgerald is considered one of the three most important American authors who wrote between the two world wars. On his father's side he was a descendant of the Scotts and the Keys who produced Francis Scott Key, the distinguished lawyer who wrote "The Star-Spangled Banner." Fitzgerald's father, Edward Fitzgerald, was unable to hold a steady job; his mother was the eccentric and powerful Mary Mc-Quillan, whose father had left her a million-dollar grocery business and a substantial personal fortune.

Fitzgerald's childhood was a pampered one—though somewhat unstable, owing to frequent moves—and included two years at the St. Paul Academy (where he published his first short story in 1909) and two years at the Newman School, a Catholic boarding school in Hackensack, New Jersey. He enrolled at Princeton University in 1913, after failing and then retaking the entrance examinations, and left Princeton in 1917 without receiving a degree. Commissioned as a second lieutenant in the U.S. Army that year, he met Zelda Sayre while on duty outside Montgomery, Alabama, in the summer of 1918.

Many short stories that Fitzgerald wrote in 1919 were rejected, but a first novel, *This Side of Paradise*, based on his life at Princeton, was published in 1920, the same year he and Zelda were married. *Flappers and Philosophers*, a collection of short stories, was published the same year, and another collection, *Tales of the Jazz Age*, followed. It is primarily on the basis of these two volumes and *The Great Gatsby* that Fitzgerald won his reputation as the "chronicler of the Jazz Age." Already in these early works two character types appeared that were frequently to recur in Fitzgerald's writings—the "flapper," or new woman, and the "sheik," or Jazz Age young man. Both types are beautiful and rich, sad and gay, witty and reserved, and independent.

Between Fitzgerald's first two novels, the couple embarked on a profligate lifestyle marked by heavy drinking, partying, and over-spending. Elements of this lifestyle appear in Fitzgerald's second novel, *The Beautiful and Damned*, which explores the character of a man spoiled by the promise of wealth. First appearing as serial install-ments in *Metropolitan Magazine* before its publication in book form in 1922, this work was not as well received as Fitzgerald's first novel.

That same year a twenty-month residence in Great Neck, New York, provided the setting for what would become Fitzgerald's most popular novel, *The Great Gatsby*. Before its publication in 1925 Fitzgerald wrote his only mature play, *The Vegetable*, which was performed in At-lantic City but which neither author nor audience found memorable.

Fitzgerald regarded *The Great Gatsby* as his best piece, and it has been called by many critics the best work of Fitzgerald's generation. The story concerns a flamboyant racketeer's efforts to recapture the heart of the upper-class girl who cast him aside when he was a young man. The novel's excellence turns on its brilliant characterization, finely drawn class distinction, and the poignant development of sev-eral themes important to all Fitzgerald's fiction: romantic love, reality and delusion, success and failure, and the evanescence of pleasure and beauty. At the time it was published, the critical response was mixed and sales were mediocre. When stage and film versions were pro-duced, however, Fitzgerald's money worries were temporarily allevi-ated.

Between May, 1924, and December, 1931, the Fitzgeralds spent five years abroad. Fitzgerald described the summer of 1926 as one of a thousand parties and no work. During this time he met Ernest Heming-way, whose work he promoted, and he published a collection of nine stories titled *All the Sad Young Men*. This volume included many weak stories as well as one of his very best, "Winter Dreams," a story that Fitzgerald described as a short version of *The Great Gatsby*. Apart from these events, this period in Fitzgerald's life is marked only by ex-cessive drinking and instability. Zelda Fitzgerald began obsessively to pursue a dance career in 1928, and a nervous collapse two years later led her to diagnosis as a schizophrenic. She repeatedly had to be placed in sanatoriums, and she remained in a sanatorium in North Carolina from 1937 until her death in a fire there in 1948.

In 1934 Fitzgerald published *Tender Is the Night*, a novel about a psychoanalyst who falls in love with and marries a wealthy patient and is subsequently ruined by her money. Reviews at the time were more or less favorable, but the book's sales were lower than those of any other of Fitzgerald's novels. Most remarkable of Fitzgerald's short-story production at this time was a set of twelve well-crafted stories about the character Basil Duke Lee, which include reminiscences of Fitzgerald's boyhood and adolescence. Successors to the Basil Duke Lee stories are Fitzgerald's five so-called Josephine Perry stories, whose central character is based on Ginevra King, with whom Fitzgerald had had early love while a young man at Princeton. Several of the Basil and Josephine stories were also collected in Fitzgerald's largest collection of short stories, *Taps at Reveille*.

During the time that Zelda was recovering from her second nervous breakdown, she wrote an autobiographical novel, *Save Me the Waltz* (1932), which gives her perspective on many events of their lives. The book, which did not sell many copies and garnered poor reviews, irritated Fitzgerald because it borrowed material from his unfinished novel and portrayed him in an unflattering way. This, in combination with his alcoholism, recurring bouts of tuberculosis, and strain over his wife's condition, pushed Fitzgerald into a precarious mental state. He recorded his struggles in three essays that were published in *Esquire* magazine and later anthologized by Edmund Wilson into a posthumous collection of Fitzgerald's writing called *The Crack-Up*.

In the summer of 1937 Fitzgerald signed a contract with Metro-Goldwyn-Mayer and moved to Hollywood. While doing piecemeal work on film scripts, he met and began a relationship with Sheilah Graham. She was with him when he died of a heart attack on December 21, 1940.

Fitzgerald's final work, the novel *The Last Tycoon*, remained unfinished at the time of his death, but it was later edited by Edmund Wilson and published posthumously. The novel explores the economic struggles and power intrigues concomitant with the Hollywood film industry. When it first appeared, reviews hinted that it might well have been Fitzgerald's masterpiece, but such praise became tempered as early as 1945.

The fate of Fitzgerald's reputation as a social historian of the age and of the upper middle class was sealed with the resurgence of interest in his work prompted by the appearance in 1951 of Arthur Mizener's *The Far Side of Paradise* and Alfred Kazin's *F. Scott Fitzgerald: The Man and His Work*. In 1958 *The Fitzgerald Newsletter* began publication, and it became the *Fitzgerald/Hemingway Annual* in 1969. Other biographies, memoirs, and criticism, the publication of his letters, and the appearance of film versions of *The Great Gatsby*, *Tender Is the Night*, and *The Last Tycoon* ensured continuing interest among readers. Although Fitzgerald generally stirs less international interest than Hemingway or Faulkner, *The Great Gatsby* has been translated into more than thirty languages and remains the most popular of his works.

From *Cyclopedia of World Authors, Fourth Revised Edition* (Pasadena, CA: Salem Press). Copyright © 2004 by Salem Press, Inc.

Bibliography

Berman, Ronald. *Fitzgerald, Hemingway, and the Twenties*. Tuscaloosa: University of Alabama Press, 2001. An explication of the cultural context of the era and how the works of these two American writers are imbued with the attitudes and icons of their day.

_____. *"The Great Gatsby" and Fitzgerald's World of Ideas*. Tuscaloosa: University of Alabama Press, 1997. Explores Fitzgerald's political and social views of his era and how he incorporated them into his seminal novel.

Bloom, Harold, ed. *F. Scott Fitzgerald: "The Great Gatsby."* New Haven, Conn.: Chelsea House, 1986. A short but important collection of critical essays. This book provides an introductory overview of Fitzgerald scholarship as well as readings from a variety of perspectives on Fitzgerald's fiction.

Bruccoli, Matthew J. *Some Sort of Epic Grandeur*. New York: Harcourt Brace

Jovanovich, 1981. In this outstanding biography, a major Fitzgerald scholar argues that Fitzgerald's divided spirit, not his lifestyle, distracted him from writing. Bruccoli believes that Fitzgerald both loved and hated the privileged class that was the subject of his fiction.

Conroy, Frank. "Great Scott." *Gentlemen's Quarterly* 66 (December, 1996): 240-245. A reconsideration of Fitzgerald on the centenary of his birth; Conroy argues that one of Fitzgerald's great strengths as a writer was his ability to make the metaphysical beauty of his female characters believable.

Eble, Kenneth. *F. Scott Fitzgerald*. Rev. ed. Boston: Twayne, 1977. A clearly written critical biography, this book traces Fitzgerald's development from youth through a "Final Assessment" that surveys scholarship on Fitzgerald's texts.

Gale, Robert L. *An F. Scott Fitzgerald Encyclopedia*. Westport, Conn.: Greenwood Press, 1998. Provides everything students should know about Fitzgerald's life and works. Indispensable.

Gross, Dalton, and MaryJean Gross. *Understanding "The Great Gatsby": A Student Casebook to Issues, Sources, and Historical Documents*. Westport, Conn.: Greenwood Press, 1998. Part of the Literature in Context series. An excellent study guide for students of the novel.

Hook, Andrew. *F. Scott Fitzgerald: A Literary Life*. New York: St. Martin's Press, 2002. Part of the Literary Lives series. Concise rather than thorough, but with some interesting details.

Jefferson, Margo. "Still Timely, Yet a Writer of His Time." *The New York Times*, December 17, 1996: C17. A brief biography of Fitzgerald on the occasion of his centennial year; Jefferson calls him one of those rare artists with a cultural radar system that is constantly picking up sensations, responses, and fresh thoughts.

Kuehl, John. *F. Scott Fitzgerald: A Study of the Short Fiction*. Boston: Twayne, 1991. Part 1 discusses Fitzgerald's major stories and story collections, part 2 studies his critical opinions, and part 3 includes selections from Fitzgerald critics. Includes chronology and bibliography.

Lee, A. Robert, ed. *Scott Fitzgerald: The Promises of Life*. New York: St. Martin's Press, 1989. An excellent collection of essays by Fitzgerald scholars, this book includes an introduction that surveys scholarship on the texts. Topics addressed include Fitzgerald's treatment of women, his notion of the decline of the West, his "ethics and ethnicity," and his use of "distortions" of the imagination.

Mangum, Bryant. *A Fortune Yet: Money in the Art of F. Scott Fitzgerald's Short Stories*. New York: Garland, 1991. Discusses all of Fitzgerald's stories, both those in collections and those uncollected, focusing on their relationship to his novels and their role as a proving ground for his ideas.

Meyers, Jeffrey. *Scott Fitzgerald: A Biography*. New York: HarperCollins, 1994. In this biography, which makes use of previously unknown materials about Fitzgerald's life, Meyers discusses how such writers as Edgar Allan Poe, Ernest Hemingway, and Joseph Conrad influenced Fitzgerald's fiction.

Miller, James E., Jr. *F. Scott Fitzgerald: His Art and His Technique*. New York: New York University Press, 1964. An expanded version of *The Fictional Technique of Scott Fitzgerald*, originally published in 1957, this book emphasizes

Fitzgerald's technique, focusing on the impact of the "saturation vs. selection" debate between H. G. Wells and Henry James; it also adds critical commentary and interpretations of the later works.

Oxford, Edward. "F. Scott Fitzgerald." *American History* 31 (November/December, 1996): 44-49, 63. A biographical sketch that notes that Fitzgerald was able to convey the energy and image of the 1920's, only to become an ironic witness to the death of that era. Discusses Fitzgerald's life with Zelda and his literary career.

Petry, Alice Hall. *Fitzgerald's Craft of Short Fiction*. Ann Arbor, Mich.: UMI Research Press, 1989. A study of Fitzgerald's short stories in relationship to his novels, American society, and his personal life. Summarizes and critiques the critical reception of his short-story collections and discusses his relationship with his editor Maxwell Perkins; analyzes all the major stories and a number of minor ones.

Tate, Mary Jo. *F. Scott Fitzgerald A to Z: The Essential Reference to His Life and Work*. New York: Facts On File, 1998. A comprehensive study of the man and his oeuvre.

Taylor, Kendall. *Sometimes Madness Is Wisdom: Zelda and Scott Fitzgerald, a Marriage*. New York: Ballantine, 2001. An examination of one of literature's most famous couples and their symbiotic marriage.

The *Paris Review* Perspective

Elizabeth Gumport for *The Paris Review*

The Jazz Age was a boom time when fast cities towered higher, skirts got shorter, and money seemed sure to blossom as perpetually as flowers. The decade was one that celebrated youth, and F. Scott Fitzgerald was no exception to this rule, riding to fame in 1920 at the age of twenty-three on the success of his first novel, *This Side of Paradise*. Born in 1896 in St. Paul, Minnesota, and thus slightly older than the iconic generation of flappers and vamps, he chronicled their frenzy, and their country's, in his novels and stories. America, he wrote, was not a place but "a willingness of the heart," and in the 1920s that meant a willingness to believe in unstoppable progress and wealth without limit. Like Jay Gatsby, his most famous creation, Fitzgerald has become a symbol of the Jazz Age, a writer who both defined and embodied the period.

Yet Fitzgerald's creations are no dusty museum pieces or historical curiosities, and in our climate of deflated stocks and deflated hopes, his writing feels more contemporary than ever. Fitzgerald's characters are always plagued by a tendency toward magical thinking, a belief that the world will arrange itself according our wishes if only we want it badly enough.

This, of course, cannot be: in "The Crack-Up," an essay about his own mental breakdown, Fitzgerald writes, "I began to realize that for two years my life had been drawing on resources that I did not possess, that I had been mortgaging myself physically and spiritually up to the hilt." He expanded on this financial metaphor in a letter to his daughter, warning her against making the same mistakes: "Our danger is imagining we have resources—material and moral—which we haven't got. One of the reasons I find myself so consistently in valleys of depression is that every few years I seem to be climbing uphill to recover from some bankruptcy. Do you know what bankruptcy exactly means? It means drawing on resources which one does not possess." What brings down a market brings down a man. The relation between the individual spirit and the spirit of the age is one of Fitzgerald's great themes. There is Gatsby, who believes money and love can alter the course of time, and there is Monroe Stahr, the doomed visionary of *The Last Tycoon*: reckless hearts in a reckless society, each inflaming the other.

Just as the crash followed the boom, so does age follow youth, and it is the joys and loss of the latter that constitute Fitzgerald's other great subject. His fiction teems with men and women wild with seemingly infinite promise and with those who have seen that promise broken by the years. "What becomes of everybody you used to know and have so much in common with?" Anthony Patch asks in *The Beautiful and Damned*. The answer is the same for everyone, including his wife, who postpones pursuing a movie career until just before her thirtieth birthday. After learning the director has offered her the part of a widow, rather than the ingenue part for which she auditioned, Gloria collapses: "'Oh, my pretty face,' she whispered, passionately grieving. 'Oh, my pretty face! Oh, I don't want to live without my pretty face! Oh, what's *happened*?'" For Fitzgerald, trouble comes when we count on something, whether wealth or beauty, to last forever.

Fitzgerald's worth, however, does not depend simply on his topicality or on some notion of his work's practical use. What endures, above all, is his language. "Fitzgerald was a better just plain writer than all of us put together," John O'Hara once said. "Just words writing." Fitzgerald excels at showing how our feelings transform our field of vision. The world changes with us, as when Rosemary visits the Divers' house for the first time in *Tender Is the Night*:

The table seemed to have risen a little toward the sky like a mechanical dancing platform, giving the people around it the sense of being alone with each other in the dark universe, nourished by its only food, warmed by its only lights. . . . the diffused magic of the hot sweet South had withdrawn into them—the soft-pawed night and the ghostly wash of the Mediterranean far below—the magic left these things and melted into the two Divers and became part of them.

For Fitzgerald, our impression of the thing is as real and powerful as the thing itself. Love is a function of the imagination, as we elevate and admire the object of our affection over and over again in our minds. "I know myself, but that is all," Amory cries at the end of *This Side of Paradise*, and, for better or worse, it is through ourselves that we know others. Like youth, love fades, and this loss brings both heart-wrecking agony and ecstasy. We cannot return to the past, though this will not prevent us from trying. Time, unconquerable, is also no match for us: we are borne away from all we once cherished, but the vividness of our memories flings us back. "After all," Fitzgerald wrote in his notebooks, "any given moment has its value; it can be questioned in the light of after-events, but the moment remains. . . . the moment of beauty was there."

Works Cited

Fitzgerald, F. Scott. *The Beautiful and Damned*. 1922. Stilwell, KS: Digireads, 2008.

_____. *The Crack-Up*. Ed. Edmund Wilson. New York: New Directions, 1945.

_____. *Tender Is the Night*. 1934. New York: Charles Scribner's Sons, 1995.

_____. *This Side of Paradise*. 1920. New York: Vintage, 2009.

O'Hara, John. *Selected Letters of John O'Hara*. Ed. Matthew J. Bruccoli. New York: Random House, 1978.

CRITICAL CONTEXTS

F. Scott Fitzgerald's American Dream_____

Jennifer Banach

Although F. Scott Fitzgerald's novels and short stories explore a broad range of themes, they have, perhaps, become best known for their treatment of the American Dream. Most critics and scholars agree that this subject remains Fitzgerald's most dynamic and significant—his signature theme, in fact—but they differ in their opinions of how Fitzgerald understood and defined it. Critics such as Marius Bewley and Malcolm Cowley, among countless others, have argued that Fitzgerald's work serves as a harsh critique of traditional notions of the American Dream, exposing it as an illusion fueled by some misguided drive born of the "nervous energy" of a postwar generation struggling to make sense of their lives and the time in which they lived (*Crack-Up* 13). However, Fitzgerald's own lifelong pursuit of wealth and fame suggests that he instead found the dream persuasive. In fact, a close examination of his work, specifically his novels and the *Crack-Up* essays written for *Esquire* magazine in 1936, demonstrates that both theories may be simultaneously correct and incorrect, revealing a view of the American Dream more nuanced than any of these critics might have it one that demands a reconsideration and redefinition of this concept that has become so central to American culture.

The American Dream has been popularly defined as the belief that, through hard work and thrift, all Americans can improve their social status and achieve wealth and success. Though the phrase did not come into currency until 1931, when James Truslow Adams made it the central theme of his history of the United States, *The Epic of America*, the American Dream has been a driving force behind American culture since the time of the Puritans (Cullen 3). Its values—the equality of all people and the rights to life, liberty, and the pursuit of happiness—are written into the country's foundational documents and are affirmed in numerous social movements bent on extending equality and freedom to the disenfranchised. As Adams defines it:

The American Dream is that dream of a land in which life should be better and richer and fuller for every man, with opportunity for each according to ability or achievement. . . . It is not a dream of motor cars and high wages merely, but a dream of social order in which each man and each woman shall be able to attain to the fullest stature of which they are innately capable, and be recognized by others for what they are, regardless of the fortuitous circumstances of birth or position. (214-15)

Even before Adams, however, writers outside the United States recognized the dream as a defining characteristic of American culture. The French American writer J. Hector St. John de Crèvecœur (known also as Michel-Guillaume Jean de Crèvecœur) discussed the idea in *Letters from an American Farmer*, which was published in London in 1782. A Frenchman who immigrated to what is now Canada before settling in New York State, he praised American egalitarianism and the unparalleled freedom and material opportunities the country offers to its citizens. Another Frenchman, the historian and political philosopher Alexis de Tocqueville, toured the United States between 1831 and 1832 and collected his observations of the fledgling nation in *Democracy in America* (1835, 1840), noting in particular the country's fluid class structure and its high valuation of equality.

Within America itself, too, citizens were early on highly conscious of the freedom and opportunities the country appeared to promise them. One of the country's founders, Benjamin Franklin, is seemingly an embodiment of the American Dream, and he wrote his autobiography, which recounts how he rose from poverty to become a wealthy and influential entrepreneur and statesman, with the intention of urging readers to achieve their full potential by adopting his program of hard work and virtuous living. In the nineteenth century, the dream lived on in authors such as Henry David Thoreau, who at the conclusion of *Walden* remarks, "I have learned this, at least, from my experiment: if one advances confidently in the direction of his dreams, and endeavors to live the life he has imagined, he will meet with a success unexpected in common hours" (313), and Frederick Douglass, who observed:

> There is genuine heroism in his [the self-made man's] struggle and something of sublimity and glory in his triumph. . . . It, better than any assertion, gives us assurance of the latent powers and resources of simple and unaided manhood. It dignifies labor, honors application, lessens pain and depression, dispels gloom from the brow of the destitute and weariness from the heart of him about to faint, and enables man to take hold of the roughest and flintiest hardships incident to the battle of life, with a lighter heart, with higher hopes and a larger courage. (qtd. in Martin 264)

The American Dream entered into the nation's fiction during the latter half of the nineteenth century as Horatio Alger flooded the country with hundreds of rags-to-riches stories of virtuous young boys whose hard work enables them to rise from modest stations as shoe shiners, salesclerks, or bellhops to become successful businessmen and entrepreneurs. Enormously popular during Alger's day, the stories reinforced the nation's foundational belief that anyone, regardless of origin, can become successful with hard work and a little ingenuity.

As the United States entered the twentieth century and World War I, however, the American Dream underwent a transformation. While industrialization and its corresponding mechanical and technical advancements provided new opportunities for financial success, the war shook the country's faith in God, tradition, and morality. As a result, the American Dream shifted from a concept centered on personal fulfillment, accomplishment, and happiness to one driven by the more hollow desire for financial achievement and celebrity. As Fitzgerald's narrator comments in *This Side of Paradise*, the youth of the 1920s were "a new generation dedicated more than the last to the fear of poverty and the worship of success; grown up to find all gods dead, all wars fought, all faiths in man shaken" (260).

The horrors of World War I and their profound effects on American society are hard to overstate. In addition to being one the largest wars in history, World War I was one of the deadliest: technological innovations in artillery and defense—such as machine guns, poisonous gases, and barbed wire—made it impossible for forces to attack one another directly without suffering massive casualties, resulting in protracted trench warfare. In 1916, a single battle between French and German troops, the Battle of Verdun, lasted ten months and resulted in nearly a million casualties. By the time the Armistice Treaty ended the war in 1918, roughly 48,000 American troops had been killed, and the Allies had lost more than 3.9 million (Burner et al. 760).

The war left few Americans unchanged. The seemingly senseless deaths and the troops' exposure to Europe's more liberal culture had upset old American traditions and societal regulations and reshaped the morals and sexual norms of the generation that had grown up in the war's shadow. As the authors of the time, such as Fitzgerald and Ernest Hemingway, documented, gender roles shifted as traditional notions of romance and love were discarded. Women—who had entered the workforce during the war and participated in the conflict as nurses, journalists, and entertainers—were becoming more independent, and in 1920 American women gained the right to vote. There was less pressure on them to choose between family life and careers or personal fulfillment, and many gained notoriety as flappers by cutting their hair into short bobs, shortening their dresses, drinking and smoking, and behaving promiscuously.

At the same time the members of Fitzgerald's generation were reeling from the cultural changes brought on by the war, the country was entering a decade of enormous prosperity. A wave of new consumer goods, such as radios, washing machines, and vacuum cleaners, were flooding the market, and goods that had before been affordable only for the rich, such as automobiles and telephones, were also becoming less expensive and within reach of the middle class. Consumption of these products in turn stimulated the production of raw materials, such as steel, oil, and rubber, and spurred the government to build highways, airports, and telephone lines. The gross national product increased significantly, as did general wages. In addition, the rise in consumption and production fed speculation and inflated stock prices. People bought stocks "on margin," paying as little as 10 percent of the stock price up front and financing the remainder with credit, and trusted that, as other people bought stocks, the prices would rise and cancel the their debts.

Prohibition was also bringing a different kind of prosperity to crime syndicates. Originally meant to curb crime and immoral behavior, the outlawing of alcohol in fact had the opposite effect as consumer demand was met by bootleggers and speakeasies. As a result, organized crime increased as consumers turned to the black market for alcohol. Racketeering and the corruption of law enforcement officials also increased as mobsters bribed officials not to interfere with their activities.

Like the war, the prosperity of the 1920s also had a dramatic impact on American society. The sense of economic security it gave created a corresponding sense of opportunity, feeding the notion that it was possible for anyone to become a self-made success. And in the spiritual void left by the war, it further strengthened the link between material wealth and the American Dream. As President Calvin Coolidge remarked, "The man who builds a factory builds a temple. . . . the man who works there, worships there."

It also resulted in the creation of a new social class, the nouveau riche, whose members, like Fitzgerald's Jay Gatsby, had risen from modest means to become fabulously wealthy. Though members of the established, "old money" upper class tended to look down on them as unsophisticated parvenus, the nouveau riche nevertheless appeared to have achieved the American Dream the rest of the country was chasing after. On the other hand, when coupled with the malaise left by the war, this prosperity also gave people license to experiment with hedonism and cast off their moral and social responsibilities to pursue their own pleasure.

A candid documenter of the Jazz Age, Fitzgerald captured these sudden cultural and economic changes in his novels and stories, and, most important, he predicted with amazing foresight that the decade's dream of material wealth would prove incapable of providing any lasting fulfillment—a prophecy that would be realized in the stock market crash of 1929. Though some reviewers criticized Fitzgerald's work as immoral for its frank depictions of the period's excesses, Edmund Wilson offers a more sympathetic and insightful view in discussing *This Side of Paradise*:

> It may be that we cannot demand too high a degree of moral balance from young men, however able or brilliant, who write books in the year 1921: we must remember that they have had to grow up in that they have had to derive their chief stimulus from the wars, the society and the commerce of the Age of Confusion itself. (12)

More specifically, as Malcolm Cowley observes, "Fitzgerald never lost a quality that very few writers are able to acquire: a sense of living in history" (57).

Fitzgerald's acuity is likely attributable to the fact that, at least superficially, he himself was a living embodiment of the American Dream. Born in 1896 in St. Paul, Minnesota, he grew up with the new century—its teens were his teens and its twenties his own. And though his family was upper-middle-class, his social status was precarious. His father, Edward, came from a prominent family, but, having no means of his own and little business acumen, he was dependent on the wealth that his wife, Mary McQuillan, the daughter of an Irish immigrant and a successful wholesale grocer, brought to the marriage. The family moved often as Edward found and lost jobs.

With the help of his mother's rich relatives, Fitzgerald was able to attend St. Paul Academy and the Newman School, both prestigious private schools. After finishing at Newman, he went on to study at Princeton University, but, distracted by extracurricular activities and clubs, he earned poor grades. In May 1917, while repeating his junior year, he signed up for a military training course and in October received his commission and left Princeton. Expecting to be killed in the war, he began writing a novel while in training at Fort Leavenworth, Kansas. Completing the novel, which he titled "The Romantic Egotist," in 1918, he submitted it to Charles Scribner's Sons, which rejected it in August despite the favorable opinion of one young editor, Maxwell Perkins, who encouraged Fitzgerald to revise and resubmit the manuscript. Two months later, Fitzgerald was standing aboard a transport ship in New York Harbor, preparing finally to be deployed, when the war ended.

During these early years, Fitzgerald fell in love with two women. Both romances would play key parts in shaping his future work, planting the seed for his fascination with the American Dream and inspiring the notion that it was somehow linked to the success or failure of love. The first woman, Ginevra King, was a Chicago debutante from a well-to-do family. The couple met at a sledding party in Fitzgerald's hometown while he was a student at Princeton. The two were quickly taken with one another, but King ended the relationship a short time later because of Fitzgerald's apparent poverty. The second, Zelda Sayre, the popular daughter of an Alabama Supreme Court judge, met Fitzgerald in July of 1918 while he was in the Army and stationed near Montgomery, Alabama. She accepted a marriage proposal from him, but, like King, was wary of his financial prospects. To reassure her and speed their marriage, after the war ended Fitzgerald set out for New York in the spring of 1919, determined to find his fortune. Instead, he wound up with a low-paying job in advertising, another rejection from Scribner's, and 122 rejection letters from magazines to which he had submitted stories (Bruccoli 93). The couple quarreled throughout these months, and, in a last-ditch effort, Fitzgerald rushed to Montgomery in June to beg Zelda to marry him. Instead, now convinced that he would never be able to provide her with the lifestyle she wished for, she broke off the engagement.

Following this rejection, Fitzgerald went on a bender in New York, then returned home to St. Paul in July, determined to make his novel a success and win back Zelda. By September, the work, retitled *This Side of Paradise*, was finished, and Scribner's finally accepted it for publication. During the last months of 1919, too, Fitzgerald began to crack the magazine market, placing short stories in *The Smart Set*, *Scribner's Magazine*, and, in early 1920, the widely read—and high-paying—*Saturday Evening Post*. At the same time, he had begun writing and visiting Zelda again, bringing her news of his impending success, and on April 3, 1920, just days after *This Side of Paradise* had sold out all three thousand of its first copies within three days of its publication, the two married in New York. By 1921, they had a child together.

Success came early and suddenly to Fitzgerald. Writing in 1932, he would recollect that, riding in a taxi through New York City one afternoon, he began "bawl[ing] because I had everything I wanted and knew I would never be so happy again" (qtd. in Bruccoli 131). His novel had brought him success, wealth, and love, but, unlike other, earlier American success stories, he never quite could trust his fortune. Years later he would recall of his early success:

> The man with the jingle of money in his pocket who married the girl a year later would always cherish an abiding distrust, an animosity toward the leisure class—not the conviction of a revolutionist but the smoldering hatred of a peasant. In the years since then I have never been able to stop wondering where my friends' money came from. (qtd. in Bruccoli 97-98)

Still, in keeping with the times, he and Zelda spent profligately. The royalties from *This Side of Paradise* had made the couple comfortable, but at the rate the Fitzgeralds were spending, the money would quickly run out. As a result, Fitzgerald hit upon the idea of using his magazine stories and the sales of film rights to support his lifestyle and his less remunerative novels (Bruccoli 133). No matter how carefully he laid his plans, however, Fitzgerald more often than not failed to stick to them and found himself dashing off stories to stay ahead of a debt rather than working on his novels.

In 1924, the couple moved with their daughter to France, where Fitzgerald became friends with other American expatriates, including his sometime friend and rival Ernest Hemingway. Shortly after the move to Europe, Fitzgerald finished work on his third novel, *The Great Gatsby*, a work that presents, most vividly, Fitzgerald's complex views of the American Dream. Despite its tremendous popularity today, the novel did not have great success at the time of its original publication, and Fitzgerald continued to rely on magazine stories for the bulk of his income. As a result, he had difficulty completing anything other than stories calibrated for popular magazines. At the same time, it was becoming clear that he and Zelda were struggling with issues no amount of money or success could alleviate. His alcoholism was escalating and preventing him from working to his fullest potential, and Zelda's mental health was deteriorating. By 1930 she had her first breakdown, and Fitzgerald had been working on his fourth novel, *Tender Is the Night*, for four years. After 1934, the year that *Tender Is the Night* was finally published to meet with lukewarm reviews and sluggish sales, Zelda would spend the remainder of her life in and out of psychiatric hospitals. Fitzgerald died in 1940 believing he was a failure.

In the years following his death, however, friends and critics worked to resuscitate his reputation, drawing attention especially to how his work combines an acute awareness of American culture with his own personal experiences. The lasting success of *This Side of Paradise, The Beautiful and Damned, Tender Is the Night*, and, especially, *The Great Gatsby* is owing to this fact: Fitzgerald's work functions both culturally and personally, providing a unique portrait of a specific time in American history while also capturing the plight of the individual with tremendous depth and emotion.

As critics such as Bewley have observed, in the absence of faith, Fitzgerald and his generation turned to the American Dream as a make-shift replacement for the now-defunct Puritanism on which the nation was founded. However, Fitzgerald was conscious of the contrast between the old religion and the new materialism at the heart of the American Dream. As Bewley explains:

> The implicit contrast between the eternal promises of the old religion and the material promises of the American dream that have so largely taken the place of any orthodoxy in America provided the most dramatic and sinister note for Fitzgerald to strike. (27-28)

As the American population was to discover with the crash of the stock market in 1929 and as Fitzgerald would experience in his own personal struggles, "the American dream could feed only on material, and therefore exhaustible possibilities" (Bewley 27). Success could resolve Fitzgerald's financial issues and make the country prosperous, but it would not overcome the personal issues that plagued Fitzgerald's family or fill the spiritual void left by the war.

Fitzgerald's work, Bewley goes on to explain, analyzes "those material possibilities on the secular level at which America believed Heaven to be attainable" (28). There is no doubt that the failed personal and cultural promises of the American Dream had a tremendous impact on Fitzgerald's view of the subject, and his work consequently exhibits an odd dualism. While he recognized that the American Dream of the 1920s is indeed linked to a quest for wealth and status, he also suggests that it is an outgrowth of a personal quest for spiritual fulfillment. Fitzgerald's characters seek wealth and success, but only in an effort to secure love; further, and in contradiction to the traditional arc of the American Dream, once his characters have attained wealth and success, they often find these insufficient or hollow or even an impediment to spiritual fulfillment. This paradox would serve as the foundation for Fitzgerald's signature style.

Fitzgerald was aware of the postwar cultural confusion, just as he was acutely aware of his role as spokesman for those who were struggling to make sense of it. In his own words, Fitzgerald acknowledged that he was aware that his job as a writer was "simply . . . telling people that [he] felt as they did" (*Crack-Up* 13). Therefore, many of his main characters were created in his own image and suffered fates similar to his own. *This Side of Paradise*, for instance, simultaneously exposes the lives and morality (or immorality, as the case may be) of the post-World War I generation and presents characters and episodes that closely mirror the events and people of Fitzgerald's own life. Its protagonist, a young midwesterner named Amory Blaine, bears a strong resemblance to Fitzgerald as he leaves his home for the East Coast and Princeton with vague expectations of finding himself and his vocation. Like Fitzgerald, he falls in love with a woman who ultimately rejects him. He, too, is called to serve in the army during World War I and, after the war, falls in love with another woman who rejects him because of his poor financial prospects.

The Beautiful and Damned, Fitzgerald's second novel published by Scribner's in 1922, contains similar themes and resemblances. It tells the story of Anthony Patch, a 1920s socialite and heir to a fortune, as he courts and marries the dazzling Gloria Gilbert and then, lacking any purpose to his life, becomes a dissolute alcoholic. The novel not only bears witness to the period's culture but is also based in large part on Fitzgerald's relationship with Zelda. It examines postwar morality while commenting on contrasting, but linked, themes such as love, money, and excess.

However, it is Fitzgerald's third novel, *The Great Gatsby*, published in 1925, that presents the most striking portrait of the realities of the post-World War I era, exposing the excess inherent in American society and its accompanying immorality. The themes of the novel were a matter of personal importance for Fitzgerald, and, accordingly, the main characters of the book closely resemble the author. The narrator, Nick Carraway, is a young man from the Midwest who, although somewhat attracted to the other characters' decadence, is ultimately uncomfortable with their unrestrained materialism and their lack of morality; the novel's central character, Gatsby, is a self-made man who, having been rejected once by a woman because of his poverty, comes to a tragic end trying to recapture her with his new wealth. Here, Daisy's initial rejection of Gatsby echoes a remark one of Ginevra King's friends reputedly made sure Fitzgerald overheard when he was courting the debutante: "Poor boys shouldn't think of marrying rich girls" (Bruccoli 64). Fitzgerald's fourth novel, *Tender Is the Night*, the story of a promising young psychiatrist, Dick Diver, who marries one of his patients and enters a personal and professional decline, in many ways also reflects Fitzgerald's own life with Zelda.

These correspondences among the novelist's life, culture, and work lend a sense of credibility to the work—no simple feat for a novelist. Characters such as Tom Buchanan, Jordan Baker, and Jay Gatsby are drawn from Fitzgerald's life, but they also stand in for larger social types—the old-money upper class and the nouveau riche parvenu. And while many of Fitzgerald's characters are capable of horrendous lies, because the characters are so true to life, readers are prepared to accept the author's larger truth about the American Dream: that it has been perpetuated not only to give hope for the fulfillment of material needs but also to fill a spiritual and emotional void.

This dualistic vision of the American Dream—one encompassing the material and the spiritual, money and love—haunts Fitzgerald's novels. Cowley explains: "In writing about the romance of money, as he did in most of his earlier novels and stories, he was dealing not only with an intimate truth but also with what seemed to him the central truth of his American age" (65). In examining the American Dream, Fitzgerald asks us, then, to consider two ideas in opposition to each other—the spiritual and romantic fulfillment that material success seems to promise and the danger of relying on the material to find happiness. Bewley draws further attention to the duality of Fitzgerald's notions when he writes, "We recognize that the great achievement of [*Gatsby*] is that it manages, while poetically evoking a sense of the goodness of that early dream, to offer the most damaging criticism of it in American literature" (47).

Still, there is more to Fitzgerald's work than scathing criticism; underlying much of his work is a veiled romanticism. Whereas previous incarnations of the American Dream tended to be forward-looking as they promised a bright future in exchange for present virtue and hard work, Fitzgerald's version is blatantly nostalgic as his characters long to recapture the beauty of vanished moments and the faith of earlier generations. Certainly, one of his greatest creations is Jay Gatsby, a romantic figure who stands amid a tumult of excess and immorality. An upstart bootlegger with shady connections, Gatsby nevertheless emerges as the novel's tragic hero, idealistic and astonishingly uncorrupted as he gazes at the green light at the end of the Buchanans' dock and seeks to recapture an irretrievable past. *Tender Is the Night* follows in the same vein with its story of the rise and fall of Dick Diver, an idealistic, promising young psychoanalyst who becomes another exhausted, dissipated failure trying to care for his mentally ill wife. As Harold Bloom and others remind us, the title and epigraph of the novel are taken from John Keats's "Ode to a Nightingale," and the works share more than a few words. Like the ode, the novel is structured around brief moments of transport in which the characters seem to exist in a time outside of time, followed by the intrusion of harsh realities (Doherty 183). It is in these novels that the dream of material wealth is bound up with dreams of love and fulfillment and ultimately proves to be the characters' downfall.

Although his first novel was enormously successful, Fitzgerald was well acquainted with both professional and personal failure. It is no coincidence that his work illuminates the disjunction between the American Dream and its nation of dreamers, yet he refused to accept the absolute corruption or abandonment of the dream. His was a dualist understanding of the American Dream, then, with which he struggled his entire life, and in Gatsby's bearing witness to the green light we find an unwavering affirmation of existential persistence and fortitude— perhaps the most certain affirmation that the author was capable of providing. Likewise, his novels and stories are filled with failed dreamers, and in his redefinition of the American Dream, Fitzgerald ultimately proposes the revival of a type of romanticism, one that persists even in the face of the impossible. It is a difficult thought: persistence in the face of almost certain failure. Still, Fitzgerald remained faithful to it. Perhaps the greatest evidence of this faith comes not from one of his characters but from Fitzgerald himself when, reflecting on the struggles of his life in *The Crack-Up*, he writes:

> The test of a first-rate intelligence is the ability to hold two opposed ideas in the mind at the same time, and still retain the ability to function. One should, for example, be able to see that things are hopeless and yet be determined to make them otherwise. . . .
>
> . . . I must hold in balance the sense of the futility of effort and the sense of the necessity to struggle; the conviction of the inevitability of failure and still the determination to "succeed"—and, more than these, the contradiction between the dead hand of the past and the high intentions of the future. (69-70)

Works Cited

Adams, James Truslow. *The Epic of America*. New York: Blue Ribbon Books, 1931.

Bewley, Marius. "Scott Fitzgerald and the Collapse of the American Dream." *F. Scott Fitzgerald*. Ed. Harold Bloom. New York: Chelsea House, 1985. 23-47.

Bloom, Harold, ed. *F. Scott Fitzgerald*. New York: Chelsea House, 1985.

Bruccoli, Matthew J. *Some Sort of Epic Grandeur: The Life of F. Scott Fitzgerald*. 2d rev. ed. Columbia: U of South Carolina P, 2002.

Burner, David, Virginia Bernhard, and Stanley I. Kutler. *Firsthand America: A History of the United States*. 4th ed. St. James, NY: Brandywine Press, 1996.

Cowley, Malcolm. "Fitzgerald: The Romance of Money." *F. Scott Fitzgerald*. Ed. Harold Bloom. New York: Chelsea House, 1985. 49-72.

Crèvecœur, J. Hector St. John de. *Letters from an American Farmer*. 1782. New York: Oxford UP, 1998.

Cullen, Jim. *The American Dream: A Short History of an Idea That Shaped a Nation*. New York: Oxford UP, 2004.

Doherty, William E. "*Tender Is the Night* and 'Ode to a Nightingale.'" *F. Scott Fitzgerald*. Ed. Harold Bloom. New York: Chelsea House, 1985. 181-94.

Fitzgerald, F. Scott. *The Crack-Up*. Ed. Edmund Wilson. 1945. New York: New Directions, 1993.

—————. *The Great Gatsby*. 1925. New York: Charles Scribner's Sons, 1953.

—————. *This Side of Paradise*. 1920. New York: Charles Scribner's Sons, 1998.

Franklin, Benjamin. *The Autobiography of Benjamin Franklin*. 1791. New York: Dover, 1996.

Martin, Waldo E. *The Mind of Frederick Douglass*. Chapel Hill: U of North Carolina P, 1984.

Thoreau, Henry David. *Walden*. 1854. Ed. Jeffrey S. Cramer. New Haven, CT: Yale UP, 2004.

Tocqueville, Alexis de. *Democracy in America*. 1835, 1840. New York: Penguin, 2001.

Wilson, Edmund. "F. Scott Fitzgerald." *F. Scott Fitzgerald*. Ed. Harold Bloom. New York: Chelsea House, 1985. 7-12.

Within and Without:
F. Scott Fitzgerald and
American Consumer Culture_____

Suzanne del Gizzo

In "The Crack-Up," the first installment of a three-part article series he wrote for *Esquire* magazine in 1936, F. Scott Fitzgerald observes, "The test of a first-rate intelligence is the ability to hold two opposed ideas in the mind at the same time, and still retain the ability to function" (69). Nowhere in his career does Fitzgerald live out this sentiment more fully than in his complex attitude toward American capitalism and consumer culture. On one hand, he—better than perhaps any other writer in American literature—captured the glamour, excitement, seduction, and power of money. We need only recall Gatsby's "blue gardens" and the limitless bubbles and rarified scents of John T. Unger's bath in "The Diamond as Big as the Ritz" to see this is true. On the other hand, Fitzgerald recognized that this privilege and beauty comes at high price. After all, the path from West Egg, Long Island, to the white canyons of New York City is marred by the grotesque ashen wasteland of the poor (and eventually Myrtle Wilson's dead body), and Braddock Washington is willing to imprison and kill men and even to attempt to bribe God to keep his diamond mountain a secret. Money and wealth are thus enchanting and dangerous, empowering and corrupting. Fitzgerald is an exemplary American writer in part because he recognizes this paradox in American life, and he, like so many of us, has no idea what to do about it. In fact, he and many of his characters (like many of us) are profoundly ambivalent about the American upper classes, simultaneously longing to join them and eyeing them with jealousy and suspicion.

Some readers are taken in by Fitzgerald's image as a high-living, flashy, Jazz Age personality and figure he only bungled his way into his two or three fine novels amid a drunken stupor. In fact, Fitzgerald himself cultivated this image in the first decade of his career. He and his wife, Zelda, became the poster children of the roaring 1920s, presenting themselves as carefree revelers who flaunted their money and their youth. Their excess is legendary; they gave doormen hundred-dollar tips and playfully penned pieces such as "How to Live on $36,000 a Year" while engaging in drunken, sophomoric stunts such as jumping into the water fountain outside the Plaza Hotel in New York City.[1] This public image, in addition to the fact that Fitzgerald never actually graduated from Princeton University, has encouraged some readers and critics to question "the fineness and discrimination of his intelligence" (Bewley 261) and "to regard [him] as an intellectual lightweight" (Donaldson, "Possessions" 199) who was essentially a talented but unfortunate victim of "swank parties, jazz tunes, alcohol, and coloured lights" (Bewley 260).

Fitzgerald scholars, however, caution against this oversimplification. As early as 1959, Marius Bewley contended that "the charge that Fitzgerald was 'taken in' by wealth is as irritating as it is untrue" (261). He observes, "There is a radical difference between coveting a 'tony' life that can only be supported by money—lots of money—and being critically and morally unable to assess the conditions under which the money must be acquired or its ultimate effects on character" (261). Bewley recognized that like Nick Carraway, the narrator of *The Great Gatsby*, Fitzgerald lived "within" and "without" the life of money and privilege he cataloged and that some of his "gaudiest celebrations of [that life] are simultaneously the most annihilating criticisms" (262). Nonetheless, Fitzgerald's attitude toward consumer culture is complex and ambivalent, and recognizing these "criticisms" requires sensitivity to the workings and logic of American consumerism.

Fitzgerald came of age as a man and a writer toward the end of a significant transition in American capitalism—the shift from a culture of production, in which one is identified and valued by what one makes, to one of consumption, in which one is defined and assessed by what one consumes or buys. In 1937, looking back on his early career, Fitzgerald observed, "America was going on the greatest, gaudiest spree in history and there was going to be plenty to tell about it" ("Early Success" 87). This "spree" of course refers to the economic boom and subsequent excessive materialism of America in the 1920s. Although spending and indulgence reached a frenzied pace by the 1920s, this behavior was several decades in the making. As social historian William Leach explains, "From the 1890s on, American corporate business, in league with key institutions, began the transformation of American society into a society preoccupied with consumption, with comfort and bodily well-being, with luxury, spending, and acquisition" (xiii). Increasingly, leisure and the acquisition of objects were presented as the right of all hardworking Americans, putting them—in a sense—on a par with the rich. Leach refers to this phenomenon as the "democratization of desire" (5); however, he also points out that although the middle and lower classes were liberated to "desire" what they wanted in the marketplace, this "democratization" and liberalization quickly became a form of limitation and imprisonment, because those in the middle and lower classes could rarely afford luxury items without incurring debt. In fact, consumer debt skyrocketed in the 1920s due to the new, nearly ubiquitous availability of credit and the destigmatization of personal debt. According to literary and cultural critic Kirk Curnutt, "by 1929 the consumer debt load in the United States exceeded $7 billion, while the percentage of disposable income that the average family saved fell by one-third from the preceding decade" (107). Such an emphasis on spending over saving marked a monumental change in American life.

The ascendency of consumer culture signaled a shift in foundational American values and traditional notions of the self. A consumer-based society entailed a departure from the Protestant work ethic, or the belief that hard work and thrift yield success and social respect, a notion that had traditionally underpinned belief in the American Dream and faith in a meritocracy. This "ethic" was replaced by one that put a premium not on work, saving, and humility but on leisure, spending, and the demonstration of wealth. Americans, however, had to learn to be consumers. Many articles of the period, with titles such as "Thrift—The New Menace" and "The Dilemma of Thrift," actively maligned citizens' tendency toward financial restraint and responsibility and encouraged prodigality and immediate satisfaction (Curnutt 105). In addition, the new consumer culture challenged Benjamin Franklin's notion that success hinges on developing and inculcating particular desirable character traits, espousing instead a world in which personality, attitude, and the image one projects publicly, bolstered, of course, by commodities—one's house, car, and so on—are of prime importance in establishing a sense of self and status.

The pressure and confusion wrought by the shift from a culture of production to one of consumption and its attendant effects on identity is at the core of most of F. Scott Fitzgerald's work, and it is particularly visible throughout his 1925 masterpiece, *The Great Gatsby*. Nick's contradictory reaction to Gatsby in the early pages of the novel, in which he presents the title character—within the space of one paragraph—as the representative of "everything for which I have unaffected scorn" and as a person who "turned out all right at the end" (6), encapsulates the ambivalence and uncertainty about these changes in American life. In short, Nick, like Fitzgerald, must hold "two opposed ideas in mind and still retain the ability to function" in order to continue with his narrative. By telling the story of the young, unwashed James Gatz's transformation into the spectacular Jay Gatsby, Nick succinctly demonstrates the swing away from character and toward acquisition and personality. The young Gatz begins in North Dakota from a Franklinian premise for success, which includes a list of improving behaviors in the back of his edition of *Hopalong Cassidy*. At some point, however, he veers off course, becoming a bootlegger with shady business "gonnegtions" who attempts to obscure the illegal and disreputable source of his money while securing his public position through the ostentatious display of objects. Nick, who hails from a solidly upper-middle-class family in the conservative Midwest, does find Gatsby suspicious and gauche, but he cannot simply condemn or dismiss Gatsby; rather, he concludes, "it was what preyed on Gatsby, what foul dust floated in the wake of his dreams that temporarily closed out my interest in the abortive sorrows and short-winded elations of men" (7). In some sense then, Gatsby is not the point of his story. He is simply the novel's most visible victim of a corrupt and morally questionable system of American consumerism and class.

This nuanced and ambiguous reaction to Gatsby is a sign of Fitzgerald's sophistication as a writer. *The Great Gatsby* and Fitzgerald's work more generally are powerful and compelling precisely because their critique of American capitalism and consumer culture is not didactic or unequivocal. Fitzgerald does not present his narratives as simple, unforgiving, ideologically fueled tirades with stereotyped characters whose likability falls out neatly along class lines. He does not discount or belittle American fascination with commodities; he understands and appreciates the enticements of the world of wealth, and he is one of the best in his business in translating them into lyrical language.

He is particularly gifted in describing objects and the power of money to transform the ordinary into the extraordinary. One of his favorite methods for achieving this effect is to present the wealthy and their objects as defying gravity: "floating rounds of cocktails permeate the garden" (41) during Gatsby's parties, Jordan and Daisy are presented as having to "[balloon] slowly to the floor" when Nick first sees them on a hot June day (12), and Gatsby himself seems to defy the law of physics as he "[balances] himself on the dashboard of his car with a resourcefulness of movement that is so peculiarly American" (68). Such descriptions highlight the supernatural properties of objects in a commodity culture while also suggesting how baseless and precarious these properties may ultimately be. Even when earthbound, Fitzgerald imbues his descriptions of objects with magical properties and endowments—turkeys are "bewitched" to a dark gold (44) and women become "orchids" (111). His gift for lyrical description, as I mentioned earlier, has sometimes led to the charge that Fitzgerald was a "victim" of the world of wealth. Such critics, however, miss the point. They do not recognize that the very opulence and excessiveness of his descriptions suggest a critique of the remarkable, magical, but ultimately deceptive and dangerous power of objects in a consumer culture, especially their seeming ability to create identity and social status. Fitzgerald's descriptive strategies emphasize that this world is not grounded in reality; rather, it is an airy, insubstantial world that has more in common with an illusory magical spell.

Fitzgerald's critique of commodity culture, however, was substantial and had much in common with some of the most pervasive social and economic theories of his day. The young author may not have read sociologist Thorstein Veblen by the time he sat down to write *Gatsby*, but literary biographer and critic Scott Donaldson has argued that Fitzgerald did know about Veblen and his work as early as 1921 ("Possessions" 201). Veblen's seminal book *The Theory of the Leisure Class* (1899) offered some of the earliest and keenest insights into the strategies and tactics of the burgeoning consumer culture in America. In particular, two concepts—"conspicuous consumption" and "pecuniary emulation"—clarified the new ways in which the acquisition of objects and notions of class or social standing were intersecting in modern industrial life. Veblen's concept of "conspicuous consumption" refers to the motivations for expenditure in a consumer-based society. According to him, consumers spend money lavishly and publicly with two aims in mind: first, the demonstration of purchasing power through the act of spending or shopping; second, the demonstration of wealth and social status through the display of objects once they are purchased. By today's standards, this observation may seem obvious, but the emphasis on the use of objects as a means to display wealth and status gave them a new significance in social life by disengaging them from their most basic, traditional purpose: to meet some particular, utilitarian need. Even more important, Veblen understood that through a phenomenon he called "pecuniary emulation" American consumer culture implicitly promised that the acquisition of objects, especially artful and purposeful acquisition, might be used as means of overcoming the limits of birth and class. Of course, Veblen recognized that such emulation was doomed to fail, since he also understood that "inherited wealth" would always remain, as Donaldson writes, "'even more honorific' than wealth acquired through one's own efforts" ("Possessions" 202). Stuart Ewen's more recent formulation of this concept of "pecuniary emulation" highlights the futility of the process; for him, the "central appeal of style [is] its ability to create an *illusory transcendence* of class or background" (qtd. in Curnutt 99; my italics).

Veblen's theories may have ultimately crystallized these ideas for Fitzgerald, but he seems to have intuited them early in life. Even as an adolescent, Fitzgerald honestly assessed the situation: "I didn't have the two top things—great animal magnetism or money. I had the two second things, tho', good looks and intelligence. So I always got the top girl" (qtd. in Bruccoli 54). He sensed that the right type of grooming, self-presentation, and dress had the power to communicate a particular impression of himself that might make up for (or at least cover up) his shortcomings. This capacity of objects and their role in self-presentation is continually explored in his writing. In his first novel, *This Side of Paradise*, the young hero, Amory, carefully tries on different fashions as a way of projecting the "right" personality that will win him popularity and favor with rich young women. Fitzgerald also experiments with this notion in reverse when the young, penniless Jay Gatsby woos the rich, desirable Daisy Fay using the "invisible cloak of his [army] uniform" (156). Because the uniform erases any indication of social standing or personal wealth, Gatsby "let [Daisy] believe that he was a person from much the same stratum as herself—that he was fully able to take care of her" (156), even though he "had no comfortable family standing behind him and he was liable at the whim of an impersonal government to be blown anywhere about the world" (156). Even in this example, which does not hinge on conspicuous consumption, Fitzgerald captures the power of objects to create or enable impressions. In both instances, but particularly in the case of Gatsby, Fitzgerald also conveys the element of imposture and performance that accompanies such self-conscious attempts at self-presentation.

Later, Gatsby purposefully utilizes conspicuous consumption and pecuniary emulation in his attempt to win Daisy. By the time they meet again on Long Island, he has carefully created the world in which he wishes Daisy to find him. He now has a narrative about his past and substantial objects that back up the story and testify to his wealth. Such efforts, however, cannot fully erase the sense of imposture and performance in Gatsby's personality. Consistently, Nick registers suspicion about the stories and the objects that surround his wealthy, mysterious neighbor. On a trip to New York in which Gatsby offers up a narrative of his past—so Nick will not think he is "just some nobody" (71)—Nick is skeptical; he remarks, "With an effort I managed to restrain my incredulous laughter. The very phrases [in Gatsby's story about himself] were worn so threadbare that they evoked no image except that of a turbaned 'character' leaking sawdust at every pore as he pursued a tiger through the Bois de Boulogne" (70). But when Gatsby produces a medal from World War I and a photograph of his time at Oxford, the objects work their magic, and Nick's skepticism is converted into faith: "Then it was all true" (71). At other times, even the most artful presentation of objects falls a bit short, such as when Nick runs into a man in Gatsby's re-creation of Oxford's Merton College library. Owl Eyes, as this man is called, appreciates the library as a setting in a complex performance, calling Gatsby a "regular Belasco" and praising him for his "realism," although he suspects that if "one brick was removed the whole library was liable to collapse" (50).[2]

Nonetheless, everything Gatsby has or does—his house, his car, his elaborate parties—is designed to demonstrate his position and wealth to Daisy. It is no mistake that their reunion scene in chapter 5 culminates with a tour of Gatsby's house during which he proudly displays possessions that testify to his accumulation of wealth since they last met—the "period bedrooms swathed in rose and lavender silk," the "toilet set of pure dull gold," and perhaps most memorably his "shirts

with stripes and scrolls and plaids in coral and apple green and lavender, and faint orange with monograms of Indian blue," sent over from
England, which prompt Daisy to "cry stormily" and profess that she
has "never seen such—such beautiful shirts before" (97-98). Clearly,
these are not just shirts; they are potent symbols of Gatsby's wealth.

The tour makes it clear that his objects are designed to secure his
new identity and make an argument for his fitness to be Daisy's lover.
At the same time, Fitzgerald communicates through Nick that Gatsby
is also trying to assess how convincing his performance is. He watches
how Daisy—the quintessential upper-class insider—reacts to his created world: "He hadn't once ceased looking at Daisy and I think he re-
valued everything in his house according to the measure of response it
drew from her well-loved eyes" (97). Fitzgerald simultaneously conveys Gatsby's achievement and his insecurity about it, which suggests
that Gatsby is not entirely comfortable in the world of the rich; he is
still plagued by feelings of imposture. Nonetheless, Gatsby has faith
that, with some adjustments in taste and presentation, he now has
enough money to win Daisy. It is here that Fitzgerald's critique
emerges; as Bewley has argued, unlike Gatsby, Fitzgerald "perfectly
understood the inadequacy of [a] romantic view of wealth" (271).

Gatsby is a sympathetic character, despite the fact that he is a criminal attempting to steal another man's wife, because he has absolute
faith in the power of money and objects to even the playing field of the
American class system. He is, as Curnutt argues, "Fitzgerald's richest
emblem of the self-deception of pecuniary emulation" (99); he really
believes he can transform himself and enter the highest echelons of society. What he does not realize is that in the eyes of the people who
populate this class he does not (and never will) quite get "it" right. Everything about him—from his large, incoherently decorated house and
pink suits to his debauched parties and tendency to call people "old
sport"—is overdone and marks him as parvenu. Donaldson observes:
"Given an opportunity, Gatsby consistently errs in the direction of os-
tentation. His clothes, his car, his house, his parties—all brand him as

newly rich, unschooled in the social graces and sense of superiority ingrained not only in Tom Buchanan but in Nick Carraway" ("Possessions" 188). He, like so many of the new rich, overcompensates in an attempt to make up for a lack of inherited wealth, but these overcompensations are quickly visible to those he most wants to impress. For example, when Tom is told that Gatsby is an Oxford man, he responds, "Like hell he is! He wears a pink suit" (129). When Daisy on a hot day remarks that Gatsby looks "so cool" and "resemble[s] the advertisement man" (125), Gatsby, Curnutt points out, "does not respond to this compliment, which to him would not be complimentary at all, for to suggest that his identity is constructed out of commodified images is to impugn the very mechanism of his self-realization" (100).

In these flawed performances and missteps, Fitzgerald subtly pairs Gatsby with another social aspirant, Tom's mistress, Myrtle Wilson. Although Myrtle is far less successful at crafting her identity than is Gatsby, like Gatsby's efforts, her attempts to assume a wealthy persona through conspicuous consumption and pecuniary emulation ring false. Fitzgerald mercilessly lampoons Myrtle's awkward performance of wealth on a trip into New York City with Nick and Tom during which she buys odd and random things, such as cold cream and perfume, meaninglessly passes over cabs until she finds a "lavender" one, and changes "costumes" (Fitzgerald's word, which signals that her behavior is a performance) three times. With each costume change, she seems to shake off the ash from her home until she assumes an "impressive hauteur" in "an elaborate afternoon dress of cream colored chiffon" (35). Her behavior becomes increasingly exaggerated as she performs for a ragtag group of people assembled in the overcrowded apartment Tom keeps for her. She freely pours whiskey, publicly reviews a shopping list for the next day (which she thinks is impressive but is actually quite modest), and laments the incompetence of the elevator boy, to whom she refers as one of "these people!" (36). Throughout the scene, Fitzgerald signals to the reader through Nick that although Myrtle believes she is living the high life, her tastes and affects—even the sensuousness of her body—give her away as solidly lower-middle-class. Her best efforts do not seem organic; it is clear that she is putting on airs.

Fitzgerald establishes critical distance from Gatsby and his view of the world in much the same way he satirizes Myrtle by registering Nick's, Tom's, and even Daisy's sense of Gatsby's performance. Gatsby's and Myrtle's flawed performances, however, are only a symptom of their larger misunderstanding of American class. Ultimately, Donaldson points out, Myrtle and Gatsby are "guilty" of the same "crucial error in judgment," namely, that "it is not money alone that matters, but money combined with secure social position" ("Possessions" 194). As Gatsby and Myrtle endeavor to acquire objects, "they are undone by the lack of cultivation that drives them to buy the wrong things" ("Possessions" 194), and in the process they reveal that they are not truly of the class they are attempting to imitate. In this way, Donaldson explains, they "fall victim to what Ronald Berman [borrowing from Pierre Bourdieu] calls 'the iron laws of social distinction'" ("Possessions" 194), or an invisible barrier—Fitzgerald calls it the "indiscernible barbed wire between [the wealthy and the less fortunate]" (155)—that has to do with intangibles such as taste and social grace. In other words, it is not just a matter of having money, but of having the right kind of money—what Veblen refers to as "inherited wealth"—which gives one not only established and recognized social status and connections but also a way of carrying oneself in the world in relation to others that cannot be flawlessly imitated.

It is for this reason that Gatsby shatters "like glass against Tom" (155) during their showdown at the Plaza Hotel. Gatsby's performance is fragile and insubstantial compared to Tom's inherited wealth and respected social status, which are grounded in his family name and pedigree. Tom will always be able to distinguish himself from Gatsby because he is a practitioner of what Veblen refers to as "conspicuous leisure," or the display of one's unemployment as a sign that one is wealthy enough not to need to work. Such a situation frees one up (even, according to Veblen, obligates one) to cultivate rarefied tastes based on extremely fine distinctions that demonstrate discrimination and social standing on a level that Gatsby cannot even imagine. Fitzgerald associates Tom with polo ponies and horses (which Gatsby does not have) because these signal not only that he has time to indulge the expensive habit but also that he has an interest in "breeding." Such an association suggests the importance of inherited qualities and ancestry as a means of distinguishing those who occupy the highest level of the class system. When Gatsby introduces Tom at one his parties as the "polo player," the difference between the two men is clear: Tom has never had a job, while Gatsby's "work" inconveniently intrudes even during his parties in the form of phone calls from mob cities such as "Detroit" and "Chicago." When Tom's suspicions are raised about Gatsby, he becomes determined to know "who [Gatsby] is" and, perhaps more important, "what he does" (115). Of course, the assumption that Gatsby "does" something already sets him apart from and beneath Tom.

Although *Gatsby* is not on any level a simple autobiographical tale, the circumstances of Fitzgerald's childhood and upbringing heightened his awareness of the issues the novel explores, and there are elements of his experience in the character of Gatsby, in particular the desire to belong to a class in which one does not entirely feel welcome. Fitzgerald's father, Edward Fitzgerald, hailed from an old, respectable southern family with an honorable name and history but no longer any significant wealth, a situation made worse by his lack of business acumen and inability to earn enough money to support his family. Fitzgerald's mother, Mary "Mollie" McQuillan, was the daughter of extremely successful Irish immigrants who, despite their wealth, had no real social standing. The match was a strange one. Edward was a dapper, cultured man who loved fashion and reading, while Mollie was generally indifferent to society and embarrassed her son by being insensitive to the nuances of dress and personal presentation. For these reasons, the Fitzgeralds occupied a marginal relationship to St. Paul's power elite. They tended to live on the outskirts of the desirable Summit Avenue neighborhood in rented apartments, but the young Scott attended the best schools and played with the children of his rich, socially established neighbors. In addition, Fitzgerald was raised Catholic in a world of Protestants at a time when Catholics were considered a marginal and even unpatriotic religious group because of their allegiance to the pope.

According to biographer Matthew J. Bruccoli, Fitzgerald's "sense of differentness in St. Paul sharpened his skills as a social observer and shaped his lifelong self-consciousness" (22). Fitzgerald explained how his upbringing had influenced his particular view of the world in a 1933 letter to his friend John O'Hara:

> I am half black Irish and half old American stock with the usual exaggerated ancestral pretensions. The black Irish half of the family had the money and looked down upon the Maryland side of the family who had, and really had, that certain series of reticences and obligations that go under the poor old shattered word "breeding" (modern form of "inhibitions"). So . . . I developed a two cylinder inferiority complex. (qtd. in Bruccoli 23)

In short, Fitzgerald always felt like an outsider, like a "poor boy in a rich boy's world," a feeling he continued to battle when, despite significant financial and academic obstacles, he entered Princeton University as a member of the class of 1917. These situations arguably helped him develop what Donaldson calls his "double vision" ("Possessions" 210) as someone both within the world of the rich and outside of it, which would uniquely position him to capture this world and critique it.

Fitzgerald's romantic life, in particular, reinforced his suspicion that there was "indiscernible barbed wire" between him and the upper-class world of many of his classmates and friends. He was never taken seriously by his first "love," the wealthy, beautiful Ginevra King of Lake Forest, Illinois. Although they shared a flirtation and exchanged letters, Ginevra later recalled that she never thought of Scott as anything special, and, according to the myths that have grown up around Fitzgerald, Ginevra's father made sure that Scott overheard his sentiment that "poor boys shouldn't think of marrying rich girls" (Bruccoli 64). Fitzgerald was nearly burned again when he fell in love with the daughter of a judge, Zelda Sayre, while stationed in the army near Montgomery, Alabama. When, after a passionate and exciting courtship, Zelda realized that the young Fitzgerald could not support her in the style to which she was accustomed, she broke off their engagement. This shock prompted him to revise his first novel, *This Side of Paradise*, which was ultimately published with great success by Scribner's.

Although he emerged triumphant—Zelda agreed to marry him once he had made money from the novel—Fitzgerald took hard lessons away from his upbringing and these early romantic experiences. He summarizes one of these lessons in the second article of "The Crack-Up" series:

> So it came out all right, but it came out all right for a different person. The man with the jingle of money in his pocket who married the girl a year later would always cherish an abiding distrust, an animosity toward the leisure class—not the conviction of a revolutionist but the smoldering hatred of a peasant. In the years since then I have never been able to stop wondering where my friends' money came from, nor to stop thinking that at one time a sort of *droit de seigneur* might have been exercised to give one of them my girl. ("Crack-Up" 77)

His experiences with Ginevra and Zelda reminded him that although, like Gatsby, he had an attractive appearance and charisma that let him walk among the wealthy, he was not really one of them. He, like Gatsby, had to work for the money he needed to win the object of his affection. His fear that one of his friends might have exercised a "*droit de seigneur*" to take Zelda away from him confirms his sense of himself as an outsider. This phrase refers to the alleged right of a lord during the Middle Ages to take the virginity of any of the women who lived on his land, including the daughters or fiancées of the peasants who worked his land. Notably, however, Fitzgerald explains that he did not become a "revolutionist" wishing to overthrow his powerful friends and their beautiful world but a "peasant" who "hated" the leisure class, which implied that he was also impressed by their power and longed to be accepted by them.

While he never became a "revolutionist," Fitzgerald's circumstances did make him an interested student of social, political, and economic literature. He read H. G. Wells and George Bernard Shaw while at Princeton and was influenced by their socialism. As early as 1924, he referred to himself as a "communist" (Gervais 117), although most Fitzgerald scholars believe he made this pronouncement more for shock value than anything else. His 1924 claim is not unlike the last chapter of *This Side of Paradise*, in which the recently impoverished young hero Amory Blaine finds himself hitching a ride from New York to Princeton with Mr. Ferrenby, an industrialist and father of one of his college friends who died in the war. The chapter is a halfhearted tirade against the injustices of the capitalist system and an announcement of Amory's intention to become a "militant socialist" (255), but Amory cannot muster the conviction to take the kind, intelligent Mr. Ferrenby (who has, after all, sacrificed his son in the war) to task over ideological issues. Amory even admits that his current disposition may have something to do with the fact that he is "very poor at present" (248). Such whims lead Ronald J. Gervais to suggest that "whatever radical leaning Fitzgerald professed, he was ultimately less interested in investigating social problems than in illuminating his own experience and feeling" (116). Gervais, however, may overstate the degree of Fitzgerald's self-centeredness here. Donaldson argues in "Fitzgerald's Political Development" that while "Fitzgerald began as a political naïf" (190), he did take politics seriously. By the 1930s, he became a serious student of Marxism and even hosted Communist Party meetings at his house outside Baltimore, La Paix, in 1932 (197). Despite his interest in socialism and Marxism, however, Fitzgerald simply was not, as were so many of his friends (and so many people of this period), ideologically driven. Even when most interested in communism, he could not uniformly dismiss the rich and American capitalism; his opinions were always tempered by a respect for individualism.

In addition, part of his inability to oppose American capitalism and consumerism outright was grounded in aesthetics. Fitzgerald struggled with the idea of the "poor" in his writing. He was aware of the poor and included them in a variety of ways in his stories, from developed characters like Myrtle Wilson to the butler whose thumb must press a little button two hundred times to extract the juice of two hundred oranges (*Gatsby* 42) to a smelly, faceless mass on subway trains (*Paradise* 237). In fact, just one chapter before Amory claims he has become a socialist in *This Side of Paradise*, he thinks: "I detest poor people . . . I hate them for being poor. Poverty may have been beautiful once, but it's rotten now. It's the ugliest thing in the world. It's essentially cleaner to be corrupt and rich than it is to be innocent and poor" (236). Amory's whole view of New York, a city he once enjoyed, has changed with his change in fortune: "It's a bad town unless you're on top of it" (238). Echoes of such sentiments are also included in *Gatsby*; an element of Daisy's appeal for the young Gatsby resides in the fact that she is "safe and proud above the hot struggles" of the poor (157).

At the same time, Fitzgerald understood the exploitation of the poor by the rich. In the well-known shopping scene from his later novel *Tender Is the Night* (1934), he penetratingly observes:

> Nicole bought from a great list that ran two pages, and bought the things in the windows besides. Everything she liked that she couldn't possibly use herself, she bought as a present for a friend. She bought colored beads, folding beach cushions, artificial flowers, honey, a guest bed, bags, scarfs, love birds, miniatures for a doll's house and three yards of some new cloth the color of prawns. . . . Nicole was the product of much ingenuity and toil. For her sake trains began their run at Chicago and traversed the round belly

of the continent to California; chicle factories fumed and link belts grew link by link in factories; men mixed toothpaste in vats and drew mouthwash out of copper hogsheads; girls canned tomatoes quickly in August or worked rudely at the Five-and-Tens on Christmas Eve; half-breed Indians toiled on Brazilian coffee plantations and dreamers were muscled out of patent rights in new tractors—these were some of the people who gave a tithe to Nicole, and as the whole system swayed and thundered onward it lent a feverish bloom to such processes of hers as wholesale buying, like the flush of a fireman's face holding his post before a spreading blaze. She illustrated very simple principles, containing in herself her own doom. (54-55)

Many scholars consider this scene to be Fitzgerald's strongest indictment of consumer culture, because he clearly links Nicole's spending to a system of exploitation and injustice and presents the "system" as a "doomed," out-of-control "blaze." Nonetheless, even here he is accused by ideologically driven socialists and Marxists of being too sympathetic to the rich. As a result, E. Ray Canterbery and Thomas Birch observe that Fitzgerald was perhaps "less interested in class struggle than in the struggle for class" (111). Certainly, Fitzgerald found the world of the rich more beautiful and inviting than the world of the poor, but he understood that it was likely unsustainable and most definitely unfair.

This unease with class distinctions and the exploitation of the poor by the rich prompts Ross Posnock to argue that, although it is difficult to make a case for Marx's "direct influence" on Fitzgerald, "Marx's critique is assimilated into [*Gatsby*'s] imaginative life" (201). In particular, Fitzgerald's intuitive grasp of Marx's concepts of "reification" and "commodity fetishism" informs not only his lyrical writing style but also his most biting critique of American capitalism and consumer culture. Marx's disciple Georg Lukács explains that "reification requires that a society learn to satisfy all its needs in terms of commodity exchange" (qtd. in Posnock 202). As a result, commodities assume "mystical" properties in our lives and are increasingly seen not as "the products of men's hands" but as "independent beings endowed with life" (qtd. in Posnock 202). In other words, we no longer see a car as just a simple machine built by other people to get us from point A to point B; rather, we see cars as part of our identity (otherwise a Hyundai would be as desirable as a BMW). Marx calls this process of attaching mystical qualities to objects "commodity fetishism" (qtd. in Posnock 203). Although initially this may appear harmless, Marx explains that the danger of rampant reification and commodity fetishism is that everything, including workers and people in general, is "transformed into a commercial commodity" (qtd. in Posnock 203). Such a process results in confusion between objects and people; "people become objects for each other, sized up as commodities to be bought or sold" (Posnock 203), while commodities are animated and even anthropomorphized.

Such logic is in part responsible for Fitzgerald's writing style. As shown before, not only does he describe objects as enchanted and endowed with human, and sometimes even superhuman, traits—such as the billboard that becomes the eyes of God—but he also captures the way in which people, particularly women, become objects: a movie star is presented as an orchid and, most notably, Daisy is figured as the "grail." His willingness to recognize in language that people and objects have become confused animates Fitzgerald's style while also providing the basis for his most trenchant criticism of consumer culture. When Gatsby sees Daisy as the "grail" (156), he confuses her with an object, albeit the most coveted object in history. This sentiment is reinforced in more disturbing passages, such as when Nick observes that "it excited [Gatsby] too that many men had already loved Daisy—it increased her value in his eyes" (156). Here, Daisy is presented as a commodity with a higher market value because she is desired or valued by others; she is a luxury item. The element of romance may soften the harshness of this statement, but ultimately Gatsby's objectification of Daisy is a symptom of the sickness and corruption that Fitzgerald attempts to capture in the novel.

After all, Gatsby's attitude toward Daisy is grounded in the same logic that makes the Buchanans detestable figures—a willingness to sacrifice people that extends from seeing them as objects. This attitude is pervasive in the novel, from small events such as Jordan downplaying the fact that her inattentiveness causes her to nearly hit a road worker with her car to large events such as Tom's misrepresentation of Gatsby's involvement in Myrtle's death. Although Gatsby adores Daisy and treats her as a well-loved object, his work in the criminal underworld implies that he too is willing to sacrifice people when necessary. Tom points out that he left a friend, Walter Chase, "in a lurch" to serve time in a jail in New Jersey when business called for it (141). Still, Gatsby is no match for Tom and Daisy, and he ultimately pays with his life for his desire to enter this cruel world, while Tom and Daisy are left untouched. Donaldson explains, "Fitzgerald is making [the point] that if you have enough money and position you can purchase immunity from punishment" ("Possessions" 196). The upper class are beyond the law, an observation seen elsewhere in Fitzgerald's work, such as when Braddock Washington imprisons and kills men, including the friends of his children, who wander onto his estate and learn about his diamond mountain in "The Diamond as Big as the Ritz." For Fitzgerald, then, consumer culture, which leads to confusion between people and objects, in turn permits unthinkable behavior that is not just illegal but also fundamentally immoral.

Although the moral confusion that results from commodity fetishism and reification is central to Fitzgerald's critique of consumer culture, he often presents the problem with characteristic subtlety. For example, the degree of moral confusion and decay in *Gatsby* is presented indirectly through Nick's increasingly disoriented and confused behavior over the course of his summer in New York. Nick begins as a very conservative midwesterner who wants to "telephone immediately for the police" (2) when he first learns that Tom has a mistress, in the opening pages of the novel. But as the novel progresses, Nick becomes increasingly tolerant of the immorality around him. He visits Tom and

Myrtle's love nest in the city, dates the inveterate liar Jordan Baker, and facilitates Gatsby's reunion with the married Daisy. He also seems to drink more than he suggests. In addition, he becomes increasingly disoriented and even manic, following random women on the street (61) and forgetting his own thirtieth birthday (143). His increasingly odd comportment suggests that this world is destructive and insalubrious. It is a beautiful promise turned bad—just as the "fresh, green breast of the new world" as it is first seen by the Dutch sailors hauntingly resonates with Myrtle's torn breast after the car accident and the cluttering of that pristine coastline with the "inessential houses" of the rich (189). In the end, Nick, trying to recover his balance, returns to the Midwest and presumably to more conservative social and traditional American values. Although Nick may escape, Fitzgerald does not suggest that he escapes unscathed. Nick may be willing to condemn Tom and Daisy as "careless people" who "smashed up things and creatures and then retreated back into their money or their vast carelessness" (187-88), but Fitzgerald also presents him as complicit in the system; he does not report Tom or Daisy as the real culprits in Myrtle's death, and, when he runs into Tom on the street, he shakes hands with him because "it seemed silly not to" (188). In such moments, Fitzgerald captures the complexity of applying systemic critique to individuals or even to oneself.

Fitzgerald's willingness to recognize such complexities allows him to offer one of the most sophisticated and compelling critiques of American capitalism and consumer culture precisely because his critique is not simple or univocal. He understands how enticing the world of the rich and beautiful is, but he also shows that this world is based on the exploitation of others. Fitzgerald may not be this world's most impassioned critic, but he is probably its most enduring and perceptive one because he is willing to view it from "within" and from "without."

Notes

1. At the time, $36,000 was a significant amount of money. It had the same buying power as approximately $453,000 in 2009 (Officer and Williamson).

2. "Belasco" refers to David Belasco (1854-1931), a well-known Broadway producer whose sets were acknowledged for their realism.

Works Cited

Bewley, Marius. *The Eccentric Design: Form in the Classic American Novel*. New York: Columbia UP, 1959.

Bruccoli, Matthew J. *Some Sort of Epic Grandeur: The Life of F. Scott Fitzgerald*. 2d rev. ed. Columbia: U of South Carolina P, 2002.

Canterbery, E. Ray, and Thomas Birch. *F. Scott Fitzgerald: Under the Influence*. St. Paul, MN: Paragon House, 2006.

Curnutt, Kirk. "Fitzgerald's Consumer World." *A Historical Guide to F. Scott Fitzgerald*. Ed. Kirk Curnutt. New York: Oxford UP, 2004. 85-128.

Donaldson, Scott. "Fitzgerald's Political Development." *Fitzgerald and Hemingway: Works and Days*. New York: Columbia UP, 2009. 189-218.

_____. "Possessions in *The Great Gatsby*." *Southern Review* 30 (2001): 187-210.

Fitzgerald, F. Scott. "The Crack-Up." *The Crack-Up*. Ed. Edmund Wilson. 1945. New York: New Directions, 1993. 69-84.

_____. "The Diamond as Big as the Ritz." *The Short Stories of F. Scott Fitzgerald*. Ed. Matthew J. Bruccoli. New York: Simon & Schuster, 1989. 182-216.

_____. "Early Success." *The Crack-Up*. Ed. Edmund Wilson. 1945. New York: New Directions, 1993. 85-90.

_____. *The Great Gatsby*. 1925. Ed. Matthew J. Bruccoli. New York: Simon & Schuster, 1995.

_____. *Tender Is the Night*. 1934. New York: Charles Scribner's Sons, 2003.

_____. *This Side of Paradise*. 1920. Ed. James L. W. West III. New York: Simon & Schuster, 1998.

Gervais, Ronald J. "Daisy or Marx?" *Class Conflict in F. Scott Fitzgerald's "The Great Gatsby."* Ed. Claudia Johnson. New York: Greenhaven Press, 2008. 113-18.

Leach, William. *The Land of Desire: Merchants, Power, and the Rise of a New American Culture*. New York: Pantheon Books, 1993.

Officer, Lawrence H., and Samuel H. Williamson. "Purchasing Power of Money in the United States from 1774 to 2008." *MeasuringWorth*. 15 Dec. 2009. http://www.measuringworth.com/ppowerus.

Posnock, Ross. "'A New World, Material Without Being Real': Fitzgerald's Critique of Capitalism in *The Great Gatsby*." *Critical Essays on F. Scott Fitzgerald's "The Great Gatsby."* Ed. Scott Donaldson. Boston: G. K. Hall, 1984. 201-13.

F. Scott Fitzgerald's Critical Reception_____

Cathy W. Barks

"I want to be one of the greatest writers who ever lived, don't you?" F. Scott Fitzgerald once said to his friend Edmund "Bunny" Wilson when they were students at Princeton. Fitzgerald made a huge literary splash at a young age, and though over the course of his life his popular and critical reputation rose and fell, he never quite met the impossibly high standards that he held for himself. When he died, at just forty-four, he was all but forgotten. His early ambition to be not only a writer but also a great one was the driving force of his existence, however, and he pursued this aspiration regardless of the many obstacles with which he struggled throughout his too brief and uneasy life. Today, his reputation is firmly established. *The Great Gatsby* is the foremost classic American novel, and scholarly and popular interest in Fitzgerald's life and his work remain high and continue to produce fresh approaches.

Fitzgerald was only twenty-four when he published his first novel, *This Side of Paradise*, and became famous almost overnight. Critically, the book was received as that of a talented, highly promising, but as yet artistically immature writer. It had all the flaws that first novels often have, plus a few, but what it did well, it did exceptionally well: it caught the rhythms, fads, and beliefs of a new generation who were different in every way from their parents. "The glorious spirit of abounding youth glows throughout this tale," wrote a reviewer for *The New York Times* (in Bryer, *Critical Reception* 21),[1] and H. L. Mencken wrote that *This Side of Paradise* was "a truly amazing first novel—original in structure, extremely sophisticated in manner, and adorned with a brilliancy that is as rare in American writing as honesty is in American Statecraft" (28). A particularly prudish critic claimed that the novel would be harmful to "the youth of the nation" because "it deals too much with the more objectionable tendencies of youth and disregards the spiritual nature which develops rapidly during these years" (32).

Today, the novel's faults are obvious, but just as obvious are the remarkably well-written passages that presage Fitzgerald's later talent as a writer of wit and grace and remarkable beauty, one who could bring the social history—the speech, clothes, dreams, and desires—of his period to life not only for his contemporaries but for subsequent generations as well. *This Side of Paradise* will not be found on any list of American classics, but bookstores still stock it, and it continues to be read with pleasure. The novel's success instantly made its young author wealthy. As soon as it was published, he married Zelda Sayre, a southerner who was known as the prettiest and most popular girl in at least three states. Because the book seemed to herald a swift change in the culture, and because Scott and Zelda were young, good-looking, and glad to put on a show, the couple soon became celebrities. Popular magazines such as the *Saturday Evening Post* paid handsome prices for Fitzgerald's short stories about flappers and college men. The stories depicted cultural changes and created them at the same time as young people eagerly read the pieces as manuals on how to be popular and up-to-date.

Next, Fitzgerald published his first collection of short stories, *Flappers and Philosophers* (1920). The stories were uneven in quality and the reviews mixed. Fanny Butcher rightly predicted that "Bernice Bobs Her Hair" and "The Ice Palace" would become classics, but Mencken wrote that the collection included "the very good and the very bad" (48), and many reviewers judged the stories as "disappointing" after the promise of the novel. Heywood Broun said that "Fitzgerald's observations" of American youth depicted in these stories "may be entirely accurate. We only doubt whether they are important" (45). The collection, nevertheless, sold well and kept Fitzgerald in the public eye. *The Beautiful and Damned*, Fitzgerald's second novel, published in 1922, also met with mixed reviews, but, like the stories, it was generally judged to be another disappointment given the bright potential of *This Side of Paradise*. Critics recognized that it was a structural improvement over the first—more sustained and consistent—but, being heavily influenced by the school of naturalism, it was less exciting than *This Side of Paradise*. Some critics objected to what they characterized as long passages of moralizing. Later that year, Fitzgerald's second volume of short stories, *Tales of the Jazz Age*, appeared. Critics again responded with mixed reviews. Margaret Culkin called it an "uneven work of genius" (147) while another reviewer called Fitzgerald the "enfant terrible of modern American literature" and a "Twentieth Century seer who knows how to write" (139). John Gunther complained that Fitzgerald had "assembled [a] mixture of bad, fair and good—but not his best" (115).

No one wanted Fitzgerald to fulfill his early promise as a writer more than did Fitzgerald himself. "I'm tired of being the author of *This Side of Paradise*," he wrote to his Scribner's editor Maxwell Perkins, "and I want to start over" (*Life in Letters* 84). He wanted to become a mature, first-rate writer, the kind of writer he admired. With *The Great Gatsby*, published in 1925, Fitzgerald realized his ambition. In just five years, he made the leap from promising writer to a writer in control of his craft. In a review of the book for *The Dial*, Gilbert Seldes wrote, "Fitzgerald has more than matured; he has mastered his talents and gone soaring in a beautiful flight" (239). Some reviewers found the novel melodramatic and some found it lurid, but most of the prominent reviewers agreed that *Gatsby* was a beautifully crafted and moving story that captured the social milieu of the day. Conrad Aiken's review for *New Criterion* was especially perceptive in its recognition of how Fitzgerald adapted film techniques such as "flash-backs and close-ups." Aiken praised the novel for its creation of a tragic hero:

> The story itself, and the main figure, are tragic, and it is precisely the fantastic vulgarity of the scene which gives to the excellence of Gatsby's soul its finest bouquet, and to his tragic fate its sharpest edge. . . . He is betrayed slowly and skillfully, and with a keen tenderness which in the end makes his tragedy a moving one. (244)

The reception that meant the most to Fitzgerald was the one he received in letters from other writers such as Willa Cather, Edith Wharton, and T. S. Eliot, major artists with established reputations and whom Fitzgerald respected.

In 1926, Fitzgerald published what would be his best collection of short stories, *All the Sad Young Men*, which included two of his best and most important stories, "The Rich Boy" and "Winter Dreams." The volume sold well and met with good reviews. One reviewer, William Rose Benét, prophetically raised the topic of time and money: "A young writer who is earning his living at literature must work fast and put his books close together. Mr. Fitzgerald has elected so to live" (268). Though it could not have been known at the time, Fitzgerald, who published his first novel in 1920, his second in 1922, and his third in 1925, with a volume of short fiction following each, had ended his early years of "fast" production.

The Great Gatsby sold well but failed to earn the large sum of money that Fitzgerald was counting on to get him out of debt and allow him to continue writing serious fiction without constant financial worries. Not long after *Gatsby* was published, Fitzgerald enthusiastically wrote to Perkins: "The happiest thought I have is of my new novel—it is something really NEW in form, idea, structure—the model for the age that Joyce and Stein are searching for, that Conrad didn't find" (*Life in Letters* 108). That novel would eventually become *Tender Is the Night*, and it would take him nine years of unrelenting struggle to complete it. The financial pressures Fitzgerald had hoped to escape, along with Zelda's deteriorating mental health and his advancing alcoholism, nagged him every step of the way. During those nine years, he made numerous false starts as he hacked out short stories for magazines and wrote for Hollywood to pay the bills.

Tender Is the Night was published in 1934 and received largely favorable, though qualified, reviews. Factors extraneous to the novel's merit greatly influenced critical opinions of it. First, because it had been so long since Fitzgerald's last novel, critics held what were probably unrealistically high expectations when the new novel finally appeared. Malcolm Cowley, for example, wrote, "'Tender Is the Night' is a good novel that puzzles you and ends by making you a little angry because it isn't a great novel also" (323). Gossip about Fitzgerald's alcoholism and deterioration also colored how the literary set viewed the author and his work. Finally, the novel was published in the midst of the Great Depression, when proletarian novels and Marxist criticism were in vogue and the dissipation and destruction of an American protagonist living on the French Riviera could seem irrelevant to some. Clifton Fadiman, writing for *The New Yorker,* complained that "the world of luxurious living" was the only world that Fitzgerald could write about (301). Still, reviewers had positive things to say, and by Depression standards the book sold well. Gilbert Seldes proclaimed that he found *Tender Is the Night* moving and unforgettable, and that Fitzgerald had written a "Superb Tragic Novel" (292).

Fitzgerald felt that his reputation now depended on this novel, and the years since *Gatsby* had been so fraught with failure and disappointment that he was desperate to redeem himself. The mixed reviews hurt him, and the long letter that Ernest Hemingway sent, saying that although he thought parts of the novel were good, others were "fake," hurt Fitzgerald even more. Hemingway later admitted to their editor, Perkins, that after his initial reaction, the novel lingered in his mind and seemed to get better and better, but his criticisms had come at the time when Fitzgerald was most sensitive to how his work was received. He was deeply disappointed in the reception of the novel that he believed to be his best. John O'Hara, a novelist who knew and much admired Fitzgerald, said that the qualified reception of *Tender* "without a doubt broke Fitzgerald's heart" (qtd. in Bruccoli, *Epic Grandeur* 367). The following year, Scribner's released what would be Fitzgerald's last book published in his lifetime, *Taps at Reveille,* another collection of short stories. The reviews in the main were positive, but Depression-era sales were poor, and Fitzgerald was exhausted.

His alcoholism accelerated, and he was repeatedly hospitalized for treatment. Any small progress was soon blotted out by painful relapses. Zelda grew sicker, too, and her hospital bills put a considerable strain on Fitzgerald. In 1935, he hit his lowest point and entered a long period of depression that would last until sometime in 1937. It was during this time that he withdrew to a cheap hotel in Hendersonville, North Carolina, not far from where Zelda was hospitalized, and, while living off apples and tins of meat, wrote the essays that make up the "Crack-Up" sequence—"The Crack-Up," "Pasting It Together," and "Handle With Care"—which were published in the February, March, and April issues of *Esquire* in 1936. In these essays, Fitzgerald wrote candidly about his disillusionment and melancholy and tried to discover what exactly had gone wrong in life and why—a practice that is common today but was highly unusual in the 1930s. The essays met with nearly unanimous disdain. Even Fitzgerald's friends reproached him. Just at the time he most needed understanding, he was further humiliated.

Nevertheless, he vowed he would get his life in order. In 1937, Fitzgerald moved to Hollywood to write for the movies and earn enough money to pay his debts. While there, he met Sheilah Graham, a gossip columnist, and fell in love. Graham provided him with the stability he needed to be reasonably happy and hopeful about the future. He tried to stop drinking and went on the wagon only to fall off again, until he finally gave up alcohol altogether. Nevertheless, the years of alcoholism had severely damaged his heath, and he died of a heart attack in 1940, when he was only forty-four years old. His reputation was at an all-time low. The younger generation thought that he had already been dead for years if they thought about him at all. Despite his bad health and relative obscurity, however, Fitzgerald had been enthusiastically and productively at work on a new novel about Hollywood, the protagonist of which was a fictionalized version of the film producer Irving Thalberg. The novel was only two-thirds finished when Fitzgerald died, but it was published after his death under the title *The Last Tycoon*. Fitzgerald's friend from Princeton, Edmund Wilson, who had by now become a prominent literary critic, edited the manuscript and published it in a volume that included *The Great Gatsby*, a few of Fitzgerald's best short stories, and several pages of Fitzgerald's notes, thereby initiating the next phase of Fitzgerald's reception—the posthumous revival of his reputation.

Margaret Marshall, writing for *The Nation*, said that Fitzgerald's notes were "intensely moving as the intimate remarks to himself of a sensitive and highly gifted human being," and she wrote approvingly about the new novel (364). In a review for *The New York Times Book Review*, J. Donald Adams wrote:

> "The Last Tycoon" . . . uncompleted though it is, one would be blind indeed not to see that it would have been Fitzgerald's very best novel and a very fine one. Even in its truncated form it not only makes absorbing reading, it is the best piece of creative writing that we have about one phase of American life—Hollywood and the movies. (366)

Stephen Vincent Benét reviewed the novel in the *Saturday Review of Literature* and wrote what has become the reassessment of Fitzgerald's work that is most often repeated, because it was so prophetic:

> The evidence is in. You can take off your hats now, gentlemen, and I think perhaps you had better. This is not a legend, this is a reputation—and, seen in perspective, it may well be one of the most secure reputations of our time. (in Kazin 131-32)

The reassessment took up again in 1945 when Wilson edited and published *The Crack-Up* and Dorothy Parker assembled *The Portable F. Scott Fitzgerald*, which included *Gatsby*, *Tender Is the Night*, and several short stories. *The Crack-Up*, in particular, initiated a more thoughtful reconsideration of Fitzgerald and his work. The volume included miscellaneous excerpts from Fitzgerald's notebooks and letters and brief tributes from other writers, but most important, it collected the autobiographical essays that Fitzgerald published in magazines between 1931 and 1937, creating a sequence, as Wilson expressed, that "vividly puts on record [Fitzgerald's] state of mind and point of view during the later years of his life" (*Crack-Up* 11). The essay "Echoes of the Jazz Age," first published in 1931, captures the period and its aftermath so well that it has become an important document in America's social history. The "Crack-Up" essays, in which Fitzgerald chronicled his breakdown and which met with such disdain when first published a few years earlier, now seemed more incisive and poignant and called for a reevaluation. Glenway Wescott, for example, wrote, "In a wonderful essay entitled *The Crack-Up* [Fitzgerald] took stock of himself, looking twenty years back at what flaws were in him or in the day and age" (323). Wescott concluded, "The great thing about Fitzgerald was his candor; verbal courage; simplicity" (334).

About the same time as the writers and critics who knew Fitzgerald went on record with tributes and reassessments, other prominent figures also started taking a fresh look at the man and his work. In the introduction to *The Great Gatsby* published by New Directions in 1945, Lionel Trilling stated, "Fitzgerald is now beginning to take his place in our literary tradition" (qtd. in Mizener, "Gatsby" 46). In an expanded version of this introduction, "F. Scott Fitzgerald," published in *The Nation* in 1945 and reprinted in *The Liberal Imagination* in 1950, Trilling further asserted, "In Fitzgerald's work the voice of his prose is of the essence of his success. We hear in it at once the tenderness toward human desire that modifies a true firmness of moral judgment. It is, I would venture to say, the normal or ideal voice of the novelist" (253).

In 1951, another New York intellectual, Alfred Kazin, gathered some of the best of the critical assessments of Fitzgerald's work written between 1920 to 1951 (and added his own) in *F. Scott Fitzgerald: The Man and His Work*, a collection that to this day is indispensable in Fitzgerald studies. In the same year, Malcolm Cowley edited and introduced *The Stories of F. Scott Fitzgerald*, in which Cowley not only revived the best of Fitzgerald's short fiction but also introduced the stories with a perceptive essay that interconnects the themes in Fitzgerald's life with those of his work and articulates Fitzgerald's role in American literary history:

> Those who were lucky enough to be born a little before the end of the old century, in any of the years from 1895 to 1900 . . . identified themselves with the century; its teens were their teens; its world war was theirs to fight and its reckless twenties were their twenties. As they launched forward on their careers they looked about them for spokesmen and the first they found was F. Scott Fitzgerald. (vii)

Cowley's essay is personal, intimate, and astute, and it remains a superb introduction to Fitzgerald and a staple in Fitzgerald studies. During this period, Arthur Mizener, a Princeton and Harvard graduate, began his career as a scholar with the goal of doing justice to Fitzgerald's work, which he felt had been neglected. The result was the first book-length biography of Fitzgerald, *The Far Side of Paradise*, published in 1951 and revised in 1965. Mizener's biography remains an invaluable, sensitive account of Fitzgerald's life and offers an insightful analysis of the work. Moreover, the biography was a huge commercial success, proving that the public's interest in Fitzgerald was once again high.

Thus the body of work on Fitzgerald in the decade following his death provides a very solid and fertile ground for the scholarship and critical inquiry that followed and today shows no signs of abating. Book-length studies, collections of essays, and individual essays in academic journals and popular magazines abound. In addition, Fitzgerald has a place in nearly every major examination of twentieth-century American literature. Students and readers of Fitzgerald today can turn to bibliographies, biographies, letters, numerous volumes of literary criticism, and works on background and context to aid in their understanding and appreciation of Fitzgerald's life and work. Some of the best of these are discussed below.

Much of Fitzgerald criticism has been biographical, and those readers interested in Fitzgerald's life might start with Mizener's *The Far Side of Paradise*. Mizener writes intelligently and perceptively about Fitzgerald's life, and his analysis of Fitzgerald's work stands as a solid critical introduction. Andrew Turnbull's *Scott Fitzgerald* (1962) is also of interest because as a child Turnbull knew Fitzgerald, and he remained close to him when he became an adult. Turnbull's biography is a dependable as well as intimate and poignant depiction of Fitzgerald. Frances Kroll Ring's *Against the Current: As I Remember F. Scott Fitzgerald* (1985) provides another warm depiction of Fitzgerald. Ring became Fitzgerald's secretary in Hollywood when she was only nineteen and was with him almost daily during the last twenty months of his life. Matthew J. Bruccoli's *Some Sort of Epic Grandeur* (1981; second revised edition, 2002) is considered the most complete of Fitzgerald's biographies. Several biographies of Zelda Fitzgerald have also been written, but the most reliable and balanced and remains the first, Nancy Milford's *Zelda* (1970), as subsequent biographies of Zelda have been marred by an overtly feminist agenda that unfairly villainizes Scott. Those interested in Zelda's writing—she published a novel, *Save Me the Waltz*, and some short stories and magazine articles—can refer to *The Collected Writings* (1991), edited by Bruccoli.

Complementing the biographies are several collections of Fitzgerald's letters, the most useful being *F. Scott Fitzgerald: A Life in Letters* (1994), edited by Bruccoli. Here, the letters are arranged chronologically and can be read as an autobiographical narrative. *Dear Scott, Dearest Zelda* (2002), edited by Jackson R. Bryer and Cathy W. Barks, is a collection of the letters that the Fitzgeralds sent to each other, spanning the time from the beginning of their courtship until Fitzgerald's death. Zelda's letters to Fitzgerald serve as a corrective to the myth that Fitzgerald stifled his wife's creativity, as they bring to light Zelda's view of their marriage in her own words. *The Romantic Egoists: A Pictorial Autobiography from the Scrapbooks and Albums of F. Scott and Zelda Fitzgerald* (1974), edited by Bruccoli, Scottie Fitzgerald Smith (the Fitzgeralds' only child), and Joan P. Kerr, is an invaluable resource that includes a large selection of pictures of the Fitzgeralds, newspaper clippings from their scrapbooks, and images of Zelda's artwork, such as the paper dolls of her family that she made for her daughter, the drawings with which she decorated the scrapbooks, and several of her paintings.

In the same vein as biography, scholars and general audiences alike have long been fascinated by the troubled friendship between Fitzgerald and Ernest Hemingway. Bruccoli reconstructs this relationship through documentary evidence such as letters, interviews, and memoirs in *Scott and Ernest: The Authority of Failure and the Authority of Success* (1978), a revision of which was published in 1994 as *Fitzgerald and Hemingway: A Dangerous Friendship*. Scott Donaldson uses these documents and conducts further research to offer a balanced, thorough, and highly engaging analysis of this complex relationship in *Hemingway vs. Fitzgerald: The Rise and Fall of a Literary Friendship* (1999). Donaldson concludes:

> What Scott loved about Ernest was the idealized version of the sort of man—courageous, stoic, masterful—he could never be. What Ernest loved about Scott was the vulnerability and charm that his invented persona required him to despise. It made for a poignant story, really: one great writer humiliating himself in pursuit of a companionship that another's hardness of heart would not permit. (322)

In addition to providing a detailed analysis of Hemingway and Fitzgerald, Donaldson's book brings the literary period to life through the personalities and relationships of many of the era's principal players.

Bibliographies, reception studies, and reference works can also be useful tools for readers and researchers. Bruccoli's *F. Scott Fitzgerald: A Descriptive Bibliography* (1972) and "Supplement" (2002) provide a definitive primary list of Fitzgerald's work. Bryer's *F. Scott Fitzgerald: The Critical Reception* (1978) reprints a wide and well-chosen selection of the reviews of Fitzgerald's work during his lifetime and is the source used in the study at hand. Mary Jo Tate's *F. Scott Fitzgerald A to Z: The Essential Reference to His Life and Work* (1998) contains entries for nearly everything a reader could want to know about Fitzgerald and his work.

From the beginning of the Fitzgerald revival to the present, readers and scholars have been interested in Fitzgerald's lyrically evocative writing style, his eloquence, his use of literary techniques, and what his fiction tells us about American life and American dreams. Among the best of these studies are Richard D. Lehan's *F. Scott Fitzgerald and the Craft of Fiction* (1966), which offers explications of the novels; Milton R. Stern's *The Golden Moment: The Novels of F. Scott Fitzgerald* (1970); and John F. Callahan's *The Illusions of a Nation: Myth and History in the Novels of F. Scott Fitzgerald* (1972), which examines the work in terms of American history, ideas, and identity. Brian Way's *F. Scott Fitzgerald and the Art of Social Fiction* (1980) is an excellent analysis of Fitzgerald's work from a British point of view.

Many fine book-length studies have been published on individual novels. Lehan's *"The Great Gatsby": The Limits of Wonder* (1990) offers an accessible analysis of that novel's text and its social and historical context. Bruccoli's *F. Scott Fitzgerald's "The Great Gatsby": A Literary Reference* (2000) gives students and general readers a wealth of information that clarifies the critical and popular significance of the novel. Stern's *"Tender Is the Night": The Broken Universe* (1994) provides a sensitive analysis of Fitzgerald's last completed novel. Along with his novels, Fitzgerald's short stories continue to be read, investigated, and enjoyed. Excellent resources for the study of the stories include Jackson R. Bryer's *The Short Stories of F. Scott Fitzgerald: New Approaches to Criticism* (1982), a collection of twenty essays; John Kuehl's *F. Scott Fitzgerald: A Study of the Short Fiction* (1991); and Bryant Mangum's *A Fortune Yet: Money in the Art of F. Scott Fitzgerald's Short Stories* (1991).

Another productive approach to Fitzgerald's work has been the analysis of the roles of women in his fiction. In *The Resisting Reader:*

A Feminist Approach to American Fiction (1978), Judith Fetterley argues that "*The Great Gatsby* is another American 'love' story centered in hostility to women and the concomitant strategy of the scapegoat" (72). Sarah Beebe Fryer, in *Fitzgerald's New Women: Harbingers of Change* (1988), on the other hand, offers analyses of Fitzgerald's major female characters from a historical perspective and concludes that the author was sensitive to and accurate in his portrayal of the conflicts women faced during the social revolution of the period. In a recent and compelling essay, "Women in Fitzgerald's Fiction" (2002), Rena Sanderson argues that Fitzgerald's "writings are strongly androgynous" and that "it was Fitzgerald's American young girl with her 'boyish' characteristics that helped dismantle established concepts of male and female nature" (162). Joan M. Allen's *Candles and Carnival Lights: The Catholic Sensibility of F. Scott Fitzgerald* (1978) remains valuable for its analysis of the role Fitzgerald's Catholic upbringing plays in his work.

Today, Fitzgerald studies continues to thrive and grow more sophisticated. First under the editorship of Matthew J. Bruccoli, then James L. W. West III, *The Cambridge Edition of the Works of F. Scott Fitzgerald* (1991-   ) offers definitive editions of Fitzgerald's works with detailed histories of their composition and facsimiles of Fitzgerald's drafts and notes. Current cultural studies approaches explore issues of consumer culture, youth culture, and celebrity culture in Fitzgerald's work—issues that link our own era to Fitzgerald's in ways that illuminate both. Important examinations of these topics can be found in three essays by Kirk Curnutt: "Youth Culture and the Spectacle of Waste: *This Side of Paradise* and *The Beautiful and Damned*" (2003), which is reprinted in this volume; "F. Scott Fitzgerald, Age Consciousness, and the Rise of American Youth Culture" (2002); and "Fitzgerald's Consumer World" (2004). Also important is Ruth Prigozy's introduction to *The Cambridge Companion to F. Scott Fitzgerald* (2002), "Scott, Zelda, and the Culture of Celebrity." Ronald Berman, in a new and valuable line of inquiry, connects Fitzgerald and his work to the social thought and intellectual history of the period in *Fitzgerald, Hemingway, and the Twenties* (2001), "Fitzgerald's Intellectual Context" (2004), and *Translating Modernism: Fitzgerald and Hemingway* (2009).

Further valuable recent essays can be found in *F. Scott Fitzgerald: New Perspectives* (2000), edited by Bryer, Alan Margolies, and Prigozy. *The Cambridge Companion to F. Scott Fitzgerald* (2002), edited by Prigozy, is a collection of essays (many of them already mentioned) that address Fitzgerald's life and work "with a full and accessible picture of each, against the background of American social and cultural change in the early decades of the twentieth century" (xv). *The Cambridge Introduction to F. Scott Fitzgerald* (2007), by Curnutt, is divided into four chapters—"Life," "Cultural Contexts," "Works," and "Critical Reception"—and is an especially fine, readable introduction to Fitzgerald that offers suggestions for further inquiry. In addition to these resources, *The F. Scott Fitzgerald Review*, which published its first issue 2002, contributes new critical essays and reviews relevant new book-length studies each year.

Decades after his final work was published, Fitzgerald continues to be an iconic figure in popular culture. *The Great Gatsby* has been adapted to film four times—1926, 1949, 1974, 2000—and though none these adaptations quite match the book's brilliance and charm, filmmakers have still not been deterred from attempting to transform the great novel into a great film. The novel has also been adapted into numerous plays and even a lavish opera commissioned by the New York Metropolitan Opera in 1999. *Tender Is the Night* was adapted as a film in 1962 and as a television miniseries in 1985, and *The Last Tycoon* was made into a movie in 1976.

College and high school English instructors continue to introduce students to *The Great Gatsby* and, thereby, Fitzgerald, and *Gatsby* is one of the most read American novels in the world. Almost seventy-five years after its publication, the Modern Library's list of the "100 Best Novels of the 20th Century" ranked *The Great Gatsby* second (first was James Joyce's *Ulysses*; "100 Best"). The novel worked its way into the fabric of America, and critiques of American life and culture in popular magazines today often refer to the characters, themes, and vision of American life that Fitzgerald depicted in it.

Readers not only admire Fitzgerald's writing, but they also often have extraordinary affection for the man himself. The prominent writer Paul Auster eloquently expresses the feelings of so many ordinary readers:

> I first read *The Great Gatsby* as a high school student more than thirty years ago, and even now I don't think I have fully recovered from the experience. Fitzgerald's book is not like other books. It does more than just tell a story—it cuts to the heart of storytelling itself—and the result is a work of such simplicity, power, and beauty that one is marked by it forever. I realize that I am not alone in my opinion, but I can't think of another twentieth-century American novel that has meant as much to me. (qtd. in Bruccoli, *Fitzgerald's "Great Gatsby"* 308)

Fitzgerald's work lasts because his vision of aspiration and loss seems to echo our own most heightened aspirations and longings back to us. The beauty of this vision and of Fitzgerald's words continues to resonate with and move readers, and his work has become an enduring part of each new generation's individual and collective imagination.

Note

1. All subsequent quotations from reviews are from items reprinted in Bryer, *F. Scott Fitzgerald: The Critical Reception*, unless otherwise noted.

Works Cited

Allen, Joan M. *Candles and Carnival Lights: The Catholic Sensibility of F. Scott Fitzgerald*. New York: New York UP, 1978.
Berman, Ronald. *Fitzgerald, Hemingway, and the Twenties*. Tuscaloosa: U of Alabama P, 2001.

_____. "Fitzgerald's Intellectual Context." *A Historical Guide to F. Scott Fitzgerald.* Ed. Kirk Curnutt. New York: Oxford UP, 2004. 69-84.

_____. *Translating Modernism: Fitzgerald and Hemingway.* Tuscaloosa: U of Alabama P, 2009.

Bruccoli, Matthew J. *F. Scott Fitzgerald: A Descriptive Bibliography.* Pittsburgh: U of Pittsburgh P, 1972.

_____. "F. Scott Fitzgerald: A Descriptive Bibliography, Supplement (2001)." *Dictionary of Literary Biography Yearbook: 2001.* Ed. Matthew J. Bruccoli with George Parker Anderson. Detroit: Bruccoli Clark Layman/Gale Group, 2002. 399-425.

_____. *Fitzgerald and Hemingway: A Dangerous Friendship.* New York: Carroll & Graf, 1994.

_____. *Scott and Ernest: The Authority of Failure and the Authority of Success.* New York: Random House, 1978.

_____. *Some Sort of Epic Grandeur: The Life of F. Scott Fitzgerald.* 2d rev. ed. Columbia: U of South Carolina P, 2002.

_____, ed. *F. Scott Fitzgerald's "The Great Gatsby": A Literary Reference.* New York : Carroll & Graf, 2000.

Bruccoli, Matthew J., Scottie Fitzgerald Smith, and Joan P. Kerr, eds. *The Romantic Egoists: A Pictorial Autobiography from the Scrapbooks and Albums of F. Scott and Zelda Fitzgerald.* New York: Charles Scribner's Sons, 1974.

Bryer, Jackson R., ed. *F. Scott Fitzgerald: The Critical Reception.* New York: Burt Franklin, 1978.

_____, ed. *The Short Stories of F. Scott Fitzgerald: New Approaches in Criticism.* Madison: U of Wisconsin P, 1982.

Bryer, Jackson R., Alan Margolies, and Ruth Prigozy, eds. *F. Scott Fitzgerald: New Perspectives.* Athens: U of Georgia P, 2000.

Callahan, John F. *The Illusions of a Nation: Myth and History in the Novels of F. Scott Fitzgerald.* Urbana: U of Illinois P, 1972.

Curnutt, Kirk. *The Cambridge Introduction to F. Scott Fitzgerald.* New York: Cambridge UP, 2007.

_____. "F. Scott Fitzgerald, Age Consciousness, and the Rise of American Youth Culture." *The Cambridge Companion to F. Scott Fitzgerald.* Ed. Ruth Prigozy. New York: Cambridge UP, 2002. 28-47.

_____. "Fitzgerald's Consumer World." *A Historical Guide to F. Scott Fitzgerald.* Ed. Kirk Curnutt. New York: Oxford UP, 2004. 85-129.

_____. "Youth Culture and the Spectacle of Waste: *This Side of Paradise* and *The Beautiful and Damned.*" *F. Scott Fitzgerald in the Twenty-first Century.* Ed. Jackson R. Bryer, Ruth Prigozy, and Milton R. Stern. Tuscaloosa: U of Alabama P, 2003. 79-103.

Donaldson, Scott. *Hemingway vs. Fitzgerald: The Rise and Fall of a Literary Friendship.* New York: Overlook Press, 1999.

Fetterley, Judith. "*The Great Gatsby*: Fitzgerald's *droit de seigneur.*" *The Resisting Reader: A Feminist Approach to American Fiction.* Bloomington: Indiana UP, 1978. 72-110.

Fitzgerald, F. Scott. *The Crack-Up*. Ed. Edmund Wilson. New York: New Directions, 1945.

_____. *Dear Scott, Dearest Zelda: The Love Letters of F. Scott and Zelda Fitzgerald*. Ed. Jackson R. Bryer and Cathy W. Barks. New York: St. Martin's Press, 2002.

_____. *F. Scott Fitzgerald : A Life in Letters*. Ed. Matthew J. Bruccoli, with Judith S. Baughman. New York: Simon & Schuster, 1994.

_____. *The Last Tycoon*. Ed. Edmund Wilson. New York: Charles Scribner's Sons, 1941.

_____. *The Portable F. Scott Fitzgerald*. Selected by Dorothy Parker. New York: Viking Press, 1945.

_____. *The Stories of F. Scott Fitzgerald*. Ed. Malcolm Cowley. New York: Charles Scribner's Sons, 1951.

Fitzgerald, Zelda. *The Collected Writings*. Ed. Matthew J. Bruccoli. New York: Charles Scribner's Sons, 1991.

Fryer, Sarah Beebe. *Fitzgerald's New Women: Harbingers of Change*. Ann Arbor, MI: UMI Research Press, 1988.

Kazin, Alfred, ed. *F. Scott Fitzgerald: The Man and His Work*. 1951. New York: Collier, 1967.

Kuehl, John. *F. Scott Fitzgerald: A Study of the Short Fiction*. Boston: Twayne, 1991.

Lehan, Richard D. *F. Scott Fitzgerald and the Craft of Fiction*. Carbondale: Southern Illinois UP, 1966.

_____. *"The Great Gatsby": The Limits of Wonder*. Boston: Twayne, 1990.

Mangum, Bryant. *A Fortune Yet: Money in the Art of F. Scott Fitzgerald's Short Stories*. New York: Garland, 1991.

Milford, Nancy, *Zelda*. New York. Harper & Row, 1970.

Mizener, Arthur. *The Far Side of Paradise*. Rev. ed. Boston: Houghton Mifflin, 1965.

_____. *"Gatsby*, 35 Years Later." *The New York Times Book Review* 24 Apr. 1960: 46.

"100 Best Novels." Modern Library. 15 Dec. 2009. http://www.randomhouse.com/modernlibrary/100bestnovels.html.

Prigozy, Ruth. "Introduction: Scott, Zelda, and the Culture of Celebrity." *The Cambridge Companion to F. Scott Fitzgerald*. Ed. Ruth Prigozy. New York: Cambridge UP, 2002. 28-47.

_____, ed. *The Cambridge Companion to F. Scott Fitzgerald*. New York: Cambridge UP, 2002.

Ring, Frances Kroll. *Against the Current: As I Remember F. Scott Fitzgerald*. San Francisco: Ellis/Creative Arts, 1985.

Sanderson, Rena. "Women in Fitzgerald's Fiction." *The Cambridge Companion to F. Scott Fitzgerald*. Ed. Ruth Prigozy. New York: Cambridge UP, 2002. 143-63.

Stern, Milton R. *The Golden Moment: The Novels of F. Scott Fitzgerald*. Urbana: U of Illinois P, 1970.

_____. *"Tender Is the Night": The Broken Universe*. New York: Twayne, 1994.

Tate, Mary Jo. *F. Scott Fitzgerald A to Z: The Essential Reference to His Life and Work*. New York: Facts On File, 1998.

Trilling, Lionel. *The Liberal Imagination*. 1950. New York: New York Review of Books, 2008.

Turnbull, Andrew. *Scott Fitzgerald*. New York: Charles Scribner's Sons, 1962.

Way, Brian. *F. Scott Fitzgerald and the Art of Social Fiction*. New York: St. Martin's Press, 1980.

Wescott, Glenway. "The Moral of F. Scott Fitzgerald." 1941. *The Crack-Up* by F. Scott Fitzgerald. Ed. Edmund Wilson. New York: New Directions, 1945. 323-37.

The Curious Adaptation of Benjamin Button:
From Fitzgerald's Satire to Fincher's Sentimentality _____

Matthew J. Bolton

The great novelist and short-story writer Jorge Luis Borges wrote of translation, "A literal translation is not literary" (qtd. in Kristal 3). Translators fail if they aim to re-create an exact and faithful version of a poem or story because "each language has its own possibilities and impossibilities" (7). In translating a powerful, enigmatic, and culturally grounded work, the translator ought to think of his or her task not as reproducing the original but as reinventing it. The translator, Borges asserts, should "take the text as a pretext" (6). Borges's position might be applied with equal validity to adaptation, which recasts a work not in a different language but in a different medium. The written word and the motion picture, for example, are as different as two different languages, for each has "its own possibilities and impossibilities." While a reader and viewer may sometimes have the impression that a film adaptation of a book is particularly faithful to its source, the media themselves are so divergent as to make this impression illusory. An adaptation may hew closely to the plot of the original story, or may reproduce its dialogue word for word, but on many other levels the materials of a short story or novel are transformed beyond recognition when recast in the medium of film. This transformation is even more apparent when a film takes great liberties with the story on which it is based.

David Fincher's 2008 film adaptation of the F. Scott Fitzgerald short story "The Curious Case of Benjamin Button" is a fascinating example of the complexities inherent in adapting a story for the screen. In the hands of Fincher and his screenwriter, Eric Roth, Fitzgerald's short, satirical fantasy becomes a sentimental romance. While the broad outline of the plot remains the same—a man is born old and grows progressively younger—the theme and tone of "Benjamin Button" change radically in the adaptation. To use Borges's terms, Fitzgerald's text is a

---

pretext for the filmmakers. Comparing the short story "The Curious Case of Benjamin Button" to the film of the same title illuminates both works as well the process of adaptation itself. While they may share a plot and a protagonist, Fitzgerald's story and Fincher's film ultimately adopt radically different visions of the relationship between body and mind and, by extension, the nature of being human.

"The Curious Case of Benjamin Button" is one of the dozens of stories that Fitzgerald wrote between the 1920 publication of his first novel, *This Side of Paradise*, and the 1925 publication of his masterpiece, *The Great Gatsby*. The 1920s were a tremendously prolific period for Fitzgerald, seeing the publication of three novels and three collections of short stories. Most of his stories first appeared in popular magazines; he published a staggering total of sixty-five stories, for example, in the *Saturday Evening Post*. Always in need of money, Fitzgerald wrote short stories in part to make ends meet. Matthew J. Bruccoli lays out the economics of Fitzgerald's career as a magazine writer and a novelist: "In 1929, the *Post* stories brought Fitzgerald $30,000, while all of his books earned royalties of $31.77 (including $5.10 for *Gatsby*)" (xiv). The simple fact that story writing was far more lucrative than novel writing helps to explain why Fitzgerald spent so much time and energy on the form. Bruccoli argues, however, that one ought not see a clear-cut division between Fitzgerald's two modes of writing. Instead, he had "one career, into which all of his work was integrated," and the stories served as a means for him to "introduce or test themes, settings, and situations that are fully developed in the novel" (xvii). Fitzgerald's stories therefore inform masterpieces such as *The Great Gatsby*, and to study the stories is to study the evolution of Fitzgerald's artistry.

Understanding the economics of Fitzgerald's writing career underscores the strangeness of "Benjamin Button" in form and content. Fitzgerald knew that for a short story to sell, it had to be pitched to a wide readership; the mass-market magazines wanted material that was readily accessible to the common reader. With its odd mixture of fantasy and satire, "Benjamin Button" missed this mark. Though the story was eventually published in *Collier's Magazine* in May of 1922, it was not an easy sell. Fitzgerald wrote to his agent, "I know that the magazines want only flapper stories from me—the trouble you had in disposing of Benjamin Button + The Diamond as Big as the Ritz showed that" (159). The difficulty Fitzgerald had in placing both of these fantasy stories refutes the idea that he was churning out cookie-cutter stories perfectly calibrated to the demands of magazine readership. He followed not only the dictates of the market but also those of his muse.

In the case of "Benjamin Button," Fitzgerald wrote that his inspiration came from a remark by Mark Twain, "to the effect that it was a pity that the best part of life came at the beginning and the worst part at the end" (159). The tone of Fitzgerald's story owes much to Twain: its wry comedy, its conversational tone, its element of the fantastic, and its social satire make it a descendant of such works as *A Connecticut Yankee in King Arthur's Court*. The story therefore could be thought of as a divertissement in which Fitzgerald essays variations on a theme by Twain. It begins with Mr. Button rushing to the hospital to see his newly delivered son. The doctor is highly indignant, calling the situation "outrageous" and demanding, "Do you imagine a case like this will help my professional reputation? One more would ruin me—ruin anybody" (160). The case is this: the infant Benjamin has been born with the body and mind of an old man. Once in the delivery room, Mr. Button sees the following:

> Partly crammed into one of the cribs, there sat an old man apparently about seventy years of age. His sparse hair was almost white, and from his chin dripped a long smoke-colored beard, which waved absurdly back and forth, fanned by the breeze coming in at the window. He looked up at Mr. Button with dim, faded eyes in which lurked a puzzled question. . . . "Are you my father?" he demanded. (162)

Benjamin's birth is patently absurd, as are the reactions of everyone around him. Much of the comedy in the first few pages of the story comes from the tension between Mr. Button's attempts to induce his son to act and dress like a child and Benjamin's own attempts to live according to the tastes and temperaments of a seventy-year-old man, for in Fitzgerald's story, Benjamin is not a child trapped in an old man's body; rather, the old body he has been born with is coupled with an old mind. Rather than play with boys his chronological own age, he would much rather sit in a rocker or smoke a cigar.

With each passing year, Benjamin's body grows younger, and his mind follows suit. When he is twenty years old, he looks fifty. For the first time, he falls in love. As Benjamin and his father drive to a formal dance, Fitzgerald's description of the countryside reveals the romantic turn that Benjamin's mind has taken:

It was a gorgeous evening. A full moon drenched the road to the lusterless color of platinum, and late-blooming harvest flowers breathed into the motionless air aromas that were like low, half-heard laughter. The open country, carpeted for rods around with bright wheat, was translucent as in the day. It was almost impossible not to be affected by the sheer beauty of the sky—almost.

"There's a great future in the dry goods business," Roger Button was saying. He was not a spiritual man—his esthetic sense was rudimentary. (170)

Mr. Button's line of dialogue undercuts the lyric description that precedes it and underscores the difference between his practicality and his son's aestheticism. Unlike his father, Benjamin is primed to fall in love. At the dance, Benjamin meets the beautiful Hildegarde Moncrief, to whom he is soon engaged. A period of comfortable married life follows, as Benjamin finds happiness in his marriage and success in his family business.

After some fifteen years, however, Benjamin "discovered that he was becoming more and more attracted by the gay side of life" (173).

He has grown ever younger while his wife has grown ever older, and he is no longer content to stay at home. Fitzgerald's narrator demurs, "And here we come to an unpleasant subject which it will be well to pass over as quickly as possible. There was only one thing that worried Benjamin Button; his wife had ceased to attract him" (173). So he follows the interests of a young man, going off to fight in the Spanish-American War and later enrolling as a freshman at Harvard. As he gets younger and younger, Benjamin finds himself playing first with high school boys, and then with his own grandson, a toddler. His memories and knowledge fall away until he is an infant in body and mind. Fitzgerald ends the story with a brilliant passage that captures the prerational consciousness of a baby, culminating in the darkness of nonexistence itself:

> And then he remembered nothing. When he was hungry he cried—that was all. Through the noons and nights he breathed and over him there were soft mumblings and murmurings that he scarcely heard, and faintly differentiated smells, and light and darkness.
>
> Then it was all dark, and his white crib and the dim faces that moved above him, and the warm sweet aroma of the milk, faded out altogether from his mind (181)

Fitzgerald's story is an unusual admixture of comic episodes punctuated by lyric descriptions such as these. Taking his cue from Twain, he has written a narrative that is first and foremost a satire. Benjamin lives an entirely conventional life, doing at each stage of development what society would expect of him. As a physically young man, he is a soldier and a student; in middle age, he is a married businessman; in his physical old age, he sits on the porch smoking a cigar. Because he is aging in reverse, however, he passes through the stages of life backward, and hence comes into constant conflict with the people around him. All of the story's comic moments arise from the tension between Benjamin's chronological age and the age of his unusual body. The story takes as its material the fantastic and the mundane as its protagonist attempts to live the most conventional of existences under the most preposterous of circumstances.

* * *

When screenwriter Eric Roth began to think of undertaking an adaptation of "The Curious Case of Benjamin Button," he felt some trepidation about putting his own hand to Fitzgerald's work. In order to give himself license to take on the story, Roth considered Fitzgerald's own feelings about "Benjamin Button." In an interview, he later recalled:

> Well, it was a little daunting to see [Fitzgerald's] name there because he's 100 times the writer I could ever be. On the other hand, I did some research on sort of what the story was to him because I didn't want in any way to mess with his legacy or anything. The best I could tell from talking to his biographers of him is that this was kind of a whimsical piece for him. He just needed some money. It wasn't something that he took deadly serious. . . . And so, I felt the freedom to take off with my own imagination. (Roberts para. 12)

Roth felt justified in working on the piece precisely because it is one of Fitzgerald's minor works. He said, "It wasn't even a short story, it was a magazine article really" (Roberts para. 12). In a different interview, Roth said that while Fitzgerald can "write him under the table," this story "was not one of his more serious efforts: he didn't take it as life and death" (French para. 4). Bruccoli argues that Fitzgerald had "one career, into which all of his work is integrated" (xvii), but Roth clearly benefited from drawing a distinction between the serious novels and the potboiler stories. Perhaps he would approach *The Great Gatsby* or *Tender Is the Night* differently, but with "Benjamin Button" Roth felt free to write an adaptation that would use the original text as a point of departure rather than as a blueprint. He felt further assured by the story's indebtedness to Twain, reasoning elsewhere in the interview that since Fitzgerald had already appropriated the main idea of his story from Twain, it was perhaps appropriate for him to do the same. To return to Borges's characterization, Roth decided that Fitzgerald's text would be only a pretext for his own adaptation.

From the start, then, Roth felt licensed to depart from Fitzgerald's story. Director David Fincher put it this way in an interview: "The way he had dealt with the pressure of bringing F. Scott Fitzgerald to the screen was to ignore the pressure of F. Scott Fitzgerald . . . and just toss it and start all over again" (Solomons). Roth's screenplay takes liberties with many of the particulars of "Benjamin Button." The action is relocated from Baltimore to New Orleans, and Benjamin's birth is relocated from the 1850s to the end of World War I. The film uses a frame story in which an elderly woman, dying in a New Orleans hospital hours before Hurricane Katrina hits, recalls her lifelong love affair with Benjamin. The most significant change, however, involves not plot but tone. Whereas Fitzgerald's story is satiric and broadly comic, Roth's screenplay is essentially a sentimental one. Roth himself has acknowledged this shift in tone:

> In the original version Benjamin is born as a fully formed 87-year-old at 5ft 8in and virtually smoking a cigar. I thought that would have lent itself to comedy and I didn't want to write a comedy, per se. I wanted to write something . . . a little more meaningful. ("Interview" para. 5; ellipses in original)

Roth begins by making Benjamin's birth more realistic: Benjamin enters the world not as a "fully formed" man, but as a wrinkled and sickly baby. The effect is no longer comic, because Benjamin's form has been defamiliarized. An old man sitting in a delivery-room cradle is funny; a baby born with the infirmities of an old man is not.

In fact, differences in tone between the comic short story and the sentimental film are rooted in their different representations of the relationship between body and mind. In Fitzgerald's story, Benjamin's body dictates the condition of his mind. As a newborn, he speaks in complete sentences and demands a cigar and a rocking chair. This is the stuff of slapstick and sight gags, for it creates a hierarchy in which the body takes precedence over the mind. In his essay "Laughter: An Essay on the Meaning of the Comic," the early-twentieth-century French philosopher Henri Bergson explores the circumstances under which the body becomes a source of humor. He writes, "The attitudes, gestures and movements of the human body are laughable in exact proportion as that body reminds us of a mere machine" (218). As an illustration of this principle, Bergson cites the following example:

> A man, running along the street, stumbles and falls; the passers-by burst out laughing. They would not laugh at him, I imagine, could they suppose that the whim had suddenly seized him to sit down on the ground. They laugh because his sitting down is involuntary. Consequently, it is not his sudden change of attitude that raises a laugh, but rather the involuntary element in this change. (215)

In Fitzgerald's story, Benjamin's consciousness and attitudes seem to be an involuntary outgrowth of his body. Born with an old body, he immediately and involuntarily behaves as an old man. His body dictates his desires, and as his body grows "younger," he wants different things. The suddenness with which he takes up college football or begins to play with toy soldiers is comic precisely because it is so mechanical; Benjamin's personality is not the product of a gradual accretion of experience but rather an extension of his changing body. At each stage of life, he instinctively wants those things that are most stereotypically associated with his age, be it a rocker, a marriage, or a rattle.

Roth's screenplay inverts the relationship between Benjamin's body and mind. Mentally and emotionally, Benjamin ages as anyone else would. His body's reverse-aging process is therefore akin to any number of genetic conditions: it is a physical condition that he must grapple with and that affects how others treat him. But Benjamin's internal life is not a mechanical response to the machinelike promptings of his body. Benjamin's initiation into adult life, for example, is comparable to that of a teenager or young man: he goes to sea, travels the world, and falls in love in the frail body of an elderly man, and the people he encounters tend to treat him according to his appearance. Yet Benjamin himself learns and grows throughout this period of his life. Whereas Fitzgerald's protagonist painlessly sloughs off experiences, regressing to ever younger stages of life, Roth and Fincher's Benjamin is always accruing experience. In fact, Roth must use a narrative sleight of hand to effect the film's conclusion: when Benjamin is stricken with Alzheimer's disease, his confusion and anger are misinterpreted as the behavior of the young boy he now resembles. Thus both versions of the story have Benjamin end his life with the body and mind of a child.

To recast "Benjamin Button" in a sentimental vein, Roth needed first to move it into the realm of the plausible. Fitzgerald offered no explanation for Benjamin's condition, but Roth must gesture toward one if he is going to create some measure of pathos and help audiences identify with his protagonist. He invents several explanations for Benjamin's bizarre condition. At the start of the film, a blind clockmaker whose son has been killed in the trenches of World War I has been commissioned to build a giant clock for the new railroad station in New Orleans. When the clockmaker unveils his creation, the spectators who have gathered to celebrate the grand opening of the station are shocked to find that the clock runs backward. The clockmaker has rigged the clock this way so that time might run backward and the soldiers killed in the trenches might come home again. That same night, Benjamin is born, and the implication seems to be that the clock's power and its maker's grief have manifested themselves in the biology of the infant. Roth told an interviewer that he introduced the clock, which appears nowhere in Fitzgerald's story, in order to make the audience suspend disbelief:

I think it was probably because I was afraid the audience wouldn't get into it right away. In other words, you have to make a sort of leap of faith. I thought at least maybe if I provide this kind of metaphor, this can be kind of an interesting way of getting into it. (Roberts para. 46)

Roth has a similar explanation for a hummingbird that appears several times throughout the film, and that like the clock serves as a sort of visual metaphor. He terms it "pure magical realism like in a Latin [American] novel" (Roberts para. 49). Clock and hummingbird alike provide analogues for Benjamin's condition, and thus move that condition from the realm of farce or satire into one of a dreamlike realism. Writing at the far side of the twentieth century, Roth has read novelists who wrote after Fitzgerald, and he is quite right to attribute his inventions of the clock and the bird to magical realism. The works of Gabriel García Márquez, Jorge Luis Borges, and other magical realists provide Roth with models for how fantastic events can be grounded in the objective discourse of the realistic novel—or, in this case, the screenplay. This is another facet of the adaptation process: the writer of an adaptation brings to the original text frames of reference and modes of thought that were not available to the text's author. Thus Roth's screenplay filters Fitzgerald's story not only through the medium of film but also through a literary genre that had not yet been developed in Fitzgerald's time.

Fincher's direction amplifies the sentimental quality of the film. The computer-enhanced graphics by which he and his effects team created the illusion of Benjamin's aging received much attention in reviews and interviews, but perhaps equally impressive is Fincher's crisp, pictorial framing of shots, which does not rely on special effects. Fincher and cinematographer Claudio Miranda offer a series of sepia-toned evocations of twentieth-century Americana, and their lingering close-ups of lead actors Brad Pitt and Cate Blanchett are charged with emotional resonance. In fact, the quality of the camera work at times outpaces the substance of the story, such that certain images and scenes seem beautiful but hollow. A. O. Scott, reviewing the film for *The New York Times*, pokes fun at Fincher's sentimental cinematography, writing, "there will be sailboats and motorcycles as the ambient light turns gold along with Mr. Pitt's hair" (para. 9). Fincher's images gesture toward an emotional weight that they cannot always support—which, in fact, is a workable definition of sentimentality itself.

The most dramatic change from short story to film, however, may lie in the importance that Roth's adaptation places on Benjamin's love story. In the original story, Benjamin falls in love and then, gradually, falls out of love again when he finds that the gap between his wife's age and his own has grown too great. There is no great sense of loss in the end of this marriage; only the narrator seems a little chagrined at Benjamin's abandonment of his wife, terming it "an unpleasant subject." His wife, Hilda, seems more annoyed at the social embarrassment of Benjamin's youthfulness than she does at his callowness. She complains, "There's a right way of doing things and a wrong way. If you've made up your mind to be different from everybody else, I don't suppose I can stop you, but I really don't think it's very considerate" (173). For Benjamin, other events are far more formative than his marriage. For example, as a man of eighteen or twenty he is accepted to Yale University, but he is thrown out when he arrives looking three times that age. After the dissolution of his marriage, Benjamin, now much older chronologically but looking like an undergraduate, attends Harvard. Thrashing Yale on the football field carries far more of an emotional charge for Benjamin than does loving and leaving his wife. The love story, such as it is, is only a minor element of the short story. With the exception of the beautiful description of the evening as it appears to a smitten Benjamin, the romantic aspects of the story are played entirely for laughs.

Roth, setting out to write something "a little more meaningful," makes the love story the central event in Benjamin's life. The one-dimensional Hilda becomes the more well-rounded character Daisy. Of course, Daisy's name registers as an homage to Fitzgerald, for Daisy

Buchanan of *The Great Gatsby* is one of the most famous characters—and objects of desire—in literature. Several critics, including Phillip French of the *Observer*, have pointed out a further parallel between Roth's Daisy and Fitzgerald's wife Zelda, in that both pursue careers in dance. It is hard, of course, to create a character who can compete for center stage with Benjamin. After all, it is Benjamin who gives the story and screenplay its title, and the narrative arc of each begins with his birth and ends with his death. But Roth's frame story expands Daisy's role, so that Benjamin's life and death are rounded and punctuated by the recollections of a dying Daisy. More important, Benjamin and Daisy encounter each other more often than do their counterparts in the short story. They first meet when Daisy is a little girl and Benjamin is an "old man" (though, of course, he is actually about her age). They meet several times over the next two decades but are always out of synch; when Benjamin is an earnest older suitor, for example, Daisy is living a carefree bohemian life in New York City. Finally, as Daisy ages and Benjamin grows younger, they reach a period of equipoise in which true love blossoms. Daisy says, "We're almost the same age. We're meeting in the middle." Benjamin answers, "We finally caught up with each other." The relationship therefore centers on the fleeting period in which they are contemporaries. Benjamin's condition imbues the relationship with a sense of urgency and loss, for they will have only a few years together before their age difference strains them to a breaking point. Whereas Fitzgerald's Benjamin will become a contemporary of and then a child to his own son, Roth's Benjamin leaves home before his daughter can witness his devolution into a teenager and a child. Perhaps nowhere in the film are the tragic and alienating implications of Benjamin's condition made clearer than in this act of self-exile.

Benjamin's intermittent wanderings—he takes trips across the globe both as a young man in an old body and as an old man in a young one—are reminiscent of those of another Roth protagonist: Forrest Gump. In fact, *Forrest Gump* is the elephant in the room in discussions of Roth's adaptation of "Benjamin Button." That earlier screenplay seems to be one of the lenses through which Roth has reimagined Fitzgerald's story. Both share a similar frame story, a Louisiana setting, a protagonist whose life is set against shifting historical backdrops, and the characters' tendency to speak in terms of proverbs, maxims, and adages. The comparison between the two films was so common that one interview with Roth begins this way:

MOVIESONLINE: One of the things I'm sure you've heard and probably makes you cringe but I do want to ask you is . . .

ERIC ROTH: I'll ask you, why is this like *Forrest Gump*?

MOVIESONLINE: Exactly. (Roberts paras. 7-9)

Roth clearly has been asked this question many times before, but his answer is still rather equivocal. He says:

Look, I wrote the other one . . . and there are certain ingredients that feel similar in this—the picaresque nature of the piece, the episodic nature, you know, the journey of a man's life per se. But I like to think at least, and I hope I'm right to some extent, that they're just very different. (Roberts para. 10)

The parallels between the two films underscore an important factor in the process of adaptation. Bruccoli has argued that Fitzgerald's work is "integrated," such that minor works like "Benjamin Button" and major ones like *The Great Gatsby* are part of a single career. But if the same is true of a writer working on an adaptation, then the process of adaptation draws the original source material into the orbit of the adapter's other work. In short, Roth is still himself even when working on Fitzgerald's story, and it should not be a surprise that in adapting "Benjamin Button" he has produced a script that is integrated with and related to his previous work. In freely adapting the short story rather than trying to create a more literal version of it, Roth seems to have fallen back on a narrative arc and tone that have worked for him in the past. Any given viewer will have to decide whether this strategy—conscious or unconscious as it may be—renders "Benjamin Button" derivative. For the reader or viewer who has an interest in the process of adaptation itself, however, the parallels between Roth's two screenplays make for a fascinating case study.

The film version of "Benjamin Button" is so different from the Fitzgerald story on which it is based that its director and screenwriter might well have been justified in considering it an entirely new work. With a few more tweaks to the script and a change of the protagonist's name, they could plausibly have disowned their source material. Yet by retaining Fitzgerald's title, they do more than put a great American author's imprimatur on their film. Fincher and Roth acknowledge both the source of their inspiration and the extent to which they have deviated from that source. Because the film and the short story share a title, a protagonist, and a premise, they stand as a case study in the process of adaptation, illustrating how a work changes as it moves across genres and media. The satiric short story and the sentimental film it inspired take fundamentally different views of the nature of the human body, and as such offer two radically different interpretations of the human experience.

Works Cited

Bergson, Henri. "Laughter: An Essay on the Meaning of the Comic." *Comedy*. Ed. Wylie Sypher. Baltimore: Johns Hopkins UP, 1956.

Bruccoli, Matthew J. "Preface." *The Short Stories of F. Scott Fitzgerald*. Ed. Matthew J. Bruccoli. New York: Charles Scribner's Sons, 1989.

The Curious Case of Benjamin Button. Screenplay by Eric Roth. Dir. David Fincher. Paramount, 2008.

Fitzgerald, F. Scott. "The Curious Case of Benjamin Button." *The Short Stories of F. Scott Fitzgerald*. Ed. Matthew J. Bruccoli. New York: Charles Scribner's Sons, 1989.

French, Philip. "*The Curious Case of Benjamin Button*." *The Guardian* 8 Feb.

2009. 17 Dec. 2009. http://www.guardian.co.uk/film/2009/feb/08/curious-case-benjamin-button-review.

"Interview: Eric Roth." *The Guardian*. n.d. 17 Dec. 2009. http://www.guardian.co.uk/benjamin-button/eric-roth-interview.

Kristal, Efraín. *Invisible Work: Borges and Translation*. Nashville: Vanderbilt UP, 2002.

Roberts, Sheila. "Eric Roth Interview, *Curious Case of Benjamin Button*." n.d. 17 Dec. 2009. http://www.moviesonline.ca/movienews_16098.html.

Scott, A. O. "It's the Age of a Child Who Grows from a Man." *The New York Times* 25 Dec. 2008. 17 Dec. 2009. http://movies.nytimes.com/2008/12/25/movies/25butt.html.

Solomons, Jason. "In the Director's Chair." *The Guardian* 4 Feb. 2009. 17 Dec. 2009. http://www.guardian.co.uk/film/video/2009/jan/29/david-fincher-benjamin-button.

CRITICAL
READINGS

Youth Culture and the Spectacle of Waste:
This Side of Paradise and
*The Beautiful and Damned*_____

Kirk Curnutt

I don't want you to see me growing old and ugly. . . .
> We'll just *have* to die when we're thirty.
>> —Zelda Sayre to F. Scott Fitzgerald, Spring 1919 (Milford 49)

"About the Fitzgerald youth," Woodward Boyd wrote in 1922 as she set out to "shoot a few arrows" through the celebrated image of the author as "disillusioned, cynical, and so young": "He is young, certainly, but not so young as to look absurd in long trousers." As she points out, when *This Side of Paradise* was published in 1920, Fitzgerald was Dickens's age when he completed *The Pickwick Papers*, only a little younger than Keats when his final poems were written, and actually older than John Dos Passos when *Three Soldiers* first appeared. "Yet Keats, Dickens, Dos Passos, and hundreds of others who wrote things before they were 25 are not judged as 'infant phenomenons' while Scott Fitzgerald, in spite of the fact that he is only two years younger than Ben Hecht, whom no one ever dreams of calling childish, still suffers under this absurd handicap," Boyd observed (Bruccoli and Bryer 340). She makes what seems an obvious point here: while neither the youngest nor the first writer to chronicle the temperament of his generation, Fitzgerald identified with the theme of youth more intently than his contemporaries did—so much so, in fact, that when Dorothy Parker set out a year after Boyd's essay to skewer the media fascination with the era's flappers and philosophers, she focused her satire on Fitzgerald's reputation as a "special correspondent from the front line of the younger generation" who bravely "broadcasts the grim warning that conditions are getting no better rapidly and that decadence, as those outside the younger generation know of it, is still in its infancy." As the author of such shocking tomes as *Anabelle Takes to Heroin*, *Gloria's*

Youth Culture and the Spectacle of Waste   **91**

Neckings, and *Suzanne Sobers Up*, Tommy Clegg, Parker's fictionalized Fitzgerald figure, specializes in exposés of the "scandalous doings of modern youth" that excite parental anxiety while earning their author a pretty penny. While Boyd claims not to understand why Fitzgerald defines himself as an enfant terrible, Parker *does*, for by "cashing in" on the youth craze, "Tommy and his little playmates don't regard being young as just one of those things that are likely to happen to anybody. They make a business of it" (156).

At first glance, Boyd and Parker seem to arrive at disparate conclusions regarding Fitzgerald's relationship with youth. For the former, the popular image of him as "frightfully disillusioned in the younger manner [is] really laughable," since his work glows with an optimism and enthusiasm that suggests "he believes anything and everything and is enchanted and ecstatic because there are so many interesting things to believe" (339).[1] For Parker, by contrast, his "lurid" tales of "debauched doings" evince entrepreneurial opportunism, for this "commercial genius who began the grand work of selling this younger generation to the public" (156) secured an enviable profit by capitalizing upon an erupting fad. Yet in the end, these essays disagree less than an initial reading suggests, for both authors acknowledge that Fitzgerald would never have achieved notoriety had a mass audience not been eager for insight into how the twentieth century's first generation, its "heirs of progress," was shaped by the emergence of modernity.

One would think that Fitzgerald's contribution to the image of the youth of the 1920s as ambassadors of "unchanneled and potentially disruptive energies" (Fass 21) would constitute a central line of scholarly inquiry. Yet, except for the obligatory admission that *This Side of Paradise* inaugurated a brief vogue for novels and films about "bright young things," the question of how his thematic obsession with youth relates to his modernist milieu is largely neglected.[2] The reason can be inferred from Theodore Roethke's comment that Fitzgerald was "born, and died a Princeton sophomore" (249). At worst, his age-consciousness strikes detractors as endemic of the immaturity of his interests; at best, it seems a romantic indulgence whose glitter and gilt distract from the professionalism of his craft. Even ardent admirers like John O'Hara find it necessary to remove Fitzgerald from his era to redeem his artistry. Although he recalled in *The Portable Fitzgerald* (1945) his intense adolescent affection for *Paradise*, O'Hara elsewhere insisted that "one of the worst things that ever happened to Fitzgerald was the simultaneous popularity of John Held's drawings," the cartoons of frolicking flappers that often adorned the covers of Fitzgerald's books: "Who would ever want to take Fitzgerald seriously if all they ever knew about him was that he wrote about those John Held girls?" (18).[3] Scholars are equally anxious about seriousness. As Matthew J. Bruccoli pointedly told an Associated Press reporter during the 1996 Fitzgerald centennial celebrations, the lost-youth legend surrounding Fitzgerald is frivolous and "detracts attention from what's important. . . . And what's important is little black marks on pieces of paper" (Thompson).

Unfortunately, such judgments overlook the deep sociohistorical importance invested in youth in this century. The phrase "youth culture" may bring to mind a never-ending cycle of teen fads, fashions, and fascinations, but its significance transcends the oversimplified images of generational identity that have stereotyped each decade's adolescents, from the 1920s' slicker to today's slacker. As Patricia Meyer Spacks has noted, American culture mythologizes youth as a time of "exploration, becoming, growth, pain," and thus, by implication, dismisses aging as a time of "stodginess, inertia, stasis;" and "absence of feeling" (4). As such, the term has become a multivalent measure of everyday life, evoking not just a demographic constituency of adolescents but a standard of psychic well-being achievable by anyone of any age with the correct salutary regard for life. As Lawrence Grossberg puts it, youth is at once a category of "chronology, sociology, ideology, experience, style, [and], attitude" (171). When referring to young people, it most often functions as an index of social change, becoming, in Grossberg's words, a "battlefield" upon which teens and adults fight "for control of its meanings, investments and powers, [as both groups attempt] to articulate and thereby construct its experiences, identities, practices, discourses and social differences" (183). Yet in its broader usage, youth is celebrated as a universal remedy for the encroachments of senescence. As advertisers incessantly inform us, we can *feel* young even if we can no longer credibly claim to *be* young—as long as we purchase their particular wares.

Given the prevalence of interest in youth, acknowledging the ways in which Fitzgerald's early writing reflects its valorization in no way devalues it as Hemingway did when he dismissed his friend's fictional corpus as a "little children's, immature, misunderstood, whining for lost youth death-dance" (Bruccoli, *Some Sort of Epic Grandeur* 374). Rather, *This Side of Paradise* and *The Beautiful and Damned* vividly record evolving ideas on youth that today are the norm. Not only do these novels critique outmoded Victorian ideals of maturation, but they explore the ambiguous power that flagrant displays of youth styles afford young people. Most intriguingly, these works reflect the anxiety of a burgeoning age-consciousness that encouraged the young to maximize their youth before losing it to middle age. As Lois tells her brother in the early short story "Benediction," "Youth shouldn't be sacrificed to age" (*Flappers and Philosophers* 141). But while Fitzgerald—long before Abbie Hoffman or Jerry Rubin—insisted that anyone over thirty was corrupt in morals and imagination, his work acknowledges the impossibility of staying young forever. The result is a fascinating tension: though these early novels idealize youth, they also recognize its imminent passing and thus illustrate the desire throughout American culture to segregate youth from age.

An obvious way that Fitzgerald's work reflects emerging attitudes toward youth is its rejection of the Victorian myth of adolescence, a critique most apparent in the structure of *This Side of Paradise*. When Scribner's declined Fitzgerald's first effort at a novel, "The Romantic Egotist," in August 1918, the austere publishing firm singled out the story's inconclusiveness as its major flaw: "Neither the hero's career nor his character are shown to be brought to any stage which justifies an ending," the rejection letter noted, adding, "This may be intentional on your part for it is certainly not untrue to life; but it leaves the reader distinctly disappointed and dissatisfied since he has expected him to arrive somewhere . . . perhaps in a psychological [sense] by 'finding himself' as for instance Pendennis is brought to do" (Bruccoli and Duggan 31).[4] By offering Thackeray's 1848 novel as a model, Scribner's was encouraging Fitzgerald to subscribe to a bildungsroman formula that dictated the protagonist's entry into an adulthood governed by genteel notions of humility, duty, and self-sacrifice. But as Fitzgerald later confessed in a preface to *This Side of Paradise* which he wrote in August 1919 but never published, he was uncertain "how [he] could intrigue the hero into a 'philosophy of life' when [his] own ideas were in much the state of Alice's after the hatter's tea-party" (394).[5] Not yet twenty-two, he knew *he* hadn't yet "arrived" at the vague "somewhere" that signaled the end of his own adolescent uncertainties. As a result, when he repaired to his parents' home in St. Paul, Minnesota, the following summer to redraft the book, eventually reinventing it as *This Side of Paradise*, he again grappled with the conclusion. While "The Romantic Egotist" ended with Stephen Palms declaring his intention to write his autobiography, his new protagonist, Amory Blaine, would finish his education brokenhearted and disillusioned, questioning the value of life's lessons. Alone among the spires and towers of the Princeton campus, Amory stretches his arms to the sky and announces, "I know myself . . . but that is all—" (260).[6] As Fitzgerald decided, "Whether [the] hero really 'gets anywhere'" would be "for the reader to decide" (*This Side of Paradise* 395).

While critics have debated the dramatic merits of the ending of *This Side of Paradise*, Fitzgerald was in fact acknowledging the newfound indeterminacy of the adolescent experience. Victorian pedagogy insisted that maturation was a fixed period in the life cycle in which youth learned "the physical and moral regimen appropriate for success" and the proper "conduct required in the world of affairs" (Kett 167). As in Thackeray's novel, this script formed the plot of dozens of popular young-adult books. According to W. Tasker Witham, "sentimental dramas" like Compton Mackenzie's *Sinister Street*, Owen Johnson's *Stover at Yale*, and Booth Tarkington's *Seventeen* portrayed growing up as a series of moral challenges. Because their heroes inevitably triumph through their character and resolve, their message was that youth's "problems will disappear in time and should not be taken seriously" (10-11).

But while these narratives popularized a teleological view of adolescence, early-twentieth-century social scientists like G. Stanley Hall rejected the determinism of "stages of life" theories of development and questioned instead the cultural prerogative to assume adult roles. In *Adolescence and Its Psychology and Its Relations to Physiology, Anthropology, Sociology, Sex, Crime, Religion, and Education* (1904)—a mammoth study often credited with establishing youth as a viable field of academic study—Hall argued that the "storm and stress" of maturation arose from an effort to reconcile the "hot life of feeling" that "has its prime in youth" with the "prematurely old and too often senile" temper of adulthood (2:59). Unlike other Victorian psychologists, Hall insisted that the young should not capitulate to this process without a fight. Artists and "gifted people," he noted, "seem to conserve their youth and to be all the more children, and perhaps especially all the more intensely adolescent, because of their gifts, and it is certainly one of the marks of genius that the plasticity and spontaneity of adolescence persists into maturity. Sometimes even its passions, reveries and hoydenish freaks continue" (1:547). Growing up, in other words, should not mean growing old. While Victorians insisted that youth was a liability, Hall and other influential social theorists defined it as an important cultural resource that needed to be preserved. The result was an increasing divergence between the idea of adolescence as a set period in the life cycle and the idea of youth as a romantic attitude or instinct symbolizing one's essential humanism. While Fitzgerald was probably unaware of Hall's work, at least one reviewer did make the connection. According to the *San Francisco Chronicle, This Side of Paradise* read like "an additional chapter to G. Stanley Hall's 'Adolescence' or a psychopathological case record" (Bryer, *Fitzgerald: The Critical Reception* 29).

The tension between Victorian and modern definitions of adolescence is prevalent throughout *This Side of Paradise*, lending dramatic coherence to the novel's otherwise episodic structure. At first, Amory's adolescence is guided by a sense of divine purpose. Fueled by the "aristocratic egotism" imparted to him by both his mother, Beatrice, and Monsignor Darcy, he approaches his youth as a series of preparatory adventures for his eventual emergence as a personage able to "see clearer than the great crowd of people . . . [to] decide firmly . . . to influence and follow his own will" (88). For Amory, growing up means disciplining the natural "energy" of youth as he "tr[ies] to orient [it] with progress" (121). Books provide convenient models for achieving this end; not surprisingly, many of the titles cited in this "romance and reading list" (*Notebooks* 158) are Victorian expositions on children's proper moral education. As a preadolescent, Amory reads Alcott's *Little Women*, R. H. Barbour's *For the Honor of the School*, and Annie Fellows Johnston's *Mary Ware*, among other didactic fictions (23). At eighteen, he devours Tarkington's *The Gentleman from Indiana* and Johnson's *Stover at Yale*, the latter becoming "somewhat of a textbook" (38) for him. Later, during his junior year at Princeton, he notes his fondness for what he calls "'quest' books" like Robert Hugh Benson's *None Other Gods* or Mackenzie's *Sinister Street*, in which heroes "set off in life armed with the best weapons . . . avowedly intending to use them as such weapons are usually used, to push their possessors ahead as selfishly and blindly as possible" (115). The books teach Amory what David Bakan calls the "promise of adolescence," the social contract which guarantees that "if a young person does all the things he is 'supposed to do' during his [maturation], he will then realize success, status, income, power" (989). By dramatizing growth as a simple process of applying set moral lessons to ethical quandaries, Amory's texts impose upon adolescence a linear structure that encourages him to think of youth as a time of "going forward in a direct determined line" (129).

Yet a series of events conspires slowly to erode his belief in the bildungsroman formula: his romance with Isabelle Borgé goes awry, he fails a crucial exam that prevents him from assuming the chairmanship of *The Princetonian*, and his family's financial setbacks diminish his privileged sense of noblesse oblige. Most importantly, Amory loses Rosalind Connage to the wealthy dullard Dawson Ryder, who can more ably finance her luxurious frivolity. As his "philosophy of success" tumbles down around him, Amory finds himself haunted suddenly by a "purposeless[ness]" and a "general uncertainty on every subject" (104). Stripped of the certainty of its entelechy, the energy of youth threatens to stagnate into ennui, the "ambitionless normality" of being "très old and très bored" (197). Continually stimulating himself through drink and minor forms of debauchery, Amory attempts to simulate the feeling of motion and purpose, yet he remains painfully aware that "life had changed from an even progress along a road stretching ever in sight . . . into a succession of quick, unrelated scenes. . . . It was all like a banquet where he sat for this half-hour of his youth and tried to enjoy brilliant epicurean courses" (215-16). Accordingly, the stories that embodied the ideals of adolescent achievement lose their allure: "Mackenzie, Chesterton, Galsworthy, Bennett, had sunk in his appreciation from sagacious, life-saturated geniuses to merely diverting contemporaries" (195).

Recognizing the inefficacy of Victorian models of maturation, Amory indulges in various "experiments in convalescence" to assuage his newfound indirection and uncertainty. He gets drunk at the Knickerbocker Bar, hoping to tumble into a "merciful coma" to avoid dealing with his disappointments (185); he quits his job at Bascome and Barlow's advertising agency, telling his employer he couldn't care less "whether Harebell's flour was any better than anyone else's" (191); he even manages to get himself pummeled by "some waiters and a couple of sailors and a few stray pedestrians" (192-93). As he tells his Princeton pal and roommate Tom D'Invilliers, the beating "was bound to come sooner or later and I wouldn't have missed it for anything. . . . It's the strangest feeling. You ought to get beaten up just for the experience of it" (192-93).

Such moments typify the disaffection of youth when the promises of adult culture seem most illusory. As Dick Hebdige writes, young people voice their dissatisfaction with the world they are inheriting "by going 'out of bounds,' by resisting through rituals, dressing strangely, striking bizarre attitudes, breaking rules, breaking bottles, windows, heads, issuing rhetorical challenges to the law." Through such acts, they invoke "the only power at their disposal: the power to discomfit. The power, that is, to pose—to pose a threat" (17-18). Youth poses this threat by utilizing the power of display; rejecting the obligations of good citizenship and economic productivity before these ideals fail *them*, young people enact what Charles Acland calls the "spectacle of wasted youth"—in effect, a symbolic theater through which they act out their status as "lost" and encourage "the adult world [to crowd] around the accident scene of contemporary youth . . . jostling and stretching to see the carnage" (132). By indulging in an "arabesque nightmare of [a] three weeks' spree," Amory externalizes the "dramatic tragedy" of his failure at Princeton *and* his loss of Rosalind. This intention is realized in the bizarre scene at Shanley's, when Amory announces to a table of casual strangers his decision to commit suicide: "This provoked discussion. One man said that he got so depressed, sometimes, that he seriously considered it. Another agreed that there was nothing to live for. . . . Amory's suggestion was that they should each order a Bronx, mix broken glass in it and drink it off" (189-90)—a plan foiled only when Amory passes out.

As he admits to himself when Prohibition "put[s] a sudden stop to the submerging of [his] sorrows," Amory's debauchery is the "most violent, if the weakest, method to shield himself from the stabs of memory, and while it was not a course he would have prescribed for others he found in the end that it had done its business: he was over the first flush of pain" (194). The passage is deceptive, however, for when the Eighteenth Amendment ends his public drunkenness, Amory finds other ways in which to dramatize his dissatisfaction. He assumes blame for the underage girl in his friend Alec's hotel room and flusters the house detective by boasting of his indifference to the corrupt old man's threats of prosecution under the Mann Act (230-33). He shocks Mr. Ferrenby and his supercilious assistant by posing as a socialist when the businessmen insist on lecturing him on the benevolence of capitalism (246-57). Nor is the audience for these supposedly shocking admissions of disdain for adult norms necessarily adults. Even by himself, Amory likes to "congratulat[e] Poe for drinking himself to death in that atmosphere of smiling complacency" (207).

The oft-disparaged "Young Irony" interlude—derided by James L. W. West III as *This Side of Paradise*'s "weakest chapter" for "introduc[ing] new inconsistencies into Amory's character" (*The Making of "This Side of Paradise"* 70)[7]—serves as the novel's most extended examination of the power that self-wastage promises youth. As Hebdige writes, part of the intrigue of ostentatious displays of youth discontent is their ambiguity: while drinking, promiscuity, and other rituals of disaffection constitute a "declaration of independence, of otherness, of alien intent, a refusal of anonymity, of subordinate status," they are also "a confirmation of powerlessness, a celebration of [the] impotence" inflicted by their alienation. "Both a play for attention and a refusal, once attention has been granted, to be read according to the Book" (35), displays like Amory's insist that youth's exile from society's promise locates them outside the norms of comprehension. If *we can't belong*, the message is, *we can't be known*. Throughout "Young Irony," Amory and Eleanor Savage revel in this ambiguity as they try to trump each other's "Bohemian naughtiness." For her, Amory's resemblance to Rupert Brooke is enough to fuel her romantic rebelliousness and prolong her entry into the prescriptive sex roles of wife and mother; for him, Eleanor represents the allure of unconventionality that proved illusory in Rosalind. If his former love needed Dawson

Ryder to support her petulant immaturity, Eleanor seems entirely self-sufficient in "the artificialities of the temperamental teens" (217). That is, Amory knows she will never demand he grow up. Indeed, immaturity for Eleanor is vital because it allows her to avoid boarding "the sinking ship of future matrimony," which she knows is her inevitable future: "If I were born a hundred years from now, well and good, but now what's in store for me—I have to marry, that goes without saying" (219).

On a horseback ride during their last night together, Amory and Eleanor test each other's commitment to their nihilism. Infuriated by Amory's insistence that she is not the atheist she pretends to be, Eleanor declares, "If there's a God let him strike me—strike me!" (220), and to authenticate her Byronism, she charges toward a cliff as if to kill herself: "Then some ten feet from the edge . . . she gave a sudden shriek and flung herself sideways—plunged from her horse and, rolling over twice, landed in a pile of brush five feet from the edge" (221). By saving herself at the last minute, Eleanor acknowledges that her disaffection is at least part *affectation*; by extension, Amory must admit that just as he "had loved himself in Eleanor, so now what he hated was only a mirror. Their poses were strewn about the pale dawn like broken glass" (222). By depicting youth's anomie as a facade, a defensive reaction against its ill-defined social integration, such scenes reveal how the young are caught between caring and not wanting to care, how their poses are attempts to avoid the painful uncertainty of the future. In this sense, "Young Irony" is essential to *This Side of Paradise*'s portrayal of the new conditions of youth, for it shows how spectacular or theatrical displays of shocking behavior are forms of both power and powerlessness that dramatize but do not provide an escape from the indeterminacy and liminality of being young.

As Stuart Hall and Tony Jefferson have argued, the strategies by which youths like Amory and Eleanor symbolically respond to their disenfranchisement are not necessarily rejections of "proper" adult behavior; rather, they exaggerate to the point of parody patterns of social

behavior otherwise deemed normal. In particular, youth cultures articulate their sense of identity through flagrant pageants of conspicuous
consumption that display affluence and prosperity while demonstrating their indifference to the value of frugality and thrift (57). What
Acland calls "the spectacle of wasted youth" is in this sense part of a
broader consumer attitude that Stuart Ewen describes as the "spectacle
of waste," a "live-for-the-moment ideology that . . . avoids the question
of the future, except insofar as *future* is defined by *new, improved*
items" and experiences promising novel pleasures (245). In a culture
that celebrates wastage as a privilege of abundance, the old adage
about youth's being wasted on the young takes on a slightly different
meaning: while the culture defines it as a quality that is conserved and
sheltered, youth is precious to the young not for its fleetingness but for
the very ease with which it can be lost. While elders covet the flame of
adolescence, the young treat youth as a commodity to be exhausted.
Wasting one's youth becomes a quintessential form of youth-culture
display, for by utilizing the one quality that is uniquely their own, the
young appropriate the central reward of the "promise"—the pleasure
of consumption—from which they are otherwise alienated. Intriguingly, Zelda Fitzgerald alludes to this idea in her 1922 essay "Eulogy
on the Flapper" when she dismisses the idea that disaffection and disillusion were detriments to her generation. By stripping youth of its innocence, she insists, they have taught young people to "capitalize their
natural resources and get their money's worth." The lost generation is
not really lost; it is "merely applying business methods to being
young" (392-93).

The pleasure of wastage is a central motif in *This Side of Paradise*,
for it represents the sensibility that Amory ultimately adopts when his
Victorian ideals of adolescence fail him. As youth erodes into that
"succession of quick, unrelated scenes," he struggles to acclimate himself to the lingering sense that maturation is a matter of loss rather than
growth. At first Amory is demoralized, but gradually he assumes a
pose of determined indifference toward the future. When Rosalind ac-

cuses him of being sentimental, he insists that he is a romantic, because "a sentimental person thinks things will last, . . . [while] a romantic person hopes against hope that they won't" (166)—a line he later repeats to Eleanor (212). Of course, when Rosalind chooses to marry for security rather than passion, his wish comes true; the experience leaves him aware that "his youth seemed never so vanished as now" (226). The broken affair leaves him with "tireless passion, fierce jealousy, [and a] longing to possess and crush," which he feels are the only "payment for the loss of his youth—bitter calomel under the thin sugar of love's exaltation" (227). Likewise, he comes to understand that through his romance with Eleanor "he lost a further part of him that nothing could restore; and when he lost it he lost also the power of regretting it" (206). In effect, what Amory must learn here is that he will receive a fair return on his youth only if he transforms the loss ailing him into a proactive principle of self-depletion. No longer believing he possesses the "qualities that made him see clearer than the great crowd of people, that made him decide more firmly and able to influence and follow his own will" (88), Amory must accept that the definitive experience of youth is not moral growth or social achievement but the pleasure afforded by its consumption.

The realization comes to him on a rainy afternoon during which he aimlessly rides atop a bus rattling its way through Manhattan. Interrogating his motives and beliefs, he decides his cynicism is honest if not virtuous. The test of his corruption, he decides, would be "becoming really insincere" by "thinking I regretted my lost youth when I only envy the delights of losing it": "Youth is like having a big plate of candy. Sentimentalists think they want to be in the pure, simple state they were in before they ate the candy. They don't. They just want the fun of eating it all over again. . . . I don't want to repeat my innocence. I want the pleasure of losing it again" (239). In many ways, the passage is even more central to Amory's education than the meditation that ends the novel, in which he declares that his generation has "grown up to find all Gods dead, all wars fought, all faiths in man shaken" (260).

The bus-top monologue reveals that Amory has accepted the irrelevance of the bildungsroman in the modern world and that wastage is the lone compensation for one's inability to become "a certain type of artist. . . . a certain sort of man" (259). Youth, he realizes, is not a formative period of promise but a momentary pleasure whose entire raison d'être is defined by its own inevitable passing.

This Side of Paradise proved one of those rare novels that is ultimately remembered more as a part of a fad than as an artistic achievement. The book's initial printing of three thousand copies disappeared from bookstore shelves within a week, while total first-year sales neared fifty thousand, more than ten times the average amount for a debut novel in the 1920s. This unexpected success proved to publishers what other sectors of the commercial marketplace were at the same time discovering: that youth was a lucrative target audience as well as a topic of cultural concern. Savvy media manipulators realized that the prominence of the "rising generation" as a social problem offered unlimited potential for generating interest in their various products and ventures. Fitzgerald was among these skilled press agents. The popularity of *This Side of Paradise* allowed him to establish himself as a spokesman for modern youth. As he wrote his Scribner's editor Maxwell Perkins in May 1922, Amory Blaine's story created his "*own personal public*" composed of "countless flappers and college kids who think I am a sort of oracle" (Kuehl and Bryer 59).[8] And as he declared in interview after interview, he imagined it his duty to limn the attitudes and mores of his peers as accurately as possible. The three-paragraph aesthetic declaration entitled "The Author's Apology," composed in 1920 for the American Booksellers Association, offers Fitzgerald's most succinct statement of this intent: "An author ought to write for the youth of his own generation, the critics of the next, and the schoolmasters of ever afterward" (*F. Scott Fitzgerald on Authorship* 35).[9]

Yet almost immediately, the problem of following up the success of *This Side of Paradise* proved a formidable challenge. Fitzgerald wanted not only to retain his popular appeal but also to strengthen his standing among those literati who dismissed him as precious and pretentious—two seemingly conflicting goals that he intended to realize by reassessing his trademark theme of generational disaffection from the perspective of naturalistic writers whom he admired, including H. L. Mencken and Frank and Charles Norris. Even before *This Side of Paradise* was published, he spoke of at least four prospective projects that never materialized. Part of the reason that "The Demon Lover," "The Diary of a Literary Failure," "The Drunkard's Holiday," and "The Darling Heart" proved false starts may have been a growing need to move beyond the critique of the bildungsroman that had formed the plot of his first novel. "It seems to me that the overworked art-form at present in America is the 'history of the young man,'" Fitzgerald publicly declared in early 1921. "This writing . . . consists chiefly in dumping all your youthful adventures into the readers' lap with a profound air of importance, keeping carefully within the formulas of Wells and James Joyce" (*F. Scott Fitzgerald on Authorship* 43). Fitzgerald was particularly irked by Floyd Dell's *Mooncalf*, which he repeatedly disparaged in 1920-21 for plagiarizing *Paradise* to cash in on its rightful popularity and praise (Bruccoli and Duggan 75). He also dismissed former influences: whereas *Stover at Yale* once served as a "textbook," Owen Johnson's *The Wasted Generation* (1921) struck him as "so obvious as to be painful," a pathetic attempt to palliate his generation's postwar disillusionment with an antiquated sentimentalism (*F. Scott Fitzgerald on Authorship* 50).

By August 1920, Fitzgerald had formulated a plot that freed him from the constraints of the "history of the young man": he would describe "the life of one Anthony Patch between his 25th and 33d years," showing how "he and his beautiful young wife are wrecked on the shoals of dissipation" (*Letters* 145). Ostensibly, in keeping with his ambition to produce naturalistic fiction, Fitzgerald planned to portray the Patches' wreckage as a symbolic testament to the amorality of the era's rampant consumerism. Yet wasted youth and its relationship to the dilemmas of maturation remained an insistent concern over the course of the composition process, albeit in a very different form than in *This Side of Paradise*. Fitzgerald's debut novel can be classified as a coming-of-age story in the sense that it attributes youth's problems to the uncertainty of the *paysage moralisé* into adulthood. But coming of age evokes something far more ominous in *The Beautiful and Damned*, as this second novel was eventually titled. If *This Side of Paradise* focuses on the difficulties of growing up, *The Beautiful and Damned* dramatizes the dread of growing old, for more than wealth or prodigality, it is the fear of aging that compels the wildly self-destructive behavior of the central characters. The result is a more complex and more compelling examination of the causes and consequences of wasted youth than the book's reception history would suggest.[10] In *This Side of Paradise*, displays of disaffection are compensation for Amory's inability to become "a certain type of artist" or "a certain sort of man." By contrast, *The Beautiful and Damned* projects a "use it or lose it" philosophy. Anthony and Gloria Patch so dread the chronological coming of senescence that they decide to squander their youth before its vibrant intensity naturally erodes. Measuring their self-wastage against clock and calendar, the couple ravage themselves prematurely because doing so is for them the only victory possible against the inevitable ravages of time. Their self-destruction is by no means as noble as Amory's; rather than rebel against the false promises of Victorian maturation, *The Beautiful and Damned* depicts wasted youth as a lifestyle adopted by dilettantes and bacchantes as well as romantic egotists. Nevertheless, the book elaborates upon Fitzgerald's belief that, given the temporal fixity of youth, its only practical value is the brief pleasure offered by its consumption.[11]

The novel builds toward a climactic revelation of this point by playing off connotations of youth as a standard of intensity, passion, and joie de vivre. Throughout the first third of the narrative, protagonists in their early twenties insist that they can retain their youthful energy and vigor as they exit their adolescence to assume adult responsibilities. Indeed, they initially believe that their enthusiasms will invigorate and transform stolid adult institutions, marriage in particular. Yet no sooner do Anthony and Gloria feel blessed with this power than an approaching birthday grips them with unrelenting age anxieties, and they are forced to acknowledge their imminent exile from the paradisiacal world of youth. Exploiting the desire to detach youth from time, Fitzgerald promptly insists it cannot be done. In the end, Anthony and Gloria succumb to a deterministic attitude toward age by dating their entry into senescence according to a specific chronological milestone—their thirtieth birthdays. Curiously, the Patches are not alone in dreading this approaching event. Fitzgerald's narrator frequently intrudes into the action with grandiloquent editorials that lament "the inevitable metamorphosis" that this milestone inaugurates. While one's twenties are "a play, most tragic and most divine," life after twenty-nine degenerates into "a succession of speeches, sweated over by the eternal plagiarist in the clammy hours and acted by men subject to cramps, cowardice, and manly sentiment" (170). By its final page, *The Beautiful and Damned* proves so insistent on this point that Fitzgerald might well have subtitled it "Life Ends at Thirty."

The yearning to believe that youth is an eternal quality that can transcend age is dramatized most vividly in the chapters detailing Anthony and Gloria's courtship. Fitzgerald introduces this desire in an atypical supernatural prelude that depicts youth as God's gift to humanity. In a dialogue with the spirit of beauty, the disembodied voice of the Lord announces his intention to reincarnate her as the "susciety gurl" Gloria Patch. "You will be known during your fifteen years as a ragtime kid, a flapper, a jazz-baby, and a baby vamp," the deity declares. "You will dance new dances neither more nor less gracefully than you danced the old ones" (29). However inadvisable, this excursion into the fantastic offers Fitzgerald's most literal representation of juvenescence as a divine blessing. If beauty is youth and youth beauty, the scene implies, that is all we on earth need to know—except, as God assures Beauty, that being young is also a lot of fun. Originally, the novel was to conclude with Beauty's return to paradise, her spirit inexorably diminished by her tenure on earth. "How remote you are," God laments. "You seem to have no heart" (Bruccoli, *Some Sort of Epic Grandeur* 157). Fitzgerald cut this second scene shortly before publication, fearing that its lack of realism would diminish the tragedy of the Patches' dissolution. Had both dialogues remained, they would have served as narrative frames illustrating the point that youth is ephemeral, even in the afterlife. Without the concluding conversation, however, God and Beauty's first exchange serves an ironic function. While the early chapters suggest that youth's spirit is eternal, the rest of the story offers ample evidence of its fleetingness.

As Beauty's earthly incarnation, Gloria embodies the illusory allure of immortal youth in the novel's introductory episodes. On her first date with Anthony, when he tells her that, at twenty-two, she looks eighteen, she insists, "I'm going to start being that. I don't like being twenty-two" (64). She claims the power to reverse the clock; when Anthony asks, "It's your world, isn't it?" she replies, "As long as I'm— young" (66). Paradoxically, her unwillingness to act her age makes her seem wise beyond her years. Anthony is often surprised by how "she seemed to grow gradually older until at the end ruminations too deep for words would be wintering in her eyes" (113). Fitzgerald does not imply here that Gloria suddenly matures; rather, Anthony wants desperately to believe that her melodramatic immaturity embodies the age-old truth of the supremacy of youthful passions over adult contentment. A simple kiss from her convinces him that "he [is] young now," and that status makes him feel "more triumphant than death" (126).

Initially, Gloria resists Anthony's matrimonial advances, claiming incompetence in domestic matters. Once convinced that he shares her youthful fervor, she plots to rejuvenate marriage with juvenescent passion. A diary passage records her pledge not to succumb to "colorless" adult complacencies: "Marriage was created not to be a background but to need one. Mine is going to be outstanding. It can't, shan't be the setting—it's going to be the performance, the live, lovely, glamourous performance, and the world shall be the scenery." Nor will she relinquish her immature selfishness in the name of motherhood. Rather than "grow rotund and unseemly" and "lose [her] self-love" by "think[ing] in terms of milk, oatmeal, nurse, diapers," she will raise only "dream children . . . dazzling little creatures who flutter . . . on golden, golden wings" (147).

Yet this optimism erodes barely six months into the Patches' union when they realize that marriage is an "extortion of youth" (156). The revelation first comes during a honeymoon visit to the Virginia home of Robert E. Lee, where tourists flock to gape at the site's newly re-stored antebellum facade. To Gloria, the estate looks like "a blondined, rouged-up old woman of sixty" (167), an aged thing competing against its lost youth. The effort to reconstruct and preserve the past violates the natural tragedy of mutability: "Beautiful things grow to a certain height and then they fail and fade off, breathing out memories as they decay" (166), she declares. "I want this house to look back on its glamourous moment of youth. . . . [because] [t]here's no beauty with-out poignancy and there's no poignancy without the feeling that it's go-ing, men, names, books, houses—bound for dust—mortal" (167). Fitz-gerald offers little justification for why Gloria, the reincarnation of eternal beauty, should suddenly sing the praises of its mortality, yet the scene marks a turning point in the Patches' attitude toward youth. Op-pressed by a sense of its ephemeralness, the couple begin "extracting poignancy from the memorable things of life and youth" (169) and pass their entire twenties measuring its slow disintegration. Certain to be soon dispossessed of it, Anthony and Gloria commence a count-down to thirty, the age at which they believe flaming youth gives way to the raked embers of middle age.

Intriguingly, the Patches' anxieties about aging are so strong that they date themselves not by their actual age but by the milestones looming on the horizon. As Fitzgerald implies, age phobias inspire the paradoxical tendency to soothe that fear by prematurely presuming oneself old. Anthony at twenty-six initiates this pattern when he be-moans his lack of accomplishment in life: "Here I am almost twenty-seven—" he declares in an argument with Gloria (211). At twenty-three, Gloria herself is "in an attractive but sincere panic" over turning twenty-four, because it means only "six years to thirty!" (192). At twenty-five, she fears turning twenty-six because she realizes that her adolescent narcissism has decayed into "something that she had hitherto never needed—the skeleton . . . of her ancient abhorrence, a conscience" (278). And by her twenty-ninth birthday, she is reduced to wondering whether "she had not wasted her faintly tired beauty, whether there was such a thing as use for any quality bounded by a harsh and inevitable mortality" (391).[12] These frequent declarations not only insist that the butterfly of youth is broken on the wheel of time but that the most crushing blows come long before they are due.

Controversially, this attitude is reiterated by Fitzgerald's intrusive narrator, who often halts the advancing plot to offer his own ruminations on the significance of chronological milestones: "It is in the twenties that the actual momentum of life begins to slacken, and it is a simple soul indeed to whom as many things are significant and meaningful at thirty as at ten years before" (169). Pessimism about the middle years even leads to the occasional, bizarre reductio ad absurdum: "At thirty an organ-grinder is a more or less moth-eaten man who grinds an organ—and once he was an organ-grinder!" (169). Just when the organ-grinder's image begins to establish a new standard for idiosyncratic symbols, Fitzgerald conveys youth's dissipating energies by referencing another peculiar occupation: "After the sureties of youth there sets in a period of almost intense and intolerable complexity. With the soda-jerker this period is so short as to be almost negligible. Men higher in the scale hold out longer in the attempt to preserve the ultimate niceties of relationship, to retain 'impractical' ideas of integrity. But by the late twenties the business has grown too intricate, and what has hitherto been imminent and confusing has become gradually remote and dim" (283-84). Why an organ-grinder would suffer the loss of these sureties more than a soda jerk is an unresolved ambiguity; yet the interjections complement Anthony and Gloria's attitude by depicting aging as an unceasing erosion of youthful vivacity. Turning thirty, Fitzgerald concludes, marks the point at which "we value safety above romance, [and] we become, quite unconsciously, pragmatic" (284).

For most critics, this editorializing tendency reflects Fitzgerald's unfortunate training in the popular-fiction market of the 1920s, which encouraged authorial intrusions to minimize textual complexity and ensure recognition of a story's point. Matthew J. Bruccoli argues that the aforementioned asides diminish the novel's artistry and that Fitzgerald "would not become a complete novelist until he learned the techniques for controlling point of view and disciplining his habit of obtruding into the narrative" (*Some Sort of Epic Grandeur* 159), a prerogative he would not achieve until *The Great Gatsby* three years later. Yet, however aesthetically flawed, the running commentary on turning thirty in *The Beautiful and Damned* echoes a contemporaneous attitude toward aging popularly known as the "fixed period" theory. This view, disseminated throughout a range of scientific discourse and public policy, held that intellectual, moral, and economic potential decline with age. The early twentieth century witnessed a cottage industry in mathematical formulas and equations claiming to calculate the physiological and psychological effects of aging. Frequently advanced as "natural laws," these theories of senescence held that "a certain number of years mark the limit of human productivity, rationality, and efficiency," and they helped create the cultural presumption that "old age was irrelevant and burdensome" (Cole 169). Fitzgerald's interjections reflect a similar attitude. Not only is the enfeebling that age brings a biological inevitability, but that structure of decline is tied to a specific chronological sequence. Thirty may mark an earlier moment of erosion than most fixed-period advocates argued, but not by much—forty was the average age at which the irrevocable diminishment of capacities was said to begin. As the narrator of *The Beautiful and Damned* insists, age is a "force intangible as air" and "more definite than death" (414).

As if to compensate for their eroding youth, Anthony and Gloria begin to affect a "magnificent attitude of not giving a damn" and hurl themselves headlong into drinking and profligacy. They host endless fetes, wreck cars, and squander their finances, all in an effort "not to be sorry, not to loose one cry of regret, . . . and to seek the moment's happiness as fervently and persistently as possible" (226). The Patches themselves are never quite able to articulate their motives for squandering what youth they still possess; Fitzgerald charges that duty to their close friend Maury Noble, who appears at select moments (much like the novel's narrator) to pontificate on the futility of ambition and effort in the adult world. In one long tirade against maturity, Maury recounts his initiation into the despair of senescence: "I grew up, and the beauty of succulent illusions fell away from me. The fibre of my mind coarsened me and my ears grew miserably keen. Life arose around my island like a sea, and presently I was swimming. . . . I reached maturity under the impression that I was gathering the experience to order my life for happiness. Indeed, I accomplished the not unusual feat of solving each question in my mind long before it presented itself to me in life—and of being beaten and bewildered just the same" (253-54). Growing up, the passage insists, offers little chance of triumphing over life's challenges. Instead, it ensures nothing but a sense of loss and defeat.

For their part, however, Anthony and Gloria fail to appreciate the significance of this dispiriting moral, and they continue their revelries with only slight awareness that both are "vaguely weaker in fibre" and that "things [have] been slipping" (278). But when Anthony's temperance-preaching grandfather happens upon one of their frequent debauches, they are disinherited and must cope suddenly with such adult inconveniences as paying their own bills. To meet expenses, Anthony embarks upon various careers but quits when he finds the work monotonous. Gloria also attempts to economize but grows bitter at her husband's laziness. By the final third of the novel, their marriage weathers adultery, alcoholism, and the humiliation of relocating to a working-class neighborhood. As refuge from this downward spiral, they act out increasingly empty gestures from their glamorous youth. Anthony resorts to drink to renew "those opalescent dreams of future [pleasure]—the mutual heritage of the happy and damned." But intoxication provides only a transitory escape from his fall: "As he grew drunker the dreams faded and he became a confused spectre, moving in odd crannies of his own mind . . . harshly contemptuous at best and reaching sodden and dispiriting depths" (388). Gloria also reverts to her girlhood by dressing dolls and rereading the romantic novels which fuel "that illusion of young romantic love to which women look forever forward and forever back" (371). But whereas being young was once a matter of acting eighteen instead of twenty-two, Gloria can no longer maintain the fantasy. Her most debilitating moment of disillusion occurs when she discovers Anthony scrounging for loose change to buy his morning drink: "For a moment she received the impression that he was suddenly and definitely old" (424).

By their thirties, then, Anthony and Gloria waste their youth and beauty. But if their dissipation is a moral failure, the squandering also realizes perfectly the logic of planned obsolescence, for they consume and exhaust the precious commodity of their twenties and all that the age symbolizes before "harsh mortality" can. Not surprisingly, the toll taken by their wastage is not most visible in their marital discontent or economic misfortunes. The real tragedy of their ruin, Fitzgerald implies, is that they have made themselves old before their time. On her twenty-ninth birthday, Gloria is horrified to discover that she looks too old to star as a silent-film vamp, a part she once effortlessly played in high society. Told she is more suited for "*a small character part supposed to be a very haughty rich widow*" (403), she rushes to the mirror, where she is stunned by the wear and tear of her features. If her beauty once seemed the very essence of vitality, she recognizes now that her eyes are "tired": "Oh, my pretty face," she cries. "Oh, I don't want to live without my pretty face!" The episode concludes with Gloria prostrate on the floor, sobbing, "the first awkward movement she had ever made" (404). As she later explains to Anthony, "I wasn't thirty; and I didn't think I—looked thirty" (428). Gloria's husband must likewise confront the withered youth in the mirror: "He faced his reflection . . . contemplating dejectedly the wan, pasty face, the eyes with their criss-cross of lines like shreds of dried blood, the stooped and flabby figure whose very sag was a document in lethargy." The vision leads to the book's strongest evidence of his decline: "He was thirty-three—[but] he looked forty" (444).

As with *This Side of Paradise*, Fitzgerald delivered his protagonists to a final recognition of their wasted youth only to confront his au-thorial uncertainty over the novel's ending. After discarding the epi-sode in which Beauty, to God's dismay, returns dispirited to heaven, he crafted an orotund coda in which he praised the Patches' faith in the glory of youth: "In the search for happiness . . . these two people were marked as guilty chiefly by the freshness and fullness of their desire. Their disillusion was always a comparative thing—they had sought glamour and color through their respective worlds with steadfast loy-alty—sought it and it alone in kisses and in wine, sought it with the same ingenuousness in the wanton moonlight as under the cold sun of inviolate chastity. Their fault was not that they had doubted but that they had believed" (Bruccoli, *Some Sort of Epic Grandeur* 157-58). Praising Anthony and Gloria for their romantic idealism satisfied the sentimental dictates of *Metropolitan Magazine*, the high-paying peri-odical that serialized *The Beautiful and Damned* in the fall of 1921. Yet Fitzgerald eventually rejected this conclusion for violating the tragic tone he desired. Had it ended with this passage, the novel would have implied that the Patches' youth had been lost, not wasted.

At his wife's recommendation, Fitzgerald concluded the novel in-stead with the Patches sailing for Europe after winning an arduous court battle over his grandfather's thirty-million-dollar estate. Gloating over his replenished wealth and social status, Anthony congratulates him-self for "show[ing] them. . . . It was a hard fight, but I didn't give up and I came through!" (448). All around him, passengers gossip about his poor health and the insanity said to accompany his courtroom travails. Their whispering confirms the long-term effects of the emotional breakdown that he suffers in the book's penultimate scene, just before their courtroom victory is announced. When a former mistress appears on his doorstep, Anthony suffers a violent blackout and reverts to his childhood. Gloria discovers him stretched out on his bedroom floor, poring over the stamp collection that he prized as a young boy. "Get out. . . . Or else I'll tell my grandfather," Anthony screams, his voice sounding "like a pert child" (447). Woefully unfit for adult responsibilities, he copes by escaping into a preadolescent world of simple, uncomplicated pleasures. The luxury of remaining childish is, of course, just what his newly refurnished wealth will allow. He can resume believing that youth is a lifestyle best enjoyed by the affluent. Yet the assumption is contradicted by his appearance, for he has been reduced to a "bundled figure seated in a wheel chair" (447). As Fitzgerald makes clear, Anthony and Gloria are neither young nor beautiful anymore, regardless of the fantasies that their fortune can now finance. Instead, they have been damned by the aging process.

* * *

The Beautiful and Damned hardly exhausted Fitzgerald's anxieties toward aging and lost youth. Rather, these issues remain a persistent— if unacknowledged—obsession throughout his major work as well as his more commercially minded short stories. In *The Great Gatsby*, Nick Carraway remembers in the midst of the climactic exchange between Gatsby, Daisy, and Tom that he has forgotten his thirtieth birthday: "Thirty—the promise of a decade of loneliness, a thinning list of single men to know, a thinning brief-case of enthusiasm, thinning hair" (106). And in a later story, "At Your Age" (1929), a fifty-year-old man hopes to revive the "warm sureties of his youth" by romancing a flapper young enough to be his daughter. The tale includes a line that could describe Fitzgerald's attitude toward the subject: "Youth! Youth! Youth!" Tom Squires tells himself. "I want it near me, all around me, just once more before I'm too old to care" (*The Short Stories* 482). Inevitably, however, such characters must admit that they have aged: "I'm thirty," Nick tells Jordan Baker when she accuses him of treating her inconsiderately. "I'm five years too old to lie to myself and call it honor" (*The Great Gatsby* 138). And as Tom Squires realizes that he has "lost the battle against youth and spring," he understands that the affair has stripped him of any illusions he had carried into middle age: "He could not have walked down wasted into the darkness without being used up a little; what he wanted, after all, was only to break his strong old heart" (*The Short Stories* 494). This age-consciousness even works its way into biographical legend. In 1950, Alice B. Toklas described Fitzgerald visiting Gertrude Stein on his thirtieth birthday complaining "that it was unbearable for him to have to face the fact that his youth was over" (1). While its accuracy is questionable—the Fitzgeralds were in Juan-les-Pins, not Paris, in September 1926—the story nevertheless furthers the myth of an artist who memorialized and moralized his generation's wasted youth. But rather than simply mourn the passing of youth, Fitzgerald was the first author to recognize the appeal of youth culture. Intrigued by and yet wary of the freedoms that new rites of passage allowed his peers, Fitzgerald poses in his early work a question that American writing would ask of its teens and twenty-somethings for decades to come: Where are you going, and where have you been?

From *F. Scott Fitzgerald in the Twenty-first Century*, edited by Jackson R. Bryer, Ruth Prigozy, and Milton R. Stern, pp. 79-103. Copyright © 2003 by University of Alabama Press. Reprinted with permission of the University of Alabama Press.

Notes

1. Boyd's desire to rehabilitate Fitzgerald's "disillusioned youth" image may have been an effort to pay him back for recommending her manuscript *The Love Legend* to Scribner's in 1922. Fitzgerald also encouraged Maxwell Perkins to accept Boyd's husband Thomas's novel *Through the Wheat* (Bruccoli and Duggan 94).

2. The major exception is Berman's *"The Great Gatsby" and Modern Times*,

which examines how Fitzgerald's most famous novel comments on various cultural phenomena of the 1920s, including the fascination with youth.

3. Held designed the book jackets for *Tales of the Jazz Age* (1922), Fitzgerald's second story collection, and *The Vegetable* (1922), his unsuccessful play. See Bruccoli, *Some Sort of Epic Grandeur* 171 and Le Vot 132.

4. It was long assumed that Fitzgerald's personal editor, Maxwell Perkins, wrote this letter (see Bruccoli and Duggan 32). Recently, however, West and others have suggested that William C. Brownell is the author (see *This Side of Paradise* xix).

5. His first reaction was hasty: before submitting the book again to Scribner's in late 1918, he "dispatched" Stephen Palms "to the war and callously slew him several thousand feet in the air, when he fell . . . down ★ ★ ★ ★ down ★ ★ ★ ★" (*This Side of Paradise* 394).

6. As West notes, this final dash turned into a period in the book's first edition. His introduction to the Cambridge edition of *Paradise* makes a convincing case for returning to the original punctuation (xxix-xxx).

7. West's dissatisfaction arises largely from evidence that Fitzgerald spliced a portion of "The Romantic Egotist" into *This Side of Paradise* without revising minor inconsistencies like Stephen Palm's hair color (blond) to match Amory's (auburn) (*The Making of "This Side of Paradise"* 68-71).

8. For a brief but illuminating discussion of Fitzgerald's reputation as a generational spokesman, see Fass, who examines how the same periodical market that rewarded Fitzgerald handsomely for his Jazz Age short stories took up "the theme of youth . . . like a literary leitmotif" as it debated the effects of modernity on the emerging generation: "The central issue was always the failure of modern society; rarely were specific solutions for the youth problem more than an afterthought. The repetition of the catalogue of youth's faults was, in fact, not intended to describe or reform. It was, instead, a form of ritual incantation which, by bringing the problem forward again and again, created a painful consciousness that became a substitute for action, and indeed, even a way of coming to terms with the situation." Like the countless articles sensationally entitled "The Revolt of Youth," "Has Youth Deteriorated?" or "These Wild Young People," both Fitzgerald's early novels and his short fiction employed the "technique of relief by exposure," for by "employing the symbols of his time to tease his readers' curiosity while he exploited their alarm," he "was able to best express the period's aching sense of frustration" (17).

9. Evidence suggests that Fitzgerald later regretted both this statement and his reputation as the voice of the "rising generation." In *The Beautiful and Damned* he attributes "The Author's Apology" to an unsympathetic character, the novelist Richard Caramel, who complains about how his propensity for "strange pronouncements" pigeonholes him in the literary marketplace. "I believe a lot of it," Caramel admits. "It simply was a mistake to give it out" (189). Later, in what can only be regarded as a bizarre metafictional commentary on his public identity, Fitzgerald has Caramel complain that "Everywhere I go some silly girl asks me if I've read 'This Side of Paradise.' Are our girls really like that? If it's true to life, which I don't believe, the next generation is going to the dogs" (421).

10. With the exception of *The Vegetable*, *The Beautiful and Damned* has generated

less critical interest than any other full-length work in its author's oeuvre. What commentary does exist treats the Patches' story as a critique of capitalist decadence. For a recent representative example of such criticism, see Craig Monk's "The Political F. Scott Fitzgerald."

11. Fitzgerald's age-consciousness surfaces in his stories as well. At times references may seem gratuitous, as in "The Ice Palace" when Sally Carrol Happer is described as "rest[ing] her nineteen-year-old chin on a fifty-two-year-old sill" (*Short Stories* 48). Elsewhere, the theme is more central to the plot. "The Curious Case of Benjamin Button" tells the story of a man born at seventy who grows younger throughout his life; the tale captures the era's belief that vitality and a healthy lifestyle could reverse the aging process. In "'O Russet Witch!'" a young man ages prematurely when he abandons his romantic illusions and settles for a dull but comfortable life whose equanimity is only occasionally interrupted by a woman who symbolizes for him the energy and power of youth. Only at sixty-five does he learn that this woman is not a supernatural being but a former dancer infamous for her role in a sensational divorce trial. The effect on Merlin is immediate: "He was an old man now indeed, so old that it was impossible for him to dream of ever having been young, so old that the glamour was gone out of the world. . . . He was too old now even for memories" (*Six Tales of the Jazz Age* 118-19).

12. In one of the novel's more glaring editorial oversights, Fitzgerald places Gloria's birthday in three different months (August, May, and February). When a reader, one George A. Kuyper, informed him of the inconsistency, Fitzgerald responded with exasperation: "My God! I can never straighten it out without rewriting the whole book. It is really a most embarrassing predicament. God! This bugbear of inconsistency!" (Bruccoli and Duggan 98).

Works Cited

Acland, Charles. *Youth, Murder, Spectacle: The Cultural Politics of "Youth in Crisis."* Boulder, CO: Westview, 1995.

Bakan, David. "Adolescence in America: From Idea to Social Fact." *Daedalus* 100 (1971): 979-95.

Berman, Ronald. *"The Great Gatsby" and Modern Times*. Urbana: U of Illinois P, 1994.

Bruccoli, Matthew J. *Some Sort of Epic Grandeur: The Life of F. Scott Fitzgerald*. New York: Harcourt Brace Jovanovich, 1981.

Bruccoli, Matthew J., and Jackson R. Bryer, eds. *F. Scott Fitzgerald in His Own Time: A Miscellany*. Kent, OH: Kent State UP, 1971.

Bruccoli, Matthew J., and Margaret M. Duggan, eds., with the assistance of Susan Walker. *Correspondence of F. Scott Fitzgerald*. New York: Random House, 1980.

Bryer, Jackson R., ed. *F. Scott Fitzgerald: The Critical Reception*. New York: Burt Franklin, 1978.

Cole, Thomas. *The Journey of Life: A Cultural History of Aging*. New York: Cambridge UP, 1991.

Ewen, Stuart. *All Consuming Images: The Politics of Style in Contemporary Culture*. New York: Basic Books, 1989.

Fass, Paula S. *The Damned and the Beautiful: American Youth in the 1920s*. New York: Oxford UP, 1977.

Fitzgerald, F. Scott. *The Beautiful and Damned*. New York: Scribner's, 1922.

_____. *Flappers and Philosophers*. Ed. James L. W. West III. Cambridge, UK: Cambridge UP, 2000.

_____. *F. Scott Fitzgerald on Authorship*. Ed. Matthew J. Bruccoli with Judith S. Baughman. Columbia: U of South Carolina P, 1996.

_____. *The Great Gatsby*. 1925. Ed. Matthew J. Bruccoli. New York: Macmillan/Scribner's, 1992.

_____. *The Letters of F. Scott Fitzgerald*. Ed. Andrew Turnbull. New York: Scribner's, 1963.

_____. *The Notebooks of F. Scott Fitzgerald*. Ed. Matthew J. Bruccoli. New York: Harcourt Brace Jovanovich/Bruccoli Clark, 1978.

_____. *The Short Stories of F. Scott Fitzgerald: A New Collection*. Ed. Matthew J. Bruccoli. New York: Scribner's, 1989.

_____. *Six Tales of the Jazz Age and Other Stories*. New York: Scribner's, 1960.

_____. *This Side of Paradise*. 1920. Ed. James L. W. West III. Cambridge, UK: Cambridge UP, 1995.

Fitzgerald, Zelda. *The Collected Writings*. Ed. Matthew J. Bruccoli. New York: Scribner's, 1991.

Grossberg, Lawrence. *We Gotta Get Out of This Place: Popular Conservatism and Postmodern Culture*. New York: Routledge, 1992.

Hall, G. Stanley. *Adolescence and Its Psychology and Its Relations to Physiology, Anthropology, Sociology, Sex, Crime, Religion, and Education*. 2 vols. New York: Appleton, 1904.

Hall, Stuart, and Tony Jefferson, eds. *Resistance through Rituals: Youth Subcultures in Post-War Britain*. London: Hutchinson, 1976.

Hebdige, Dick. *Hiding in the Light: On Images and Things*. New York: Comedia, 1988.

Kett, Joseph F. *Rites of Passage: Adolescence in America 1790 to the Present*. New York: Basic Books, 1973.

Kuehl, John, and Jackson R. Bryer, eds. *Dear Scott/Dear Max: The Fitzgerald-Perkins Correspondence*. New York: Scribner's, 1971.

Le Vot, André. *F. Scott Fitzgerald: A Biography*. Trans. William Byron. Garden City, NY: Doubleday, 1983.

Milford, Nancy. *Zelda: A Biography*. New York: Harper & Row, 1970.

Monk, Craig. "The Political F. Scott Fitzgerald: Liberal Illusion and Disillusion in *This Side of Paradise* and *The Beautiful and Damned*." *American Studies International* 33 (1995) 60-70.

O'Hara, John. *Assembly*. New York: Random House, 1961.

Parker, Dorothy. "Professional Youth." *Saturday Evening Post* April 28, 1923: 14, 156-57.

Roethke, Theodore. *Straw for the Fire: The Notebooks of Theodore Roethke, 1943-63.* Ed. David Wagoner. Garden City, NY: Anchor, 1974.

Spacks, Patricia Meyer. *The Adolescent Idea: Myths of Youth and the Adult Imagination.* New York: Basic Books, 1978.

Thompson, Anne. "Late Author Connects Jazz Age to Generation X." *Montgomery (AL) Advertiser* September 23, 1996: D2.

Toklas, Alice B. "They Who Came to Paris to Write: Impressions, Observations and Asides by Gertrude Stein's Closest Companion." *New York Times Book Review* August 6, 1950: 1, 25.

West, James L. W., III. *The Making of "This Side of Paradise."* Philadelphia: U of Pennsylvania P, 1983.

Witham, W. Tasker. *The Adolescent in the American Novel, 1920-1960.* New York: Frederick Ungar, 1964.

F. Scott and Zelda Fitzgerald in American Popular Culture_____

Ruth Prigozy

F. Scott and Zelda Fitzgerald are today, and indeed, have been for the past twenty years, indissolubly tied to American popular culture. Scarcely a week passes that we do not notice an allusion to one or both of them in our mass media. In a best-selling paperback mystery, a leading character marries a beautiful but hopelessly mad woman who slashes the bathroom mirror with lipstick before shattering it and then bleeding on the floor. He later tells his friend, "I've got Zelda for a wife" (Patterson 1984, 31). In a 1970s film, *Getting Straight*, the protagonist, played by Elliott Gould, rebels against his questioners at an M.A. oral examination when they state that Nick Carraway and Gatsby have a homosexual relationship, that Jordan Baker is probably a lesbian, and that Fitzgerald, Gould's favorite author, was driven by "a terrible need to express homosexual panic through his characters." The candidate, outraged yet afraid at first to offend his mentors, finally retorts, "It's possible . . . but it's gonna be a surprise to Sheilah Graham. Sheilah is not gonna believe that." He then explodes in fury and throws away his academic career, salvaging his soul in the process. And in the Fall of 1993, the Turner Network presented a barely fictionalized television drama on the Fitzgeralds' troubled marriage, *Zelda*, with the glamorous Natasha Richardson in the title role and Timothy Hutton as Fitzgerald. (Both actors playing the diminutive Fitzgeralds are over six feet tall, suggesting perhaps contemporary media inflation of celebrities.) These three examples, drawn from three mass media, are not unique. Fitzgerald has been played on the screen by Gregory Peck, and countless one-man and one-woman shows have played throughout the country purporting to disclose the inner struggles of either Scott or Zelda. For better or worse, mostly worse, they are part of our lives, appropriated probably forever into mainstream American culture.

Why Scott and Zelda? Other major American writers, from Mark

Twain and Jack London to Ernest Hemingway, have entered the public's consciousness without the spousal link. Indeed, although she was a more talented writer than Zelda, there has never been, to my knowledge, a conference dedicated to Martha (Gellhorn) and Ernest Hemingway. Clearly the Fitzgeralds' lives together had a mythic quality, and their symbiosis made both their successes and their tragedies, like the actors who impersonate them today, larger than life. As Mary Gordon has remarked, "The case of Zelda and Scott Fitzgerald . . . as creator and object of creation, may be unique in the history of literature—at least in the history of literary married couples" (Introduction, *Zelda: The Collected Writings* xvii). Further, they were extraordinarily attractive, and both worked studiously at developing public personalities that at first enchanted and later repelled the audience they had always courted. Fitzgerald had, as Scott Donaldson has noted (190), a "histrionic" personality, which coincided with Zelda's lifelong need for self-dramatization. So they became popular culture icons, and the story, so irresistible in its dimensions, has become fixed in the imagination of a mass public larger and more curious than they had ever imagined. There is another dimension to the connection between the Fitzgeralds and American popular culture: I do not wish to offer another biographical sketch, but it is a fact that Fitzgerald knew and liked that culture, that he drew on the stories of his youth to re-tell episodes from his own life, that he was a fan of movies, musical comedy, popular songs, songwriters, and stars, and that the study of the Fitzgeralds and popular culture involves a dialectic between their public performance and public image on the one hand and their use of popular culture in their creative language on the other.

For the purposes of this paper, I am defining popular culture as one "well-liked or widely favored by many people" (Storey 7), a commercial culture created for mass consumption, and a culture whose "texts and practices . . . are seen as forms of public fantasy . . . a collective dream world" (11). Popular culture is not a fixed entity; it emerged after the industrial revolution and the urbanization of America, and because it is not historically fixed, it is highly responsive to economic and social change. It is often distinguished from "high culture," but the cross-over is not only from "high" to "popular" but the reverse as well. (And we have not even mentioned the category of "pulp," which too has managed to infiltrate formerly fixed categories.) Popular culture, in the world of the twenties, meant the illustrated magazines (a negligible element in contemporary life), newspapers, bestsellers, drama, and movies. As technology grew and shifted over the next seventy years, television largely supplanted popular magazines and forced changes in movies and the movie-going public. Thus, this discussion of the Fitzgeralds and popular culture reflects the changes in that culture throughout the twentieth century.

I will trace the relationships between the Fitzgeralds and popular culture through three stages, reflecting American cultural life in our century: first, the creation of the legendary couple in the mass media of the 1920s and their disappearance during the Depression; second, the Fitzgerald revival of the 1950s signaled by the almost simultaneous publication of Budd Schulberg's *The Disenchanted* and Arthur Mizener's *The Far Side of Paradise*, and lasting through the 1960s; and third, the revisionist legend propelled by Nancy Milford's biography of Zelda from the 1970s to the present day. Finally, in the light of what we have discerned from this study as well as recent developments that portend a shift in perception, I will try to predict the future of F. Scott and Zelda Fitzgerald in American popular culture. In addressing this subject, I hope to illuminate the relationship between American culture and the American artist and perhaps offer additional insights into that uneasy alliance between a writer and that vast audience to which he or she aspires. For the relationship between a successful writer and the public is never simple: whether he courts its favor and develops the kind of persona suitable to a mainstream audience, like Hemingway, Fitzgerald, and Mailer, or rejects it and remains personally unrecognizable like Bellow, or in an extreme case, Salinger (although his hermetic existence exerts its own fascination on an admittedly smaller public), the public arena is seductive, the rewards for personal notoriety great, and the temptations eternal. For Fitzgerald, there was never a doubt.[1]

The Fitzgeralds Create a Legend

Scott and Zelda Fitzgerald were throughout their life together acutely conscious of their public image, as attested to by their scrapbooks into which they pasted newspaper articles about themselves as well as brief mentions, photographs from magazines and newspapers and from their own collections, reviews of Fitzgerald's books and films adapted from books and stories, theater reviews of his play and dramatic adaptations, Zelda's varied artistic endeavors, and even advertisements which alluded to either of them. Near the end of his life, Fitzgerald pasted in his scrapbooks clippings which compared other writers to him, or even mentioned his name in passing, heading the page, "The Memory Lingers On" (*Romantic Egoists* 204-205). From the start, immediately following the success of *This Side of Paradise* (1920), the Fitzgeralds courted public attention, and in that quest, the press was a strong ally in creating their public personas. Today, we are accustomed to manipulation of the press by celebrities, but in the twenties, only a skilled self-publicist could dictate the form his public image would take, and the Fitzgeralds had an innate instinct about their own popular appeal. Critics have noted that even a close friend of Fitzgerald, Alex McKaig, was distrustful of the couple's antics—even those likeliest to provoke a storm of criticism. He wondered if the couple's brawls were "all aimed to hand down the Fitzgerald legend" to a public eager to read of their exploits.[2] After his death, Zelda wrote to Scottie, "Daddy loved glamour and I also had a great respect for popular acclaim" (qtd. in Mellow 491), so it is fair to conclude that much of what they did in those apparently unthinking times in the twenties was in some way aimed at keeping their image alive for the public and further enhancing their legend. James Mellow's description of their "invented lives" is only half the story; popular culture itself dictated the terms of that invention, and Fitzgerald was, from childhood, adept at self-promotion. In "My Lost City" (1932) (*Crack-Up*), he remembers how the "offices of editors and publishers were open to me, impresarios begged plays, the movies panted for screen material. To my bewilderment, I was adopted . . . as the arch type of what New York wanted." He recalls that he "was pushed into the position not only of spokesman for the time but of the typical product of that same moment. I, or rather it was 'we' now, did not know exactly what New York expected of us and found it rather confusing. Within a few months after our embarkation on the Metropolitan venture we scarcely knew anymore who we were and we hadn't a notion what we were. A dive into a civic fountain, a casual brush with the law, was enough to get us into the gossip columns . . ." (27). And he reveals what the publicity, the notoriety, the public life meant to him: success is linked with "eternal youth" (33). The narrator of that and other autobiographical essays, Fitzgerald's literary persona, is recasting earlier events as part of a lifelong pattern of constructing a popular image; we cannot take at face value his apparent bewilderment at his notoriety. As Budd Schulberg has noted, "He himself had been a prime mover in this god-making and god-smashing" (*Four Seasons* 142).

Fitzgerald was a keen observer of the cultural marketplace. He once suggested to Scribner's that they reprint Scribner titles in low-priced editions, suggesting that "known titles in the series" would "carry the little known or forgotten" (*Life in Letters* 57-58). He decided to remake his image before *Gatsby* appeared, writing Perkins, "I'm tired of being the author of *This Side of Paradise* and I want to start over" (84). He was an expert judge of advertising, and directed his publisher where to advertise his books, and what kind of blurbs, if any, were to be printed in his jackets. And he advised Ernest Hemingway, no amateur at creating his own legend, that a published Hemingway parody "would make you quite conscious of your public existence" (151). His investment in his self-created image was so great that we can comprehend and sympathize with his outrage over Zelda's effort to tell their story in *Save Me the Waltz*: "My God, my books made her a legend and her single intention in this somewhat thin portrait is to make me a non-entity" (209). So intent was Fitzgerald in controlling the public's perception of him, that he wrote to Perkins in 1933 suggesting how his new novel should be advertised so as to preserve the precarious balance he always sought between the popular figure and the serious writer: "For several years the impression has prevailed that Scott Fitzgerald had abandoned the writing of novels and in the future would continue to write only popular short stories. His publishers knew different and they are very glad now to be able to present a book which is in line with his three other highly successful and highly esteemed novels, thus demonstrating that Scott Fitzgerald is anything but through as a serious novelist" (*Life in Letters* 241).

What was the public image of the Fitzgeralds in the 1920s, and how did it arise? Clearly, the daily press, in feature stories, news articles (public relations pieces), photos, and gossip columns and the popular magazines with their lavish illustrations were the prime shapers of the legend of F. Scott and Zelda Fitzgerald.

From the outset, the Fitzgeralds readily granted interviews to reporters. Their physical attractiveness was a key element in their successful seduction of the media. One reporter marvels at the "blue-eyed, frank faced, fastidiously dressed author" (Bruccoli and Bryer 256), and another notes Zelda's beauty, concluding, "The two of them might have stepped, sophisticated and charming, from the pages of any of the Fitzgerald books" (Bruccoli and Bryer 278). A woman reporter confesses archly after noting how handsome Fitzgerald is, "My interest was perhaps a bit more than professional" (Bruccoli and Bryer 278). Thomas Boyd's 1922 description is representative of the journalist's vision of the authors: "His eyes were blue and clear; his jaw was squared at the end which perceptibly protruded; his nose was straight and his mouth, though sensitive looking, was regular in outline. His hair which was corn-colored, was wavy. His were the features that the average American mind never fails to associate with beauty. But there was a quality in the eye with which the average mind is unfamiliar" (Bruccoli and Bryer 247). That last quality is, of course, intellect, or genius, and Fitzgerald sought to portray himself as both hedonistic and intellectual at the same time. Boyd concludes, "To be with him for an hour is to have the blood in one's veins thawed and made fluent" (Bruccoli and Bryer 252). Years later, when Fitzgerald could no longer control the press and his own public persona, he was to read Michael Mok's notorious description which stands in such stark and painful contrast to those of a decade earlier: "His trembling hands, his twitching face with its pitiful expression of a cruelly beaten child" (Bruccoli and Bryer 294).

As the image of the fun-loving Fitzgeralds captured the public imagination, Fitzgerald would consistently remind readers that he was a serious writer. (Later, when his exploits became less attractive, and his need for the money that his stories brought in became greater, he tried to distance himself from the image he had so consciously created in the early 1920s, and to remind his public that he was a writer first.) Even in the earliest interviews, he called attention to his drinking, which was not nearly the problem that it would become in just a few years. On the one hand, he boasts of drinking, and on the other asserts that he does not let it interfere with his artistry. He cannot drink and write, he tells Boyd, "for me, narcotics are deadening to work. I can understand anyone drinking coffee to get a stimulating effect, but Whiskey—oh, no" (Bruccoli and Bryer 253). In "The Author's Apology," which appeared in the third printing of *This Side of Paradise* (April 1920) distributed to the American Booksellers Association convention, however, Fitzgerald, under an extremely flattering photograph, advises them to "consider all the cocktails mentioned in this book drunk by me as a toast to the American Booksellers Association" (Bruccoli and Bryer 164). In 1926, he was quoted in the *New Yorker* as saying, "Don't you know I am one of the most notorious drinkers of the younger generation?" (Bruccoli and Bryer 443). And in 1929, he published a clever, tongue-in-cheek "short Autobiography" in the *New*

Yorker tracing his life from 1913 through the present in terms of varied alcoholic beverages consumed through the years.

The same interview pattern was repeated so frequently that it seems clear it was orchestrated by the Fitzgeralds and the press. After answering the obligatory questions on the current state of flapperdom, Fitzgerald would launch into a stream of apparently spontaneous observations on the state of the world, on marriage, on the modern woman, on writers both classical and modern, on the Leopold-Loeb case, and even on the future of America from a Spenglerian perspective. His magazine pieces attempted to shock (mildly, of course) the mass-audience readership, but more important, to establish Fitzgerald as the authority on male-female relationships of the era, unafraid to reject the sexual codes which were no longer as widely held as both he and the reporters would have the reader believe. The Fitzgeralds were challenging public notions of sexual morality in the traditionally conservative, pseudo-rebellious fashion characteristic of the popular media. None of their apparently outrageous remarks would have been truly shocking to the audience reading their breezy comments in *Metropolitan*, or the New York Evening *World*. Indeed, remarks like, "I believe in early marriage, easy divorce, and several children" (Bruccoli and Bryer 184) are thrown out for their shock effect with no serious discussion of their implications. He wasn't a bit perturbed when a reporter said, "He is an actor . . . vivacious, imaginative, forceful—slightly imbalanced. The latter is his chief charm" (416).

Fitzgerald played with publicity with childlike ingeniousness, little suspecting that a sensation-seeking biography seventy years later would devote pages to his public and probably facetious confession of a "pedentia complex" (Bruccoli and Bryer 416), his exaggeration of his psychological quirk as a four-year-old child (*Ledger* 155). As in *Vanity Fair* essays today, the reader's interest is piqued, but the "shocking" revelations generally prove to be far less revealing than the headlines and advertising suggest. In this particular instance, the accuracy of the biographer's discovery of Fitzgerald's "foot fetish" and all of its psycho-sexual implications is highly questionable, if not laughable. He writes, to confirm his assertions, that Frances Ring told him that Fitzgerald "always wore slippers and never went about in bare feet" (Meyers 13). In an interview Mrs. Ring stated that she was asked by this biographer what kind of clothes Fitzgerald wore, and she replied, that because he arose late and preferred to work before he dressed, he usually wore a bathrobe and slippers during the day (telephone interview, 10/7/94). She was horrified, she says, to find her words distorted to support the lurid conjectures of her interviewer. She also explains Sheilah Graham's remarks about Fitzgerald's not taking his shoes and socks off at the beach (Graham, *Rest of the Story* 197, 33) as stemming not from a "mysterious shyness" (he had told Sheilah about his childhood complex), but from his extreme hypochondria in his last years. He was always worried about TB, about colds, about flu, and indeed, did not play tennis and swim with Sheilah at their Malibu home. In support of Mrs. Ring's version, we should look at the photographs of Fitzgerald with bare—and well-formed—feet clearly displayed at the beach in four photographs reprinted in *The Romantic Egoists*, in Hyeres in 1914 (117), in Vevey in 1930 (177), at Lake Annecy in 1936 (181), and at Myrtle Beach in 1938 (219). Thus do myths begin and grow until they enter into popular culture; this particular one is foolish and irrelevant, but it is a good example of the kind of mythologizing to which the lives of the Fitzgeralds *have* been subject over the years.

Interviews with Zelda and her own pieces for the popular press from this period are designed to reinforce the public's perception of the two of them as overgrown children having a riotous good time, very much in love, and happily married. Her apparent unconventionality (masking the real disturbances she experienced) is part of her charm, and in no way threatens her marriage or her role as wife and, later, mother. Indeed, Zelda is for her public the new flapper grown up. One of the popular essays published under Fitzgerald's name, but written by Zelda, states that flapperdom is a necessary brief period in a young woman's development that will better prepare her to be safely settled as wife and mother. Zelda writes (in Scott's name), "I believe in the flapper as an artist in her objective field, the art of being—being young, being lovely, being an *object*" [italics mine] (Bruccoli and Bryer 398). In another flapper piece, she argues that if women are allowed to be free and to express themselves fully when young, there will be fewer divorces and women will be content to marry and settle down (Bruccoli and Bryer 392). Zelda publicly presents herself as a partner in the Fitzgeralds' life-as-extravaganza. Her tongue-in-cheek review of *The Beautiful and Damned* offers as a reason for purchasing the book the "aesthetic" one that "there is the cutest cloth-of-gold dress for only three hundred dollars in a store on Forty-Second street" (*Collected Writings* 387). Zelda never challenges the frivolous, Southern belle persona publicly. (All of the interviewers comment admiringly on her Southern drawl, her indolence around the house, her easy charm.) And as early as 1924, both of the Fitzgeralds were eager to tell the world that Zelda was a writer too, with a "queer decadent style. Scott incorporates whole chapters of his wife's writing into his own books" (Bruccoli and Bryer 419). Just as everything else they wrote and enacted for public consumption is exaggerated, if not a set of elaborate fantasies, we should note that the source of contemporary mythology surrounding Fitzgerald's putative use of Zelda's material lies in the couple's public role-playing, as fabricated as everything else they concocted for public consumption those days. That mythology, which I shall address later, is as suspect as such early Fitzgerald public pronouncements as "I am a pessimist, a communist (with Nietzschean overtones), have no hobbies except conversation—and I am trying to repress that" (Bruccoli and Bryer 270) or his statements in a 1928 interview (where he again boasts of his drinking prowess), in which he informs the reporter that "happiness consists of the performances of all the natural functions, with one exception—that of growing old. Sunday, Washington, D.C., cold weather, Bohemians, the managing type of American woman, avarice, and dullness are his principal dislikes" (Bruccoli and Bryer 282).

Magazine illustrations and photographs in newspapers and magazines also helped feed the Fitzgeralds' mythmaking enterprise. Perhaps the most characteristic shot of the couple was originally published in *Hearst's International* in 1923 (*Romantic Egoists* 105) along with the often reproduced photo of the family in their Paris apartment at Christmas. The Fitzgeralds' faces were not only good-looking, but they were ideally suited to the 1920s need for models illustrating the culture of youth, and they exploited their own personal appeal accordingly. Their pictures accompanied the movie magazine articles written during their 1927 trip to Hollywood. Magazine illustrations of Fitzgerald's fictional heroes all look like taller versions of Fitzgerald, and all of his characters, whether true to the story or not, are dressed in elegant evening clothes. John Held cartoons accompanied their dual articles on "What Became of Our Flappers and Sheiks" for *McCall's* (October 1925, *Romantic Egoists* 132-133), and James Montgomery Flagg's glamorized drawing of Scott and Zelda accompanied the *College Humor* 1928 essay, "Looking Back Eight Years" (*Romantic Egoists* 162-163). The headline for a Westport, Connecticut, newspaper photograph of the Fitzgeralds in 1920 is "Illustrating His Own Title!" (*Romantic Egoists* 72). The caption continues, "This fortunate youngster has won not only an enviable reputation as a writer but also an undeniably charming wife to share with him the joys of '*This Side of Paradise*.'" The comic essay "The Cruise of the Rolling Junk" for *Motor* magazine (1924) is accompanied by photos of the Fitzgeralds in matching white touring outfits which were to scandalize observers in small Southern towns on the route to Montgomery (Meyer 69). Fitzgerald's famous profile adorned advertisements for his novels, and in the advertisement for *Scribner's Magazine*'s serialization of *Tender Is the Night*, "Richard Diver: A Romance," (January 1934, *Romantic Egoists* 194), the portrait forever links the author and the hero of his novel. Further publicity photographs for the novel use *both* Fitzgeralds, in recognition of the public's memory of the couple when both commanded attention. Perhaps the most memorable illustration of the Fitzgeralds was Reginald Marsh's drawing for the drop curtain of *Greenwich Village*

Follies showing Zelda's dive into a downtown New York fountain and Fitzgerald with a group of young literary celebrities riding down Seventh Avenue. Photographers and illustrators could not resist their appeal; as John Dos Passos described them, "there was a golden innocence about them and they both were so hopelessly good looking" (Mellow 161). Virtually every reporter commented on his coloring, her complexion, their eyes, and their style. Zelda was, in those years, Scott's equal in physical attractiveness, and the combination of outrageous behavior, youthful exuberance, and personal beauty secured their place in the public eye.

Their public image was further enlarged by the gossip columnists who reported their exploits, by occasional editorials criticizing Fitzgerald's "attempts to be an aristocrat" (Louisville *Courier Journal*, April 4, 17, 1922, Bruccoli and Bryer 410), and above all by the impression they made on their circle of friends and acquaintances who would remember, with Donald Ogden Stewart, "I felt like some embarrassed spectator caught by the unexpected rising of the curtain on the stage of a comedy in which the two stars were competing for the spotlight" (179); or with Gilbert Seldes, who recalled, "The two most beautiful people in the world were floating toward me" (Milford 127).

Fitzgerald's early magazine pieces are pseudo-confessionals where he eagerly seizes on whatever print opportunities are available to define himself for his public. Thus "Who's Who and Why" (1920) (his first public print appearance for a mass audience—readers of the *Saturday Evening Post*) also marks the beginning of his self-created legend, shrewdly re-writing the text of his life so that, for example, there is no hint of his dismal performance at Princeton. The essay is a brief autobiography culminating in an account of his brilliant success, written as though in dazed wonder, but there is considerable calculation behind the simple recitation (*Afternoon* 83-86). Similarly, his mock confessionals, "How to Live on $36,000 a Year" (*SEP* 5 April 1924) and "How to Live on Practically Nothing a Year" (*SEP* 20 September 1924) are ironic and humorously self-deprecating yet convey the excitement, a "kind of unconscious joy" the couple experienced in those early years. Their self-revelation was itself self-creation in its most extreme form. The author's self-stated fear of "conventionality, dullness, sameness, predictability" (*American Magazine* September 1922, Bruccoli and Bryer 213), his lack of patience with the older generation, his distaste for the parasitic leisure class, the diatribe against education for women, along with his advice to insure that the new generation will avoid the fate of its elders, was Fitzgerald's way of seizing public attention at the outset. He was then forced by the confessions themselves to continually raise the stakes, until the lives of the Fitzgeralds (which later would include their daughter) soon became the popular myth they had always planned, but larger, and ultimately more destructive to them, than they could have realized at the outset. Fitzgerald quotes in "My Lost City" (*Crack-Up* 28) a headline he read years earlier "in astonishment": "Fitzgerald Knocks Officer *This Side of Paradise*." He notes his difficulty remembering this and other exploits from the heady period of his success, admits ruefully how ephemeral that success was, and, at the same time, attempts to cast an elegiac glow on events that might have been too humiliating and self-destructive to report unless they were transmuted into a portion of the ongoing legend of his life.

The Fitzgeralds were equally aware of other popular media. As a young boy, he was captivated with the theater and described in his scrapbook his first appearance in a play, "The Coward" (1913), as "The great event" (*Romantic Egoists* 18). The theatrical season in New York in the 1920s was particularly exciting to a young man who had long worshipped musical comedy and had written his own at Princeton. Zelda's love of the theater was as intense as Scott's, and her self-dramatization was integral to her personality at a young age. When these two people at the height of their success met the Broadway of the 1920s, the effect on both was electric. They saw Ina Claire, Theda Bara, Marilyn Miller, and the Barrymores, and in their delight at the dramatic spectacles, they were moved to enact dramas of their own. A public greedy for stories about celebrity hijinks relished the dramatic antics of the Fitzgeralds, which gossip columnists painted in expectedly sensational colors. Today we cannot dissever the real from the fabricated, so successful were they at self-publicizing. But they have surely provided fodder for those contemporary biographers who have sought to sensationalize and trivialize their lives.

Fitzgerald's interest in the theater remained unabated throughout his lifetime, although his involvement in Hollywood drew his attention to that popular medium. He was enormously pleased by the success of Owen Davis's stage version of *Gatsby*, directed by George Cukor in 1926 ("Cukor's Breakthrough," McGilligan 52), particularly since the theatrical world "had not anticipated such a shrewd adaptation" by a playwright "best known for his hundreds of cheap melodramas and Hippodrome extravaganzas" (52). The play had a substantial run, 113 performances, affording some compensation for the failure of his own work, *The Vegetable* (1923), which had a disastrous opening night when the audience walked out during the second act fantasy (Bruccoli 187).

Fitzgerald was a movie fan too. As Schulberg has noted, he "believed in films as an ideal art form for reaching out to millions who might never have read a serious novel" (98). Movies, for Fitzgerald, were foremost a popular entertainment. He declared in 1921, "I like to see a pleasant flapper like Constance Talmadge or I want to see comedies like those of Chaplin's or Lloyd's. I'm not strong for the uplift stuff. It simply isn't life to me" (Bruccoli and Bryer 245). He was always looking for opportunities to see his work adapted for film, remarking to Perkins in 1924 that he thought he had hard luck with the movies. "I must try some love stories with more action this time," he wrote (*Life in Letters* 82). Before the publication of *Gatsby* he was interested in moving-picture bids, and in 1936, he proposed to Harold Ober a movie about a ballet dancer based on Zelda's life (*Life in Letters* 297). "Of course," he wrote, "the tragic ending of Zelda's story need not be repeated in the picture. One could concede to the picture people the fact that the girl might become a popular dancer in the Folies Bergère" (296). He proposed an alternate ending that reveals how well he understood the popular marketplace: "One could conceive of a pathetic ending à la Hepburn in which because of her idealism she went on being a fifth rate 'figurine' in ballets all over Europe—this to be balanced by a compensatory love story which would make up for the failure of her work" (296). I have elsewhere described his lifelong admiration for Griffith (Prigozy, "Griffith's Girls"). He recalls in 1935 how as a young author in the 1920s he had tried to interest Griffith in a film about Hollywood and a studio romance (*Life in Letters* 297), indicating how apt a student he was of public taste, for shortly thereafter such self-reflexive films as *What Price Hollywood?* (1932) and *A Star Is Born* (1937) showed how accurately he took the public pulse. Beginning with the sale of "Head and Shoulders" (1920) to Metro Studios for $2500 as a vehicle for the popular actress Viola Dana (produced as *The Chorus Girl's Romance*, 1920), Fitzgerald was tireless in seeking opportunities to see his fiction translated into film. Indeed, in the same year, he sold the options for "Myra Meets His Family" (1920) and "The Offshore Pirate" (1920), and signed a contract with Metro for future film rights to his short stories. His lifelong association with Hollywood would last until his death. In 1939, whether it was true or not, he was proud to inform Harold Ober that Alfred Hitchcock had put him at the top of his list as a possible writer for *Rebecca* (*Life in Letters* 291).[3]

Fitzgerald's connection with movies extended beyond film adaptations of his own work. He and Zelda wanted to play the leads in a possible adaptation of *This Side of Paradise*, and during his 1927 Hollywood sojourn, Louis Moran arranged a screen test for him which proved unsuccessful. As Alan Margolies has pointed out, screenwriter Edwin H. Knopf and director King Vidor believed that the lives of Scott and Zelda Fitzgerald could provide material for a popular movie. An early version of the 1935 film *The Wedding Night*, with Gary Cooper and Helen Vinson, and featuring Anna Sten, was known as "Broken Soil," and it was based on their lives—indeed their names are Scott Fitzpatrick and Zelda; the author in the screenplay has as his publisher Scribner's, and his first book is titled *This Side of Heaven*. As Margolies tells us, both Knopf and Vidor knew Fitzgerald from the 1920s into the 1930s, and although the filmed version differs from the early screenplay, there is still some resemblance to the famous couple (Margolies 224-225). The story of Fitzgerald and Hollywood has been told many times, including Fitzgerald's allusions to movies in many fictional works. But that the Fitzgeralds as a couple would themselves become the subject of popular films—in their own time and years later—is another illustration of their absorption into American popular culture.

Fitzgerald was aware that he was no longer a literary or public celebrity in the 1930s, although brief items about the Fitzgeralds' several moves in the early thirties found their way into mostly local newspapers. He was deeply concerned about his reputation both as a popular and serious writer, desperate for the public attention that had attended him so devotedly a decade earlier. As Scott Donaldson has suggested, "The Crack-Up" essays were in part public confession, in part an effort to re-cast his private life into a public image with which readers who might have forgotten him could identify. Letter after painful letter to Zelda, to Perkins, to Ober attempt to explain the public's neglect. On the one hand, he would tell Zelda, in 1940, that "a whole new generation grew up in the meanwhile to whom I was only a writer of *Post* stories" (*Life in Letters* 466), and on the other, in the same year, he would tell her of a "new idea . . . a comedy series which will get me back into the big magazines—but my God I am a forgotten man" (439). To Perkins, he would write, "But to die, so completely and unjustly after having given so much" (445). He is mourning, of course, his neglect as a serious writer, but again, he is looking for any way back into public favor—even taking the route of the "commercial" stuff he claimed had destroyed his reputation. In his last letters, he frequently linked the public image of the Fitzgeralds with the unaccountable public neglect, writing to Zelda in 1940, "It was partly that times changed, editors changed, but part of it was tied up somehow with you and me—the happy ending" (467-468).

Both the Fitzgeralds were largely forgotten in the 1930s, save for brief newspaper accounts of the 1934 exhibition of her paintings. As one biographer has noted, "The press was less interested in the work than in the resurrection of a legendary figure from the Jazz Age" (Mellow 427), and photographs of Zelda in *Time* magazine were not flattering. Accounts of the exhibition all noted that Zelda had been released from a mental institution to attend the opening.

Scott Fitzgerald's brush with the press in the 1930s took the form of the notorious interview with the *New York Post*'s Michael Mok in 1936, who established the picture of the writer that would remain with the public for years to come: a foolish, drunken failure whose degradation was matched only by that of his mad, suicidal wife. Anthony Powell, meeting Fitzgerald in 1937, noted, "It was almost as if he were already dead; at best risen from the dead, and of somewhat doubtful survival value" (Dardis 3). Powell was then surprised to discover that the mythical failure was very much alive, sober, and anything but the broken man he and the few who still recalled the writer expected. Even Sheilah Graham, who was to create a new public Fitzgerald mythology for later generations, remembered him at their first meeting only as a figure out of the past: "I thought, he's the writer of the gay twenties, of flaming youth, of bobbed hair and short skirts and crazy drinking—the jazz age. I had even made use of his name: in SHEILAH GRAHAM SAYS when I wanted to chide women for silly behavior, I described them as passé, as old-fashioned F. Scott Fitzgerald types, though I had never read anything he wrote" (Graham 174). Ironically, Fitzgerald was to spend the most memorable days of his last years with one of that great public who knew him only by his popular reputation, who had never read his books.

It is now part of the legend that when Fitzgerald died in 1940, he was remembered as "the best chronicler of a short and parochial chapter in American history," "part and parcel of the twenties," who "dramatized an American state of mind, wild and reckless, and when it petered out, as much from emptiness as anything else, he, too, petered out—tragically and completely" (Bryer 202-204). His genius was trivialized in the *New York Times* as a "real talent which never fully bloomed" (Bruccoli and Bryer 469). Friends of Fitzgerald paid tribute to the forgotten author in a special edition of *The New Republic* in 1941, remembering him fondly, with Glenway Wescott, as "a kind of king of our American youth" in the 1920s (Kazin 116). Budd Schulberg, reminiscing in the same issue, connected Fitzgerald's rise and fall to the massive social upheavals of his era (one of the first of many attempts to connect Fitzgerald's life to American history): "My generation thought of F. Scott Fitzgerald as an age rather than as a writer, and when the economic stroke of 1929 began to change the sheiks and flappers into unemployed boys or underpaid girls, we consciously and a little belligerently turned our backs on Fitzgerald" (110). Fitzgerald finally achieved in death a new, if smaller, public life, as our American failure—and the legend of Fitzgerald the failure would haunt the second stage of Fitzgerald's life in popular culture. By the 1950s, not only would the public meet the failed alcoholic writer, but they would be reintroduced to his wife, now a pathetic madwoman whose life had literally gone up in flames.

The Fitzgerald Revival in the 1950s

The Fitzgerald revival in the 1950s was inaugurated by Budd Schulberg's best-selling novel, *The Disenchanted* (1950), a thinly veiled portrait of Fitzgerald as a failed alcoholic has-been writer, Manley Halliday, who accompanies a young man—like Schulberg himself—to a college winter carnival to write a screenplay. The book was a huge success, and was followed almost immediately by Arthur Mizener's scholarly biography, *The Far Side of Paradise* (1951). Schulberg and Mizener were in close contact, and much of the material in the Mizener book about the Hollywood years was in fact the product of a Mizener-Schulberg collaboration which Sheilah Graham felt it necessary to correct in both *Beloved Infidel* (1958) and in *The Rest of the Story* (1964). Schulberg was then, and always has been, happy that the "one-two punch" of those books "brought to Scott . . . the new generation of readers, admirers, and enthusiastic critics he had been hoping for in vain throughout the thirties" (Schulberg, *Four Seasons* 140), and indeed, Schulberg has been actively involved in contemporary tributes and conferences devoted to Fitzgerald.

Both books stressed Fitzgerald's great success and equally stunning failure, and they stimulated ruminations among scholars and journalists about the price of success and failure in America. Indeed, America in the 1950s was embarking on a postwar period of expansions; as in Fitzgerald's own youth, life seemed to be starting all over again as if we could put behind us the traumas of a war, the dropping of the atomic bomb, and the revelations of the Holocaust. New York City was once again a magnet that drew young writers and artists. (Dan Wakefield has recently compared his youthful days as a writer in New York with Fitzgerald's in *New York in the Fifties*, 1992.) Treatises on the lonely crowd and the man in the gray flannel suit led to speculation on the meaning as well as the price of success in America. Undoubtedly, as Malcolm Cowley has suggested, Fitzgerald's "was a story that appealed to something deep in the American psyche" (Cowley, *FHA* 12). For Americans, he suggests, the words "success" and "failure" had always been weighted, the question "Will I be a success?" giving way to "Mightn't it be better to be a failure, that is, to fall from some dizzy height and yet in the end to be better than those who kept on rising? By 1950 Scott and Zelda had become the hero and heroine of an American legend" (12). Leslie Fiedler's 1951 essay "Some Notes on F. Scott Fitzgerald" (Fiedler 174-182) was written during the revival spurred by the Schulberg-Mizener books, and he asked why we had seized on Fitzgerald as a great writer. Discounting, as too many of the popular sociologists and psychologists of the era consistently did, the brilliance of the writing, Fiedler attributed the revival to nostalgia for the 1920s, but beyond everything else the seduction of Fitzgerald's failure for the American public. Quoting Schulberg's line, "Nothing fails like success," he feels that for American artists, whose prototype was Poe,

"Nothing succeeds like failure," that "Fitzgerald *willed* his role as a failure" (176), Fiedler links Fitzgerald's failure to his great flaw, alcoholism, decries the author's penchant for "composing himself," and concludes, "when the lives of Scott and Zelda are forgotten, or when they have become merely chronologies without legendary distortions and pathos, his books will be less rewarding" (178). The words "success" and "failure" in the 1950s would become associated with Fitzgerald as with no other American writer. In his recent book on Fitzgerald and Hemingway, Matthew Bruccoli quotes from Prince Michael Roumanoff, whose description of Fitzgerald in Lillian Ross's 1950 *New Yorker* article became the popular starting point for a discussion of Fitzgerald in the 1950s: "Scott Fitzgerald was a failure as a success—and a failure as a failure" (Bruccoli 7). Unquestionably, the Schulberg-Mizener books forced that legend into popular culture mythology, while at the same time, writers like J. D. Salinger and Dan Wakefield were responding to the words behind the image. The revelations by Mizener about Zelda Fitzgerald's insanity and death served both to keep her image alive and to enhance the mythology of Fitzgerald's all too public rise, fall, and posthumous resurrection.

Schulberg's *The Disenchanted* introduced the subject of glamorized failure in the scene in which Manley Halliday is dying and thinks, "Take it from me, baby, in America nothing fails like success" (388) and Halliday is the consummate American failure. In the 1950s and subsequently, Schulberg has stated that Halliday is a composite of many writers he knew (particularly with regard to popular culture— "unlike my Manley Halliday . . . Scott was quite the opposite of a film snob," *Four Seasons* 97), but the book was so superficially accurate that readers and reviewers accepted it as a barely fictionalized account of Fitzgerald's last years. It was a bestseller and brought Fitzgerald's name back into the arena of popular culture.[4] Author James M. Cain praised the novel in the *Times*, while disparaging Fitzgerald's artistry. However, Alfred Kazin in the *New Yorker* (February 17, 1951) perhaps spoke for many writers and scholars when he challenged Schulberg's portrait: "Schulberg pities Fitzgerald, but he does not really approve of him, with that approval which starts from creative sympathy and understanding. That is the trouble with the book all along." Burke Wilkinson's laudatory essay in the *New York Times Book Review* (December 24, 1950) surveyed the writer's career and hailed Schulberg's book for re-introducing Fitzgerald to the American reading public. But *The Disenchanted* and the Mizener biography also spawned new criticism of the Fitzgeralds' lives, as in the *New Leader* (March 12, 1951), which intoned, "The secret of the problem of F. Scott Fitzgerald is that the author and his wife actually believed that money could buy happiness" (Bryer 219).

One of the more interesting contributors to the popular Fitzgerald mythology in the 1950s was his old friend Ernest Hemingway. In January 1951, *Life* magazine ran an article on the Mizener biography, which was being serialized in *The Atlantic*, and included five pages of photographs of pages from Fitzgerald's scrapbooks. Hemingway was outraged by the captions and headings the *Life* editors wrote, particularly the subheading, "The rediscovered novelist of the 20s was beset by drink, debt, a mad wife" (qtd. in Bruccoli, *Fitzgerald and Hemingway* 219). Hemingway's anger at the article's criticism of writers and artists of the twenties, although it did not mention him, led him to write to Harvey Breit of the *New York Times Book Review* and to Malcolm Cowley castigating the "Schulberg-Mizener axis" (222). Publicly, he responded only by citing as among six titles he would like to have read had they been published, "*Longevity Pays: The Life of Arthur Mizener* by F. Scott Fitzgerald, and *The Schulberg Incident* by F. Scott Fitzgerald" (222). Whatever outrage Hemingway might have felt at the time, it did not prevent him from adding to the public mythology of Fitzgerald the failure. I have discussed his chapters on Fitzgerald in *A Moveable Feast* elsewhere[5] but the Hemingway portrait of Fitzgerald, very precise, and very damning, particularly the last line of the description, "The mouth worried you until you knew him and then it worried you more" (149), fed into the image of Fitzgerald created by Mizener and

Schulberg. Because those memories of Fitzgerald were published in *Life* (April 10, 1964), they were assured a wide readership. And Hemingway's dislike and distrust of Zelda Fitzgerald, whom he described as "more jealous of his work than anything" (183), as well as his confession that he knew she was crazy at the outset, enhanced her image as one of the prime causes of Fitzgerald's failure. As if that were not sufficient to garner public attention, his remarks about the size of Fitzgerald's male organ generated a very public debate in the pages of *Esquire* (December 1966, 188). Titled "Scott, Ernest and Whoever," it was an unprecedented controversy to which *Esquire* editor Arnold Gingrich and Sheilah Graham added their perspectives. *Getting Straight* certainly indicates the extent to which the debate had become part of Fitzgerald's popular culture persona. One of the first plays on the friendship between the two authors, *Before I Wake*, opened at the Greenwich Mews Theater in 1968 (October 13, 1968). Ninety-five percent of the dialogue was drawn from the letters between the two writers and to others commenting on each other. Both writers were now in the public domain.

In 1958, the dramatic version of *The Disenchanted* opened on Broadway to generally excellent reviews (December 3, 1958, Coronet Theater). Again, the Fitzgerald-as-failure story became public entertainment, as critics described it as "the story of the waning life and ebbing faculties of F. Scott Fitzgerald" (John Chapman, *Daily News*, December 4, 1958); or "He and his wife led a gay life. He made money fast, and she spent it faster. Eventually, both were broken physically" (Robert Coleman, *Daily Mirror*, December 4, 1958); or "the destruction of a writer haunted by the past, possessed by the demands of the present, weary, disillusioned, overwhelmed on every side by the practical realities that he has never faced" (Brooks Atkinson, *New York Times*, December 4, 1958). But the film version was never made, largely as the result of efforts by Sheilah Graham and Scottie Fitzgerald, who threatened legal action (Graham, *Rest of the Story* 14). (Schulberg has indicated that he and Graham, after a long misunderstanding, reviewed the events which she had challenged and mended fences, *Four Seasons* 122.)[6]

Sheilah Graham's book *Beloved Infidel* (1958), a genuinely moving account of Fitzgerald's last years, was her attempt to offer a corrective to the Schulberg-Mizener version of that period, and to tell the public about their love. It too became a bestseller, and was made into a 1959 Cinemascope film which Schulberg describes as "just as screwed up as *Winter Carnival*" (*Four Seasons* 142). Articles by Frances Ring (1959) and Budd Schulberg (1962) in *Esquire* responded to public fascination with Fitzgerald's Hollywood years, and Calvin Tompkins' well-received *Living Well Is the Best Revenge* (1962) shed light on the Fitzgeralds' sojourns on the French Riviera with Gerald and Sara Murphy. Andrew Turnbull's 1962 sympathetic biography of Fitzgerald was widely reviewed throughout the United States and became a bestseller. Although it was a warm response to Turnbull's boyhood friendship with the author, it did little to dispel the contemporary popular view of the author.

Perhaps the best contemporary view of the Fitzgeralds as they appeared to the American public in these years is that of Wakefield, who recalls meeting a friend accompanied by a girl identified as "Zelda." It is not her name, but "she could have passed for a twenties flapper that night. She loved the legend surrounding Zelda and Scott Fitzgerald, our generation's idols of literary glamour and doom" (39-40). In the seventies, both the glamour and the doom would be held up to new scrutiny as the scholarly world joined the media marketplace to create a new image of Scott and Zelda Fitzgerald that has persisted to the present.

The Revisionists: 1970 to the Present

Public perception generally lags behind that of critics and scholars. During the early 1970s, the influence of Hemingway's and of Sheilah Graham's revelations shaped the popular culture images of the Fitzgeralds, even though Nancy Milford's revisionist biography, *Zelda*, was published in 1970, creating a new interpretation of the couple which has lasted until the present. Thus, the early 1970s television dramatization of their lives on ABC-TV with Jason Miller and Tuesday Weld presented the story of the Fitzgeralds and of Sheilah Graham according to the accepted biographies of the 1960s. Nancy Milford's frankly feminist book drew upon new material to cast Zelda in the light of an artist whose talents were thwarted by a husband who was fearful that she would use material drawn from their lives together that properly belonged to him as the established writer and financial support of the family. In her introduction, she proclaims her emotional involvement with her subject: "Reading Zelda's letters to her husband moved me in a way I had never been moved before . . ." (xiii). One might be equally moved by his letters to her and others, revealing his desperation about earning enough to support her and their daughter, and by Sheilah Graham's memoir of her desperate efforts to save his life and work. Milford paints Zelda as "the American girl living the American dream" who "became mad with it" (xiv). Milford passes quickly over the many mental illnesses in the Sayre family, choosing to stress Zelda's relationship with Scott as the chief contributor to her breakdown, although she does provide sufficient instances of Zelda's youthful bizarre escapades to raise questions about her mental and emotional balance. Unfortunately, she relies upon Sara Mayfield's biased memories (later appearing in Mayfield's *Exiles from Paradise*) which recall Zelda as not mentally ill (for her, Scott was the unbalanced one), and as the true genius of the family. Milford's book appeared at a crucial period for women in America, indeed, at the beginning of the women's movement which needed heroines, particularly women whose creativity had been stifled by a patriarchal society. What figure better fits that paradigm than Zelda Fitzgerald, and what better male oppressor than F. Scott Fitzgerald? Scottie Fitzgerald Smith perhaps put it best in her comment on the phenomenon of her mother's new status in life and letters:

I was surprised when Women's Lib finally became part of our national consciousness to find that my mother was considered by many to be one of the more flamboyant symbols of the movement. To a new generation, the generation of her grandchildren, she was the classic "put down" wife, whose efforts to express her artistic nature were thwarted by a typically male chauvinist husband. . . . Finally in a sort of ultimate rebellion, she withdrew altogether from the arena; it's a script that reads well, and will probably remain part of the "Scott and Zelda" mythology forever, but is not, in my opinion, accurate. (Preface, *Collected Writings of Zelda Fitzgerald* v)

Scottie was correct, of course, for to the revisionists, Zelda was a literary talent of the first rank. Mary Gordon sees her work as a *Bildungsroman*, "a female self coming to maturity in the age of the flapper" (Gordon, introd. *Collected Writings* xxi). Gordon sides with Zelda in her accusations against her husband, and advises that we should apply new criteria to Zelda's writing, "discarding the notion that the formal, finished and pared down is aesthetically superior to the associative and fragmentary" (xvii), that we give a more "open" reading to her work, "to make a place for the 'You see what I means,' and the 'Can't you understands'" (xvii). Feminist critics have been unwilling to look at the Fitzgeralds' troubled relationship from both perspectives: he *had* to support his family; he was the professional writer; he had been working on *Tender Is the Night* for years (interrupted by his having to earn money to pay for her care), and was understandably disturbed by her use of the same material for her book. They had both concocted the story of his use of her work years earlier; it now became an issue for her. Was she, as Hemingway asserted, deeply jealous of his success, or was she a writer who deserved recognition in her own right? (Considering their publicly created personas, that judgment would have been difficult to make in any event.) I am not going to offer answers here to fuel a new controversy, save to state that there are passages of brilliant writing in her stories and her novel, but that she is finally a highly gifted amateur who would not have received the recognition now accorded her had she not first been married to F. Scott Fitzgerald, and then experienced the heady success of the twenties, collapsed pathetically in the thirties, and died tragically in the forties.

But the new image of the Fitzgeralds was intriguing to the popular audience, which now had not only Scott's failure to relish but his abuse of Zelda and her emergence as a heroine-victim. This last image, along with that of her abusive, manipulative alcoholic husband, has been kept alive in American popular culture—in film, in theater, in the popular press, and notably in popular biographies like those of the four "M"s: Milford, Mayfield, Mellow, and Meyers.

Among the many dramatizations based on the lives of the Fitzgeralds according to the new gospel, the most representative is perhaps that by Tennessee Williams, who creates in Zelda his own double, as he did in Blanche DuBois: the troubled, misunderstood Southern belle, confined to a mental institution. Williams' 1980 play, *Clothes for a Summer Hotel*, opened in 1980 and drew heavily on material in Milford's book, with Scott complaining, with regard to *Save Me the Waltz*, "Didn't I have to pay for her treatment, for Scotty's Vassar?" (Williams 34). The couple talks about their fame, their picture in *Cosmopolitan*, and has Zelda mourn their "storybook marriage, legendary. Yes, well, legends fade" (74). She concedes their marriage had been as Scott described it, a "monumental error, and that it had been a mistake for us ever to have met" (74). As the reviewers noted, this is a ghost play which offers "no more about the Fitzgeralds and their companions than we might have picked up from stray accounts over the years without ever having cracked one of the novels or books about the pair" (Douglas Watt, New York *Daily News*, March 27, 1980). One reviewer found it hard to find Zelda, the central character, sympathetic: "For much of the play she wears a shabby tutu, which has a forlornly comic sense of grace, quite undone by the dancers' leggings on her thighs. . . . For the most part, she whines. She nags Scott or taunts him. It is hard to find her tragic or even sympathetic" (Howard Kissel, *Women's Wear*

Daily, March 27, 1980). Other figures from the Fitzgerald legend appear—Gerald Murphy, Ernest Hemingway, Mrs. Patrick Campbell, but the play simply rehashes the popular mythology with little of the poetry Williams usually brings to his drama. Joel Siegel, reviewing the play on television, said, "Until I double-checked my Playbill I was sure I'd walked into a play about Ed and Pegeen Fitzgerald by Tennessee Ernie" (New York, ABC-TV News, March 26, 1980).

In her 1985 memoir, Frances Ring noted Fitzgerald's entry into the world of television, his stories and novels providing material for countless adaptations which she describes as "Scott's lucrative life after death" (145). In the Fall of 1993, Turner Network Television offered a dramatization of the lives of the Fitzgeralds which accurately reflects their image in popular culture today. The dramatization (based largely on the Milford biography) opens with their meeting at a dance in Alabama in 1918. From that moment and throughout the film, Scott is rarely, if ever, shown without a flask or glass. In their first encounter, Zelda, whose daring is her most notable attribute, says, "I've always wanted to swim naked" and promptly sheds her clothes; their naked swim fits the classic "meet cute" Hollywood scenarios from the 1930s and 1940s. Every aspect of their lives is reduced, trivialized, exaggerated, vulgarized, and Maxwell Perkins, Hemingway, and Edmund Wilson are bit players in this sordid tale of a couple of losers. Throughout, their sexual lives are held up to scrutiny, as are their Jazz Age escapades and their troubled marriage. The obligatory sequences depicting Scott's lack of sympathy for Zelda's artistic endeavors and her relationship with the French aviator are familiar, yet somehow strange, episodes in this visual medium which cruelly caricatures the couple. When Zelda says, "Scott and I don't believe in self-preservation" and jumps from the roof of a villa into a pool (followed by Scott), we can only laugh at the gross lack of subtlety that has made their lives into television trash. But it does tell us what F. Scott and Zelda Fitzgerald signify in American popular culture in the 1990s: a morality tale directed at the excesses of the 1980s which so resembled those of the

1920s. The Fitzgeralds are thus portrayed for the general public as object lessons, combining popular notions of female victimization with failure to conform to broadly acceptable norms of behavior.

Undoubtedly several recent biographies have contributed to the skewed popular culture vision of F. Scott and Zelda Fitzgerald. For James Mellow, Fitzgerald's life interferes with judging his art, and he consistently denigrates Fitzgerald's short stories, perhaps taking the author's rationalizations for truth without reading the stories himself. Because Mellow is unsympathetic to Fitzgerald the person, he draws upon several versions of a story (without any direct evidence) to portray the writer as a thoroughly unsympathetic drunk (the episode at the train station at Ellerslie is a good example of Mellow's technique, 325-327). He trots out the old homosexuality stories, and provides grim details about Scott and Zelda's charges and countercharges regarding sexual performance. His disapproval makes his biography truly reflective of its title, *Invented Lives*. Sara Mayfield's biography is so biased that it cannot be taken seriously, so I shall not linger on such foolish conclusions as Scott being responsible for Zelda's madness, that *he* had the split personality, that he encouraged her to be dependent on him and kept her in hospitals so that he might be free (a charge made by members of her family), that *Save Me the Waltz* is superior to *Tender Is the Night*, or that incredible conclusion that she is the genius, he the mere talent. Jeffrey Meyers' biography is the latest assault on the couple, as it assiduously digs out whatever "dirt" he believes lies under an already picked-over corpse. Thus his psychosexual diagnoses, his sensationalized "discoveries" of Fitzgerald's past flames, his incapacity to portray either of the Fitzgeralds as the creative figures they were leave the reader repelled. He has turned Scott and Zelda into tabloid personalities, the Roseanne and Tom Arnold of the Jazz Age.

All of these biographies have turned the writer and his wife into vulgarized figures easily recognized by a mass public which does not distinguish between great talent and dross, so intermingled are they today in the pages of *People Magazine* and *Vanity Fair*, and even *The New Yorker*.

The Future of the Fitzgeralds in Popular Culture

Is the dismal picture I have described to be the final incarnation of the Fitzgeralds in American popular culture? I think not; in fact, I believe the tide has already turned. There has been, for the past fifteen years, a strong link between academics and the mass market. As the film *Getting Straight* suggests, the mass market may turn on the new revelations and reject them in the name of common sense. Even the academics themselves may discern the excesses that biographers with biased agendas have committed. The Meyers book was rejected both by critics and the public, and at the 1994 Hemingway-Fitzgerald Conference in Paris, the only standing ovation was accorded Frances Ring, who advised us to "throw the gin down the drain" and to think of what the Fitzgeralds really were and what they accomplished. "She was more than a pretty face and he was more than a handsome playboy. She had a sharp intelligence and creative gifts that were adrift in an aimless sea. She was a product of the era in which she lived when women were dependent 'girls' or obedient wives. . . . Why make comparisons? They were two different people linked by the public spectacle of their marriage, but still separate in the degree of their talent. A writer was all he ever wanted to be. . . . But she drifted in and out of the arts. Her painting reflected her exaggerated erratic personality, decorative though it was. And her obsession with the ballet ultimately defeated her. Yes, she was searching, desperately for some gratification of her very own and it was a valid search, but it was her illness, not Scott that interfered with achievement." Mrs. Ring recalls Fitzgerald at the end, and asserts, "he wasn't finished. He wasn't a failure though he was poor. . . . He believed in his talent; he believed in *The Last Tycoon*. So let us give him credit for his own resurrection and let's finally pour the gin down the drain."

On what would have been Fitzgerald's 98th birthday, Garrison Keillor and a group of St. Paul residents led a birthday parade and celebration before dedicating the Fitzgerald Theater in the city of his birth. The announcement of the dedication states, "Fitzgerald was a beautiful writer, his best writing as graceful and truthful as ever, and he was a heroic man who was defeated and kept on fighting." Perhaps we have all tired of the old stories and are ready to look more charitably on a great writer and his talented wife whose personal lives held both laughter and sadness, and whose gifts deserve to live in the glow of that public affirmation they so tirelessly sought.

From *Zelda and Scott/Scott and Zelda: New Writings on Their Works, Lives, and Times*, edited by Donald R. Noble, pp. 63-91. Copyright © 2005 by Whitston Publishing. Reprinted with permission of Whitston Publishing.

Notes

1. For a thorough discussion of Hemingway's public personality and celebrity, see John Raeburn's *Fame Became of Him*.

2. See Nancy Milford, *Zelda*, p. 109, and James Mellow's account, in *Invented Lives*, p. 123.

3. Movies made from Fitzgerald stories during his lifetime also include *The Offshore Pirate*, *The Beautiful and Damned*, and *The Great Gatsby*. He also wrote titles (to convey dialogue), a scenario and a screenplay for three silent movies in 1923-1924 (Meyers 168). After his death, five films were made from his works or from works about him: *The Great Gatsby* (1949); *The Last Time I Saw Paris* from "Babylon Revisited" (1954); *Beloved Infidel* (1959); *Tender Is the Night* (1962); and *The Last Tycoon* (1976).

4. Tom Dardis comments on Schulberg's role in creating what Dardis sees as an inaccurate picture of Fitzgerald in Hollywood, and ponders Schulberg's motives, which he finds suspect. See Dardis, p. 26.

5. Ruth Prigozy, "Fitzgerald and Hemingway: A Matter of Measurement."

6. Schulberg regards Andrew Turnbull's account of the *Winter Carnival* episode as stemming from "pure malice," its errors later inherited by Henry Dan Piper, in *F. Scott Fitzgerald: A Critical Portrait*.

Works Cited

Anderson, W. R. "Rivalry and Partnership: The Short Fiction of Zelda Fitzgerald." *Fitzgerald/Hemingway Annual* (1977): 19-42.

Bruccoli, Matthew J. *Fitzgerald and Hemingway: A Dangerous Friendship*. New York: Carroll & Graf, 1994.

_____. *Some Sort of Epic Grandeur: The Life of F. Scott Fitzgerald*. New York: Harcourt Brace Jovanovich, 1981.

_____ and Jackson R. Bryer, editors. *F. Scott Fitzgerald in His Own Time*. Ohio: Kent State University Press, 1971.

_____, Scottie Fitzgerald Smith and Joan P. Kerr, editors. *The Romantic Egoists*. New York: Scribner, 1974.

Bryer, Jackson R. *The Critical Reputation of F. Scott Fitzgerald*. N.P. Archon Books, 1967.

Cowley, Malcolm. "The Fitzgerald Revival: 1941-53." *Fitzgerald/Hemingway Annual* (1974): 11-13.

_____. *A Second Flowering: Works and Days of the Lost Generation*. New York: Viking, 1973.

_____. *Think Back on Us. . . . A Contemporary Chronicle of the 1930s: The Literary Record*. Carbondale & Edwardsville: Southern Illinois University Press, 1967.

Dardis, Tom. *Some Time in the Sun*. New York: Scribner's, 1976.

Donaldson, Scott. *Fool for Love: F. Scott Fitzgerald*. New York: Congdon & Weed, 1983.

Fiedler, Leslie. "Some Notes on F. Scott Fitzgerald." *An End to Innocence*. Boston: Beacon Press, 1955.

Fitzgerald, F. Scott. *Afternoon of an Author*. Edited by Arthur Mizener. New York: Scribner's, 1958.

_____. *The Beautiful and Damned*. New York: Scribner's, 1922.

_____. *The Crack-Up*. Edited by Edmund Wilson. New York: New Directions, 1945.

_____. "The Cruise of the Rolling Junk." Bloomfield Hills, Michigan & Columbia, South Carolina: Bruccoli Clark, 1976.

_____. *The Great Gatsby*. New York: Scribner's, 1925.

_____. *The Last Tycoon*. New York: Scribner's, 1941.

_____. *Ledger (A facsimile)*. Edited by Matthew J. Bruccoli. Washington Bruccoli Clark/NCR Microcard Books, 1973.

_____. *A Life in Letters*. Edited by Matthew J. Bruccoli. New York: Scribner's Macmillan, 1994.

_____. *Tender Is the Night*. New York: Scribner's, 1934.

_____. *This Side of Paradise*. New York: Scribner's, 1920.

Fitzgerald, Zelda. *The Collected Writings*. Edited by Matthew J. Bruccoli. New York: Charles Scribner's Sons, 1991.

Graham, Sheilah. *Beloved Infidel*. New York: Henry Holt & Co., 1958.

_____. *The Rest of the Story*. New York: Coward-McCann, 1964.

Hemingway, Ernest. *A Moveable Feast*. New York: Scribner's, 1964.

Kazin, Alfred, editor. *F. Scott Fitzgerald: The Man and His Work*. Cleveland: World Publishing Co., 1951.

Long, Robert Emmet. "Fitzgerald and Hemingway on Stage." *Fitzgerald/ Hemingway Annual* (1969): 143-144.

Margolies, Alan. "F. Scott Fitzgerald and *The Wedding Night*." *Fitzgerald/Hemingway Annual* (1970): 224-225.

Mayfield, Sara. *Exiles From Paradise*. New York: Delacorte Press, 1971.

McGilligan, Patrick. *George Cukor: A Double Life*. New York: St. Martin's Press, 1991.

Mellow, James. *Invented Lives: F. Scott and Zelda Fitzgerald*. New York: Ballantine Books, 1986.

Meyers, Jeffrey. *Scott Fitzgerald: A Biography*. New York: HarperCollins, 1994.

Milford, Nancy. *Zelda*. New York: Harper & Row, 1970.

Mizener, Arthur. *The Far Side of Paradise*. New York: Houghton Mifflin, 1949,

Patterson, Richard North. *Escape the Night*. New York: Ballantine, 1984.

Petry, Alice Hall. "Women's Work: The Case of Zelda Fitzgerald." *Lit* 1 (1989): 69-83.

Prigozy, Ruth. "From Griffith's Girls to Daddy's Girl: The Masks of Innocence in *Tender Is the Night*." *Twentieth Century Literature* 26 (Summer 1980): 189-221.

_____. "A Matter of Measurement: The Tangled Relationship between Fitzgerald and Hemingway." *Commonweal* (29 October 1971): 103-109.

Raeburn, John. *Fame Became of Him: Hemingway as Public Writer*. Bloomington, Indiana: University of Indiana Press, 1984.

Ring, Frances Kroll. *Against the Current: As I Remember F. Scott Fitzgerald*. Berkeley: Creative Arts Book Co., 1985.

_____. Telephone interview. 7 October 1994.

Schulberg, Budd. *The Disenchanted*. New York: Random House, 1950.

_____. *The Four Seasons of Success*. Garden City, New York: Doubleday, 1972.

Shorer, Mark. *The World We Imagine*. New York: Farrar, Straus & Giroux, 1968.

Stewart, Donald Ogden. "Recollections of Fitzgerald and Hemingway." *Fitzgerald/ Hemingway Annual* (1971): 177-189.

Storey, John. *An Introductory Guide to Culture Theory and Popular Culture*. Athens, Georgia: University of Georgia Press, 1993.

Turnbull, Andrew. *Scott Fitzgerald*. New York: Charles Scribner's Sons, 1962.

Wakefield, Dan. *New York in the Fifties*. Boston/New York: Houghton Mifflin, 1992.

Williams, Tennessee. *Clothes For a Summer Hotel*. New York: New Directions, 1983.

Wilson, Edmund. *Letters On Literature and Politics*. Edited by Elena Wilson. New York: Farrar, Straus & Giroux, 1977.

Scott Fitzgerald's Romance with the South_____

Scott Donaldson

I

I suppose that poetry is a Northern man's dream of the South.[1]

Scott Fitzgerald's attitudes toward the American South were shaped by the two most important relationships in his life: with his wife, Zelda Sayre of Alabama, and with his father, Edward Fitzgerald of Maryland. Born and bred in the North, Fitzgerald nonetheless developed an early tug toward the country of his father's youth, sympathizing with the lost cause of the Confederacy and admiring the impeccable manners of the Old South. This tendency to glamorize the South, inherited from his father, Scott Fitzgerald never lost. Settling into a house in the San Fernando Valley in 1938, he at first found the place, which Sheilah Graham had located, rather drab, but when Buff Cobb came for a visit, admired the garden, and remarked that its fence pickets looked "like little gravestones in a Confederate graveyard," Fitzgerald ran inside to tell Sheilah that Buff had "made the place livable! We've got romance in the house."[2]

The case was different with the reckless young girl who caught him on the rebound at a 1918 dance in Montgomery, materializing before his eyes in her fluffy organdy beneath a wide-brimmed hat as "the very incarnation of a Southern belle."[3] Perhaps Fitzgerald fell in love with the image as much as with the girl; she brought glitteringly alive to him his own ties to the South. Together they took flower-scented walks where the wall "was damp and mossy . . . [and] the wisteria along the fence was green and the shade was cool and life was old."[4] To celebrate their engagement, they strolled past the headstones of the Confederate dead, and Zelda told him he would never understand how she felt about those graves, but he insisted that he did—and proved it in "The Ice Palace." To Fitzgerald their marriage was symbolic, "the mating of the age" between the golden beauty of the South and the brilliant success of the North.[5] But Zelda like any mere mortal was inadequate to the ideal; their marriage fractured even before her beauty faded and her mind fissured. As early as 1922, the honeymoon barely over, he wrote Edmund Wilson of "the complete, fine and full-hearted selfishness and chill-mindedness of Zelda."[6] The threat of that disillusionment, suggested by his novels, is still more precisely spun out in half a dozen stories Fitzgerald wrote, during the 1920's about the confrontation of a young man from the North with the girl he loves from the South— stories which could hardly be more autobiographical.

This theme lies persistently at center stage in "The Ice Palace" (1920), which contrasts the Southern—Sally Carrol Happer, indolence, heat, and a sense of the past peculiar to Tarleton, Georgia—with the Northern—her fiancé Harry Bellamy, vigor, cold, and the three-generation newness of St. Paul, Minnesota. During their engagement, Sally Carrol travels north to meet Harry's family and is appalled by the howling winds and fierce cold of the Northern winter, a coldness she observes too in Harry's friends who do not trouble to pay gallant compliments to her. As to Harry's family, she gets along fine with Mr. Bellamy, who had been born in Kentucky, but not with Mrs. Bellamy, who objects to Sally Carrol's smoking and, not understanding about double names in the South, persists in calling her "Sally," a name she hates.

In Tarleton, she had been content to drop syllables, fall asleep on automobile rides, stretch out on the worn couch in the library, or droop, too tired to yawn, her nineteen-year-old chin resting "on a fifty-two-year-old sill." In the North, by way of contrast, everyone is hyperactive, and the Bellamys' home, though it has "a lot of expensive things in it that all looked about fifteen years old," is not, somehow, comfortable.

In Georgia, Sally Carrol had wandered through graveyards, conjuring up romantic visions for those who lay, like "Margery Lee," beneath the sun- and rain-washed headstones. How awful, she thinks in Minnesota, to be buried beneath great piles of snow and the chilling north wind. These graveyard reflections foreshadow the climactic incident of the story, when she is temporarily interred, having lost her way among its labyrinthine passages, in the magnificent but terrifying Ice Palace, whose walls of ice are forty inches thick. Escaping this "icy breath of death" she bids adieu to Harry and their love and returns to her warm and languid Tarleton.[7]

"The Ice Palace" is Zelda's story. Fitzgerald admitted to Alexander McKaig that her ideas had been "entirely responsible" for this story, and for another of 1920, "The Jelly-Bean."[8] But it is her story in another, more significant way, for the action is filtered through the consciousness of her fictional double, Sally Carrol. The sympathies of the reader are almost entirely enlisted on Sally Carrol's side, and on the side of the South in the clash of cultures (Fitzgerald introduces a college professor who philosophizes mournfully on the strains of dullness and melancholia among Scandinavian races). Sally Carrol is frightened and lost in the frozen wastes of the North: we tremble for her. But she is also lovely and intelligent, and despite her comic lassitude retains a certain dignity: we are charmed by her.

The romantic appeal of the South was obviously mingled in Fitzgerald's mind with the golden girl. For Southern young men he has only scorn: in his fiction they are weak, indolent, and not especially bright. It is the Southern girl in whom Fitzgerald invests his romantic illusions— and it is by the Southern girl, too, that these illusions are shattered.

In two stories first printed in 1924, "Gretchen's Forty Winks" and "'The Sensible Thing,'" he sketches out the sources of this disillusionment. Gretchen, married to young advertising man Roger Halsey, "was a Southern girl, and any question that had to do with getting ahead in the world always tended to give her a headache." Totally selfish, she insists on entertaining herself with another man while her husband struggles through six weeks of day-and-night work to establish himself in the advertising business. "I'll go out with him all I want," she tells Roger when he objects. "Do you think it's any fun living here with you?" In a slick magazine ending (the story ran in the *Saturday Evening Post*), Roger succeeds and Gretchen spurns the other man, who suffers a nervous breakdown, but her "complete, fine, and full-hearted selfishness" has obviously stretched the bonds of matrimony to the breaking point.[9]

"'The Sensible Thing'"—"about Zelda and me, all true," Scott assured Maxwell Perkins—reflects Fitzgerald's abiding resentment at Zelda for stringing him along and torturing him with other beaus during their courtship. George O'Kelly, an MIT-trained construction engineer clerking in an insurance office, is desperately in love with Jonquil Cary of southern Tennessee. He leaves his job in a vain and humiliating attempt to persuade her to marry him (it's "the sensible thing" to wait until he's successful), then travels to Peru where, in just over a year, he moves from "poverty into a position of unlimited opportunity." But the Horatio Alger yarn has a bittersweet conclusion. Returning to see Jonquil, who is ready to accept him now, he realizes that the bloom is off their romance: "There are all kinds of love in the world, but never the same love twice." She has failed him. He could not idealize a woman guided by her head and not her heart, by calculation and not love.[10]

Fitzgerald's ultimate rejection of the Southern belle did not come, however, until 1929, with "The Last of the Belles." The setting is Tarleton, Georgia, during World War I, and the young lady is Ailie Calhoun, "the Southern type in all its purity. . . . She had the adroitness sugar-coated with sweet, voluble simplicity, the suggested background of devoted fathers, brothers and admirers stretching back into the South's heroic age, the unfailing coolness acquired in the endless struggle with the heat. There were notes in her voice that ordered slaves around, that withered up Yankee captains, and then soft, wheedling notes that mingled in unfamiliar loveliness with the night." She is, in short, all artifice (Fitzgerald knew what he was doing with Ailie's "adroitness sugar-coated" and her "soft, wheedling notes"), and she holds in thrall several of the young pilots who are training nearby. A heartless coquette, Ailie is as easily reconciled to the death-by-suicide of one of her rejected admirers (once she is assured that no one will know he has died for her) as she is willing to add to her string the most prized beau of a close friend. The hapless narrator Andy returns after the War to confess his love for Ailie, but she demands not merely love but worship. Dejectedly, he tours the now deserted site of the wartime camp, looking for his youth "in a clapboard or a strip of roofing or a rusty tomato can." But it is no good: his youth like the camp has been dismantled, and "in another month Ailie would be gone, and the South would be empty for [him] forever."[11]

Like Basil in "Basil and Cleopatra," another story of 1929, Andy has confused place and person, so that "Wherever she was, became a beautiful and enchanted place. . . . He thought the fascination was inherent in the locality, and long afterwards a commonplace street or the mere name of a city would exude a peculiar glow, a sustained sound, that struck his soul alert with delight."[12] But Basil decides not to pursue his beloved Minnie Bibble (Fitzgerald would not have used that name for a Southern heroine in 1920), and Andy, if he still cherishes Ailie's memory and the South he associates with it, knows both that the dream is over and that Ailie was, after all, unworthy of the dream.

The Southern belle that Scott Fitzgerald had bodied forth with the charming and vulnerable Sally Carrol in 1920 was transformed by 1929 into the vicious and cruelly aristocratic Ailie Calhoun. The girls come from the same town, they shop at the same drug store together, but there is a world of difference between them. The fictional approach mirrors the distortion of the dream: Sally Carrol tells her own story, but Andy narrates "The Last of the Belles," despite his incurable love possessing the insight to dissect the unlovely personality of Ailie Calhoun. Once Andy had come to the wartime camp as if "on a magic carpet that had landed on the Southern countryside," and had parked on dates "under the broken shadow of a mill where there was the sound of running water and restive squawky birds and over everything a brightness that tried to filter in anywhere—into the lost nigger cabins, the automobile, the fastnesses of the heart. The South sang to us—" but the carpet had whisked him back to his home in the North, the brightness had faded, and the song had turned to dissonance.[13]

The parallel is too close to be accidental. As the decade wore on, the fascination that Zelda and the South held for Scott Fitzgerald wore off, and he was faced with the inescapable fact that he was locked with his wife in a struggle for survival. In "Two Wrongs," printed in 1930, Fitzgerald suggests one way the struggle might have ended. In that story, Bill McChesney, Irish, a drunken producer down on his luck, is married to Emmy Pinkard, dancer, of Delaney, South Carolina. She succeeds as a dancer; his health cracks.[14]

In fact, of course, it was Zelda who cracked, and Fitzgerald, left in charge of their daughter Scottie's upbringing, made certain that she avoided those Southern influences which, he felt, had incapacitated Zelda. So he sent her to Miss Walker's and then to Vassar in the Northeast, though not without misgivings. Scottie must not, he warned her, let the atmosphere of wealth and social snobbery at such schools turn her head. Thus, when Scottie proposed inviting ninety guests to her coming-out party in Baltimore, her father cut the list to sixty (counting on ten or twelve refusals) and chastised her for putting on airs. "If I thought that the Ethel Walker School was going to give you a peculiar idea of what your financial resources are, it would have been far, far better to send you to a modest school here in the Carolina mountains."[15] But this was an empty threat, for Fitzgerald was unalterably opposed to sending Scottie to a Southern school. Still more frightening dangers lurked there than in the East. Though the American South was "tropical and early maturing," it had not learned the lessons of other warm climates—"it has never been part of the wisdom of France and Spain to let young girls go unchaperoned at sixteen and seventeen." When Scottie visited her aunt Cecilia Taylor in Norfolk, Fitzgerald cautioned Mrs. Taylor twice in the same letter against letting his daughter consort with any "sixteen-year-old boys who have managed to amass a charred keg and an automobile license as their Start-in-Life . . . I mean that, about any unreliable Virginia boys taking my pet around. I will never forget it was a Norfolk number . . . who gave me my first drink of whiskey."[16]

Southern boys, then, were not to be trusted; in fact an air of moral carelessness and intellectual laziness lay over the whole region. (Fitzgerald referred to several of Scottie's friends as "feebs of the Confederacy.") When it was proposed, after she had graduated from Miss Walker's, that Scottie spend the summer visiting her aunt in Virginia and her mother in Alabama, Fitzgerald sent her instead to a summer session at Harvard. "You remember," he reminded Zelda in June 1940, "your old idea that people ought to be born on the shores of the North Sea and only in later life drift south toward the Mediterranean in softness? . . . I want Scottie to be hardy and keen and able to fight her own battles and Virginia didn't seem to be the right note however charming."[17]

The strain of environmental determinism apparent in this letter to Zelda (borrowed perhaps from Oswald Spengler, whose *Decline of the West* represented the culminating point of the educational program Fitzgerald mapped for Sheilah Graham) dictated that Scottie should avoid the insidious appeal of warmer, softer climes and grow up tough and strong in a hardier region. "Scottie at her best is as she is now with a sense of responsibility and determination. She is at her absolute worst when she lies on her back and waves her feet in the air," Scott wrote Zelda in August 1939. "I am not particularly sorry for a youngster who is thrown on his own at 14 or so and has to make his way through school and college, the old sink or swim spirit—I suppose, *au fond*, the difference of attitude between the North and the old South."[18]

II

When Zelda cuttingly referred to his father as an Irish policeman, Fitzgerald retaliated by slapping Zelda hard across the face.[19]

You could call Scott Fitzgerald's father a failure, you could say that he lacked the vigor required of the successful businessman—in fact, his son said these things about Edward Fitzgerald more than once. But not even Zelda, who of course knew where to plant the barb, could with impunity reduce Scott's father to the status of an Irish cop on the beat. Despite his lack of achievement, Edward Fitzgerald remained always for his only son a figure deserving of respect for his style, his manners, and his breeding. If the stock was tired, it was also very old American stock; and Scott Fitzgerald was proud of his paternal ancestry. Forever analyzing himself and his origins, Scott tended to see his father and mother as almost polar opposites. In the Basil Duke Lee stories (how unmistakably Southern that name), Fitzgerald revisited his adolescence and recalled the sense of social inferiority *vis-à-vis* well-bred young ladies that derived from being his mother's son. Basil's background strongly resembles that of his creator: "Basil's father had been an unsuccessful young Kentuckian of good family and his mother, Alice Reilly, the daughter of a 'pioneer' wholesale grocer. As Tarkington says, American children belong to their mother's families, and Basil was 'Alice Reilly's son.' Gladys Van Schillinger, on the contrary—"[20] As the quotation suggests, Fitzgerald was rather ashamed of his mother, not only for her lack of family distinction but also because her extravagant dress and behavior made that lack constantly apparent. Scott's 1933 letter to John O'Hara clarified where his loyalty lay: "I am half black Irish and half old American stock with the usual exaggerated ancestral pretensions. The black Irish half of the family had the money and looked down upon the Maryland side of the family who had, and really had, that certain series of reticences and obligations that go under the poor old shattered word 'breeding' (modern form 'inhibitions'). So being born in that atmosphere of crack, wisecrack and counter-crack I developed a two-cylinder inferiority complex."[21] As John Kuehl has observed, given Fitzgerald's tendency to "identify autobiographical and historical events," it seems probable "that his financially inept but 'Old American stock' father came to symbolize pre-Civil War southern aristocracy while his mother's financially successful but 'black Irish' relatives came to represent post-Civil War northern *nouveaux riches*."[22]

In fact, Edward Fitzgerald qualified as the product of pre-Revolutionary, not merely pre-Civil War, breeding. Through his mother, he was related "to the Scotts, the Keys, the Dorseys, the Ridgeleys, the Tildens and the Warfields," all of whom (save for the Keys) "had been in Maryland since the first half of the sixteen hundreds."[23] But it was the connection that stretched back to Francis Scott Key which Scott Fitzgerald, like his mother, most coveted. Mrs. Fitzgerald used to advise Scott's boyhood playmates of this relationship, adding that her son "was second to none in honor of his birth," and Fitzgerald himself, inheriting her socially insecure over-aggressiveness, later claimed the famous Key as his great-grandfather or great-uncle. Actually, Scott's father's great-great-grandfather was the brother of Francis Scott Key.[24]

Fitzgerald derived more than an aristocratic bloodline from his father. In a reminiscence written shortly after his father's death in 1931, Scott observed that "always deep in my subconscious I have referred judgments back to him, what he would have thought, or done. . . . He loved me—and felt a deep responsibility for me. I was born several months after the sudden death of my two elder sisters—he felt what the effect of this would be on my mother, that he would be my only moral guide. He became that to the best of his ability." Only slightly altered, the same words are applied to Dick Diver's father in *Tender Is the Night*.[25]

The morality Edward Fitzgerald taught his son depended upon a code of honor, an awareness of the existence and rights of others (here Scott's father was working against his mother's tendency to spoil the boy), and a highly developed "sense of the fundamental decencies" which, Nick Carraway observes on the first page of *The Great Gatsby*, he had inherited from his father. But it was the way this moral standard found expression—the manners that derived from the code—that Scott Fitzgerald most admired in his father. "Southern manners are better," he wrote Scottie in June 1940, and added, "especially the rather punctilious deference to older people."[26] As the context of the letter makes clear, Fitzgerald was cautioning his daughter against any youthful inclination to condescend to her elders. It was a lesson he had well learned from his own father. "Once when I went in a room as a young man," so Edward Fitzgerald told his son, "I was confused so I went up to the oldest woman there and introduced myself and afterwards the people of that town always thought I had good manners." Recalling that incident in "The Death of My Father," Fitzgerald concluded that his father had acted "from a good heart that came from another America—he was much too sure of what he was . . . to doubt for a moment that his own instincts were good. . . ."[27]

The same incident is recorded in "The Romantic Egotist," Fitzgerald's first draft for *This Side of Paradise*, where the young protagonist reflects on the difference between himself and his father. "Father had a distinct class sense—I suppose because he was a Southerner. He used to tell me things as precepts of the 'School of Gentlemen' and I'd use them as social tricks with no sense of courtesy whatever."[28] Though he could hardly become a Southern gentleman himself, Fitzgerald felt a deep nostalgic affection for his father's native state. Maryland, he wrote in 1924, was the "loveliest of states, the white-fenced rolling land. This was the state of Charles Carroll of Carrollton, of colonial Annapolis in its flowered brocades. Even now every field seemed to be the lawn of a manor. . . . Here my great-grandfather's great grandfather was born—and my father too on a farm near Rockville called Glenmary." Maryland became for him an idyllic place, and he resisted any disturbing manifestations of reality. Thus Jason, the protagonist of "Lo, the Poor Peacock," drives the seventy miles from Baltimore to his grandfather's farm in a haze, passing "villages he had never wanted to ask the names of, so much did he cherish the image of them in his heart. . . ."[29]

For most of four years, from 1932 to 1936, the Fitzgeralds lived, in three separate locations, in and around Baltimore, while Zelda underwent care at the Phipps Clinic and Sheppard-Pratt Hospital. During this period it became finally clear that Zelda would require more or less permanent institutional care, and Scott suffered his own "Crack-Up."

Despite these woes, however, Fitzgerald felt more at home in Maryland than anywhere else on earth. "Baltimore is warm and pleasant," he wrote in September 1935. "I love it more than I thought—it is so rich with memories—it is nice to look up the street and see the statue of my great uncle and to know Poe is buried here and that many ancestors of mine have walked in the old town by the bay. I belong here, where everything is civilized and gay and rotted and polite." And the thought of being buried there, snuggled up alongside Zelda in "some old graveyard," he added, was really a happy one "and not melancholy at all." The next year, after moving to North Carolina, he wrote Baltimore friends that though he "was never a part of Baltimore" he loved the place and would have been content there, were he not such a wanderer.[30]

If Fitzgerald the wanderer had a spiritual home, it was located neither in Zelda's Alabama nor in the hills of Carolina and Virginia whence he periodically retreated to dry out or refresh himself, but in the flatlands of his father's Maryland. Contributing a foreword to a book of etchings showing *Colonial and Historic Homes of Maryland* (1939), Fitzgerald acknowledged that "there must be hundreds and hundreds of families in such an old state whose ancestral memories are richer and fuller than mine," but stated that he considered himself "a native of the Maryland Free State through ancestry and adoption," mentioned such names of family legend as "Caleb Godwin of Hockley-in-ye-Hole, or Philip Key of Tudor Hall, or Pleasance Ridgeley," and, to underscore his rights, signed himself "Francis Scott Key Fitzgerald."[31]

When he was a little boy, Edward Fitzgerald stood on the fence outside his Maryland home "watching the butternut battalions of Early stream by on their surprise attempt at Washington, the last great threat of the Confederacy." This story was one that he later told his son, along with other Civil War yarns. Much of his early childhood in Minnesota, Fitzgerald later recalled, was spent in asking his father such questions as:

"—and how long did it take Early's column to pass Glenmary that day?"
(That was a farm in Montgomery County.)

and:

"—tell me again how you used to ride through the woods with a spy up be-hind you on the horse."

or:

"Why wouldn't they let Francis Scott Key off the British frigate?"[32]

Edward Fitzgerald's sympathies, and Scott's, rested with the Confederacy; son like father was imbued with the romance of the lost Southern cause. All of American history, in fact, fascinated Edward Fitzgerald, and he so transmitted his enthusiasm that his son "remembered from his sixth year books about the Revolution and the Civil War" and had before his twelfth year begun to write his own history of the United States. This interest in the American past, together with "certain ineradicable" romantic tastes in poetry (which included Poe and Byron), Edward Fitzgerald bequeathed to his son.[33]

But it was the Civil War stories that fixed themselves most firmly in Scott's mind, so that much of his juvenile writing (and some of his late fiction as well, since an incident about a spy hung by his thumbs appears in "The End of Hate," the last serious story published in Fitzgerald's lifetime) took the Civil War as its setting. Two stories written at St. Paul Academy, when Scott was fourteen and fifteen years old, for example, spin improbable tales of Southern gallantry. One of them, "The Room with the Green Blinds," is a story of vengeance and mistaken identity. John Wilkes Booth, it turns out, has escaped punishment for assassinating President Lincoln, and survives shut up in a Georgia mansion. The governor of Georgia, whose son has been executed in Booth's stead, discovers Booth's hiding place and takes revenge by killing him. Then the governor and the young man who serves as narrator swear to carry the secret of Booth's survival and eventual demise to the grave.[34]

No less romantic, the other story, "A Debt of Honor," introduces a theme which Fitzgerald would often re-explore. Pvt. Jack Sanderson, a Virginia soldier, falls asleep on sentry duty and is pardoned from death for his dereliction by the intervention of Gen. Robert E. Lee, who reasons that the boy is "awfully young and of good family too." Given another chance, Jack redeems himself with an act of personal heroism that puts the Union troops to flight. No matter that Sanderson has died in his bravery: "He had paid his debt."[35] This 1910 story, like Fitzgerald's 1913 Civil War play, *Coward*, takes as its hero a Southern lad who first fails, then gloriously succeeds for his cause. This theme of failure and success, and the thin line between them, was to become an obsession in the mature Fitzgerald's treatment of such protagonists as Jay Gatsby and Dick Diver. It is not improbable that this theme first presented itself to the young Fitzgerald in the person of his father, a failure by the conventional standards which his son could not repudiate, yet nonetheless "a Southern gentleman" whose well-bred display of "reticences and obligations" provided for his son a model of behavior he could only hope to emulate. His father had not succeeded in business, but unlike Zelda he lived up to Scott Fitzgerald's picture of him as an aristocratic and admirable representative of the Old South. In Fitzgerald's last years, he expressed his desire to lie in a grave alongside his parents in Rockville County, Maryland. The request was denied; as a fallen-away Catholic Fitzgerald was judged unworthy of admission.[36] His bones lie nearby, in another cemetery in the same county—not exactly where and among the company he would have liked, but close enough to look on through the window of his soul.

From *The Southern Literary Journal* 5 (1973): 3-18. Copyright © 1973 by the Department of English and Comparative Literature of the University of North Carolina at Chapel Hill. Reprinted with permission of the University of North Carolina Press.

Notes

1. "The Last of the Belles," *The Stories of F. Scott Fitzgerald*, ed. Malcolm Cowley (New York: Scribner's, 1956), p. 251.

2. Sheilah Graham, *Beloved Infidel* (New York: Henry Holt, 1958), pp. 266-67.

3. Andrew Turnbull, *Scott Fitzgerald* (New York: Scribner's, 1962), pp. 86-87.

4. Turnbull, pp. 275, 101-102.

5. Nancy Milford, *Zelda* (New York: Harper & Row, 1970), p. 306.

6. F. Scott Fitzgerald to Edmund Wilson, [January, 1922], *The Letters of F. Scott Fitzgerald*, ed. Andrew Turnbull (New York: Scribner's, 1963), p. 331.

7. F. Scott Fitzgerald, "The Ice Palace," *Flappers and Philosophers* (New York: Scribner's, 1921), pp. 49-86.

8. Turnbull, p. 115.

9. F. Scott Fitzgerald, "Gretchen's Forty Winks," *All the Sad Young Men* (New York: Scribner's, 1926), pp. 239-67.

10. F. Scott Fitzgerald, "'The Sensible Thing,'" *All the Sad*, pp. 217-38; Arthur Mizener, *The Far Side of Paradise* (New York: Vintage, 1959), pp. 89, 99; F. Scott Fitzgerald to Maxwell Perkins, [circa June 1, 1925], *Letters*, p. 189.

11. F. Scott Fitzgerald, "The Last of the Belles," *Stories*, pp. 240-53.

12. F. Scott Fitzgerald, "Basil and Cleopatra," *Afternoon of an Author* (New York: Scribner's, 1958), p. 50.

13. F. Scott Fitzgerald, "The Last of the Belles," *Stories*, p. 248.

14. F. Scott Fitzgerald, "Two Wrongs," *Stories*, pp. 287-304.

15. F. Scott Fitzgerald to Frances Scott Fitzgerald, 12 December 1936, *Letters*, p. 13.

16. F. Scott Fitzgerald, "Echoes of the Jazz Age," *The Crack-Up*, ed. Edmund Wilson (New York: New Directions, 1956), p. 15; F. Scott Fitzgerald to Mrs. Richard Taylor, 11 June 1935, *Letters*, pp. 417-18.

17. F. Scott Fitzgerald to Frances Scott Fitzgerald, 15 June 1940, *Letters*, p. 80; F. Scott Fitzgerald to Zelda Fitzgerald, 7 June 1940, *Letters*, pp. 118-19.

18. F. Scott Fitzgerald to Zelda Fitzgerald, 4 August 1939, *Letters*, p. 108.

19. Milford, p. 140.

20. The names Duke and Lee have obvious Southern resonances. Turnbull suggests that Fitzgerald may have derived the name Basil Duke Lee from Basil Duke, author of the standard biography of Zelda's most famous ancestor, the Confederate guerrilla General John Hunt ("Raider") Morgan: Turnbull, pp. 338-39; F. Scott Fitzgerald, *Crack-Up*, pp. 233-34.

21. F. Scott Fitzgerald to John O'Hara, 18 July 1933, *Letters*, p. 503.

22. *The Apprentice Fiction of F. Scott Fitzgerald*, ed. John Kuehl (New Brunswick, N. J.: Rutgers University Press, 1965), p. 35.

23. Turnbull, p. 337.

24. Turnbull, pp. 12, 114, 6-7.

25. "The Death of My Father," *Apprentice Fiction*, pp. 2-3; F. Scott Fitzgerald, *Tender Is the Night* (New York: Scribner's, 1962), p. 203.

26. F. Scott Fitzgerald to Frances Scott Fitzgerald, 7 June 1940, *Letters*, p. 76.

27. "The Death of My Father," *Apprentice Fiction*, p. 3.

28. Quoted in Robert Sklar, *F. Scott Fitzgerald: The Last Laocoön* (New York: Oxford, 1967), p. 27.

29. F. Scott Fitzgerald, "The Cruise of the Rolling Junk," *Motor* (February 1924), pp. 62-63; F. Scott Fitzgerald, "Lo, the Poor Peacock," *Esquire* (September 1971), p. 156.

30. F. Scott Fitzgerald to Laura Guthrie, 23 September 1935, *Letters*, p. 531; quoted in Thelma Nason, "Afternoon (and Evening) of an Author," *Johns Hopkins Magazine* (February 1970), pp. 10-12.

31. *Colonial and Historic Homes of Maryland*, foreword, Francis Scott Key Fitzgerald (Baltimore: The Etchcrafters Art Guild, 1939).

32. *Ibid.*

33. Mizener, pp. 12, 14-15; F. Scott Fitzgerald, *Crack-Up*, p. 174.

34. "The Room with the Green Blinds," *Apprentice Fiction*, pp. 39-43.

35. "A Debt of Honor," *Apprentice Fiction*, pp. 36-38.

36. Turnbull, p. 321; Mizener, pp. 325-26.

Fitzgerald's Brave New World_____

Edwin S. Fussell

Think of the lost ecstasy of the Elizabethans. "Oh my America, my new found land," think of what it meant to them and of what it means to us.

—T. E. Hulme, *Speculations*

I

Ultimately, Fitzgerald's literary stature derives from his ability to apply the sensibilities implied by the phrase "romantic wonder" to American civilization, and to gain from the conjunction a moral critique of that civilization. As this predominant motive took shape in Fitzgerald's writing, he approached and achieved an almost archetypal pattern that can be isolated and analyzed, admired for its aesthetic complexity and interest and valued for its ethical and social insight. Certainly, this pattern does not run through all Fitzgerald's fiction; but its significance is underscored by the fact that it appears in his two finest novels and in several of the best stories. It is important to us, because it embodies above all Fitzgerald's understanding of the past and the present—perhaps the future—of his America.

Fitzgerald's story, roughly, is of the New World, or, more exactly, of the work of the imagination in the New World. It has two predominant patterns, quest and seduction. The quest is the search for romantic wonder, in the terms which contemporary America offers for such a search; the seduction represents capitulation to these terms. Obversely, the quest is a flight: from reality, from normality, from time, fate, and the conception of *limit*. In the social realm, the pattern of desire may be suggested by the phrases "the American dream" and "the pursuit of happiness." Fitzgerald begins by showing the corruption of that dream in industrial America; he ends by discovering that the dream is universally seductive and perpetually unreal. Driven by forces that compel him towards the realization of romantic wonder, the Fitzgerald hero is destroyed by the materials which the American experience offers as objects of passion; or, at best, he is purged of these unholy fires, and chastened.

In general, this quest has two symbolic goals. There is, for one, the search for eternal youth and beauty, the myth of Ponce de Leon. (It is a curious coincidence that Frederick Jackson Turner used the image of "a magic fountain of youth" to describe the unexhausted frontier.) The essence of romantic wonder appears to inhere in the illusion of perennial youth and grace created by the leisure class of which Fitzgerald usually wrote; thus the man of imagination in America is seduced by his illusion that these qualities inhere in a class that is charming, vacuous, and irresponsible. This kind of romantic quest which becomes escape is equated further, on the level of national ideology, with a transcendental and Utopian rejection of time and history and, on the religious level which Fitzgerald persistently but hesitantly approaches, with a blasphemous rejection of the very condition of human existence.

The second goal is, simply enough, money. The search for money is the familiar American commercial ideal of personal materialistic success, most succinctly embodied for our culture in the saga of Benjamin Franklin. It is the romantic assumption of this aspect of the "American dream" that all the magic of the world can be had for money. Largely from the standpoint of the middle-class radicalism of the American progressive tradition, Fitzgerald examines and condemns the plutocratic ambitions of American life and the ruinous price exacted by this dream. But the two dreams are, of course, so intimately related as to be one: the appearance of eternal youth and beauty is centered in a particular social class whose glamour is made possible by a corrupt social inequality. Beauty, the object of aesthetic contemplation, is commercialized, love is bought and sold. Money is the means to the violent recovery of an enchanting lost youth. It is no accident that the word "pander" turns up in the key passage of *The Great Gatsby*.

In contrast, Fitzgerald affirms his faith repeatedly in an older, simpler America: the emotion is that of pastoral, the social connotations agrarian and democratic. In such areas Fitzgerald continues to find fragments of basic human value, social, moral, and religious. But these affirmations are largely subordinate and indirect: Fitzgerald's attention was primarily directed to the symbolism of romantic wonder proffered by his time and place and, like the narrator of *Gatsby*, he was "within and without, simultaneously enchanted and repelled by the inexhaustible variety of life." Through a delicate and exact symbolism, he was able to extend this attitude of simultaneous enchantment and repulsion over the whole of the American civilization he knew. His keenest perception was the universal quality of the patterns he had been tracing, his greatest discovery that there was nothing new about the Lost Generation except its particular symbols. The quest for romantic wonder and the inevitable failure were only the latest in a long series. It was thus that Fitzgerald conceived the tragedy of the American experience.

Fitzgerald approached this major theme slowly and more by intuition than design. In a hazy form it is present in such early stories as "The Offshore Pirate" and "Dalyrimple Goes Wrong." It is allegorized in "The Diamond as Big as the Ritz" and fumbled in *The Beautiful and Damned*.

But it is "May Day," significantly motivated by Fitzgerald's first sharp awareness of American society, which is, for one tracing Fitzgerald's gradual realization of this major theme, the most illuminating production of his early career. Its formal construction on social principles ("Mr. In" and "Mr. Out") is obvious enough; what has not been sufficiently remarked is the way Fitzgerald's symbolic method extends his critique from the manners of drunken undergraduates to the pervasive malaise of a whole civilization. The hubris with which these characters fade from the story may be taken as an example of how dramatically the story indicts the materialistic hedonism and the vulgar idealism that Fitzgerald is diagnosing as American shortcomings:

Then they were in an elevator bound skyward.

"What floor, please?" said the elevator man.

"Any floor," said Mr. In.

"Top floor," said Mr. Out.

"This is the top floor," said the elevator man.

"Have another floor put on," said Mr. Out.

"Higher," said Mr. In.

"Heaven," said Mr. Out.

Set against the tale's controlling symbol, the universal significance of this passage frames its particular historical implications. The scene is an all-night restaurant, and the preliminary setting emphasizes social and economic inequality, the brutalization of poverty and the apparent wonder of wealth. As a Yale junior is ejected for throwing hash at the waiters, "the great plate-glass front had turned to a deep creamy blue . . . Dawn had come up in Columbus Circle, magical, breathless dawn, silhouetting the great statue of the immortal Christopher, and mingling in a curious and uncanny manner with the fading yellow electric light inside." The final significance of the symbol can only be established after one considers the conclusion of *The Great Gatsby*, but the intention is clear enough: Fitzgerald is measuring the attitudes and behavior of the Lost Generation by means of a symbol of romantic wonder that is extensive enough to comprehend all American experience. The contrast amounts to the ironic rejection of all that this generation believes in, the immaturity and irresponsibility of its quest for "experience," when such a quest is juxtaposed with one (Columbus') that suggests the fullest possibilities for romantic wonder. There is the added implication that some kind of conscious search for experience is at the heart of American cultural history, but that the quest had never taken so childish a form. This, Fitzgerald seems to be saying, is what has become of Columbus' dream—this is our brave new world.

II

With *The Great Gatsby* (1925), Fitzgerald first brought his vision of America to full and mature realization. Notwithstanding its apparent lack of scope, this is a complex and resonant novel, and one with a variety of significant implications. No single reading, perhaps, will exhaust its primary meanings, and that which follows makes no pretense of doing so. But there is, I think, a central pattern that has never been sufficiently explored—this pattern is the story of America, or of the New World, the story that Fitzgerald had been intuitively approaching since he began to write.

Gatsby is essentially the man of imagination in America, given specificity and solidity and precision by the materials which American society offered him. "If personality is a series of successful gestures, then there was something gorgeous about him, some heightened sensitivity to the promises of life, as if he were related to one of those intricate machines that register earthquakes ten thousand miles away." It is Gatsby's capacity for *romantic wonder* that Fitzgerald is insisting upon in this preliminary exposition, a capacity that he goes on to define as "an extraordinary gift for hope, a romantic readiness." And with the simile of the seismograph, an apt enough symbol for the human sensibility in a mechanized age, Fitzgerald has in effect already introduced the vast backdrop of American civilization against which Gatsby's gestures must be interpreted. The image is as integral as intricate; for if Gatsby is to be taken as the product and the manifestation of those motivations caught up in the phrase "the American dream," he is also the instrument by means of which Fitzgerald is to register the tremors that point to its self-contained principles of destruction. "What preyed on Gatsby, what foul dust floated in the wake of his dreams" is ostensibly the stuff of the novel, the social content of Fitzgerald's universe of fiction. But it is essential to realize that Gatsby, too, has been distorted from the normative by values and attitudes that he holds in common with the society that destroys him. Certainly, in such a world, the novel assures us, a dream like Gatsby's cannot remain pristine, given the materials upon which the original impulse toward wonder must expend itself. Gatsby, in other words, is more than pathetic, a sad figure preyed upon by the American leisure class. The unreal values of the world of Tom and Daisy Buchanan are his values too, they are inherent in his dream. Gatsby had always lived in an imaginary world, where "a universe of ineffable gaudiness spun itself out in his brain"; negatively, this quality manifests itself in a dangerous tendency toward sentimental idealization: his reveries "were a satisfactory hint of the unreality of reality, a promise that the rock of the world was founded securely on a fairy's wing."

Daisy finally becomes for Gatsby the iconic manifestation of this vision of beauty. Little enough might have been possible for Gatsby anyway, but once he "wed his unutterable visions to her perishable breath, his mind would never romp again like the mind of God." One notes how steadily if surreptitiously, through his metaphors and similes mainly, Fitzgerald is introducing the notion of blasphemy in conjunction with Gatsby's Titanic imaginative lusts. But the novel makes only tentative gestures in the direction of religious evaluation; Fitzgerald's talent indicated that Gatsby's visions be focussed rather sexually and socially. After this concentration of Gatsby's wonder on Daisy has been established, Fitzgerald can go on to an explicit statement of her significance to the thematic direction of the novel: Gatsby, we are told, was "overwhelmingly aware of the *youth* and mystery that *wealth* imprisons and *preserves*, of the freshness of many clothes, and of Daisy, gleaming like silver, safe and proud above the hot struggle of the poor" (my italics). Her voice is frequently mentioned as mysteriously enchanting—it is the typifying feature of her role as *la belle dame sans merci*—and throughout the action it serves to suggest her loveliness and desirability. But only Gatsby, in a rare moment of vision, is able to make explicit the reasons for its subtle and elusive magic: "It was full of money—that was the inexhaustible charm that rose and fell in it, the jingle of it, the cymbals' song of it. . . . High in a white palace the king's daughter, the golden girl. . . ."

Possession of an image like Daisy is all that Gatsby can finally conceive as "success"; and Gatsby is meant to be a very representative American in the intensity of his yearning for success, as well as in the symbols which he equates with it. Gatsby performs contemporary variations on an old American pattern, the rags-to-riches story exalted by American legend as early as Crèvecœur's *Letters from an American Farmer.* But the saga is primarily that of a legendary Benjamin Franklin, whose celebrated youthful resolutions are parodied in those that the adolescent Gatsby wrote on the back flyleaf of his copy of *Hopalong Cassidy.* As an indictment of American philistinism, Fitzgerald's burlesque is spare and sharp; what accounts for its impression of depth is Fitzgerald's fictionally realized perception that Gatsby's was not a unique, but a pervasive American social pattern. Grounding his parody in Franklin's *Autobiography* gave Fitzgerald's critique a historical density and a breadth of implication that one associates only with major fiction.

The connection between Gatsby's individual tragedy and the tragedy of his whole civilization is also made (and again, through symbol) with respect to historical attitudes. Gatsby's relation to history is summed up in his devotion to the green light that burns on Daisy's dock. When Nick first sees Gatsby, he is in an attitude of supplication, a gesture that pathetically travesties the gestures of worship; Nick finally observes that the object of his trembling piety is this green light which, until his disillusion, is one of Gatsby's "enchanted objects." In the novel's concluding passage, toward which all action and symbol is relentlessly tending, one is given finally the full implications of the green light as symbol ("Gatsby believed in the green light, the orgiastic future").

Gatsby, with no historical sense whatsoever, is the fictional counterpart of that American philistine maxim that "history is bunk"; and he may recall, too, for those interested in such comparisons, the more crowing moods of Emerson and Thoreau, and the "timelessness" of their visions and exhortations. But for Fitzgerald, this contemptuous repudiation of tradition, historical necessity, and moral determinism, however un-self-conscious, was deluded and hubristic. When he finally came to see, as he did in *Gatsby*, that in this irresponsibility lay the real meaning behind the American obsession with youth, he was able to know Gatsby as a miserable, twentieth century Ponce de Leon. And his fictional world was no longer simply the Jazz Age, the Lost Generation, but the whole of American civilization as it culminated in his own time.

In the final symbol of the book, Fitzgerald pushes the personal equation to national, even universal, scope, and in a way that recalls the method of "May Day." The passage has been prepared for in multiple ways; indeed, nearly all the material I have been citing leads directly into it. Even the "new world" theme has been anticipated. Fitzgerald is commenting on Gatsby's state of disillusion just before his death:

> he must have felt that he had lost the old warm world, paid a high price for living too long with a single dream. He must have looked up at an unfamiliar sky through frightening leaves and shivered as he found what a grotesque thing a rose is and how raw the sunlight was upon the scarcely created grass. A new world, material without being real, where poor ghosts, breathing dreams like air, drifted fortuitously about. . . .

Such, then, was the romantic perception of wonder, when finally stripped of its falsifying illusions. Gatsby finds himself in a "new world" (Fitzgerald's symbol for the American's dream of irresponsibility takes on ironically terrifying overtones here) in which his values and dreams are finally exposed. And so Fitzgerald moves on to his final critique:

> And as the moon rose higher the inessential houses began to melt away until gradually I became aware of the old island here that flowered once for Dutch sailors' eyes—a fresh green breast of the new world. Its vanished trees, the trees that had made way for Gatsby's house, had once pandered in

whispers to the last and greatest of all human dreams; for a transitory enchanted moment man must have held his breath in the presence of this continent, compelled into an aesthetic contemplation he neither understood nor desired, face to face for the last time in history with something commensurate to his capacity for wonder.

The most important point to be made about this passage is its insistence that Gatsby's abnormal capacity for wonder could have, in the modern world, no proper objective. The emotion lingered on, generations of Americans had translated it into one or another set of inadequate terms, but Gatsby, like all his ancestors, was doomed by demanding the impossible. There is, too, the ironic contrast between the wonder of the New World, and what Americans have made of it (the same point that Fitzgerald made in similar fashion with the Columbus image in "May Day"). But there is a final, more universal meaning, implicit in the language of the passage—the hope that the new world could possibly satisfy man's lusts was, after all, "the last and greatest of all human dreams," unreal. The most impressive associations cluster around the word "pander"—a word that implies, above all, the illicit commercialization of love, youth, and beauty—which effectually subsumes most of the central meanings of the novel. Because of the verbal similarity, it is valuable to compare this phrase "pandered in whispers" with Fitzgerald's remarks (in "My Lost City" [1932], an essay collected in 1945 in *The Crack-Up*) about New York City, a good instance of how the myths of Benjamin Franklin and Ponce de Leon could be blended in his mind—"it no longer whispers of fantastic success and eternal youth." The two parallel themes do, of course, come together in the novel; in fact, they are tangled at the heart of the plot, for the greatest irony in Gatsby's tragedy is his belief that he can buy his dream, which is, precisely, to recapture the past.

III

Tender Is the Night (1934) at once restates the essential theme and complicates it. Because of the greater proliferation of symbolic statement here, it is less easy to define the novel's main designs, and yet they are remarkably parallel to those already traced out for *The Great Gatsby*. This becomes apparent if one examines carefully the implications of the leading characters and the meaning of their narrative; attention to the metaphoric and symbolic overtones of the novel further corroborates the impression that, beneath this greater wealth of detail, Fitzgerald is still telling the same story.

Dick Diver is, like Gatsby, the American as man of imagination. His chief difference from Gatsby is that he dispenses romantic wonder to others, in addition to living for it himself; Gatsby tries to purvey dreams, but doesn't know how. But to Rosemary Hoyt, Dick's "voice promised that he would take care of her, and that a little later he would open up whole *new worlds* for her, unroll an endless succession of magnificent possibilities" (my italics). Dick is the man with the innate capacity for romantic wonder, but now a member of the American leisure class of the 'twenties, now declined to an "organizer of private gaiety, curator of a richly incrusted happiness." His intellectual and imaginative energies have been diverted from the normal creative channels they might have taken and are expended on the effort to prevent, for a handful of the very rich, the American dream from revealing its nightmarish realities.

Although Dick is given a more positive background than Gatsby, he is equally a product of his civilization and he has its characteristic deficiencies: "The illusions of eternal strength and health, and of the essential goodness of people; illusions of a nation, the lies of generations of frontier mothers who had to croon falsely that there were no wolves at the cabin door." And this inherent romantic has been further weakened by the particular forms of sentimentality of his own generation: "he must press on toward the Isles of Greece, the cloudy waters of unfamiliar ports, the lost girl on shore, the moon of the popular songs. A part of

Dick's mind was made up of the tawdry souvenirs of his boyhood. Yet in that somewhat littered Five-and-Ten, he had managed to keep alive the low painful fire of intelligence."

Such is the man, essentially noble like Gatsby, but with the fatal flaw of imagination common to and conditioned by the superficial symbols and motivations of his civilization, who is brought against the conditions of temptation represented by Nicole. She is the granddaughter of a "self-made American capitalist" and of a German Count, and her family is placed in perspective by Fitzgerald's frequent analogies with a feudal aristocracy. "Her father would have it on almost any clergyman," such as Dick's father; "they were an American ducal family without a title—the very name . . . caused a psychological metamorphosis in people." Yet behind this facade of glamour and power lies unnatural lust and perversion. Nicole's father, this "fine American type," has committed incest with his daughter—the very incarnation of the American vision of youth, beauty, and wealth—and made her into a psychotic whom young Dr. Diver must cure. As Nicole says, "I'm a crook by heritage."

Through Nicole, Fitzgerald conveys, as he had with Daisy, all that is sexually and socially desirable in youth and beauty: "there were all the potentialities for romantic love in that lovely body and in the delicate mouth. . . . Nicole had been a beauty as a young girl and she would be a beauty later." Apparently she is eternally youthful, and only at the end of the novel is it discernible that she has aged. Her face, which corresponds in symbolic utility to Daisy's voice, is lovely and hard, "her eyes brave and watchful, looking straight ahead at nothing." She is an empty child, representative of her social class, of the manners and morals of the 'twenties, and of the world of values for which America, like Dick, was once more selling its soul. But it is, more than anything else, Nicole's semblance of perpetual youth that allows Fitzgerald to exploit her as a central element in the narrative correlative he is constructing for his vision of American life. Occasionally, there is a treatment of Nicole that goes beyond social criticism, entering, if obliquely and implicitly, the area of religious vision:

The only physical disparity between Nicole at present and the Nicole of five years before was simply that she was no longer a young girl. But she was enough ridden by the current youth worship, the moving pictures with their myriad faces of girl-children, blandly represented as carrying on the work and wisdom of the world, to feel a jealousy of youth.

She put on the first ankle-length day dress that she had owned for many years, and crossed herself reverently with Chanel Sixteen.

But while Fitzgerald could upon occasion so extend the significance of his narrative, he never neglected to keep it firmly grounded in a specific social and economic world, and it is in this realm that most of his correspondences are established:

Nicole was the product of much ingenuity and toil. For her sake trains began their run at Chicago and traversed the round belly of the continent to California; chicle factories fumed and link belts grew link by link in factories; men mixed toothpaste in vats and drew mouthwash out of copper hogsheads; girls canned tomatoes quickly in August or worked rudely at the Five-and-Tens on Christmas Eve; half-breed Indians toiled on Brazilian coffee plantations and dreamers were muscled out of patent rights in new tractors—these were some of the people who gave a tithe to Nicole, and as the whole system swayed and thundered onward it lent a feverish bloom to such processes of hers as wholesale buying, like the flush of a fireman's face holding his post before a spreading blaze. She illustrated very simple principles, containing in herself her own doom, but illustrated them so accurately that there was grace in the procedure.

The social structure of *Tender Is the Night* is epic in scope and intention, though it has the grace and concentration of lyric; at its base are criminal injustice and inhuman waste—at its apex is Nicole, "the king's daughter"—beautiful, forever young, and insane.

In the central scenes of temptation (Book II, chapter v), Fitzgerald quite deliberately allows Nicole to expand into her full symbolic significance, thus revealing that the larger thematic pattern of *Tender Is the Night* must be read against the largest context of American life. Throughout the chapter runs the *leitmotif* of Fitzgerald's generalizing commentary, beginning with the passage: "the impression of her youth and beauty grew on Dick until it welled up inside him in a compact paroxysm of emotion. She smiled, a moving childish smile that was like all the lost youth in the world." This mood of pathetic nostalgia is quickly objectified in the talk of Dick and Nicole about American popular songs; soon Dick feels that "there was that excitement about her that seemed to reflect all the excitement of the world." So ends the first of the two scenes that form this chapter. The second meeting of the two opens on a similar key: "Dick wished she had no background, that she was just a girl lost with no address save the night from which she had come." This time they play the songs they had mentioned the week before, "they were in America now." And Fitzgerald drives home the point in his last sentence: "Now there was this scarcely saved waif of disaster bringing him the essence of a continent. . . ."

At first Dick laughs off the notion that Nicole's family has bought him, but he gradually succumbs, "inundated by a trickling of goods and money." And Nicole is, once more, the typifying object of her class and society in the particular terms she imposes for the destruction of his moral and intellectual integrity: "Naturally Nicole, *wanting to own him, wanting him to stand still forever*, encouraged any slackness on his part" (my italics). And so, although the pattern is more complex than in *Gatsby*, practically the same controlling lines of theme can be observed. The man of imagination, fed on the emotions of romantic wonder, is tempted and seduced and (in this case, nearly) destroyed by the American dream which customarily takes two forms: the escape from time and the materialistic pursuit of a purely hedonistic happiness. On the historical level, the critique is of the error of American romanticism in attempting to transcend and escape historical responsibility. On the economic level, the critique is of the fatal beauty of American capitalism, its destructive charm and irresponsibility. And on the level of myth, one need mention only the names of Benjamin Franklin and Ponce de Leon to recall the motivations of the quest that Fitzgerald recurrently explores. Thematically, the lines come together when Nicole attempts to own Dick and therefore escape Time, as when Gatsby tries to buy back the past.

It is Fitzgerald's skill in elaborating a more complicated symbolization of unreality that makes *Tender Is the Night* more impressive than *The Great Gatsby*. In Rosemary Hoyt, who brings from Hollywood to Europe the latest American version of the dream of youth and innocence, Fitzgerald has another important symbol and center of consciousness. It is through her perception, for instance, that Fitzgerald gives us his first elaborate glimpses of the Divers and of the American leisure class. Because of Rosemary's acute but undisciplined perceptions, Fitzgerald can insist perpetually on the ironic tensions between the richest texture of social appearance and the hidden reality of social evil; her "naivete responded wholeheartedly to the expensive simplicity of the Divers, unaware of its complexity and its lack of innocence, unaware that it was all a selection of quality rather than quantity from the run of the world's bazaar; and that the simplicity of behavior, also, the nursery-like peace and good will, the emphasis on the simpler virtues, was part of a desperate bargain with the gods and had been attained through struggles she could not have guessed at."

Rosemary manifests the effects of Hollywood sentimentality and meretriciousness on the powers of American perception and imagination. The image-patterns that surround her movement are largely concerned with childhood; she is "as dewy with belief as a child from one of Mrs. Burnett's vicious tracts." Immature and egocentric, she provides one more symbol of the corruption of imagination by American civilization; both deluded and deluding, she has no opportunity for escape, as there is for Nick Carraway and Dick Diver. It is Diver who sounds the last important note about her: "'Rosemary didn't grow up.'" That she is intended symbolically, Fitzgerald makes clear in his account of her picture "Daddy's Girl": "There she was—*so* young and innocent—the product of her mother's loving care; embodying all the immaturity of the race, cutting a new cardboard paper doll to pass before its empty harlot's mind."

Nicole and Rosemary, then, are for this novel the objectified images of Fitzgerald's "brave new world." Only occasionally does Dick Diver escape the limits of this terrifying world. Once, the three of them are sitting in a restaurant, and Dick observes a group of "gold star mothers": "in their happy faces, the dignity that surrounded and pervaded the party he perceived all the maturity of an Older America. For a while the sobered women who had come to mourn for their dead, for something they could not repair, made the room beautiful. Momentarily, he sat again on his father's knee, riding with Moseby while the old loyalties and devotions fought on around him. Almost with an effort he turned back to his two women at the table and faced the whole new world in which he believed." In the gradual failure of this illusion comes Dick Diver's salvation; as the dream fades, he is enabled to recover a fragment of reality.

IV

For purposes of corroboration, one can add a certain amount of documentation from Fitzgerald's non-fictional writings, as collected in the posthumous *Crack-Up*. And the point that most needs buttressing, probably, is that Fitzgerald saw in the quest for romantic wonder a recurrent pattern of American behavior. This attitude seems strongly implied by the stories themselves, but it is additionally reassuring to find Fitzgerald writing, in a letter to his daughter: "You speak of how good your generation is, but I think they share with every generation since the Civil War in America the sense of being somehow about to inherit the earth. You've heard me say before that I think the faces of most American women over thirty are relief maps of petulant and bewildered unhappiness" (p. 306). A brief sketch of a "typical product of our generation" in the *Note-Books* indicates further what qualities were involved in this "sense of being about to inherit the earth": "her dominant idea and *goal* is *freedom without responsibility*, which is like *gold* without metal, spring without winter, *youth without age*, one of those maddening, coocoo *mirages of wild riches*" (p. 166—my italics). And that this personal attitude, translated into the broader terms of a whole culture, represented a negation of historical responsibility is made sufficiently clear in another *Note-Book* passage: "Americans, he liked to say, needed fins and wings. There was even a *recurrent idea* in should be born with fins, and perhaps they were—perhaps money was a form of fin. In England, property begot a strong place sense, but Americans, restless and with shallow roots, America about an education that would leave out history and the past, that should be a sort of equipment for aerial adventure, weighed down by none of the stowaways of inheritance or tradition" (p. 109—my italics). Still another passage, this time from one of the "Crack-Up" essays, makes it equally clear that Fitzgerald habitually saw the universal applicability of all he was saying about the ruling passion in America: "This is what I think now: that the natural state of the sentient adult is a qualified unhappiness. I think also that in an adult the desire to be finer in grain than you are, 'a constant striving' (as those people say who gain their bread by saying it) only adds to this unhappiness in the end—that end that comes to our youth and hope" (p. 80).

And yet, for all the failure and futility that Fitzgerald found in the American experience, his attitude remained one of acceptance, and not one of despair. There was no cynicism in his "wise and tragic sense of life." The exhaustion of the frontier and the post-war expatriate movement marked for him the end of a long period in human history and it was this period, the history of the post-Renaissance European man in America, that he made his subject. After he had explored his materials to their limits Fitzgerald knew, at his greatest moments, that he had discovered in an archetypal pattern of desire and belief and behavior compounded the imaginative history of modern civilization. One final passage from the *Note-Books* may substantiate our impression that

Fitzgerald could, on occasion, conceive his subject in all the range and heroism of the epic mode:

> He felt then that if the pilgrimage eastward of the rare poisonous flower of his race was the end of the adventure which had started westward three hundred years ago, if the long serpent of the curiosity had turned too sharp upon itself, cramping its bowels, bursting its shining skin, at least there had been a journey; like to the satisfaction of a man coming to die—one of those human things that one can never understand unless one has made such a journey and heard the man give thanks with the husbanded breath. The frontiers were gone—there were no more barbarians. The short gallop of the last great race, the polyglot, the hated and the despised, the crass and scorned, had gone—at least it was not a meaningless extinction up an alley.

American Riviera:
Style and Expatriation in *Tender Is the Night*_____

Michael K. Glenday

Among its many enlightenments, Andrew Turnbull's biography *Scott Fitzgerald* establishes a truth essential to understanding the life of its subject: 'With Europe and the Murphys, Fitzgerald came as close as he ever would to finding perfection in the real world, and in a way the rest of his life was a retreat from this summit' (176). By the sands of Antibes in the home they built and named Villa America, the Murphys created a salon—the centre, as Dirk Bogarde was to describe it, 'of a gorgeous, glittering carousel [. . .] Looking back at them today sprawled in the sun, laughing and dancing, is a little like turning the pages of old bound copies of *Vanity Fair* and *Tatler.* Scintillating, beautiful, remote and far out of reach' (8). For Archibald MacLeish, too, 'there was a shine to life wherever they were [. . .] a kind of inherent loveliness' (Vaill 7), and wherever in *Tender Is the Night* Fitzgerald provides a vision of graceful expatriation, there the Murphys are, shining still as the very spirit of expatriate style. They were the creators of those 'many fêtes' that the novel's winsome dedication seems to gift and bless them with, as though in a deed of reciprocal generosity. In a letter to Gerald Murphy, Fitzgerald acknowledged both extensive debts and a profound *entente*: 'the book was inspired by Sara and you, and the way I feel about you both and the way you live, and the last part of it is Zelda and me because you and Sara are the same people as Zelda and me' (Tomkins 5).[1] The way the Murphys lived would indeed become the luminous blueprint for an American arcadia in *Tender*, and though Fitzgerald would often create permutations on the theme of paradise lost in his life and writing, only here in his final completed novel does he succeed in tracing fully the tragic arc of sublimity declining to ruin.

'Please do not use the phrase "Riviera" [. . .] not only does it sound like the triviality of which I am so often accused, but also [. . .] its very mention involves a feeling of unreality and unsubstantiality' (*Life in Letters* 247). So wrote Fitzgerald to his editor Max Perkins in 1934, setting out his ideas for the dust-wrapper text of *Tender Is the Night*, and fearing that in the debt-haunted America of the 1930s an emphasis upon Riviera glamour would potentially damage the novel's sales. Yet his recognition that together with its reputation for triviality, the Riviera would generate a further set of images concerning 'unreality' is of more interest in retrospect. In a letter to Fitzgerald written soon after the novel's publication, Gerald Murphy would also invoke unreality, though as a key feature of the book's meaning and truth. If Andrew Turnbull saw that Fitzgerald had discovered 'perfection in the real world' of Europe and the Murphys, Murphy himself realized that *Tender Is the Night* folded this perfect reality into the artifice of an even more transcendent design:

> I know now that what you said in *Tender Is the Night* is true. Only the invented part of our life—*the unreal part*—has had any scheme, any beauty. Life itself has stepped in now and blundered, scarred and destroyed. (Tomkins 124-25, my emphasis)[2]

Looking back through the atmosphere of Fitzgerald's novel, Murphy was able to see that expatriation had partly provided him with the climate in which creativity could flower, if not with the prerequisite condition for entry into the beautiful land of unreality/artifice. In another related phrase invoking the potential of the human imagination, Murphy also told Fitzgerald, 'it's not what we do, but what we do with our minds that counts' (Tomkins 123), thus giving modern inflection to that dangerous liaison which for Henry James had so characterized the European scene for American visitors. In James' fiction, the European environment is often experienced as a beguiling playground in which Americans are transformed into lotus-eaters. So Roderick Hudson declares himself to be 'an idle useless creature, [who] should probably be even more so in Europe than at home' (22). Activity for James' expatriates is often sublimated by their attraction to European passivity. As Hudson muses, 'it is evidently only a sort of idealised form of loafing: a passive life in Rome, thanks to the number and quality of one's impressions, takes on a very respectable likeness to activity' (23). Although Fitzgerald's novel too is concerned with expatriation as *flânerie*, it also counters this with a revised model of the expatriate *engagé*, the 'man with repose' (the phrase is Diver's own, coined in the opening paragraph of Book 1, chapter xii), one who could, like Murphy himself, exemplify a model of calm and creative being, of 'what we do with our minds', self-consciously trying for new means of survival amidst the ruins of an inter-war Europe.

It was Edmund Wilson who first persuaded the young Fitzgerald to continue his cultural education in France, urging him to 'come to Paris for the summer. Settle down and learn French and apply a little French leisure and measure to that restless and jumpy nervous system. It would be a service to American letters: your novels would never be the same afterwards' (Wilson 63). Wilson was right about that, for having enrolled in Gerald and Sara Murphy's school of style in the summer of 1924, Fitzgerald found there, along with 'many fêtes', the influence of a refined *ménage* which seemed to him an ideal expression of human life. But in the aftermath of the Great War, such a context could also embody style as heroism. As Fitzgerald himself remarked, Dick Diver 'is after all a sort of superman [. . .] an approximation of the hero'; he recognises that 'taste is no substitute for vitality but in [*Tender Is the Night*] it has to do duty for it. It is one of the points on which he must never show weakness as Siegfried could never show physical fear' (Turnbull, *Letters* 587). For Fitzgerald, as for his American contemporary Ernest Hemingway, style, taste, deportment, became an index of existential integrity. 'Grace under pressure' was Hemingway's definition of courageous poise,[3] and grace and style were two sides of the same coin, a currency that becomes the gold standard by which Diver judges himself and others. The novel lays stress upon his exceptionalism in this regard, as his tranquil enclave is progressively attacked by the invasion of 'life itself', stepping in to blunder, scar and destroy. In many ways this novel is about betrayal, Dick Diver's 'betrayal at the hands of a world he thought he could manipulate' (Vaill 229), a betrayal so closely based upon Gerald Murphy's own. Murphy remembered telling Fitzgerald:

> For me only the invented part of life is satisfying, only the unrealistic part. Things happened to you—sickness, birth, Zelda in Lausanne, Patrick in the sanatorium, Father Wiborg's death—these things were realistic, and you couldn't do anything about them. 'Do you mean you don't accept these things?' Scott asked. I replied that of course [I] accepted them, but I didn't feel they were the important things really [. . .] The *invented* part, for me, is what has meaning. (Vaill 226)[4]

Reality in this sense is something that one is the victim of, arriving upon one's head in random blows of unreasonable fate. It is certainly no coincidence that the sign outside Villa America, the Murphys' home in Antibes (which would become the Divers' 'Villa Diana' in the novel), was designed by Murphy himself to show a dramatically split graphic, with the broken star and stripes in sharp contrast to each other. As described by Amanda Vaill, 'The effect is striking visually, but also metaphorically: somehow the villa, like its owners, exists in two worlds at once—France and America, the real and the imagined' (160).

And in *Tender Is the Night* it was that 'unreal' world, that imagined great good place, which had its fleeting correlative in the beach apartheid close by Gausse's Hôtel des Étrangers. There, for those within Dick Diver's orbit of invention, the unimportant matter of 'reality' gives way to something else, 'something [that] made them unlike the Americans [Rosemary] had known of late' (6). This 'something' is rooted in Diver's ability to create a new, playful sense of being for his group of fellow expatriates. His first appearance is indeed that of a master of comic invention, 'a fine man in a jockey cap and red-striped tights', entertaining his guests, who are captivated by his vitality. Rosemary understands that 'under small hand-parasols' (5) this group of Americans are being subtly altered by Diver's 'quiet little performance' (6), becoming, in fact, something atypical in the process as he 'moved gravely about with a rake, ostensibly removing gravel and meanwhile developing some esoteric burlesque held in suspension by his grave face' (6). The narrator's identification of the particular type of comedy is important: burlesque is a generic term for parody, caricature and travesty and is particularly effective when customs, manners, institutions—individually or as types—are ripe for debunking. Targeting the ridiculous by incongruous imitation, burlesque presents the trivial with ironic seriousness. Audience pleasure comes largely from recognizing the subject of the ridicule, and in this scene Dick Diver provides a textbook burlesque directed at a subject identified in Mrs Abrams' comment to Rosemary a few lines later, 'there seems to be so darn much formality on this beach' (7). The phrase reiterates the narrator's own earlier scene-setting comments upon expatriate beach-life on the summer Riviera, where in tedious occupancy 'British nannies sat knitting the slow pattern of Victorian England [. . .] to the tune of gossip as formalized as incantation' (4). A stultifying formality therefore reigns supreme here, as 'a dozen persons kept house under striped umbrellas, while their dozen children pursued unintimidated fish through the shallows' (4). This is the dominant reality in place at Antibes, 'the atmosphere of a community upon which it would be presumptuous to intrude' (5).

While there is certainly a strong element of *épater le bourgeois* in Diver's stylized performance, this first glimpse reveals even more about the style of his relationship to those in his circle—the effort to control the discourse, the ability to define for them an alternative, more charged correspondence between inner life and outer reality. The language gives it away—his group being 'held in suspension by his grave face', an early instance of that magical dialectic so manifest at the Divers' dinner parties at Villa Diana, where leisure and conviviality transcend themselves to approach an ultimate civility of human relationship and therefore to inhabit 'the rarer atmosphere of sentiment':

There were fireflies riding on the dark air and a dog baying on some low and far-away edge of the cliff. The table seemed to have risen a little toward the sky like a mechanical dancing platform, giving the people around it the sense of being alone with each other in the dark universe, nourished by its only food, warmed by its only lights. And, as if a curious hushed laugh from Mrs. McKisco were a signal that such a detachment from the world had been attained, the two Divers began suddenly to warm and glow and expand, as if to make up to their guests [. . .] for anything they might still miss from that country well left behind. (34)

Here, the imagery of transcendence is considerably more advanced: the table becomes a stage, the guests transported as though to a *chambre séparé* where an occult, hierarchical bonding can take place. The cameo scene at the beach had introduced the idea of Diver as gifted entertainer, a man capable of holding his audience in suspension—an image repeated here in the wonderfully exact conceit of the table as a floating 'mechanical dancing platform'—and in the scene above he appears more completely as a magus bestowing an almost mystical union, stemming from his apparent *expansion* of presence. The scene is justifiably renowned. It is perhaps the most elaborate instance of Fitzgerald's notion of Diver as 'after all a sort of superman', endowed with special powers that allow him to 'warm and glow and expand' in a spirit of ultimate conviviality. In terms of this essay the scene also personifies Murphy's idea of life as invention, of the transformative fruits of 'what we do with our minds' as well as exemplifying a new vision of an enlightened leisure class. That idea finds its way without amendment into Fitzgerald's imagination of the Divers, as Abe North tells Rosemary that Dick and Nicole 'have to like [the beach]. They invented it' (17).

In a letter of 1934 to Max Perkins, Marjorie Kinnan Rawlings wrote of *Tender* as 'a book disturbing, bitter and beautiful. [. . .] Fitzgerald visualizes people not in their immediate setting, from the human point of view—but in time and space—almost, you might say, with the divine detachment' (Tarr 140). The novel's vision of serenity is of course intensified by the bitter cargo that lies in wait for Dick Diver and others in his circle, but in a scene such as the above, Rawlings is absolutely right—the angels do hold sway. Fitzgerald admired Matthew Arnold and agreed with his warnings about the gathering threats to civilized values posed by the modern world. In *College of One* Sheilah Graham remembers how he stressed the need to defend against this, recalling his approval of Arnold's line: 'the question, how to live, is itself a moral idea' (99). The above scene responds to this question (which is also a question about the virtues of style) in its celebration of life shared with intensity of purpose, a mystical, almost Yeatsian vision of unity. In referring to the novel's 'divine detachment' was Rawlings alluding specifically to just 'such a detachment from the world' as described in the above passage? As Yeats' charting of spiritual transcendence in 'Sailing to Byzantium' is based upon a necessary renunciation of the physical world, since 'That is no country for old men' (217), so the Divers also dispel any regrets for what the narrator calls 'that country well left behind' (34).

The Divers' dinner party presents a paradigm of carefully cultivated licence, of the freedoms deriving in part from what Henry James called 'dispatriation'.[5] Perhaps such a scene comes as close to a vision of benign exile as it is possible to get. R P. Blackmur, however, pointed to one important paradox at the heart of American expatriates' generic experience, noting that they 'sought to be exiled, to be strangers in a far land, and sweetly to do nothing; that is to say, they wanted to be men of the world divorced from the world' (69). So one version of expatriation is manifest in a rare kind of worldly transcendence, mediated through invention/artifice, but Fitzgerald's expatriates also take their place as 'men of the world' in Blackmur's terms. As Malcolm Bradbury has written, Dick and Nicole Diver 'belong willingly enough to history, which, as Fitzgerald aptly says, manifests itself day-to-day, as style. [. . .] Thus they live, like the Fitzgeralds themselves, by history's daily workings, through styles and images, this week's haunting jazz songs and the summer's new resorts' (355). The Divers certainly show themselves to be alive to the appeal of the avant-garde. They are 'too acute to abandon its contemporaneous rhythm and beat' (76), but even here Dick is untrammelled, inventive (this characteristic Fitzgerald also derived from Gerald Murphy, who is described most wonderfully by André Le Vot as 'the corsair of La Garoupe [. . .] a fount of fashions [. . .] there was something in him of the impresario' [207]) and influential. In a Europe that was becoming increasingly stylocentric, they set the fashions that others followed: 'the sailor trunks and sweaters they had bought in a Nice back street' were 'garments that afterward ran through a vogue in sills among the Paris couturiers' (281). Be it a small patch of sand on a Riviera beach or a dinner party, the Divers' style is appreciated by the *gens de monde*. In a description that recalls Jay Gatsby's lustrous automobile, 'bright with nickel [. . .] and terraced with a labyrinth of wind-shields that mirrored a dozen suns' (*The Great Gatsby* 51), Fitzgerald even has Dick commandeer 'the car of the Shah of Persia' so that his party guests can see Paris on a joyride: 'Its wheels were all silver, so was the radiator. The inside of the body was inlaid with innumerable brilliants' (77).

In a 1927 interview Fitzgerald indicated his appreciation of Gallic civilization in matters of taste and breeding, remarking that 'France has the only two things toward which we drift as we grow older— intelligence and good manners' (Le Vot 223). Intelligence, good manners, and what Henry Dan Piper would call 'the tragic power of charm' (211)[6] are all in view when Rosemary first meets Dick Diver. In his voice she finds immediately that promise of romantic, almost effortless invention: 'he would open up whole new worlds for her' (16). She intuits quickly that Diver, Barban and North are different from the men of her previous acquaintance, 'the rough and ready good fellowship of directors [. . .] and the indistinguishable mass of college boys' (19). In contrast these people manifest a new kind of self-possession. Rosemary sees that they share an essential difference, one that at this early stage seems Fitzgerald's answer to the jibe at American expatriate degeneration in Hemingway's *Fiesta* (1927):

'You're an expatriate. You've lost touch with the soil. You get precious. Fake European standards have ruined you. You drink yourself to death. You become obsessed by sex. You spend all your time talking, not working. You are an expatriate, see? You hang around cafes.' (133)

Instead of atrophy in the type, however, Rosemary finds integrity, for '[even] in their absolute immobility, complete as that of the morning, she felt a purpose, a working over something, a direction, an act of creation different from any she had known' (19). These men are not only integrated with their immediate environment, they are also involved creatively with it, intuitive *auteurs*. It is perhaps also significant that the group is here easily embraced by organic, natural imagery: they are 'complete' like the morning itself—they have not, in fact, 'lost touch with the soil'. Compare this depiction to the narrator's treatment of the effeminate Campion in the same section: he is the man *without* repose, rejected by the natural as he 'tried to edge his way into a sand-coloured cloud, but the cloud floated off into the vast hot sky' (11).

Barban, Diver, North: each in his own distinctive way personifies a version of selfhood that challenges orthodoxy; each exemplifies a disjunction between ego and collectivity that enables him to exploit possibilities of feeling and response which others have either abandoned or failed to realize. In this sense *Tender* is a novel that confronts concepts of identity and convention. The condition of being an expatriate can be precisely that—a condition of being. Yet there are those who are able to escape confinement within expatriate stereotypes, to escape the poverty of encountering life through a toneless lens. The novel's twelfth chapter begins with the characters (Diver, the Norths, Rosemary) poking fun at neurotic American mannerisms, played off against Dick Diver's notion of himself as the 'man with repose' (51). Scrutinizing their fellow diners in a high-class Paris restaurant, they put Diver's claim that 'no American men had any repose, except himself' (51)[7] successfully to the test, as one by one they show the signs of nervous impulse: 'a man endlessly patted his shaven cheek with his palm, and his companion mechanically raised and lowered the stub of a cold cigar. The luckier ones fingered eyeglasses and facial hair [. . .] or even pulled desperately at the lobes of their ears' (52). This scene is a vignette of all that bourgeois respectability cannot contain, being maladjusted to its environment, a condition exacerbated for these Americans by their displacement in Europe. It is a society of no repose, peopled by a moneyed class that is ill at ease with itself, filled with wanderers who are uncomfortable with themselves and their bodies.[8] If this is typical of post-war expatriate café society, it is a society without wit or elegance. The patrons' restless tics and twitches are signs of a more general enervation in the culture.

Fitzgerald's chronicle of modern neurosis interacts with the surrounding sociological, cultural, economic setting. Expatriation is a factor in all of those contexts and style is used as an index of the eclipse of the old order. As Nicole Diver realizes when she and Dick visit the beach at Antibes together for the last time, its boundaries have quite literally disappeared, crumbled beneath the sand: 'Let him look at it—his beach [. . .] he could search it for a day and find no stone of the Chinese wall he had once erected around it, no footprint of an old friend' (280). In its stead there is a new style of expatriate presence—an idiom of abject mediocrity, the presence of no style at all. This new reality is entirely without nuance, a democratized mass without discrimination. Fitzgerald's narrator is withering in judgement here, telling us that 'Now the swimming place was a "club", though, like the international society it represented, it would be hard to say who was not admitted' (281). As in the novel's opening scenes on the beach, body and form are used to indicate essential values. There are still the beach umbrellas, but simply too many to matter, so many in fact that Nicole has to watch 'Dick peer about for the children among the confused shapes and shadows of many umbrellas' (280). When the bodies are individuated, they are unlovely, a perception apparently acknowledged even by their owners, since 'few people swam any more in that blue paradise [. . .] most of Gausse's guests stripped the concealing pajamas from their flabbiness only for a short hangover dip at one o'clock' (281). Here is repose without style. If the Divers, and the Murphys on whom their lives were based, were 'masters in the art of living' (Tomkins 7) on the Riviera, they were shown the way by convincing old-world aristocrats who had come there to die—in the grand style. In a passage stripped almost verbatim from another published in *The Saturday Evening Post* of 1924,[9] Fitzgerald's narrator paints a beguiling picture of that *ancien régime*. The very names of Cannes, Nice, Monte Carlo whisper 'of old kings come here to dine or die, of rajahs tossing Buddha's eyes to English ballerinas, of Russian princes turning the weeks into Baltic twilights in the lost caviare days' (15). Though Diver is no blue-blood,[10] the narrator's description of him as representing 'the exact furthermost evolution of a class' (21) suggests that in sensibility if not in breeding he is the natural inheritor of what is left of that civilization.

Certainly Diver's return is to a place that has by 1929 become effete, and the narrator is careful to make that return carry overtones of *lèse majesté*: 'Probably it was the beach he feared, like a deposed ruler secretly visiting an old court' (280). In valediction, 'his beach' has become, in the narrator's words (though the strong implication is that they represent Nicole's thoughts), 'perverted now to the tastes of the tasteless' (280), an intriguing use of language that suggests the rape of a natural environment by a counterworld of vulgar kitsch. All of the subtlety, the deep amity that went into the Divers' art of living has given way to rampant philistinism. The Riviera summers of a lost, aristocratic order are most certainly gone, buried under a whole apparatus of meretricious form. Both style and the natural (for in Fitzgerald's aesthetic, they are congruent) have been overwhelmed by an odious flourishing of 'new paraphernalia': 'the trapezes over the water, the swinging rings, the portable bath-houses, the floating towers, the searchlights from last night's fetes, the modernistic buffet, white with a hackneyed motif of endless handlebars' (281). Diver was right to fear the beach, or at least what has been done to it. Again we see that in this novel style is emblematic of cultural change, though in this case the change is an affliction. Nicole 'was sorry' (280) for Dick, whose instincts seem lost amid such meaninglessness. Yet of the two, Nicole is better equipped to adjust towards the future: whatever one side of her ancestry suggests, her essential self easily shakes free of old-world values. The capacity to adapt to modern conditions, however unseemly, is an integral part of her deepest structure. She is in this respect profoundly centred in the modern. Whereas for Dick adaptation often involves an imaginative assimilation of new prospects, for Nicole change is rather a matter of reversion to origins, since she 'had been designed for change, for flight, with money as fins or wings. The new state of things would be no more than if a racing chassis, concealed for years under the body of a family limousine, should be stripped to its original self' (280). In this radical sense she is much more at home in the new world than her husband, whose expatriation, as the above return to the beach suggests, has become akin to a state of profound homelessness. Indeed, his exiled condition will increasingly resemble that of a refugee, driven from place to place by social upheaval and personal crisis. In this sense Diver is a representative figure, for as George Steiner has written, the twentieth century inaugurated 'the age of the refugee', an environment of extreme alienation: 'No exile is more radical, no feat of adaptation and new life more demanding. It seems proper that those who create art in a civilization of quasi-barbarism which has made so many homeless, which has torn up tongues and people by the root, should themselves be poets unhoused and wanderers across language' (11).

Faced by the 'feat of adaptation' now required of him in this subverted culture, Diver's capacities are ineffectual. He is defeated not by European standards, but, as Hemingway's Bill Gorton put it, by 'false European standards' which have turned the simplicity of the Divers' beach colony into a mixture of amusement park and 'club'. Modernity is here defined by such pretence and artificiality, and although Jacqueline Tavernier-Courbin is right to draw attention to the sensuality of the novel's Riviera setting, to its appeal deriving from 'a life lived in closer harmony with the body and with nature' (226), she over-emphasizes the contrast between Dick and Nicole in this regard, for he is more than capable of sensual engagement. It is indeed Nicole herself who acknowledges this, remembering wistfully their *vie plaisante*—a life emanating from Dick's openness towards natural energy, 'the ritual of the morning time, the quiet restful extraversion towards sea and sun—many inventions of his, buried deeper than the sand under the span of so few years' (281). For Nicole now, Dick has become 'a tarnished object of art' (282) and her new state of resurgent vitality can only emerge fully once she has departed his orbit, 'his beach'. The narrator goes so far as to tell us that 'she hated the beach, resented the places where she had played planet to Dick's sun' (289). The operative term in this figure is, however, that of life as playful invention. Nicole refuses any longer to be defined in these terms, opting instead for the reality of banal betrayal.

In 1935 Gerald Murphy wrote to Fitzgerald of his premonitory fear that his happiness would be lost to 'life itself', telling him that 'in my heart I dreaded the moment when our youth and invention would be attacked in our only vulnerable spot, the children' (Tomkins 125). Diver's 'inventions', now buried under Riviera sand, are exactly analogous to Murphy's youthful fount of 'inventions': both have been destroyed by the advance of an amoral realism. For though George Steiner has reminded us that 'the liberating function of art lies in its singular capacity to "dream against the world," to structure worlds that are *otherwise*' (34), Fitzgerald's novel insists that the imagination of Dick Diver can only resist reality's darkening shadow for so long. Nicole is right—Dick has indeed become 'a tarnished object of art', and as his own 'dreams against the world' are increasingly threatened by the appeal of baser appetites, so Nicole is the beneficiary. Her affair with Barban is conditioned not by the application of style or tasteful discrimination but by the appeal of an opposing motive—the attraction of moral chaos: 'all summer she had been stimulated by watching people do exactly what they were tempted to do and pay no penalty for it'

(291). As she crosses herself with Chanel Sixteen and waits for Barban, her 'earnest Satan' (294), she has no vision, no plan; she only knows that the change is coming and that she will not stand in its way. Her primary desire at this stage is not even marital emancipation, instead 'she enjoys the caviare of potential power [. . .] she wanted a change' (291). With 'the plush arrogance of a top dog' (301) she knows that nothing can prevent her taking what she wants and needs: a new freedom, an unfettered licence to indulge her passion.

For the present Nicole is a free agent, but Fitzgerald's narrator clearly signals that in the future her moral bills will be called in. Adultery ensures her entry to the post-war mess of collapsing values, to what Adamov called '*le temps de l'ignominie*'[11] (106). Her 'vulgar business' (291) with Barban is, she realizes, an unemotional act of self-indulgence. In the final push to claim her freedom and at the same time give Doctor Diver *his* liberty, she uses all weapons at her disposal, even her 'unscrupulousness against his moralities' (302). Just like the new breed of expatriates who 'pay no penalty' for self-indulgence, so Nicole has the freedom of knowing that she need never commit herself to anything. Her visionary reach is, however, limited, and 'she does not seem [. . .] to anticipate the subsequent years when her insight will often be blurred by panic, by the fear of stopping or the fear of going on' (291). For now, however, an act of easy betrayal is the line of least resistance, and after her return to Diver from Barban '[she] wandered about the house rather contentedly, resting on her achievement. She was a mischief, and that was a satisfaction' (300). As Fitzgerald's narrator reminds us, one of Nicole's most potent weapons is that she is equipped 'with the opportunistic memory of women'; this allows her to tell Barban accomplished lies about her passion for him, and hardly to remember the times 'when she and Dick had possessed each other in secret places around the corners of the world' (300). Yet what Tavernier-Courbin calls 'the complicated and intellectual world of Dick Diver' survives as the truest one nevertheless, and in the end Nicole's rebellion could never damage it radically, nor defeat his deep-rooted moral intelligence, 'sometimes exercised without power but always with substrata of truth under truth which she could not break or even crack' (301). In the end, 'Nicole felt outguessed, realizing that [. . .] Dick had anticipated everything' (311).

J. Gerald Kennedy finds correctly that writing by American expatriates 'tends to reflect both an intensified awareness of place and an instinctive preoccupation with the identity of the alienated self' (26), and indeed the final scenes of *Tender* show that, for Diver, place was in the end perhaps even more important than people.[12] There is both practicality and humour in his farewell to his Riviera housekeepers: 'he kissed the Provençal girl who helped with the children. She had been with them for almost a decade and she fell on her knees and cried until Dick jerked her to her feet and gave her three hundred francs' (311). He dispenses with the formality of polite manners at the close as he tells his fellow expatriate Mary North, 'You're all so dull' (313). When, demanding a final showdown with Diver, Barban interrupts the Divers' joint visit to the barber at the Carleton Hotel in Cannes, Fitzgerald even provides a considerable element of the ludicrous in Diver's matter-of-fact refusal to allow him any opportunity for macho posturing or the confrontation he wanted. This interruption is only the first of a series of apparently farcical breaks in the proceedings, one of which is the commotion caused by the incongruous arrival of the Tour de France outside. The meeting subsequently takes place nearby, at the ironically named Café des Alliés, but not before Tommy gets his row from a still fully towelled and resentful Nicole: '"But my hair—it's half cut"' (307). She 'wanted Dick to take the initiative, but he seemed content to sit with his face half-shaved matching her hair half-washed', his dishevelled appearance being obviously reflected in the exhausted back-markers and losers of the Tour de France, 'indifferent and weary' (310). Yet Diver is still the master of ceremonies, maintaining a code of permissible expression: '"Well, then," said the Doctor, "since it's all settled, suppose we go back to the barber shop"' (310), thus concluding a scene of abject reality which could not be transfigured. 'So it had happened—and with a minimum of drama' (344), and Nicole was right—Dick had anticipated everything.

His final action is, explicitly, to 'take a last look at Gausse's beach' rather than at its many occupants, who in those last moments include Nicole and Baby Warren, and finally Nicole and Tommy. It may be hardly surprising that the sight of Nicole and Tommy is precisely what he wishes to avoid at the last, but even the elements are now armed against his moods: '[a] white sun, chivied of outline by a white sky' (311-12) delineates betrayal in sharp relief, etched as myth, 'a man and a woman, black and white and metallic against the sky' (313). Colour and realistic perspective are here subordinated to the bleak mono-chrome of archetype. For although Dick is looking down on the beach and thus on his wife and her lover 'from the high terrace' (314) above, Fitzgerald chooses sky, rather than the more logical sand, to provide the boundless backdrop for a mythic theme. Any poetry of place, of subtle invention is impossible in such a harsh light. The Riviera set is still dazzling, but Diver's show is over. Perhaps in the end the beach was the only place that Diver could call home, the only place in which he had been not estranged, but in ownership, as Nicole recognizes: '"This is his place—in a way, he discovered it. Old Gausse always says he owes everything to Dick"' (312). Indeed this impression had from the start been facilitated by Fitzgerald's language, which domesticated the beach in homely metaphor as a 'bright tan prayer rug' (3). It may be Gausse's beach in fact, but it was more creatively and exclusively '[our] beach that Dick made out of a pebble pile' (20).

For Fitzgerald himself what might be termed 'good expatriation' was very much linked to relative isolation from the crowd, more akin to voluntary exile than expatriation. 'No one comes to the Riviera in summer, so we expect to have a few guests and to work' (161), says Nicole in a dream of hope. Loneliness as a theme increasingly became a defining zone in Fitzgerald's life and work, one in which his charac-ters were tested and challenged. In loneliness he found a kind of eman-cipation, a freedom from the tyranny of social obligations. He also saw himself as constitutionally suited to the classic model of the sequestered artist.[13] For Fitzgerald on the Riviera in his annus mirabilis of 1924, expatriation was about being alone to work, with loneliness as the key to great things—and he knew it, writing in a letter of that year as he worked on *The Great Gatsby*: 'I hope I don't see a soul for six months [. . .] I feel absolutely self-sufficient + I have a perfect hollow craving for lonliness [*sic*] [. . .] I shall write a novel better than any novel ever written in America' (*Life in Letters* 68). Yet only a year later he would pen a bittersweet testimony to this paradise lost to the crowd of expatriates who joined him in France, good expatriation turned bad, as he told John Peale Bishop in a famous letter: 'there was no one at Antibes this summer except me, Zelda. The Valentinos, the Murphy's, Mistinguet, Rex Ingram, Dos Passos, Alice Terry, the McLieshes [*sic*] [. . .] just a real place to rough it and escape from the world' (*Life in Letters* 126). Similarly Dick Diver's final meeting with Nicole and Tommy is interrupted not only by the arrival of the Tour de France, but by the ominous figure of an American photographer, in search of Riviera gold and in his way an eloquent expression of all that has gone wrong with Diver's world. Roughing it in splendid isolation on the Riviera is no longer an option with company like his. Rarely was publicity more unwelcome, and privacy more endangered:

> They were suddenly interrupted by an insistent American, of sinister aspect, vending copies of The Herald and of The Times fresh from New York. [. . .] He brought a gray clipping from his purse—and Dick recognized it as he saw it. It cartooned millions of Americans pouring from liners with bags of gold. 'You think I'm not going to get part of that? Well, I am.' (309)

This invasion is malign and inexorable, the sullying of the private by the public, a note struck again in the novel's penultimate chapter when Diver notices that 'an American photographer from the A. and P. worked with his equipment in a precarious shade and looked up quickly at every footfall descending the stone steps' that led to Gausse's beach (312). The wolves are now at the very door of Diver's domain, drawn by the scent of exclusivity and difference. The result is a phenomenon we have all had to get used to in the years since, the surrender of the private sphere to the public, with a concomitant erosion of the virtues of private discourse, including inward imaginative energies.

This essay began with memories of the Murphys and their special charisma for F. Scott Fitzgerald, who in *Tender* was able to deepen their influence through his vision of their enlightened expatriation. It is fitting, then, to close with Gerald Murphy's own memory of Fitzgerald, provoked by having seen the 1964 film version of *Tender.* Murphy went to the cinema without Sara, who had refused to go, presumably because she feared that moving pictures would do no more justice to the reality of Riviera life in the early 1920s than did the kind of photography satirized by Fitzgerald in the novel. If so, she was right. Murphy recalled that as he watched the movie the vast auditorium was completely empty apart from himself and 'an elderly charwoman sweeping the back rows' (Tomkins 128). The film 'disregarded everything except the battle of the sexes and dismissed the lure of the era with a nostalgic ridiculing of the Charleston' (Tomkins 128). Bad it was, yet Murphy remembered that, driving home afterwards in the snow,

> I had a really vivid recollection of Scott on that day, years and years ago, when I gave him back the advance copy of his book and told him how good I thought certain parts of it were [. . .] and Scott took the book and said, with that funny, faraway look in his eye, 'Yes, it has magic. It has magic.' (Tomkins 128)

Critical Insights

Notes

1. Cf. André Le Vot: 'Gerald-Scott, Sara-Zelda, Scott-Sara in juxtaposition, permutation, fascination with themselves and each other. The identification would be complete in the various phases of *Tender Is the Night* [. . .] seen through the worshiping eyes of Rosemary against a background of sea and sun, Dick Diver in the opening chapters is Gerald, serene and magnanimous, ready to dare anything and do anything' (Le Vot 208). The admiration was reciprocal. According to Le Vot, 'Gerald wrote a kind of love letter to the Fitzgeralds on September 19, 1925 [. . .] he described exactly that process of symbiosis that would form the composite character of the Divers in *Tender Is the Night*. "We four communicate by our presence [. . .] so that where we meet and when will never count. Currents run between us regardless: Scott will uncover values for me in Sara, just as Sara has known them in Zelda through her affection for Scott"' (Le Vot 209).

2. 'This was the period when Baoth, the sturdiest of Murphy's children, died of meningitis at school before his parents could reach him [1935]. Patrick was to die two years later' (Le Vot 261).

3. The famous phrase was used in a letter Hemingway sent to Fitzgerald from Paris in April 1926: 'Was not referring to guts but to something else. Grace under pressure. Guts never made any money for anybody except violin string manufacturers' (Baker 200).

4. James R. Mellow used the phrase for the title of his 1984 biography *Invented Lives: F. Scott and Zelda Fitzgerald*.

5. James' term denotes the dwindling of American roots in conditions of exile, and in 1898 he wrote with extraordinary prescience of the emergence and effect of forces responsible for what would now be referred to as globalism: 'Who shall say, at the rate things are going, what is to be "near" home in the future and what is to be far from it? [. . .] The globe is shrinking, for the imagination, to the size of an orange that can be played with' (cited by Weintraub, *The London Yankees* 380).

6. 'The tragic power of charm had been the book's main theme ever since he had first conceived of it in the Murphys' garden at Antibes back in 1925' (Piper 211).

7. Nicole Diver, too, is associated with repose: 'she liked to be active, though at times she gave an impression of repose that was at once static and evocative' (26).

8. This critique seems aimed especially at American men. One of the 'well-dressed American' men, who nevertheless shows clear signs of uneasy comportment and 'spasmodic' mannerisms, 'had come in with two women who swooped and fluttered unself-consciously around a table' (51). Although these women are not identified explicitly as American, their relaxed occupation of this public space does suggest that at least in this scene Fitzgerald may have intended a gendered contrast.

9. 'The Riviera! The names of its resorts, Cannes, Nice, Monte Carlo, call up the memory of a hundred kings and princes who have lost their thrones and come here to die, of mysterious rajahs and boys flinging blue diamonds to English dancing girls, of Russian millionaires tossing away fortunes at roulette in the lost caviar days before the war.' 'How to Live on Practically Nothing a Year', *The Saturday Evening Post*, 20 September 1924. Reprinted in *Afternoon of an Author* 104.

---

10. Unlike Nicole, whose breeding ensures that the decline of old European aristocratic manners will be countered genetically by the ascendant American plutodemocracy: 'Nicole was the grand-daughter of a self-made American capitalist and the grand-daughter of a Count of the House of Lippe Weissenfeld' (53).

11. Arthur Adamov was a Russian émigré who had arrived in Paris in 1924, where he edited an avant-garde periodical, *Discontinuité*, and associated himself with the nonconformity of early modernism. His autobiography *L'Aveu* [*The Confession*] is a classic statement of the metaphysics of exile. There he diagnoses the post-war epoch as one sickening due to the loss of any sense of the sacred, peopled by neurotics who are afflicted by the disappearance of ultimate meaning in the world.

12. In this regard, it may be significant that as Dick fades from Nicole's view in the novel's last chapter, his final notes to her are from the small towns of upstate New York. Perhaps the implication is that American repatriation has provided him not with the spiritual integrity or reconstitution of homecoming, but rather with fragmentation of self. Identity is again associated with place, though here it is scattered, and as we are told in the novel's final words, Dick is also scattered, dispersed 'in one town or another' (315).

13. Fitzgerald told Laura Guthrie 'I am really a lone wolf. [. . .] Everyone is lonely—the artist especially, it goes with creation. I create a world for others' (Turnbull, *Scott Fitzgerald* 265).

Works Cited

Adamov, Arthur. *L'Aveu*. Paris: Sagittaire, 1946.

Baker, Carlos, ed. *Ernest Hemingway: Selected Letters 1917-1961*. Frogmore, St Albans: Granada, 1981.

Blackmur, R. P. *The Lion and the Honeycomb: Essays in Solicitude and Critique*. London: Methuen, 1956.

Bogarde, Dirk. 'Paying the Cruel Price of Careless Happiness'. *Daily Telegraph* 8 November 1998: 8.

Bradbury, Malcolm. *Dangerous Pilgrimages: Trans-Atlantic Mythologies and the Novel*. London: Secker and Warburg, 1995.

Bruccoli, Matthew J. *Some Sort of Epic Grandeur: The Life of F. Scott Fitzgerald*. London: Hodder and Stoughton, 1981.

_____, and Judith S. Baughman, eds. *F. Scott Fitzgerald: A Life in Letters*. New York: Scribner's, 1994.

Fitzgerald, F. Scott. 'How to Live on Practically Nothing a Year'. *Afternoon of an Author: A Selection of Uncollected Stories and Essays*. Ed. Arthur Mizener. New York: Scribner's, 1957. 100-16.

_____. *Tender Is the Night*. New York: Scribner's, 1934.

Graham, Sheilah. *College of One*. Harmondsworth: Penguin, 1969.

Hemingway, Ernest. *Fiesta*. London: Cape, 1959

James, Henry. *Roderick Hudson*. London: Rupert Hart-Davis, 1961.

Kennedy, J. Gerald. *Imagining Paris: Exile, Writing and American Identity*. New Haven and London: Yale University Press, 1993.

Le Vot, André. *F. Scott Fitzgerald. A Biography*. New York: Doubleday, 1983.

Mellow, James R. *Invented Lives: F. Scott and Zelda Fitzgerald*. Boston: Houghton Mifflin, 1984.

Piper, Henry Dan. *F. Scott Fitzgerald: A Critical Portrait*. New York: Holt, Rinehart and Winston, 1965.

Steiner, George. *Extraterritorial: Papers on Literature and the Language Revolution*. New York: Atheneum, 1971.

Tarr, Rodger L., ed. *Max and Marjorie: The Correspondence Between Maxwell E. Perkins and Marjorie Kinnan Rawlings*. Gainesville: University Press of Florida, 1999.

Tavernier-Courbin, Jacqueline. 'The Influence of France on Nicole Diver's Recovery in *Tender Is the Night*'. *French Connections: Hemingway and Fitzgerald Abroad*. Ed. J. Gerald Kennedy and Jackson R. Bryer. New York: St Martin's Press, 1998. 215-32.

Tomkins, Calvin. *Living Well Is the Best Revenge: Two Americans in Paris 1921-1933*. London: André Deutsch, 1972.

Turnbull, Andrew. *Scott Fitzgerald*. Harmondsworth: Penguin, 1970.

_____, ed. *The Letters of F. Scott Fitzgerald*. Harmondsworth: Penguin, 1968.

Vaill, Amanda. *Everybody Was So Young: Gerald and Sara Murphy—A Lost Generation Love Story*. London: Warner Books, 1999.

Weintraub, Stanley. *The London Yankees: Portraits of American Writers and Artists in England 1894-1914*. London: W. H. Allen, 1979.

Wilson, Edmund. *Letters on Literature and Politics, 1912-1972*. Ed. Elena Wilson. New York: Farrar, Straus and Giroux, 1977.

Yeats, W. B. 'Sailing to Byzantium'. *The Collected Poems of W. B. Yeats*. London: Macmillan, 1973. 217-18.

Tender Is the Night and the Calculus of Modern War_____

James H. Meredith

Despite conventional wisdom on the topic of Fitzgerald and war—that because he was not a combatant, war therefore had little effect on him and his work—it is important to understand the ways in which he thought World War I had fundamentally and irretrievably changed Western civilization. Fitzgerald did not write combat literature that emphasizes the naturalistic aspects of modern war, as his old friend Hemingway did most notably in *A Farewell to Arms* (1929), but he did write one of the most engaging war novels, *Tender Is the Night*, about the aftermath of World War I. In this essay, I shall explore the ways in which *Tender* functions as a war novel, as opposed to combat fiction, differences that can best be understood when the novel is contrasted with other World War I fiction, such as Henri Barbusse's *Under Fire: The Story of a Squad*. Moreover, the broader social implications of war in *Tender*, such as Dick Diver's war neuroses, are easier to contextualize in relation to such works as Stendhal's *The Charterhouse of Parma* and William Makepeace Thackeray's *Vanity Fair*, novels about war during the Napoleonic period. I shall argue that, while in these nineteenth-century novels war is not shown as having had a lasting psychological effect on society, in *Tender* Fitzgerald clearly shows the lasting psychological impact of World War I. By addressing these and other issues in *Tender*, I hope that the critical tide will continue to turn, and that Fitzgerald will be recognized as an important writer about war and its aftermath in the twentieth century.

Before understanding how the war transformed European society forever, it is essential to reinforce how it first changed combat conditions. In *The Face of Battle*, John Keegan writes about the Somme:

Despite the immense growth of complexity of the machinery and business of war which had taken place in Western armies since 1815, the Battle of the Somme was to be in many ways a simpler event than Waterloo—not, indeed, in terms of the strains of management it threw on commanders and their staffs, but in the range and nature of the encounters between different categories of armed groups which took place on the ground. [. . .] The nearest thing to single combat in trench warfare ('him or me' bayonet thrusting excepted) was perhaps the 'game of bombing up the traverses,' of which the most striking feature, so characteristic of the First World War, was that one did not see one's enemy. (242)

For all its complicated logistical manifestations, the Somme simplified the individual's combat role, essentially meaning that the human being was lost on the battlefield. The soldier became just another asset in modern, industrialized warfare that needed to be managed, and as a consequence a complete psychological reorientation about the nature of war took place. Interestingly enough, this reorientation, this dehumanizing objectification of the human on the battlefield, had much to do with a whole host of emerging post-war psychological problems, such as shell shock or war neuroses, that occurred on and off the World War I battlefield and became more clearly manifested after the war. In other words, the dehumanized battlefield led to the spiritual waste land in the 1920s and, one could argue, eventually led to the ugliness of fascism in the 1930s and another world war in the 1940s.

In *Tender Is the Night*, Dick Diver's famous monologue, given while he and an entourage are touring the post-war ruins of the Somme battlefield, clearly illuminates this disillusionment that the dehumanized World War I combat experience created in post-war Europe (56-57). The sense of modern tragedy and despair that is so profoundly conveyed in this novel stems from what Diver feels was lost—his 'beautiful lovely safe world'—on that Picardy field on the banks of the Somme in 1916. While, of course, the trends towards modernism predate the war, World War I was a dramatic catalyst for the complex modern world that *Tender* so sensitively conveys—a world in which the calculus of intimate relationships has to include a father who is also a lover of his daughter and a psychiatrist who is also the husband of his patient—where daughter and patient are the same. In the novel, of course, Nicole and her father have a brief sexual relationship that leads to her eventual mental collapse (129). Subsequently, Nicole, who is receiving mental treatment in Switzerland, meets Diver while he is wearing the uniform of a noncombatant. While he is away performing his duty in a military psychiatric unit, Nicole and Diver correspond, and they form an epistolary relationship, which ends up being the basis of their long-term relationship both as husband and wife and as doctor and patient (121-25). These relationships are complicated and based on a calculus of unusual, modern psychological alliances.

In her article 'From Griffith's Girls to *Daddy's Girl*: The Masks of Innocence in *Tender Is the Night*', Ruth Prigozy writes:

> *Tender Is the Night* (1934) extends and deepens Fitzgerald's historical perspective as it reveals not only a nation's unrealized past and feckless present, but also its futile, diminishing future. Fitzgerald traces American history through the central metaphor of the novel, the incestuous father-daughter relationship, actual in the Warren Family and mythic in the title and scenario of Rosemary Hoyt's great Hollywood success, *Daddy's Girl*.
>
> Father-daughter intimacy, a prevalent motif in nineteenth-century literature and drama survived into the twentieth century, indeed was given another life by the newest, most popular form of mass culture, the movies; it was reflected too in popular songs, comic strips, and even in current events in the 1920s, an era when life began more and more to imitate the popular arts. (190)

Prigozy continues her argument by stating that *Daddy's Girl*

> suggests the complex ideas Fitzgerald was working out in the novel—the role of women in the economic structure of American society, the illusions of the nation endlessly rekindled by the movies, the ambiguous nature of love—marital, familial, sexual—and finally, the decline of a civilization

which, after a bloody, disillusioning war, sought sanctuary in the nursery, free of claims of adulthood—morality, rationality, responsibility for others. (190)

Prigozy goes on to demonstrate how incest represents in Fitzgerald's fiction the degradation of modern culture, which, as my essay attempts to demonstrate, was significantly brought on by the brutality and dehumanization of modern warfare. Since she is created with all of these issues in mind, it is no accident that Diver's primary, immediate audience for this speech on the Somme battlefield is Rosemary Hoyt, the under-age star of *Daddy's Girl*.

Tender Is the Night is arguably one of the best novels about the aftermath of the Great War, rivalling Virginia Woolf's *Mrs Dalloway* in complexity. However, it should be clearly stated here that *Tender* (for that matter, like *Mrs Dalloway*) is not a combat novel but rather is a war novel, which means that it concerns itself more with the lasting, comprehensive effect of the war than with the immediate impact of combat on the individual soldier. In *Mrs Dalloway*, one sees the obvious effect of combat on Septimus Warren Smith (whose middle name, interestingly, is also the maiden name of Nicole in *Tender*), and it ends in his suicidal plunge from a window in his home. Septimus represents post-war soldiers, post-war survivors, who were haunted by their war experiences and unable to live with their psychological condition. On the other hand, Clarissa Dalloway represents the noncombatant who also has suffered some form of trauma from the war. As Trudi Tate puts it in *Modernism, History and the First World War*, '[for] many people, the trauma did not end with the war' (147). The main point here is that *Tender*, like *Mrs Dalloway*, is a war novel, primarily concerned with social conditions after the conflict had ended.[1]

By way of comparison, a good example of a World War I combat novel, as opposed to a war novel, is Henri Barbusse's *Under Fire: The Story of a Squad*. Published in 1916, Barbusse's novel narrates, in naturalistic detail, the wretched life of a French combatant:

We threw ourselves flat on the ground, closely, desperately, and waited there motionless, with the terrible star hanging over us and flooding us with daylight, twenty-five or thirty yards from our trench. Then a machine-gun on the other side of the ravine swept the zone where we were. Corporal Bertrand and I had had the luck to find in front of us, just as the red rocket went up and before it burst into light, a shell-hole, where a broken trestle was steeped in the mud. We flattened ourselves against the edge of the hole, buried ourselves in the mud as much as possible. (225-26)

This type of warfare clearly illustrates what Martin Van Creveld, in *Technology and War: From 2000 BC to the Present*, describes as a revolutionary change in the way infantry fought. Creveld writes that the 'tactical significance of this was that, perhaps for the first time since the invention of organized warfare, infantry no longer fought standing erect on their feet and organized in formation' (171). While learning not to stand up on the battlefield may have been a matter of survival at the Somme, it certainly is a clear indication that the modern era ushered out any romantic notions of war and ushered in degrading, dehumanized warfare.

Further in this same passage, Barbusse describes the various conditions of corpses who were once his comrades:

Barque in his rigidity seems immoderately long, his arms lie closely to the body, his chest has sunk, his belly is hollow as a basin. With his head upraised by a lump of mud, he looks over his feet at those who come up on the left; his face is dark and polluted by the clammy strains of disordered hair, and his wide and scalded eyes are heavily encrusted with blackened blood. [. . .] Eudore seems very small by contrast, and his little face is completely white, so white as to remind you of the befloured face of a pierrot, and it is touching to see that little circle of white paper among the grey and bluish tints of the corpse. Biquet, the Breton, squat and square as a flagstone, appears to be under the stress of a huge effort. [. . .]

Barque and Biquet were shot in the belly; Eudore in the throat. (227-28)

What is particularly interesting about these two scenes is that despite the danger, there seems to have been no direct contact with the human enemy. While there is plenty of description of the enemy's technology and warfare's destructive power, there is otherwise no face-to-face encounter. If this novel is any indication, then one could deduce that while representative World War I combat narrative seems to include specific descriptions of modern weaponry and naturalistic descriptions of corpses, the living human presence of the enemy is not necessarily featured. Although there are examples of narratives containing actual encounters with the enemy, these encounters do not seem to have been the most lasting traumatic experience for the World War I soldier. Rather, the most traumatizing experience seems to have been the soldiers' dehumanization by the overwhelming technologizing of the battlefield, particularly in their inability to orient themselves in an upright, human way.

While World War I combat literature concentrates on the immediate battlefield experiences that not only caused lasting trauma for the soldiers but also filtered through and traumatized the whole culture as a consequence, for its part, war literature concentrates on the rippling cultural aftermath of that initial combat trauma. As such, World War I becomes the first war to develop an extensive collection of both combat and war literature. Leo Braudy, in *From Chivalry to Terrorism: War and the Changing Nature of Masculinity*, explains the development in this way:

> Henri Barbusse's *Under Fire* appeared in 1916, Ernest Jünger's *Storm of Steel* in 1920, John Dos Passos's *Three Soldiers* in 1921, Jünger's memoir-essay *Copse 125* in 1925, and Hemingway's *A Farewell to Arms* and Erich Maria Remarque's *All Quiet on the Western Front* both in 1929. They were only the most prominent in a great flood of poems, novels, memoirs, and recollections written by participants in the war—the first war in history to be so voluminously documented, in part because it was the first war to draw so heavily upon a literate, self-conscious male community. (398)

Samuel Hynes, in *The Soldiers' Tale: Bearing Witness to Modern War*, further reinforces this point and gives a fuller explanation:

> [The] tale of the Great War didn't come from the ranks, it came from the middle-class volunteers who became the war's junior officers. That's understandable. The middle class is the great self-recording class, the class that keeps diaries and journals and considers that the preservation of one's daily life is an appropriate and interesting activity for an individual. In modern times it has also been the imagining class, out of which comes most of the novels and poems and plays that constitute Western literature. (32)

In *The Great War and Modern Memory*, Paul Fussell explains why it was so important for these middle-class combatants to record their experiences faithfully: 'Everyone who remembers a war first-hand knows that its images remain in the memory with special vividness. The very enormity of the proceedings, their absurd remove from the usages of the normal world, will guarantee that a structure of irony sufficient for ready narrative recall will attach to them' (326). Hence, '[r]evisiting moments made vivid for these various reasons becomes a moral obligation' (327).

Thus, if revisiting moments of war in fiction becomes a moral obligation for a participant writer, the whole aesthetic balance of the novel shifts from its traditional historical position. That is, if a writer of combat literature remains obsessed with his 'moral obligation' to revisit moments on the battlefield, then the historical position of his work likewise remains centred in the war itself. However, a war writer focuses his or her historical perspective on the aftermath, as Fitzgerald did in Diver's trip to the Somme. This differentiating shift in the moral and aesthetic calculus of war literature is a major feature of modernism. Braudy states it thus:

Since the heroic battles of classical and Renaissance epics, there had been few works in European literature that took war as their basic setting, unless, as in Shakespeare's history plays, their story was of kings. By contrast in novels such as Henry Fielding's *Tom Jones* and Laurence Sterne's *Tristram Shandy* in the eighteenth century, or Stendhal's *Charterhouse of Parma*, Thackeray's *Vanity Fair*, and even Tolstoy's *War and Peace* in the nineteenth, war was more important as scene and setting than as central issue. (398)

One of the distinguishing features of modernist literature, therefore, is the shifting of the central issue, the historical position of its aesthetic balance along a narrative axis of combat versus non-combat scenes and experiences of war. For example, the central issue in Barbusse's *Under Fire* is combat, whereas it is the war's aftermath in *Tender Is the Night*. However, both novels remain representative modernist fictions because the war, in one form or another, is the major theme. Fitzgerald avoids the naturalistic details of combat because, for one thing, he did not want to draw inordinate attention to his lack of combat experience; but, more importantly, Fitzgerald's sensibilities always favoured social issues. As I have stated in another context· 'War [combat] itself is not the central feature in Fitzgerald's fiction, but it is rather another part of the social fabric of the modern world, an essential factor that a serious writer had to confront whether he had participated in combat or not. As such, Fitzgerald's work concentrates on the bitter peace rather than the bloody war' (Meredith 165). And *Tender* clearly illuminates just how bitter the post-World War I peace became—a peace filled with complex relationships, marital infidelities, mental illnesses and personality disorders, and alcoholism, to name only a few of the problems.

Milton Stern, who has long recognized Fitzgerald's contribution to war fiction, writes that [unlike] the work of most of Fitzgerald's best-known contemporaries, *Tender Is the Night* is not generally thought of as a war novel because it is not set in war. But no novel written in the so-called 'lost generation' more deeply or centrally probes the significance of the war's legacy. [. . .]

World War I changed the human universe, quite literally. The Western world, especially, was never the same again. The war was the last cataclysmic gasp of British and French empire; it was the devastating interruption of an attempt at German empire; it brought about fundamental change in governmental structures and social functions. In its aftermath of enveloping cynicism and profoundly anarchic disillusion, it gave enormous impetus to everything antiestablishmentarian, socially and politically, and to everything existential, personally and culturally. (103)

* * *

While my essay is not meant to provide a lengthy comparison and contrast between *Tender Is the Night* and the great war novels of Stendhal and Thackeray, it is essential, merely as a matter of perspective, to recognize the latter works as definitive war literature. As literary models of Waterloo and its post-war effect on Europe, Stendhal's *The Charterhouse of Parma* and Thackeray's *Vanity Fair* are influential novels for modernist war literature writers; F. Scott Fitzgerald certainly found them to be so, but, of course, only up to a certain point.[2] In other words, while *Tender* is definitive war literature, in a similar vein to these two nineteenth-century works, Fitzgerald's novel is also significantly different from them, just as conditions on the nineteenth-century battlefields were very different from those in World War I.

Both Stendhal and Thackeray have very little concern with actual combat conditions. Although he is at one time armed with a soldier's rifle, and even takes aim and fires a shot at another man, more often than not Stendhal's Fabrizio merely wanders the Waterloo battlefield quixotically rather than in a soldierly way. In fact, he is a parody of a soldier. As such, he represents more the errant knight in Cervantes'

Don Quixote than the trained soldier in Barbusse's *Under Fire*. In fact, Fabrizio even admits: "'I know that I am ignorant, but I want to fight and I've made up my mind to go where that white smoke is'" (Stendhal 37). Dressed in costume, rather than properly wearing the uniform of the French Sixth Light Cavalry, Fabrizio eventually ends up on foot and he directly encounters the 'enemy', a Prussian hussar: 'He heard two shots fired right next to his tree; at the same moment he saw a cavalryman in a blue uniform galloping in front of him, heading to his left. "He's more than three paces away," Fabrizio calculated, "but at this range I can't miss"' (51). And he does not. Yet that is the extent of Fabrizio's combat experience—except for the fact that he is wounded by a 'comrade', a French soldier, during the great retreat from the battlefield. Despite having been shot, and quite possibly having killed another man, and subsequently being wounded himself by a cavalryman's sabre, Fabrizio seems never to show signs of psychologically suffering from his 'combat' trauma.

In *Vanity Fair: A Novel without a Hero*, where the noise of combat is off in the near distance from Brussels in Quatre Bras and Mons, Rebecca and the rest of the camp followers are waiting out the battle of Waterloo, instead of directly participating in it. In the novel, Thackeray bluntly writes: 'We do not claim to rank among the military novelists. Our place is with the noncombatants. When the decks are cleared for action we go below and wait meekly. We should only be in the way of the maneuvers that the gallant fellows are performing overhead' (334). Moreover, war seems neither to have any psychological effect on anyone in this novel, combatant or noncombatant, nor to be a deciding condition in the aftermath. Although the Napoleonic Wars began in 1792 with the First Coalition, 23 years before the final battle at Waterloo, there is little evidence, if either of these nineteenth-century novels is any indication, of shell shock, combat fatigue, or what is today called post-traumatic stress syndrome. Therefore, while the Napoleonic period significantly altered the geographical and political map, in these novels at least the wars are not shown to have effected any noticeable change in the psychological landscape of Europe. The situation is, however, very different in the case of World War I in Fitzgerald's *Tender Is the Night*.

Unlike those of the nineteenth-century novels, his noncombatants seem to be deeply altered by the war. Fitzgerald writes:

> On the way to the clinic he [Franz] said: 'Tell me of your experiences in the war. Are you changed like the rest? *You* have the same stupid and unaging American face, except I know you're not stupid, Dick.'
>
> 'I didn't see any of the war—you must have gathered that from my letters, Franz.'
>
> 'That doesn't matter—we have some shell-shocks who merely heard an air raid from a distance. We have a few who merely read newspapers.'
>
> 'It sounds like nonsense to me.' (119)

For all of his intelligence, education and sophistication, Diver is arguably unaware of the pervasive post-war trauma that has seemingly blanketed Europe like a fog, affecting even himself. Yet Fitzgerald's modern novel demonstrates that pervasive war trauma turned out to be anything but nonsense. In *Shell Shock: Traumatic Neurosis and the British Soldiers of the First World War*, Peter Leese describes some of the symptoms of combat stress diagnosed in a group of soldiers who actually saw combat. The list of symptoms includes 'recurrent dreams and nightmares, hallucinations and insomnia, as well as paralysis, hysterical gait, tics or stereotypical movements, fits, mental regression, somnambulism and severe depression' (95). While as a noncombatant Diver would only have had a secondary or milder form of war stress, he does seem to be affected; his problems seem to be manifested primarily in recurrent dreams (there is evidence in the novel that Diver continues to have dreams about the war [179]), insomnia, mental regression, and at times severe depression, all of which are self-medicated by alcohol. Overall, Diver's war neuroses seems particularly evident in his gradual but obvious emotional disintegration, as is particularly seen in his regressive move back to upstate New York, and in his continual and inordinate self-absorption and self-destruction.

In a way similar to Fabrizio's experience in war, Diver also quixotically wanders the battlefield, but in his case it is after the war, and his wanderings also demonstrate aspects of severe self-absorption and mental regression, reactions which are not evident in Stendhal's hero. Diver states:

> 'See that little stream—we could walk to it in two minutes. It took the British a month to walk to it—a whole empire walking very slowly, dying in front and pushing forward behind. And another empire walked very slowly backward a few inches a day, leaving the dead like a million bloody rugs. No Europeans will ever do that again in this generation.' (56-57)

Although they concern a passage from another Fitzgerald novel, and involve a different concept of relative time, Ronald Berman's comments in his essay 'Fitzgerald: Time, Continuity, Relativity' are apt here: 'Fitzgerald invokes cosmic movement for more than romantic purposes: it allows him to imply the passage of more than one kind of time. And something familiar is made relative in time as it moves. We lose the capacity to quantify, although time is itself quantity' (51). The 'cosmic movement' in this passage is the historical British Army's assault against the German lines during the Battle of the Somme. Besides the concept of spent empires and historical time, the most important idea expressed here is the differences in relative time under contrasting conditions. The two-minute walk in peacetime would equal a month during the war, even though both are covering the same distance. The difference, of course, would be that during the war there would be opposition to face on a dehumanized battlefield—not merely machine guns, artillery shells and hand grenades, but psychological resistance as well, both from the faceless enemy and from within the soldiers themselves. Such psychological tensions directly created the post-war condition of Woolf's Septimus Warren Smith and Fitzgerald's Abe

North and as a consequence indirectly caused Diver's. Trudi Tate writes that 'the idea of civilians suffering from war neuroses was by no means unknown during the Great War, and it turns up in a number of works of fiction. [. . .] F. Scott Fitzgerald refers bluntly to "noncombatant war neuroses" in *Tender Is the Night*' (1934). Tate also notes that '[c]ivilians exposed to violence and terror, whether public and shared (railway accidents, floods, war) or individual and private (rape), can suffer from serious traumatic symptoms' (15). Despite (or perhaps because of) all these complex connotations in Diver's speech, the simple, overarching symptom of his trauma can be overlooked, which is regressive self-absorption. After all, Diver says that it was his 'beautiful lovely safe world' that blew itself up here.

Despite his sensitivity to individual psychology, Diver still cannot fully grasp the extent to which World War I altered the spiritual calculus of the entire Western world, not just his world, but everybody's world. When Diver says that 'this [the Somme] was a love battle— there was a century of middle-class love spent here. This was the last love battle' (57), he does not quite seem to understand the literal, terrible actuality of what he says. After this war, human experience, especially love, would never be the same. If his own experience is any indication, the Battle of the Somme truly was the last 'love battle' of the old world. Stern writes:

> Until Dick is ruined—he had always known that he needed a little ruin and that the price of his intactness was incompleteness—he cannot know in his bones the extent of the truth he was uttering during his visit to the trenches. [. . .] But until he truly and profoundly recognizes the nature of the new world that has replaced the old one, his nostalgic sense of the past is marred by a faintly professional sentimentality that tends to reduce history to one of his therapeutically ego-soothing, sensitive performances as the unparalleled social host. (76)

In other words, his response is regressive, not progressive.

While Diver is pontificating regressive, romantic platitudes about the war to Rosemary, Abe, the lone battlefield survivor among the group, pretends to throw a grenade and showers dirt and debris on the group. Abe yells out, "'The war spirit's getting to me again. I have a hundred years of Ohio love behind me and I'm getting to bomb out this trench." His head popped up over the embankment. "You're dead—don't you know the rules? That was a grenade'" (57-58). Hauntingly, Abe's words echo through the post-war battlefield: yes, both he and Diver are dead, but in a way that neither man can quite comprehend at the time. Both men are spiritually dead, traumatized in their own different ways (and at different levels, which is why Diver survives longer) by the war and its aftermath. But then again, the post-war culture that both men are 'living' in is dead as well. No, Diver does not know the rules; how could he, he was not a combatant during World War I, when the cardinal rule was that there was to be no human contact with the enemy, real or imagined. The calculus of the dehumanized battlefield, where it would have been better for the individual soldier to know the person he was either going to kill or be killed by, led to the calculus of the dehumanized, post-war battlefield of life, where individuals were hurt more by those they were closest to—by a wife, a husband, or a father. However, modernist writers, including Fitzgerald, all sensed that their milieu, the post-war 'waste land' culture, was indeed, in T. S. Eliot's words, 'breeding/ Lilacs out of the dead land, mixing/ memory and desire, stirring/ dull roots with spring rain' (ll. 1-4).

From *Twenty-first Century Readings of "Tender Is the Night,"* edited by William Blazek and Laura Rattray, pp. 192-203. Copyright © 2007 by Liverpool University Press. Reprinted with permission of Liverpool University Press.

Notes

1. For more analysis of these two novels in the broader context of World War I, see my *Understanding the Literature of World War I*, 149-78.

2. While I have not found direct evidence that Fitzgerald read Stendhal's *The Charterhouse of Parma*, Matthew Bruccoli, in *Some Sort of Epic Grandeur*, argues that Fitzgerald considered *Le Rouge et le Noir* an important novel and that it served as a model for his failed Philippe series (383), which was begun straight after the publication of *Tender Is the Night*. It follows that if Fitzgerald read *Le Rouge et le Noir*, he probably also read *The Charterhouse of Parma*. Moreover, Steven Curry and Peter Hays, in 'Fitzgerald's *Vanity Fair*', write: 'In his critical biography of Fitzgerald, *The Far Side of Paradise*, Arthur Mizener records an exchange between Fitzgerald and a correspondent of *Hound & Horn* concerning the literary influences on *The Great Gatsby*: when the correspondent "ventured a guess that Thackeray had been an important influence on the book", Fitzgerald replied, "I never read a French author, except the usual prep-school classics, until I was twenty, but Thackeray I had read over and over by the time I was sixteen, so as far as I am concerned you guessed right"' (63). Two issues are important here. Firstly, I conclude that Stendhal's *The Charterhouse of Parma* could be one of those French classics Fitzgerald mentions here. Secondly, I would suggest that Thackeray's *Vanity Fair* would have been an even more important influence on his writing of *Tender* than it had earlier been for writing *The Great Gatsby*. Beyond this speculation, however, my argument ultimately is not about whether Fitzgerald was influenced by these nineteenth-century novels, but rather that *Tender* is as accurate in depicting post-World War I society as Stendhal and Thackeray were in portraying the aftermath of the Napoleonic Wars.

Works Cited

Barbusse, Henri. *Under Fire. The Story of a Squad*, 1926. Trans. W. Fitzwater Wray. London: Dent, 1974.

Berman, Ronald. *Modernity and Progress: Fitzgerald, Hemingway, Orwell*. Tuscaloosa: University of Alabama Press, 2005.

Braudy, Leo. *From Chivalry to Terrorism: War and the Changing Nature of Masculinity*. New York: Viking, 2005.

Bruccoli, Matthew J. *Some Sort of Epic Grandeur: The Life of F. Scott Fitzgerald*. Second Revised Edition. Columbia: University of South Carolina Press, 2002.

Curry, Steven, and Peter L. Hays. 'Fitzgerald's *Vanity Fair*'. *Fitzgerald/Hemingway Annual 1977*. Ed. Margaret M. Dugan and Richard Lyman. Detroit: Gale, 1977. 63-75.

Eliot, T. S. 'The Waste Land'. *Selected Poems*. New York: Harcourt Brace, 1930. 49-74.

Fitzgerald, F. Scott. *Tender Is the Night*. New York: Scribner's, 1934.

Fussell, Paul. *The Great War and Modern Memory*. New York: Oxford University Press, 1975.

Hynes, Samuel. *The Soldiers' Tale: Bearing Witness to Modern War*. New York: Penguin, 1997.

Keegan, John. *The Face of Battle*. New York: Viking, 1976.

Leese, Peter. *Shell Shock: Traumatic Neurosis and the British Soldiers of the First World War*. London: Palgrave, 2002.

Meredith, James H. 'Fitzgerald and War'. *A Historical Guide to F. Scott Fitzgerald*. Ed. Kirk Curnutt. New York: Oxford University Press, 2004. 163-213.

_____. *Understanding the Literature of World War I*. Westport, CT: Greenwood Press, 2004.

Prigozy, Ruth. 'From Griffith's Girls to *Daddy's Girl*: The Masks of Innocence in *Tender Is the Night*'. *Twentieth Century Literature* 26 (summer 1980): 189-221.

Stendhal. *The Charterhouse of Parma*. 1839. Trans. Richard Howard. New York: Modern Library, 2000.

Stern, Milton R. '*Tender Is the Night* and American History'. *The Cambridge Companion to F. Scott Fitzgerald*. Ed. Ruth Prigozy. Cambridge: Cambridge University Press, 2002. 95-117.

Tate, Trudi. *Modernism, History and the First World War*. Manchester: Manchester University Press, 1998.

Thackeray, William Makepeace. *Vanity Fair: A Novel without a Hero*. 1848. New York: Penguin, 2003.

Van Creveld, Martin. *Technology and War: From 2000 BC to the Present*. New York: Free Press, 1971.

A Stricken Field:
Hemingway, Fitzgerald, and Medievalism During the Thirties_____

Michael Reynolds

The relationship between Ernest Hemingway and Scott Fitzgerald, in both its literary and legendary forms, has been so often revised by memory and desire that we can only speak of probabilities, not certainties. The residual evidence, for the most part now public, is as deceptively simple on its surface as the outside of a telephone interchange box; to sort out the maze of colored wires inside, however, requires the acuity of a neurosurgeon. This metaphor, which holds at almost every level of their relationship, is a particularly apt description of their shared interest in medievalism. Because the story of that interest is not linear, the reader must put the parts together for himself.

Part One: The End of Something

Hemingway and Fitzgerald, we have been told, first met in 1925 in a Paris bar, but both writers were well aware of each other before their first shared drink. During the Chicago summer of 1921, Hemingway read and was influenced by Fitzgerald's *This Side of Paradise*, the structure of which he considered for his own fledgling war-novel in progress.[1] In August, Hadley, his wife to be, cautioned Ernest against structuring his fiction like Scott's college novel, which she found "too patchwork." She reminded Ernest how she had wanted "a long stretch of the same form when Fitzgerald got to pitching from letter to narrator" (*Young Hemingway* 241-242). Three years later on the basis of *In Our Time*, whose author he had not met, Fitzgerald recommended Hemingway to Max Perkins as a potentially rising star.

This now legendary relationship between Hemingway and Fitzgerald, once so filled with humor and camaraderie, reached its nadir early in 1936. That was the year Roosevelt tried to balance the budget of a struggling economy, which immediately got worse; those citizens who had jobs were making thirty percent less money than they had in 1929.[2] It was the year that Margaret Mitchell and William Faulkner published their rather different neo-medieval versions of the defeated South, its lost gallantry and its disabled families.[3] Between January and April of that year, in *Esquire* magazine Scott Fitzgerald published three loosely related essays detailing his fall from grace into spiritual isolation, essays we call *The Crack-Up*.

Writing lyrically, if somewhat vaguely, about his inability to write, Fitzgerald repented of being "a mediocre caretaker" of his own talent, and one who let himself "be snubbed by people" with no more ability or character than himself. He was through with caring about others, he said, for he was no longer able to stand the sight of almost all his former acquaintances, particularly writers. For moral support he had only his childhood dreams of heroic deeds on fields of sport or war (*Crack-Up* 71-73). Somewhat ironically, this first essay appeared in the same issue as Hemingway's "Wings Always over Africa," a natural historian's take on the Italian dead in the Ethiopian War.

When Ernest read Scott's essay, he was unamused but untouched, even though he was, presumably, one of the writers no longer to be tolerated. "Once a fellow writer always a fellow writer," Ernest joked with John Dos Passos, telling him that Max Perkins "says he [Scott] has many imaginary diseases along with, I imagine, some very real liver trouble" (*Selected Letters* 433). But when the second essay, "Pasting It Together," appeared, Hemingway was appalled. Not only was Scott wallowing in self-pitying rhetoric, but he was also referring to Hemingway by implication if not by name. "I saw honest men through moods of suicidal glooms," Fitzgerald wrote, "some of them gave up and died; others adjusted themselves and went on to a larger success than mine" (*Crack-Up* 77). Ernest must have seen allusions to his own "suicidal gloom" during his 1926 divorce after which he had written Scott that he was "all through with the general bumping off phase" (*Selected Letters* 232). Fitzgerald went on to refer to a contemporary who "had been an artistic conscience," and whose "infectious style" he was barely able to avoid imitating (*Crack-Up* 79). Hemingway, who did not want to be remembered as Fitzgerald's artistic conscience, wrote Max Perkins that he "felt awful about Scott," whose public whining he took as the act of a coward. "It is a terrible thing for him to love youth so much that he jumped straight from youth to senility without going through manhood. But it's so damn easy to criticize our friends and I shouldn't write this. I wish we could help him" (*Selected Letters* 437-438). Honest work was the only treatment Hemingway could recommend.

After *The Crack-Up*, there was nothing left to discuss from Hemingway's point of view. In April of 1936, shortly after reading Fitzgerald's third installment in *Esquire*, Ernest completed his own version of the writer in despair, "The Snows of Kilimanjaro," with its now suppressed references to Fitzgerald's admiration of the very rich.

> He remembered poor Scott Fitzgerald and his romantic awe of them and how he had started a story once that began "The very rich are different from you and me." And how some one had said to Scott, yes, they have more money. But that was not humorous to Scott. He thought they were a very glamorous race and when he found they weren't it wrecked him just as much as any other thing that wrecked him. (*CSS* 53)

Although Fitzgerald and his apologists have, at some length, described the unfairness of this comment by the dying narrator of "Snows," we have not seen the story as Hemingway's answer to *The Crack-Up*. Harry Walden berates himself for the same never-dids that Fitzgerald bemoans in his essay. Both are writers of squandered talent, never having written the fiction of which they were capable. True to his early advice to Scott—"use your hurt"—Hemingway compiled a collection of unwritten short stories inside of a short story about a writer who failed his talent by not writing those stories. "Snows of Kilimanjaro" is, among other things, an object lesson to Fitzgerald: here is what he could have done with his hurt.

Although we have no Hemingway letters to Fitzgerald written after *The Crack-Up*, Scott would haunt him to the end of his life and well into ours, as seen in Hemingway's posthumous *A Moveable Feast*. Fitzgerald, who canonized himself as the authority on failure and Ernest the authority on success, either missed the point of their conversations or chose to ignore it. From beginning to end, it was neither success nor failure about which their relationship circled; the focal question was always how does it behoove a writer to behave in our time when the traditional guides—family, church, community, and state—no longer provide convincingly moral imperatives. Refurbished medievalism wasn't the only available answer, but it is a palpable presence for both writers, a presence better understood in a broader cultural context.

Part Two: The Education of Young Men, Sad and Otherwise

In their disparate youths, Hemingway and Fitzgerald absorbed various elements of medievalism from the ambient cultural air of the Midwest, air redolent with the literary deeds of British heroes, for as Spengler suggested and Fitzgerald seems to confirm in *Tender* and *Tycoon* (Moyer), civilization was the tawdry extension of a past culture no longer redeemable, and American civilization, cut off from its cultured British roots, had declined without ever having been a distinct culture.

Despite Mark Twain's attempt to make buffoons of King Arthur's court and to mock the courtly lover, everyone knew, at the turn of the last century, there was not yet an American literature. We remained a country in love with the English past. Tennyson, Scott, Shakespeare, and Chaucer were required high-school reading in any college preparatory curriculum, and Kipling was ubiquitous. In Oak Park schools, Hemingway read *Idylls of the King*, *The Cloister and the Hearth*, *Ivanhoe*, General Prologue to the *Canterbury Tales*, and the Knight's

Tale at least twice. When he was courting his first wife by mail, she referred to him as her "gentil, parfect, knight." In Paris, soon after meeting the Fitzgeralds, the Hemingways were reading and discussing George Moore's *Heloise and Abelard*, a medieval romance that accompanied Hemingway back to Key West and eventually to Cuba (Reynolds, *Reading*). Fitzgerald's medieval reading was at once more structured and perhaps less effective. At Princeton he took the standard regime in British and French literature, but there is little corroborative evidence that it made much of an impression. Fitzgerald regularly flunked or barely passed courses, in part because he seldom attended classes. Almost every year he exceeded his fifty allowed cuts, which forced him to take an extra course the following year. In the fall of 1915, Fitzgerald's sophomore English course included Spencer, Marlowe, Sidney, and Chaucer; in French literature, he studied the Romantic Movement. However, John Peale Bishop and Edmund Wilson were more important intellectual influences than were his academic tutors. His out-of-class reading of British decadents and the Irish generation from the 1890s was probably more formative than any of his class reading except for Keats, whose unrequited, ever young, and undisappointed "Urn" lover becomes one of Scott's stock male characters (Bruccoli 43-79). With Fitzgerald, the question is—almost always—How to Love. With Hemingway, the question is—most frequently—How to Lose. Both questions, as this disjunctive discourse hopes to show, found partial answers in the authors' helter-skelter absorption of medievalism.

Part Three: An Idea Almost as Big as the Ritz

When Woodrow Wilson's Progressive Era went bankrupt in the aftermath of World War One, and Western Europe reeled under a series of self-serving and short-sighted treaties guaranteed to produce another war, and when England's remaining young men sat down to tell sad stories about the demise of empire, and a displaced American summed it all up in a poem called *The Waste Land*, when all of these omens were obvious as chalked messages on the sidewalk, several texts captured the fears of the post-war generation: Sigmund Freud's *Civilization and Its Discontents* (1930); Oswald Spengler's *Decline of the West* (1932, one-volume edition); Matthew Arnold's *Culture and Anarchy* (1932); and Reinhold Niebuhr's *Reflections on the End of an Era* (1934, the same year that Hemingway was writing *Green Hills of Africa* and Fitzgerald published *Tender Is the Night* and four chapters of his medievally set Phillipe novel). Some citizens actually read Spengler and company; most absorbed their fears through the media's discussion; others simply agreed with the titles: civilization was in decline and many were discontented.

That year Hemingway wrote his own epitaph for America mired in the Great Depression: "A country, finally, erodes and the dust blows away, the people all die and none of them were of an importance permanently, except those who practiced the arts, and these now wish to cease their work because it is too lonely, too hard to do, and is not fashionable" (*Green Hills* 109).

Part of the American cultural discontent resulted from the impact of new technology in the home. Parents who had grown up with horse-drawn carriages, gas lighting, live theater, dreamy waltzes, and light opera gave birth to a generation who dated in automobiles, listened to raunchy blues singers on the phonograph, talked for hours on the telephone, watched scantily clad young lovelies at the moving pictures, and found their parents altogether out of date. It was the generation that learned to kiss and smoke from the movies, learned to drink from pocket flasks, and began dancing to a beat their parents did not know.

Simultaneously in America and England, neo-medievalism with its chivalric ideals appeared if not as a counter statement to modern times, at least as an alternative set of values. In England, two Oxford intellectuals came of age whose fiction and non-fiction would reaffirm medieval ideals: C. S. Lewis with his *Narnia* novels and his *Allegory of Love* and Tolkien with his *Hobbit* and his *Lord of the Rings* trilogy. As the Thirties came to a close and the great crusade to free Europe from the fascists began to mount its forces, Lewis argued that: "The medieval ideal taught humility and forbearance to the great warrior because everyone knew by experience how much he needed that lesson. It demanded valor of the urbane and modest man because everyone knew that he was, as likely as not, to be a milksop" (*Living Age* 110). A generation of urbane and modest young men were soon to be taught that forbearance was deadly and humility unbecoming to a warrior; they would leave their names and their bones in Normandy and the Ardennes, across North Africa and the South Pacific.

Publishers' records from the period lend support to Lewis' position that the medieval ideal "was something that needed to be achieved, not something that can be relied on to happen" (*Living Age* 111). Between 1928 and 1937, six editions of Malory's *Morte d'Arthur* and thirty-nine editions of all or part of *Idylls of the King* appeared; fifty-two books on King Arthur and his Knights of the Round Table were written; over one hundred books were published about the Middle Ages. That generation on the edge of what we would call "the last good war" came of age with chivalric ideals close at hand. The same semester that Hitler invaded Poland, Stanford University, in response to "the growing interest in medieval studies," began an experimental curriculum whose core courses included: Chivalry, The Church Fathers, Medieval Mysticism, Medieval Technology, and Medieval Heresies (White 55-57).

Meanwhile in Peoria, Hackensack, and Amarillo, grown men became Knights of Columbus, Knights of Pythias, Knights of Rhodes and Malta, Knights of St. John, Teutonic Knights, and, of course, Knights of Labor. Knighthood was also flourishing in the backwash of the new technology. Popular fiction gave us *Knights of the Air and of the Wing*; *Knights of the Wheel*; *Knights of the Cockpit*. There came *Knights Riding* and *Flying*. Knights were found in every clime: *Knights of the Desert, Knights of the Boomerang, Knights of El Dorado, Knights of the Moon, Knights of the Horseshoe*, of the *Saddle*, and of the *Silver Shield*. These stalwarts rode in various dress: *Knight*

Errant in Chaps, Knight in the Tiger's Skin, Knight in a Slouch Hat, and *Knight in Motley.* They also had a variety of interests, these modern chevaliers: *Knight of the Pen, Knight of the Virgin, Knight of the Road, of the Range, of the Shire,* and *of the Snow Storm.* In February 1937, the medieval comic strip *Prince Valiant* first appeared in American newspapers. Like any idea watered down for mass consumption, this popularization of medieval values was but a shadow of the more rigorous medievalism that Hemingway and Fitzgerald were moving toward throughout the decade. When Fitzgerald's last half-courtly lover, Dick Diver, retreated into obscurity, Scott turned to Phillipe, Count of Darkness, a harder man by far, a man in need of love but with little of the "Urn" lover's patience. Phillipe and later Monroe Stahr both want to control others, manipulate, consolidate the fiefdom at hand. Hemingway's medievally-based characters from the Thirties are hard where Jake Barnes and Frederic Henry were soft. Harry Morgan and Robert Jordan also need a woman, but their mental hardness, worn like armor, keeps them focused on the tasks, the challenge at hand.

Part Four: All Along the Watch Tower

In November of 1934, Fitzgerald, whose first chapter of *Phillipe, Prince of Darkness* had appeared in the previous month's *Redbook*, asked Max Perkins about the setting for Hemingway's next book (*Green Hills of Africa*), "I hope to God," he wrote, "it isn't the crusading story he once had in mind, for I would hate like hell for my 9th century novel to compete with *that*" (*Dear Scott* 212). To understand Fitzgerald's concern, its immediate foreground must be considered.[4]

Between 1922 and 1927, Hemingway's appreciation of medieval cathedrals and their attendant way of life was richly developed in Paris (Notre Dame), during his several visits to Chartres, and during his summers in Spain (Burgos, Zaragoza). In 1927, traveling the "Milky Way" from Paris across the Pyrenees and down the spine of Spain, he followed the medieval pilgrimage route to the Cathedral of St. James at Santiago de Compostela.[5] By 1924, Hemingway was discussing *The Song of Roland* with friends. During the summer of 1925, before his romance with Pauline Pfeiffer led to his Catholic conversion, Hemingway created a Catholic narrator for *The Sun Also Rises*. In that novel of a misdirected pilgrimage, Jake Barnes, the would-be-good Catholic, prays and confesses as he is able.

In April of 1925, just as *The Great Gatsby* was published, Fitzgerald, the lapsed Catholic, first met Hemingway, Catholic to be, in Montparnasse, two months before Ernest and Hadley left for Pamplona and the events that produced *The Sun Also Rises*. From their first encounter, the Hemingway-Fitzgerald relationship was strained by the differing needs of both men. Scott, the failed collegian, was continually trying to educate or improve any man, woman, or child who came within his reach. Hemingway, the high-school graduate sensitive about not having gone to college, resented Scott's instruction. Hemingway, never able to suppress his competitive drive, always wanted to displace Fitzgerald in the marketplace, in the heart of Max Perkins, and finally in the literary history of their time. These conflicting drives are present in the composition history of *The Sun Also Rises*. Fitzgerald's now famous critique of Hemingway's typescript has that genial but slightly superior tone of the upperclassman explaining to the green freshman that certain things simply aren't done by Princeton men. In Hemingway's unpublished preface to the novel, he warns his reader that his generation "that is lost has nothing to do with any Younger generation about whose outcome much literary speculation occurred in times past. This is not a question of what kind of mothers will flappers make or where is bobbed hair leading us."[6] This blatant belittling of Fitzgerald, consigning him early to the museum of ideas, has that bluster of the new kid on the block marking off his turf.

In March of 1926, with his new Scribner's contract in his pocket, Hemingway made notes toward his next novel, which he titled "A New Slain Knight," taken from the medieval poem "The Twa Corbies."

Quoting four lines in his notebook, Hemingway was clearly focused on the bleaker version of the poem where the ravens sit down to feast on the dead knight whose lady has already "tane anither mate." Having by this time thoroughly digested *The Great Gatsby*, Hemingway planned to write a "picaresque novel" about an escaped convict. "It will not be the story of a weak disappointed youth caught and sucked up by fate," he promised himself. "It will be the story of a tough kid lucky for a long time and finally smashed by fate."[7] This less than kind, left-handed judgment of Jimmy Gatz as a "disappointed youth" shows Hemingway chafing from his recent and profitable negotiations with Scribner's, in the same month when Fitzgerald, Scribner's golden boy, was publishing *All the Sad Young Men* (February 1926).

In May 1927, Ernest and his new wife, Pauline Pfeiffer, climbed the battlements of Aigues Morte, the beautifully defended castle built by sainted Louis IX as a gathering and launching point for the ill-fated seventh and eighth crusades. Four months later, he returned to his notes for "A New Slain Knight," no longer the narrative of an escaped criminal, but a father-son story of a divorced revolutionist, which floundered about for twenty chapters before Hemingway abandoned it. But the title and its object, the fallen knight on the field of battle, were with him for the rest of his life. Instead of the "tough kid smashed by fate," Hemingway began a different story about the somewhat passive Frederic Henry who is only slightly smashed and whom no one would call "tough." However, the book's title, *A Farewell to Arms*, came from George Peele's poem which embodies the chivalric ideal once embraced by warrior knights.

In March of 1929, the Hemingways and the Fitzgeralds both, but separately, returned to Paris. Despite Hemingway's request to Max Perkins that he not give Scott the Hemingway address, the two writers did spend time together that year. Both were at a changing point: Fitzgerald had not published a novel in five years and would not for another five; Hemingway, riding a crest, would not publish his next full-fledged novel for another ten years. Each, in his own way that year in

Paris, was searching for a new course amid the floating wreckage of the Twenties, wreckage at home and abroad which between them Scott and Ernest had documented in *Gatsby* and *The Sun*.

It was during that Paris spring of 1929 that Fitzgerald and Hemingway discussed the possibilities of using a medieval setting for their fiction. We can see Hemingway's interest in the crusader bound on a holy mission reflected in his reading at Sylvia Beach's lending library where he borrowed Coulton's *Life in the Middle Ages* and Villehardouin's *Chronicles of Crusaders*, and he apparently bought a copy of Haye's *Ancient and Medieval History* published that year.[8] In 1933, Hemingway invented a medieval quote to title his new collection of short stories.

> Unlike all other forms of lutte or combat the conditions are that the winner shall take nothing; neither his ease, nor his pleasure, nor any notions of glory; nor, if he win far enough, shall there be any reward within himself. (*Winner*, frontis)

A year later, 1934, Fitzgerald began his ninth-century story of Phillipe, Count of Darkness, who returns to the Loire Valley to claim his patrimony in a time of civil chaos. In his notebook Fitzgerald wrote: "Just as Stendhal's portrait of a Byronic man made *Le Rouge et Noir* so couldn't my portrait of Ernest as Phillipe make the real modern man" (*Notebooks* #1034). Twenty years later, Hemingway amused himself and his fourth wife, Mary, by pretending to be a medieval knight as they drove down the Loire Valley (Baker; Stoneback).

Part Five: Closing the Circle

For both Hemingway and Fitzgerald, the love of knights was rooted in *Morte D'Arthur* and *Idylls of the King*, but first and always in Chaucer's Knight who "loved chivalrie, trouthe and honour, freedom and curteisie . . . and though that he were worthy, he was wys, And of his

port as meeke as is a mayde. . . . He was a verray, parfit gentil knight."
With that worthy knight, you may recall, there rode his young squire,
hot and lusty we are told. The beginning and the end, youth and age,
they were, those two pilgrims, not unlike Fitzgerald and Hemingway,
each bound on his own life's journey. If with Fitzgerald the question
most frequently is how to love, or what happened to love, with Hemingway the question becomes how to live and die alone. Fitzgerald
turns outward toward the social world; Hemingway, inward toward the
dark self. These two views are not competitive, but complementary;
one does not have to choose between them. And both views have their
attendant devils.

Hemingway's earliest fictions were about young men trying desperately to please either women or fathers, but he quickly gave up that
theme. The post-1930 Hemingway character is most often focused on
his duty or his profession; for him, it is no longer a question of whether
he will lose: losing is a given, a constant in the equation that he learns
to accept. The variables are how will he lose and on whose terms. Like
Chaucer's aging knight, Hemingway's characters between 1930 and
1950 are battle-scarred veterans, tender towards women when women
are in sight, but relentless in battle; Harry Morgan, Robert Jordan, Colonel Cantwell, Thomas Hudson—each in his own way chivalric—
form a progression as Hemingway experimented with medieval values
in contemporary settings. Harry Morgan, in modern idiom, "does what
a man has to do" to support his family; he lives violently and dies broken, but true to himself. Robert Jordan is much closer to the crusader
knight, fighting not for an ideology but to free a land important to himself. When all is doomed, the attack botched, the bridge probably no
longer important, Jordan, true to his duty, dies in its perfect execution.
With Maria he is the careful, considerate lover so long as she does not
come between him and the bridge. Colonel Cantwell, the warrior at
rest, is the aged courtly lover; Renata, his inviolate princess; Venice,
their romantic domain. If we are less satisfied with Cantwell than with
Jordan, it may be that for Hemingway courtly love does not translate as

well as the crusader's zeal. One might note that the Colonel, like Fitzgerald and Monroe Stahr, is dying from failure of the heart. For
Thomas Hudson, artist and warrior, the question of courtly love is
moot. He tells us that love is past, honor long lost, only duty remains.
"Duty," he says, "you do."

Jordan, Cantwell, and Hudson live and die epitomizing the advice
that Chaucer's knight gives us at the end of his tale:

> Thanne is it wysdom, as it thunketh me,
> To maken vertu of necessitee
>
> . . .
>
> and certeinly a man hath moost honour
> To dyen in his excellence and flour,
>
> . . .
>
> Thanne is it best, as for a worthy fame,
> To dyen whan that he is best of name.

Throughout the Thirties and Forties, Hemingway's characters accept
"necessitee" and die in the "best of name."

If Hemingway chose the crusader as a model, Fitzgerald chose the
squire. The book of courtly love seems written with many of Fitzgerald's unrequited characters in mind, "the young man who performs a
grand deed for the sake of his beloved and who sometimes breaks
against her selfishness" (Bruccoli 35). Keats' "Urn" lover is the prototype: always seeking, never satisfied but never disappointed. Jay
Gatsby, that unlikely courtier whose perfect gestures continually be-
tray him, lives and dies by the rules of courtly love. Dick Diver, meek
perhaps to a fault, self-destructs in his need to be kind, brave, wise, and
loved "if he could fit it in." That Daisy and Nicole never quite match
their courtly lovers' expectations does little to dampen their male ardor.
Phillipe, Count of Darkness, and Monroe Stahr came too late and too
little to balance the cult of love that Fitzgerald embraced.

Part Six: Knights' Gambit

A cold December day, 1929, in the Palace Hotel for consumptives, Montana-Vermala, Switzerland. Looking out across the frozen valley of the Rhone beneath them, they could see the snow fields white in the sun, but here there was no skiing, no drinking, no loud laughter. This was a different winter. Nine days earlier in New York City, madcap Harry Crosby lay down with a lover in a borrowed bed to put a bullet through his lullaby. On Wall Street the bull market had been drawn and quartered. In his chilled room at the Palace, Patrick Murphy, son of Gerald and Sara, was beginning his eight-year journey into death by tuberculosis. Gathered round were his parents, Ernest and Pauline, Scott and Zelda, John and Katy Dos Passos, Dotty Parker and Donald Ogden Stewart: the last time this group would gather.

Ten Decembers later, another field of snow, this time the mountains of Idaho, 1939: Ernest alone in the Sun Valley Lodge for the moderately wealthy. Patrick Murphy is two years dead, having outlived his brother Baoth, dead of meningitis in 1935. In Key West, Pauline has locked and left the Hemingway house, taking their children with her; Ernest's second marriage is finished. Zelda Fitzgerald has found her last home in Highland Hospital for the mentally ill. John Dos Passos and Ernest, having divided over the Spanish Civil War, are no longer speaking. Scott Fitzgerald, with twelve months to live, is in Hollywood planning *The Last Tycoon*. Ernest has written an epigraph for Martha Gellhorn's new novel, an epigraph that claims to be "from a Medieval chronicle." It reads:

> There were young knights among them who had never been present at a stricken field. Some could not look upon it and some could not speak and they held themselves apart from the others who were cutting down the prisoners at my Lord's orders, for the prisoners were a body too numerous to be guarded by those of us who were left. Then Jean de Rye, an aged knight of Burgundy who had been sore wounded in the battle, rode up to the group of young knights and said, "Are ye maidens with your downcast eyes?

Look well upon it. See all of it. Close your eyes to nothing. For a battle is fought to be won. And it is this that happens if you lose." (*Stricken Field*, epigraph)

That's what they all eventually did, lose; some in flames, some forgotten, some lonely. They died by automobile, by failing heart, by shotgun to the forehead. And with them died the last of the nineteenth century, the last literary generation that century coughed up to modern times. That they took with them to the grave their codes of behavior is altogether fitting. What chance would courtly love have in a discourteous age; who among the tabloid generation would value honor or duty? Fitzgerald and Hemingway were children of the last century abandoned into this one, searching for a moral imperative to give guidance. Fitzgerald chose love; Hemingway, duty. That neither choice held back the night is not the fault of the choosers.

From *Zelda and Scott/Scott and Zelda: New Writings on Their Works, Lives, and Times*, edited by Donald R. Noble, pp. 131-145. Copyright © 2005 by Whitston Publishing. Reprinted with permission of Whitston Publishing.

Notes

1. Hadley Richardson to Ernest Hemingway (24 August 1921), Hemingway Collection. John F. Kennedy Library. The war novel was among the manuscripts stolen in the Paris train station in December 1922.

2. *Historical Statistics of the United States*, Bicentennial Edition, Part 1 (Washington, D.C.: Bureau of the Census, 1975) pp. 166-225.

3. *Gone with the Wind* and *Absalom, Absalom!*

4. This essay will not repeat what H. R. Stoneback has already done so well in his forthcoming essay, "A Dark, Ill-Lighted Place: Fitzgerald and Hemingway, Phillipe Count of Darkness and Phillip Counter-Espionage Agent." As usual, Stoneback has opened new country to the trophy hunter. My understanding of Hemingway's use of the pilgrimage in his fiction is indebted to Stoneback's several essays over the last twenty years.

5. Ernest and Pauline spent the month of August at Santiago in 1927, 1929, and 1931.

6. Item 202C, Hemingway Collection, John F. Kennedy Library.

7. Hemingway Notebook dated March 1926, owned once by Toby Bruce and copied in the Baker Collection at Princeton.

8. He also owned a copy of Lecky's *History of European Morals Augustus to Charlemagne* (1869) which he took to Cuba with him in 1940.

Works Cited

Arnold, Matthew. *Culture and Anarchy.* Cambridge: The University Press, 1932.

Baker, Carlos. *Ernest Hemingway, A Life Story.* New York: Scribner's, 1969.

Bruccoli, Matthew J. *Some Sort of Epic Grandeur.* New York: Harcourt Brace, 1981.

Chaucer, Geoffrey. "The General Prologue," and "The Knight's Tale," *The Works of Geoffrey Chaucer.* Edited by F. N. Robinson. 2nd edition. Boston: Houghton Mifflin, 1957.

Fitzgerald, F. Scott. *The Crack-Up.* Edited by Edmund Wilson. New York: New Directions, 1945.

_____. *Dear Scott/Dear Max.* Edited by John Kuehl and Jackson Bryer. London: Cassell, 1971.

_____. *The Great Gatsby.* New York: Scribner's, 1925.

_____. *The Notebooks of F. Scott Fitzgerald.* Edited by Matthew J. Bruccoli. New York: Harcourt Brace, 1978.

_____. *Tender Is the Night.* New York: Scribner's, 1934.

Freud, Sigmund. *Civilization and Its Discontents.* London: Hogarth Press, 1930.

Hemingway, Ernest. *The Complete Short Stories of Ernest Hemingway.* New York: Scribner's, 1987.

_____. *Green Hills of Africa.* New York: Scribner's, 1935.

_____. *Islands in the Stream.* New York: Scribner's, 1970.

_____. *Selected Letters of Ernest Hemingway.* Edited by Carlos Baker. New York: Scribner's, 1981.

_____. *The Sun Also Rises.* New York: Scribner's, 1926.

_____. *Winner Take Nothing.* New York: Scribner's, 1927.

Lewis, C. S. "Importance of an Ideal." *Living Age* (October 1940): 109-111.

Moyer, Kermit. "Fitzgerald's Two Unfinished Novels: The Count and the Tycoon in Spenglerian Perspective." *Contemporary Literature* xv 2 (Spring 1974): 238-256.

Niebuhr, Reinhold. *Reflections on the End of an Era.* New York: Scribner's, 1934.

Reynolds, Michael. *Hemingway: An Annotated Chronology.* Detroit: Omnigraphics, 1991.

_____. *Hemingway's Reading, 1910-1940.* Princeton: Princeton University Press, 1981.

_____. *The Young Hemingway.* New York: Blackwell, 1986.

Spengler, Oswald. *Decline of the West* (one-volume edition). New York: Alfred A. Knopf, 1932.

White, Lynn. "An Undergraduate Curriculum in Medieval Studies." *School and Society* (8 July 1939): 55-57.

Will the Real Pat Hobby Please Stand Up?_____

Milton R. Stern

In the critical activity of rediscovering, reviving, or redressing, there always is at least the faint effluvium of crusade that permeates the proceedings. In the spirit of the campaign, critical affirmations tend to become overstated, and the phenomenon of mild overheating is true of responses to the Pat Hobby stories. The reaction is occasioned by the relative neglect of these vignettes (compared to the attention paid to Fitzgerald's novels and the more familiar short stories) and by the negative responses in many of the reviews that greeted the edition collected in 1962 by Arnold Gingrich from the pages of *Esquire*, where the Hobby stories had appeared in an unbroken monthly series from January 1940 through May 1941.[1]

They "could just have well remained in whatever mellowing archives old *Esquire* magazines are kept in," wrote one reviewer. The stories are "wearying," asserted another. "There's more life and poignancy in the Fitzgerald-Gingrich correspondence that makes up the introduction than in the whole Pat Hobby saga." And a third concluded that the stories are "stiff" and "tiresome. The fact that 21 years have passed before anyone thought it necessary or desirable to collect them is the tipoff."[2]

As everyone knows by now, the Pat Hobby stories are a series of short fictions bordering on sketches, featuring an ignorant, unintelligent, unprincipled, desperate, seedy, little gray has-been of a screenwriter whose life and values illustrate, both sadly and comically, the grubbily materialistic debasement of the human spirit in the gross vulgarity of Hollywood. Pat is a plagiarist and thief. He is an opportunistic blackmailer. He is a parasitic scrounger. He is a rummy and a liar. He is a fumbling womanizer. He is a witless gambler. He is obtuse, unimaginative, stupid, talentless, and abysmally fatuous. In a letter to Gingrich, Fitzgerald called him "a complete rat." He is that. But his wobbly life is such a soup of failure that in its bathetic and sometimes hilarious trickle from soggy misadventure to soggy misadventure, it also evokes disdainful sympathy for poor Pat—one wants to call him "poor Pat."

When Gingrich's edition appeared, with knowing certainty most of the reviewers treated the Pat Hobby series as disguised but transparent versions of Fitzgeraldana, autobiography at one remove. Presumably, the episodes provided a glimpse not only into the oxymoron of Hollywood as a comic Greek tragedy, an Attic abasement of morons, but also of the real Pat Hobby as a Mr. Hyde persona of Francis Scott Key Fitzgerald's worst fears and guilts about himself.

The crusading counterattack is represented fiercely by an essay from a French academic, Elizabeth M. Varet-Ali. It offers the voice of the avenging critic-angel finally, by God, setting things right so that "*The Pat Hobby Stories* will at last be allowed to take the place they deserve. . . ." Varet-Ali sees in the series a coherent thematic center in which the real Pat Hobby is something quite other than an alter-ego for Fitzgerald, and Hollywood is something much more than materials for local color vulgarity. The real Pat Hobby is a metaphor for the tenuousness of American identities; Hollywood is a metaphor for the national fatuities of a culture that determines and dissolves human identity; and the stories are a chronicle of the connection between the culture and the tenuousness of identity: "As a genuine product of the studios . . . [Pat] is at once base agent, pale imitator, and true victim of the system. . . . His outrageous blunders, his incompetence, are the replica of what takes place every day around him." Varet-Ali continues:

> In terms of human appeal, the absence of commentary makes the portrait at times unbearable in its harsh detachment. . . . What the ruthless portrait suggests is that Hollywood, the nation's most popular symbol of Art and Success, perhaps soon its main access to anything like culture, in fact relies on the tritest themes, the grossest illiteracy, and the basest motives and make-believe illusions imaginable. No wonder it can breed (with a few exceptions) such a race of "ignoramuses," "mental cadavers," and "submicroscopic protozoa" . . . and rats as Pat Hobby belongs to.[3]

In these observations, Varet-Ali comes at the center of the stories, though there still remains the question of the extent to which a discoverable central theme is a guarantee of literary quality. Among the commentators, both the attackers and the redeemers have some justice on their side.

The sparse reprinting of the Pat Hobby stories reflects Fitzgerald's mixed legacy of art and fluff and the relative worth of the stories. If we add Bruccoli's 1989 collection of Fitzgerald's short stories to Bryer's meticulous 1982 bibliography of collections, we find that the many compilations of Fitzgerald's selected stories reprint only six of the seventeen Hobby pieces—and this tally does not account for the collections that include *no* Pat Hobby stories.[4] "A Patriotic Short," which Fitzgerald thought too "confused" and among "the less interesting," has been reprinted five times; "Two Old-Timers," which Fitzgerald considered among the "weakest" of the pieces, has been reprinted six times; "'Boil Some Water—Lots of It'" four times; "Teamed with Genius" three times; and "No Harm Trying," which Fitzgerald judged "not up to" the good ones, twice.[5]

However, frequency of reprints, oddly enough, by no means reflects the amount of attention Gingrich's collection attracted when it first appeared. Bryer provides a comprehensive list of reviews of Fitzgerald story collections up to 1982, and they reveal the moment of revival interest in Fitzgerald rather than the literary merit of the fiction, Bryer lists thirty-nine reviews of *Flappers and Philosophers* from 1920 through 1921. Reflecting Fitzgerald's meteoric arrival with *This Side of Paradise* and the impetus of *The Beautiful and Damned*, there were fifty-six reviews of *Tales of the Jazz Age* from 1922 through 1923. Bryer finds forty-two reviews of *All the Sad Young Men* during 1926; and—by the time *Tender Is the Night* was published the falling off had become noticeable—*Taps at Reveille* was greeted with twenty-six reviews in 1935. Thereafter, the number of reviews Bryer found traces a clear pattern of neglect and rediscovery. For 1945, the year that Edmund Wilson began the Fitzgerald revival with his edition of *The*

Crack-Up, Bryer lists two reviews of Dorothy Parker's *Portable F.*
Scott Fitzgerald; and for 1951, the year that Arthur Mizener and
Malcolm Cowley firmly established the revival, Bryer finds only
twelve notices for Cowley's epochal *Stories of F. Scott Fitzgerald*. But
with the revival, the short prose pieces began to acquire greater prominence. Mizener's *Afternoon of an Author* garnered fifty-two reviews in
1957 and 1958 according to Bryer and then a glut on the market at the
turn of the decade diminished reviewer interest in new Fitzgerald titles.
The reissue of *Flappers and Philosophers* received thirty-two notices
in 1959, and in 1960 new reprints of *Taps at Reveille* and *Tales of the
Jazz Age* were given only thirty and twenty-eight reviews, respec-
tively.[6]

Exactly here is where Pat Hobby lifts his stolen hat and bows. In
1962, after a two-year breathing space in the revivalistic glut, reviewers were again interested, for Bryer found *sixty-three* of them paying
heed to Gingrich's edition of the stories, producing the second highest
number of notices for any collection of Fitzgerald's short fiction.[7] And
across the spectrum, the reviews revealed the representative nature of
the Hobby pieces. As in the 1950s the essence of critical response fractured into three clear categories.

There were those who said, "Oh dear, not again. Let Fitzgerald rest.
Is there no end to the same old stuff? He doesn't hold up, his stuff is
dated, its interest is for addicts only." There were those who read admiringly, moved that Fitzgerald remained undimmed by time, shining
as freshly and brightly as ever. Those readers concluded that as the
years go by Fitzgerald emerges more and more compellingly as one of
the classics. A third group felt that in retrospect Fitzgerald's short
pieces are a mixed bag, the newly republished stuff not as good as
his well-known best stories, but many of them quite good indeed. For
all readers, however, there was agreement about the forceful substan-
tive presence of nostalgia, dolor, spree, waste, horror, and regret—
of disintegration—in Fitzgerald's good and very good stories. Evocative of so much reviewer response, in this, as in all ways, the Pat Hobby

stories remain paradigms not of the best, but of the general average of Fitzgerald's short fiction.

Like the ironic contradictions between Fitzgerald's confused legacy of self-evaluation and the editorial selection of Pat Hobby stories, the stories are in no way more representative of the fate of Fitzgerald's short fiction than in the contradiction between popular notice and critical neglect. Gingrich's edition might have generated sixty-three reviews, but, except for a small handful of essays on the Pat Hobby stories, there has been very little notice taken of these pieces, even in books whose central subject matter is that of the Pat Hobby stories: Fitzgerald and Hollywood. One entire book on Fitzgerald's fiction in films and his work in films offers only three short paragraphs on the Pat Hobby stories. John Kuehl's recent book on Fitzgerald's short fiction allows five pages for all seventeen stories, but devotes those pages to a summary of representative plot and characterization and to the point that the style of the stories is that of Fitzgerald the leaver-outer. Bryant Mangum's 1991 book devotes six pages to the Pat Hobby stories, providing intelligent précis and the observation that they share a triangular structure connected by three variously related points: failure, hope of success, and failure. In his study of Fitzgerald in Hollywood, Aaron Latham makes only fleeting mention of two Pat Hobby stories, "Teamed with Genius" and "Mightier Than the Sword," which Fitzgerald thought was one of the two weakest of all the Hobby episodes.[8]

This lukewarm critical response was first articulated by Cowley in his 1951 introduction: "Most of the Hobby stories weren't very good by [Fitzgerald's] own standards, but they caught the Hollywood atmosphere and they also made fun of the author's weaknesses, thereby proving that Fitzgerald hadn't lost his ironic attitude toward himself or his gift of double vision." Perhaps the coexisting tugs toward praise and denial are summed up in two pieces of scholarship of the 1970s. In a periodical piece, John O. Rees argued that Fitzgerald's "fine, undervalued comic gift relaxes occasionally, among too many easy targets here, but it has not deserted him; we see his grotesques in the glaring sunshine of the working day." Fitzgerald's fine touches give us the nuances of authority: "Like Pat himself, his Hollywood has its bizarre authenticity, its small but undeniable share of felt life." And as for style, the "prose is tempered to the macho requirements of the old *Esquire*, but it is not without charm; it bespeaks a departure, as much as a falling-off, from Fitzgerald's earlier lyricism. This style is as supple as ever, and its wry, spare cadences are well suited to the gimcrack world it portrays." And if memory is a theme in all of Fitzgerald's fiction, it is centrally and especially so in the Pat Hobby stories.[9]

Rees's essay sums up the arguments of the defenders as Walter Wells's does those of the detractors:

> *The Pat Hobby Stories* . . . remain the hastily written ephemera of . . . [a still-gifted] craftsman. Few of the stories possess any plot complexity, or demonstrate any compensating subtleties of character, theme, or technique. On the contrary, their narrative technique is occasionally quite clumsy, and their exposition, as in "Putative Father," embarrassingly stilted. Their irony, sole *raison d'être* for a number of the stories, is often heavy-handed; plot structures are forced; and circumstances contrived. . . . The *Stories* are, in short, hurried fictions which bear the scars of deadline.
>
> While grinding out his monthly Pat Hobby submissions to *Esquire*, Fitzgerald was giving artistic priority—and the last of his real talent—to his own Hollywood novel.

Yet, Wells concludes, in their limitations, the Pat Hobby stories reflect essential topics in Fitzgerald's fiction: breakdown of identities, appearance versus reality, and disintegration as the central theme.[10]

Perhaps the Hobby stories might be summed up in an observation that Bruccoli made in the introduction to *The Price Was High* about the stories he collected in that volume: "It is becoming fashionable to claim that Fitzgerald was better as a short story writer than as a novelist. This [is a] truly eccentric notion. . . . Certainly it would be preferable for Fitzgerald to have written another novel instead of the stories collected here."[11]

The zephyrs of controversy still stir occasionally around the matter of literary quality. Is the real Pat Hobby a product of hasty hackwork put together for the money, or is he in fact the vehicle for carefully revised fictions that deserve greater recognition? Here, too, the truth seems to be both. The unhappy facts of the Gingrich-Fitzgerald correspondence make it clear that in their initial composition the stories *were* rushed piecework hastily written for the money. For much of the time that Fitzgerald was writing them he was freelancing at Universal Studios during weekdays. On weekends he wrote stories. Note the proximities of the dates. On September 16, 1939, the first story, "A Man in the Way," came in to *Esquire*. On September 21 Fitzgerald submitted not only a revision of the story but also a second episode, "'Boil Some Water—Lots of It.'" On September 27 he sent the revisions of the second piece, and on October 2 Gingrich received the third Hobby, "Teamed with Genius." On October 6 the revision of "Teamed with Genius" arrived together with a second revision of "'Boil Some Water—Lots of It.'" On October 14 Fitzgerald gave the magazine the fourth and fifth Hobbys, "Pat Hobby's Christmas Wish" (published first, in the January 1, 1940, issue, which appeared in the last week of December as the Christmas issue) and "Pat Hobby's Preview." On October 27 "No Harm Trying" arrived, followed by "Pat Hobby's College Days" on November 8. Five days later, Gingrich received "Pat Hobby's Young Visitor" (published as "Pat Hobby, Putative Father"), and then there was a period of silence during which, Fitzgerald explained, he had "been sick in bed again and gotten way behind."[12] On December 19 he sent in "Two Old-Timers," and on Christmas Day he dispatched "Mightier Than the Sword."

Thereafter, in the new year, there were longer intervals between appearances of the "scenario hack" to whom Fitzgerald was "getting rather attached." On January 8 Fitzgerald sent "A Patriotic Short." On February 6 "Pat Hobby and Orson Welles" arrived, and on Valentine's Day "On the Trail of Pat Hobby." On March 9 Gingrich became privy to "Pat Hobby's Secret," which was followed by "Pat Hobby Does His

Bit" on March 18. On March 28 *Esquire* enjoyed a view of "Homes of the Stars," and in early summer, on June 25, Gingrich had "Fun in an Artist's Studio," the last of Pat Hobby's sad flings.[13]

When one empathetically contemplates this composition schedule and considers that not only was Fitzgerald giving most of his time to Hollywood during the regular workweek but also that he was working as much as he could on *The Last Tycoon*, and that for much of the period his working time was diminished by ill health, the evidence becomes quite clear. Despite somewhat longer interruptions between pieces in 1940, and despite the most affectionate pro-Fitzgerald crusading spirit, one has to conclude that the Pat Hobby stories *were* a job of quick piecework ground out for money.

On the other hand, when one considers that these rushed creations were subjected to revisions and rerevisions and that Fitzgerald tinkered with their arrangement and worried Gingrich about the order of the sequence; when one considers how intensely and nimbly Fitzgerald was able to work when he was writing well; and when one considers Fitzgerald's many heartfelt and verifiable statements in his correspondence about his pride in his professional expertise and his care with his short fiction, it seems equally mandatory to conclude that though the Pat Hobby stories were in fact hastily thrown off, at least in first draft, they were not necessarily therefore all junk.[14]

Fitzgerald was not a double-talker, but he left a double legacy when he evaluated his work as a short-story writer. By the end of the 1930s—he created Pat Hobby in 1939—he was humbled, uncertain, and financially desperate, yet heartbreakingly tenacious about his own sense of his literary worth. That combination brought his judgments to very different conclusions from one day to the next. In his introduction to *The Pat Hobby Stories*, Arnold Gingrich provides material that allows us to reconstruct some of Fitzgerald's fluctuating judgments.

In October 1939 Fitzgerald considered the sixth Hobby story he wrote—published tenth in the series—"No Harm Trying," "not up to the last story ['Pat Hobby's Preview']." He followed "No Harm Trying" with "Pat Hobby's College Days," of which he said, "This is an in and outer, but," justifying its quality, "I think certainly *as good* as the last" (emphasis mine). On Valentine's Day of 1940, Fitzgerald wrote that "Pat Hobby's College Days" "seems the weakest of all to me." Yet in January he had written to Gingrich, "The weakest of the Hobby stories seems to me to have been 'Two Old-Timers' and 'Mightier Than the Sword': If you could hold those out of type for a while I might be able either to improve them later or else send others in their place." Commenting on "On the Trail of Pat Hobby," Fitzgerald wrote, "This is a short, but it seems to me one of the very funniest of all. . . . I think this really has a couple of belly laughs." But in a letter of March 15, Fitzgerald ranked "On the Trail of Pat Hobby" along with "Two Old-Timers," "Pat Hobby's Preview," "Pat Hobby's College Days," "A Patriotic Short," and "Mightier Than the Sword" as "the less interesting of the series." In March he again designated the group as "the least good of the stories."[15]

When he mailed in "Pat Hobby's Secret" (March 1940), he told Gingrich,

> I think this one should go in as early as possible (that is if you agree with me that it is one of the best). The strongest should come first in comedy because once a character is really established as funny everything he does becomes funny. At least it's that way in life.
>
> If you agree then, I hope you have this substituted for any of the earlier stories except . . . ["Pat Hobby and Orson Welles," "No Harm Trying," or "Pat Hobby, Putative Father"]. It is better than any of the others I feel sure.

Fitzgerald's desire to move stories toward the beginning of the series was a reflection of his rankings. He wanted to put the ones he thought best in early. "Don't you think it's one of the best?" he asked Gingrich when he submitted "Homes of the Stars." He asserted that "this is good enough to be shoved ahead of . . . the least good of the stories. This could come after 'Pat Hobby Does His Bit.'"[16]

With "Fun in an Artist's Studio," he sent Gingrich a request to "put it ahead of those I have designated in other letters as being mediocre"; and when he sent in a revision of "A Patriotic Short," he asked Gingrich to "insert it before any others as far as possible." But in July 1940 Fitzgerald wanted to move the previously denigrated "No Harm Trying" to appear immediately after "Pat Hobby Does His Bit" as "next in order of merit." And then, on October 15, he wired Gingrich that his previously highly rated "PATRIOTIC SHORT SO CONFUSED IT WILL STOP INTEREST IN SERIES. . . . CANT YOU SET IT UP AGAIN. . . . YOUR LETTER PROMISED TO HOLD IT OUT." His uneven, oscillating judgments reflected the rush of his production. Fitzgerald worried about the arrangement of the series, but he also became confused about that arrangement and in any event he necessarily was compelled to bow to Gingrich's order of publication. Gingrich, after all, had to plan issues ahead of time with the materials he was certain he had on hand. In the fate of the arrangement, in Fitzgerald's judgments about worth, and in the connection between publication and Fitzgerald's frenzy about money, the Pat Hobby stories are a paradigm of the history of much of Fitzgerald's short fiction.[17]

There is another critical doubleness that makes one conclude "both . . . and" rather than "either . . . or" in considering the quality of the Pat Hobby stories. An absolutely essential yet overlooked critical point is that it makes all the difference in the world if one is reading the Pat Hobby stories as a book or if one is reading any one of the stories as an individual piece.

In the enthusiasm of his introduction to the Pat Hobby stories, Arnold Gingrich exulted in the collection as the first edition of a new Fitzgerald book. He insisted that people would have to recognize that in revising and fussing about the stories, Fitzgerald had created another *book*, one that he thought of as a book and that should be designated a book. Fitzgerald "began thinking of them, after the first three were written, as a collective entity," reconsidering their order and relationship for "the over-all delineation of the character of Pat Hobby."

Although the stories do not constitute a novel, Gingrich admitted, they are, nevertheless, a "full-length portrait" that Fitzgerald "thought of . . . as a comedy." At the lowest ebb of Fitzgerald's fame and reputation, except "for the then current Pat Hobby stories, none of his work was any longer in the public eye," and Fitzgerald cared about their quality: "I can't calm down after a story till I know if it's good or bad."[18]

But the stories are a collection. They are not a fully organized single fiction. They do not maintain the evolutionary development of form or narrative that arises from the organic arrangement of parts in a book. If they are to be seen as what amount to chapters in a book, the Pat Hobby stories, in their relation to each other, offer a series of similar episodes rather than developmental, cumulative organization of shape in one unified incremental structure. For all that he foresaw the possibilities of a book in Pat Hobby, Fitzgerald much more immediately saw his own financial desperation. *Esquire* policy allowed for advances on stories, for the advances cemented a hold on an author, in effect guaranteeing first option on future output. And as his correspondence with Gingrich makes sadly clear, Fitzgerald wanted payment for each story on or before delivery, sometimes even before he wrote it. All he could do was wring his hands and lament the fact that the monthly installments did not appear in an order devoutly to be wished. As he wrote to Gingrich, "It was too bad to begin the Pat Hobby series with that story ['Pat Hobby's Christmas Wish'] because it characterizes him in a rather less sympathetic way than most of the others. Of course he's a complete rat, but it seems to make him a little sinister which he essentially is not. Do you intend to use the other stories in approximately the order in which they were written?"[19]

If they are read as a book, the stories suffer badly from too much repetition in too brief a space (the Gingrich edition contains 158 small pages of large type). In the inescapable need to reintroduce Pat Hobby with each new story, according to the demands of that story as a free-standing individual entity in a monthly magazine that the reader might not have seen before and might not see again, Fitzgerald had to repeat many basic details. Most of the instances in which Pat's identity is created—the fact that, though sadly fallen in the 1930s, in his former estate in the 1920s he had been married three times, had made two to three thousand dollars a week during the heyday of silent films, and had had a uniformed chauffeur; the fact that he is both schlemiel and schlimozzle, a conscienceless but wistful hanger-on at the studios and a fervent worshipper at the Santa Anita track—would have been deleted or revised if Fitzgerald truly had been writing the stories as a book. But when read together in one volume the stories provide justification for commentators who complained of stiffness and tiresomeness in the prose. Just as the calendar of submissions speaks with sad eloquence about the Pat Hobby stories as pieces rushed for the money, so the wearisome repetitiousness, when traced out, becomes undeniably clear. It would be wearisomely repetitious to trace all the wearisome repetitiousness; a brief and incomplete demonstration of only three central details—Pat's age, his salary, and his Hollywood longevity—illustrate the point.

Pat is first introduced as "a man of forty-nine" on page 10. Thereafter, as we proceed through the series we are told that "Pat was forty-nine" (13); that "now he was forty-nine" (21), that Pat's strength was that "of his forty-nine years" (27); that Pat is admonished, "Don't give up at forty-nine" (30); that Pat is a "venerable script-stooge of forty-nine" (52) with "old eyes" (53) and, in fact, "red old eyes" (54); that he sees out of eyes "not so very bloodshot" (62); that Pat has "red-rimmed" eyes (72); that Pat was "a dolorous and precarious forty-nine" (82) and "tightened" his "red-rimmed eyes" (83). "'I'm in my forties,' said Pat, who was forty-nine" and who had "dismal, red-streaked eyes" (93). We are told that Pat's date "would never let those red-rimmed eyes come close" (100); that Pat is "only a writer—at forty-nine" (103) and that the director "glanced into Pat's red-rimmed eyes" (104); that "Pat was forty-nine with red-rimmed eyes" (128); that he was "Pat Hobby, a man of forty-nine" (136), and that "we perceive . . . through the red-rimmed eyes of Pat Hobby" (142) that "a man forty-nine is not considered human" (152).

Similarly, Pat's longevity in Hollywood and the facts of his diminished salary (now $250 to $350 a week) are given again and again by Fitzgerald, and not always consistently from story to story. On page 1 we are told that as a scenarist Pat has "twenty years' experience," and on page 4 he complains about "three-fifty a week, when I used to get two thousand." Thereafter, the reader is informed that Pat "had thirty [screen] credits; he had been in the business, publicity and script-writing, for twenty years" (15). Jack Berners, the producer, will give Pat "two weeks . . . at two-fifty" (19).

"'Two-fifty!' objected Pat. 'Say there was one time you paid me ten times that!'" (19). Fitzgerald continues the point with the information that "Pat had been in Hollywood since he was thirty—now he was forty-nine" (21); that Pat had been "flung" a "timely bone of three weeks at three-fifty" (22); that Pat whines, "I been in the industry fifteen years, Jack. I've got more screen credits than a dog has got fleas" but that nevertheless he will be paid "just what Republic paid you last month—three-fifty a week" (29). Had Orson Welles, "like Pat, been in Hollywood over twenty years? Did he have credits that would knock your eye out? . . ." (41). We are informed that, credits and all, poor Pat is "lucky to get a few weeks at three-fifty" (42); that "ten years ago he had camped beatifically in the range of . . . [three thousand dollars a week]—now he was lucky to get a few weeks at $250" (53); that a producer offers him "four weeks at two-fifty" (59), and that Pat "had collaborated in over two dozen moving picture scripts, most of them, it must be admitted, prior to 1929" (62); that Pat could only hope to be put on a picture "at three-fifty a week" (63), and at work could only complain about "this miserable, uncertain two-fifty a week" (66); that Jack Berners will pay Pat his "last writing price, two-fifty for the week" (87); that, challenged, Pat insists, "I been in this business twenty years" (93), and again, "I been here twenty years" (95); that Pat "was an old timer in pictures; he had once known sumptuous living, but for the past ten years jobs had been hard to hold" (102-3). "You're on the payroll," he's told, "at two-fifty a week for three weeks" (104). He's good for a "small chore . . . one week at two-fifty" (115), even though the studio "had been home to him for twenty years" (121). "Pat Hobby, who was an old-timer," explains that "I been in this business, publicity and script, for twenty years" (143) and that "I got credits going all the way back to 1920" (144), but "I only get three-fifty now" (145). And, as is always the case, "Pat's four weeks at two-fifty would be up tomorrow" (151).

It would be critically stupid to fault Fitzgerald for the reiterations caused by the necessities of writing individual stories as individual stories. But unfortunately, the repetition has a precisely definable cumulative effect concerning the stories as a book. It causes the reader to begin to skim, to skip the familiar background details, and to look for events that make one story's worth of essential background different from another's. That is, the book form nudges readers into a desire for fiction that turns upon event, either in inventiveness of episode or intricacy or twist of plot. And that is the single most unfair demand to level against these stories. They were not written primarily for twist or complexity of plot. Approximately one-third of them ("Pat Hobby's Christmas Wish," "A Man in the Way," "'Boil Some Water—Lots of It,'" "Teamed with Genius," "Pat Hobby's Secret," and "No Harm Trying") depend conventionally on plot, but for the most part the Pat Hobby stories are deliberately free from concoction and commentary; they are episodes, satiric revelations of exactly the subject matter Varet-Ali (and several others) have identified. Approximately one-third of them ("Pat Hobby Does His Bit," "Pat Hobby's Preview," "A Patriotic Short," "Fun in an Artist's Studio," "Two Old-Timers," and "Mightier Than the Sword") seem deceptively plotless, almost like sketches, but they too, like all the stories, are episodes in satiric revelation. Even the O. Henry-like endings that Fitzgerald seems to employ in some of them are reversals not only for exploitation of a popular market (they are, partly, that), but also and—primarily—for the ironic upsetting of

Hobby's hopes as a metaphor for the squandering and debasement of human desires in stupidity, bad luck, and vulgar trivialization.

The "plotless" style of these stories is a foreshadowing of what came to be the norm in popular magazines of literary sophistication such as the *New Yorker* and was a culmination of literary battles that influenced Fitzgerald's style. Fitzgerald had been intrigued by the clever plotting of O. Henry; moreover, he grew up in and was swayed by the traditional chronological development of story by serious artists he admired and respected, Henry James and Edith Wharton. On the other hand, he was enormously impressed and educated by experiments in narrative voice and chronology by those who had learned from and gone beyond James, especially Conrad and Joyce. No history of literary style need be recounted here. The barest outline will suffice to locate the Pat Hobby stories in the context of Fitzgerald as short-story writer.

As coercive, commonly held, unifying beliefs and value systems disintegrated throughout the postmedieval Western world in the more liberal diversities of modern pluralism and secularism, the source of reality shifted for artists from external depiction to internal experience. The merger of mimesis and oneiros gave primacy to setting, action, dialogue, and form itself as signs of interior meaning. Those denominated naturalists insisted on unvitiated, objectively unadorned presentation of everything external to human will and fate as forces meaningless in themselves but totally identifying and deciding human will and fate. The symbolists insisted on uncensored presentation of interior perspective as the determinant of the meaning of the externals. In the modernist merger of realist and romantic, these otherwise opposing parties of metonymy and metaphor met in an insistence on style as truth—dialogue, event, sentence structure, and characterization pared down to and symbolic of the essentials of experience. These essentials are organized not according to conventional and chronological development of narrative progress in the artificially arranged plotting of beginning, middle, and end, of rising action, climax, and falling action, but according to the episodic and epiphanic nature of experience. Probability (within the nature of the experience presented) and irony (in America after the disillusion of the Civil War and increasingly after World War I) replaced coincidence, contrived twist, and dramatic convenience.

The experimental modernists led to the disappearance of the commenting narrator and an entire style of storytelling and form in the triumph of epiphany over traditional plotting of event. In style and narrative event, Flaubert and Chekhov "replaced" Dumas and de Maupassant as progenitors and models. In the American extension in which Fitzgerald was active, Sherwood Anderson and Ernest Hemingway replaced O. Henry and Booth Tarkington. The conquest was completed in the 1920s, and by 1939, when Fitzgerald began composing the Pat Hobby stories, magazines such as *Esquire* indicated the extent to which the effects of the modernist revolution had established the mode of the literary marketplace. Not only because of its marketing attempt at male sophistication but also because of its attempt at *modern* sophistication, *Esquire* cultivated a macho, cosmopolitan, ironic style whose terseness bespoke both aims. With the stripped-down, realistically presented externals in his fiction creating the unstated internals, Hemingway, of course, was *Esquire's* prize stable horse, and his influence on Fitzgerald should be reckoned as part of the magazine's demands in the dynamics of development in Fitzgerald's style. The Runyonesque and Lardneresque nuances of the prose in the Pat Hobby stories are not exclusively attributable to the success enjoyed by Runyon and Lardner in the literary marketplace. Nor are those nuances by any means exclusively attributable to Fitzgerald's deep affection and respect for Ring Lardner. Rather, they must be seen in their fullest context; for Fitzgerald, Hemingway summed up the import of artistic nuances in all the intellectual, experiential—and victorious—reverberations of the serious literary marketplace.

Fitzgerald's letters reveal hard-guy attitudes as well as what their author saw as an invaluable "female" sensibility within himself. In overall tone, however, the letters clearly come from a man who can be tough but not macho, who is romantic but not sentimental, who is vulnerable but courageously perseverant even when cynical. Yet, Fitzgerald's voice tends to change tonally in his letters to Hemingway. It becomes marginally harder, more smart-guy and macho; deeply and subtly Fitzgerald felt a need, conscious or otherwise, to pander to Hemingway. The variation of voice is a revelation of Fitzgerald's sense of subordination to Hemingway, who was a threatening presence in the problematical relationship between the two men. It is sufficient to say that for Fitzgerald, widely and profoundly, consciously and unconsciously, Hemingway summed up an entire chapter of history in the development of Western literature. On a smaller, more conscious, and more immediate level for Fitzgerald, Hemingway summed up success in the modernist modes of the serious literary marketplace; and, on the smallest, most conscious, and most immediate level, Hemingway summed up the stylistic contexts of *Esquire* magazine. The style of the Pat Hobby stories, at the point Fitzgerald's life had reached in 1939, is an eloquent and profound statement of Fitzgerald's sense of place within the history of the literary marketplace.

But the *individual* genius of F. Scott Fitzgerald requires that one define it by historical contexts only very cautiously. In his own prodigious talent Fitzgerald hardly played the sedulous ape. He retained to the end his own distinctive style. It has become a commonplace to assert that *The Great Gatsby* represents Fitzgerald's breakthrough into mastery of modernist economy and dense organization, that *Tender Is the Night* is a relapse into lyricism, and that with *The Last Tycoon* Fitzgerald was regaining the true path that, as he said in his letters, he had found and wished he had stuck to after *The Great Gatsby*. However, Fitzgerald himself felt that *The Great Gatsby* was held together in part by overlapping blankets of prose, and no reader with any sensibility can be unaware of its lyricism. Furthermore, the incredible history of versions and revisions and hopes for further revisions of *Tender Is the Night* invites examinations and explications that reveal the novel to be as fully economical and densely organized as anything Fitzgerald ever wrote. And the prose of *The Last Tycoon* fragment contains passages as lyrically evocative as anything in either *The Great Gatsby* or *Tender Is the Night*. In all three masterpieces there is romantic lyricism as well as the ethic of modernist literary economies.

In sum, the Pat Hobby stories do not mark a "new" style in Fitzgerald. Along with others of his 1930s prose pieces *as well as several stories of the 1920s* they signal the marketplace dominance of Hemingwayesque modernism that always had been *a part* of Fitzgerald's own style. The Pat Hobby stories are a stripping away of evocative lyricism, largely in a diminution of descriptive passages. In the consequent relative bareness of the style lies the reason that as a book *The Pat Hobby Stories* do not quite match the evocative power of the best of the Hollywood novels, Nathanael West's *The Day of the Locust*. From the descriptive full development of several characters to the description of houses, furniture, and the "neon piping" around the Los Angeles canyon rims at sunset, West creates an intensely evocative sense of Southern California *place* as national mortuary of the soul. In the Pat Hobby stories, Fitzgerald limited himself to one *aspect* of his stylistic capacities, not because the subject was Hollywood but because the context was *Esquire*. As *The Last Tycoon* indicates, to the end Fitzgerald remained unbeatable at evocative description and characterization when he created it for a book; had that book been finished it would have been *the* great American Hollywood novel. Fitzgerald set aside his heaviest artillery in writing the Pat Hobby stories because he was writing not a book but one brief short story at a time with *Esquire*'s space restrictions and narrative preferences. Fitzgerald's aim, after all, was to focus each time on one character and one occupation and one constantly ironic fate. It would be unfair and wrong to fault *Esquire*. It did not hurt Fitzgerald's talent and it provided him both a living and an exercise in the current idiom of respected style.

The success of the style depends upon Fitzgerald's control of the bareness. Most of the stories are essentially even in quality, so one may select at random. The very first, "Pat Hobby's Christmas Wish," becomes as good an example as any for a glimpse of the effects of stylistic strength and weakness.

There are moments in this story when the satiric quotidian style of a character's dialogue becomes that of the invisible narrator, and at that instant the writing seems merely cheap and rushed: Pat "had been hired to script an old-fashioned horse-opera and the boys who were 'writing behind him'—that is working over his stuff—said that all of it was old . . ." (2). Given what one expects about the mind of Hopper, a coworker from whom this information extends, "horse-opera" and "boys" are perfectly appropriate. They are working parts of the modernist trick of implying that the reader, without receiving commentary, is at once objectively observing a moment of experience, and yet is also aware of a perception in which the experience exists within the character's texture of sensibility. "Horse-opera" and "boys who were 'writing behind him'" work the difficult trick exactly. But the material within the dashes ("—that is working over his stuff—") belongs entirely to Fitzgerald, who is explaining to the reader, and who, in his persona of totally removed, satiric, olympian narrator, has a very different mode. Given the distancing occasioned by the style's unadorned, uninterpretive terseness of statement, even the echo of a hint of an intruding narrator is obtrusive, and disconcertingly so when suddenly that narrator's idiom is indistinguishable from the patois of the character. The momentary merger unnecessarily raises disruptive questions about the problem of the omniscient narrator as persona.

Yet, in the same passage in which he falters, Fitzgerald also displays superb control over the bare, episodic quality of the story, whose experientially realistic non sequiturs turn out not to be non sequiturs at all, but the introduction of a beautifully crafted development of relation between character and event. While waiting for his new secretary, Pat reminisces with Hopper:

He broke off as the sight of a woman, pad in hand, entering his office down the hall recalled him to the sorry present.

"Gooddorf has me working over the holiday," . . . [Pat] complained bitterly.

"I wouldn't do it."

"I wouldn't either except my four weeks are up next Friday, and if I bucked him he wouldn't extend me."

As he turned away Hopper knew that Pat was not being extended anyhow. He had been hired to script an old-fashioned horse-opera and the boys who were "writing behind him"—that is working over his stuff—said that all of it was old and some didn't make sense.

"I'm Miss Kagle," said Pat's new secretary.

She was about thirty-six, handsome, faded, tired, efficient. She went to the typewriter, examined it, sat down and burst into sobs. (2)

Abjuring embellishment or explanation, Fitzgerald works the very cadences of the sentences to create tone. The intonation of series in the last two sentences suggests the impersonality of a shopping list, reverberating against the impersonality of the situation: the loneliness of those few who have to work on Christmas Eve in the large institution that is indifferent enough about their feelings to require their holiday presence in the first place. Miss Kagle's bursting into sobs is given force by the unexpected connotational difference between the act and the style of its presentation. Except for a very few moments, that kind of swift and sophisticated stylistics characterizes Fitzgerald's expert control of economical bareness throughout the prose in all the Pat Hobby episodes.

In the first seven short sentences of the story, Fitzgerald has managed to convey all of the following: (1) a hard-boiled, satiric tone ("It was Christmas Eve in the studio. By eleven o'clock in the morning, Santa Claus had called on most of the huge population according to each one's deserts. . . . And tips of fifties, tens and fives from producers, directors and writers fell like manna upon the white collar class"

[1]); (2) the fact that Pat Hobby is cheap, broke, penurious, or all three (he had gotten rid of his secretary the day before in order to avoid buying her a Christmas present); (3) the fact that there is an intense caste system in the Hollywood studios, and those who *have* get more than those who haven't; (4) the fact that Hobby knew that the new secretary whose momentary arrival he awaited would not expect a Christmas gift on her first day on the job; (5) the knowledge that Pat Hobby would be self-seeking and unscrupulous; and (6) the knowledge that he is a very low man in the caste system. Moreover, most of the reader's knowledge is implanted by implication in a few selected facts rather than by direct statement from narrator to reader.

Fitzgerald catches the exact gesture in swift strokes. This is the selection of details to signal the end of Miss Kagle's sobbing:

"Nothing's as bad as it seems," . . . [Pat] assured her unconvincingly. "What's it, anyhow? They going to lay you off?"

She shook her head, did a sniffle to end sniffles, and opened her note book. (3)

The sureness of that last sentence provides the concrete visibility of the entire scene. In a similar manner, with three quick half-lines Fitzgerald completes the foundation for the rest of the story:

"Who you been working for?"
She answered between suddenly gritted teeth.
"Mr. Harry Gooddorf." (3)

The skillfully highlighted sobbing and the gritted teeth lay to rest any doubts the reader might have about the conspiracy formed by these two newly met strangers to blackmail Mr. Harry Gooddorf, Pat for a sinecure at the studio, Miss Kagle for revenge against a lover whose mistress and secretary she had been until he noticed that she had begun to age. And, of course, the blackmail "evidence" being mistakenly construed as proof of murder, the conspiracy comes, like all of Pat's shabby hopes, to nothing.

As plot and characterization join through economical sureness of detail, in one hilarious and inventive word Fitzgerald can characterize the pretentiousness and abysmal ignorance of Pat Hobby as Hobby dictates a scene to Miss Kagle:

> "Ext. Long Shot of the Plains," he decreed. "Buck and Mexicans approaching the hyacenda."
> "The what?"
> "The hyacenda—the ranch house." (4)

Had Fitzgerald not been impelled by financial desperation to hurry the job, his revision practices would have maintained all the Hobby tales at that same level of sweet control and invention. But the rush shows occasionally. In "Pat Hobby's Christmas Wish," the word *put* creates just the right touch as Pat says, ". . . if I put 'you rat' the scene won't have any force" (4). But when the same word becomes the author's, there is an instant of stylistic jarring in which Fitzgerald did not yet realize that he had not quite come back up out of the mind of the character into his own: "He substituted the word 'Scram!' for 'Get out of my sight!', he *put* 'Behind the eight-ball' instead of 'In trouble' . . ." (36; emphasis mine).

There are several indications of haste or carelessness here and there. In "Pat Hobby's Christmas Wish," Fitzgerald has Miss Kagle buy Pat a linen handkerchief—on Christmas morning. In "Pat Hobby's Preview," Pat starts out with twelve dollars. Fitzgerald then has Pat buy "a two-dollar shirt changing into it in the shop and a four-dollar Alpine hat—thus halving his bank account which, since the Bank Holiday of 1933, he carried cautiously in his pocket" (97). Within a few paragraphs Fitzgerald has Pat make "a further inroad on his bank account to pay for his six whiskeys"—and then Pat takes his date "into the restaurant for dinner" (98). Even at Great Depression prices and with all his magic, Fitzgerald can't bring that one off. It is also highly improbable that because the star broke his leg an entire crew would leave the location ("Pat Hobby Does His Bit") and unwittingly abandon the unconscious Pat Hobby to lie interminably in the road in the protective casement of iron that the director locked him in as protection in a stunt shot. It is mildly annoying that Fitzgerald's arithmetic is off in figuring the amount that Eric, the script boy, has left after Pat has taken his extortionist cut ("No Harm Trying"). But *most* of these occasional signs of carelessness are minor enough that neither the firmness nor the patina of the stories is destroyed.

What is not salvageable is a regression into the kind of story idea that once might have sold to the *Saturday Evening Post* or *Redbook* or the *Woman's Home Companion* in the happier finances and light-hearted receptivity of an earlier day. Neither the romantically far-fetched nor the absurd in plot material married well with the realistic style of the stripped-down Fitzgerald in the grimmer ambience and marketplace of the late 1930s. Within the irony-seeking modernist insistence on the probabilities of the kind of experience presented, "Pat Hobby, Putative Father" seems silly because of the unlikelihood that any woman who would have married Pat would have gone off to become a great and sacred lady of India, making Hobby's unknown son a Rajah princeling. Similarly, "Pat Hobby's College Days" falls apart because it hinges unbelievably on the inability of Pat's secretary to dispose of his empty booze bottles in any buildings of the studios or in any of the canyons or coastline around Los Angeles. These two tales and the moments in which control of style slips lend an air of shallowness to the stories as a book. Yet, except for those two stories and despite the scarce moments of disrepair, the Pat Hobby series, read as individual pieces at separate sittings, are successful and even glowing works of real craftsmanship whose style and theme meaningfully reflect significant literary and cultural history as well as the development of a component part of Fitzgerald's style.

The one strength of the book format is its intensification of theme.

No observer of style and theme in the Pat Hobby stories can fail to see that the theme is as consistently and coherently organized as the style. In these episodes Fitzgerald continues one of the purposes that is at the center of his better-known and highly admired stories as well as of *The Great Gatsby*, *Tender Is the Night*, and *The Last Tycoon*: an exploration of belonging, of the precariousness of personality in a world in which one's very identity is dependent upon modes of behavior and appearance most shallowly conceived. For Pat, *being* is money, cars, women, recognition; without the kind of success that Hollywood spotlights, one is just one of "them," the dead: the faceless, nameless, envious, worshipful, nonentities jostling restlessly in the darkness beyond the brilliance of the roped-off walkway down which the fluorescent insiders prance on their way to the exclusive preview. From Pat's perspective in a Great Depression world where there were either no jobs or, if one were lucky, wages of eighteen dollars or so for a forty-eight-hour workweek, to work at an ordinary job for ordinary pay in the ordinary world of ordinary days is the obscure and sullen dusk of death. In this urgent sense of being or not being, the frantically unprincipled Pat will do anything to hang on in any way to any scintilla of existence. Every aspect of existence in Hollywood confirms Pat's desperate definition of life and death. And the house of life is the studio.

In "Pat Hobby's Preview," Pat and his date are not allowed into the theater, which is showing a new film whose screen credits, for a rare and blessed change, exhibit Pat's name as one of the writers. Inside are the living luminaries. Outside are the nonexistent. Fitzgerald, without a word of comment, creates the situation and the setting, the watching crowd, as the total source of identity. When the doorkeeper consigns Pat to the oblivion of insignificance by refusing him admittance, Pat's date immediately dissociates herself from him: "Nothing in her face indicated that he was anything but what he thought he was—all alone" (99). Among the insignificant there is neither vivifying solidarity nor solacing identity:

Though the preview crowd had begun to drift away, with that vague American wonder as to why they had come at all, one little cluster found something arresting and poignant in the faces of Pat and Eleanor. They were obviously gate-crashers, outsiders like themselves, but the crowd resented the temerity of their effort to get in—a temerity which the crowd did not share. Little jeering jests were audible. (100)

But then, because the movie is so rotten that his cowriter doesn't want his name on it, his collaborator strides out of the theater and in angry, condescending disgust gives Pat his tickets. In the obtuse and callous gracelessness that characterizes Hollywood and for which Pat is the paradigm, Hobby is perfectly happy to enter, even this way, into the region of the blessed:

> He seized Eleanor's elbow in a firm grasp and steered her triumphantly towards the door:
> "Cheer up, baby. That's the way it is. You see?" (101)

As one of the best and funniest of the stories, "Pat Hobby and Orson Welles" brilliantly exploits every detail of a slapstick situation to indicate why the real Pat Hobby, ineffectively predatory, totally insensitive, and graceless Pat Hobby, is also poor Pat Hobby. The archetypal has-been, Pat forlornly clings to a bygone identity from the days of the silents, using his cachet from other days to buy a bit of time and space among the living. As long as he was still recognized by the guards and allowed to enter the studios (admission and exclusion are constant motifs in these stories), he *belonged*, even if only as a shadowy scrounger. But a new ukase from the gods has wiped out what is left of Pat's capital. Again and again the Pat Hobby stories become translations into a breezy American idiom and Hollywood locale of Kafka's *The Castle*. New guards are posted at all the studio gates to remedy lax admissions practices. Everyone will need a valid pass.

The guards humiliate Pat and condemn him by denying his craved identity: no pass, no membership. Hysterically he tries to use his contacts in the studio hierarchy to secure a pass for readmission, but Pat remains in the commoner's outer darkness: "On the third day he was frantic with gloom. He had sent note after note to Jack Berners [a sympathetic producer] and even asked Louie [the studio bookie] to intercede—now word came that Jack had left town. There were so few friends left. Desolate, he stood in front of the automobile gate with a crowd of staring children, feeling that he had reached the end at last" (44).

Through a lucky near-accident at the gate, Pat shares a ride with Mr. Marcus in his limousine. Mr. Marcus, God (the ultimate financial power) in the studio, recognizes Pat from the old days and the two men reveal a mutual fear of change, both of them reactionaries who find their security in very different levels of the status quo. Pat has felt a displacing threat in the looming of newness associated with the advent of l'enfant terrible, Orson Welles:

> "Who's this Welles?" Pat [had] asked of Louie, the studio bookie. "Every time I pick up a paper they got about this Welles."
> "You know, he's that beard," explained Louie. (41)

In the Welles-less security of the limousine and the old times, Pat and Marcus sentimentalize about the superiority of the simple life: "'That's what I'd like,' said Mr. Marcus gloomily. 'A farm—with chickens. Maybe a little nine-hole course. Not even a stock ticker'" (46). But Pat is not talking nine-hole pastoralism. In his elemental need for a pass that will readmit him to the heavenly castle and permit him to live, he feels his very life threatened by the inexorable march of progress. Whatever function the likes of Pat Hobby might pretend to in the industry, the likes of Orson Welles would find no place for it:

> "Mr. Marcus," he said so sincerely that his voice trembled, "I wouldn't be surprised if Orson Welles is the biggest menace that's come to Hollywood for years. He gets a hundred and fifty grand a picture and I wouldn't

be surprised if he was so radical that you had to have all new equipment and start all over again like you did with sound in 1928."

"Oh my God!" groaned Mr. Marcus.

"And me," said Pat, "all I want is a pass and no money—to leave things as they are."

Mr. Marcus reached for his card case. (47)

Orson Welles never enters the story in person. He is a menacing background presence in Pat's preposterously reactionary sense of things:

> At this studio . . . [Pat] never felt unemployed—in recent times of stress he had eaten property food on its stages—half a cold lobster during a scene from *The Divine Miss Carstairs*; he had often slept on the sets and last winter made use of a Chesterfield overcoat from the costume department. Orson Welles had no business edging him out of this. Orson Welles belonged with the rest of the snobs back in New York. (44)

Quickly Pat becomes a butt of jokes. With winks and nudges among themselves, the lower castes within the gates begin to call Pat "Orson," a development in which "for the first time in his life . . . [Pat] began to feel a loss of identity" (47). Fitzgerald makes the issue focal: "Now to lose one's identity is a careless thing in any case. But to lose it to an enemy, or at least to one who has become scapegoat for our misfortunes—that is a hardship" (47-48). In the ultimate practical joke, Jeff Boldoni, the makeup man, convinces Pat that he really does look like Orson Welles, and to prove it, if Pat will allow Boldoni to fashion a Wellesian "muff" on Pat's face, Boldoni will lend him the "ten smackers" (49) for which seedy, needy Pat yearns. Pat does not suspect that the beard can be removed only with a thorough soaking. Jeff offers to drive Pat to a shooting set where bearded men are needed and slyly places a sign reading ORSON WELLES in the windshield as Pat rides in the back seat. Jeff then proceeds to drive Pat all over the lot as people gawk. Perceiving the slowly oncoming automobile, an elderly man in an obviously important group falls to the sidewalk:

> "My God, did you see that?" exclaimed Jeff. "That was Mr. Marcus."
>
> He came to a stop. An excited man ran up and put his head in the car window.
>
> "Mr. Welles, our Mr. Marcus has had a heart attack. Can we use your car to get him to the infirmary?" (51)

In the spacious pecking order of Hollywood success, "those few who decide things are happy in their work and sure that they are worthy of their hire—the rest live in a mist of doubt as to when their vast inadequacy will be disclosed" (47). Confronted with merely himself as *the* New World identity on the golden throne, the poor real Pat Hobby breaks under the burden. The mighty Orson can fell both high and low, but Pat bolts from the car, rushes from the lot, flees *out* through the gates, and throws himself into Mario's bar, where "three extras with beards stood at the rail" and where Pat can exercise his belonging and his "simple life" at the only level he can manage any longer:

> With a trembling hand he took the hard-earned ten dollar bill from his pocket.
>
> "Set 'em up," he cried hoarsely. "Every muff has a drink on me." (51)

Taken together, the stories are compounded of hints about the problematic, unstable, and platitudinous nature of identity precariously based upon the fatuous surfaces that debase all possibilities of being to showbiz clichés. In "Pat Hobby, Putative Father," when Pat bids goodbye to his son, about whom he really feels and knows nothing except that the young man might be a source of income, "he turned away—feeling like—like Stella Dallas" (69). As in "Pat Hobby Does His Bit," he cannot be said to have profound feelings, and his sense of self arises from the vulgar sentimentality factory: ". . . working or not Pat liked to pass his days in or near a studio. He had reached a dolorous and precarious forty-nine with nothing else to do" (82). His pride, any essential independent self, is gone; in "Pat Hobby's Preview," Pat eats insults with neither resentment nor regret just as long as for a moment it can "be like old times walking with a cute little blonde past the staring crowds on the sidewalk" (96). All he needs is the artificial inflation, no matter how temporary, that a job at a studio gives him. In "No Harm Trying," even the "prospect of a job. . . . anesthetized the crumbled, struggling remnants of his manhood, and inoculated him instead with a bland, easy-going confidence. The set speeches and attitudes of success returned to him" (103).

His criterion for being remains one of belonging to the charmed circle of those who lunched with the president and who had swimming pools. In "A Patriotic Short," what he remembers as the sign of his own humanity was "how he had arrived at the studio in his car driven by a Filipino in uniform; the deferential bow of the guard at the gate which had admitted car and all to the lot, his ascent to that long lost office which had a room for the secretary and was really a director's office . . ." (116-17). We find, when "On the Trail of Pat Hobby," that, shallow to the core, the real Pat Hobby in his decay has nothing but unreality. All that's left as his "destination, his refuge, was the studio, where he was not employed but which had been home to him for twenty years" (121). Poor Pat Hobby because the residual precipitate of the phony is the real Pat Hobby, and that, for Fitzgerald, is the pity and the terror. Americans have lost America by identifying it with everything that Hollywood is and spawns, and thereby have lost themselves.

Consequently, neither Fitzgerald nor the Pat Hobby stories conveniently single out the executives as villains. Some are crass and vulgar and stupid, but then so is low-man Pat and so are the crowds beyond the velvet ropes. The moving picture is not one in which greedy manipulators exploit the long-suffering, resistant, producing masses, but one in which manipulator, mass, and all are joined in a national, symbiotic, and ugly dissolution of humanly meaningful culture. In fact, some of those on top are people of superior sensibility. If, as in "Pat Hobby's Secret," "perversely Pat Hobby's sense of justice was with the producer, not the writer" (53), F. Scott Fitzgerald also found that often the Monroe Stahrs were superior to the people who worked for them. And on a lower level in the Pat Hobby stories, producers Harry Gooddorf, Jack Berners, and Carl Le Vigne are characters endowed by their sympathetic creator with patience, forgiveness, sympathy, and intelligence.

Like Fitzgerald's problematic sympathies, an evaluation of the Hobby stories requires a divided allegiance. "Pat Hobby, Putative Father" and "Pat Hobby's College Days" would be best removed, and there is residual foolishness in the idea that anyone vaguely resembling Pat Hobby, even at the height of his career, would have been chosen by the moguls to represent the writers and take the place of "Doug" Fairbanks at a luncheon with the president of the United States ("A Patriotic Short")—unless one sees this story as a paradigmatic condensation of the collective theme of all of them. But gems such as "Two Old-Timers," "Pat Hobby's Christmas Wish," "No Harm Trying," "Fun in an Artist's Studio," and "On the Trail of Pat Hobby" survive the collateral irritations of some of the book around them. The more the Pat Hobby stories are reread, the more professionally effective their hard-boiled style becomes.

Whatever the mixture of ingredients that produced Fitzgerald's evaluation at any given time, since his death his pronouncements about his work have left a double critical heritage to all commentators, among whom the unwise choose one legacy over another. The complexity and changefulness of his assessments of his self and his short stories were expressed in letters and essays; they have been cited so variously and quoted so frequently elsewhere in this volume and in all the critical literature that here they only need be summarized.[20] They are especially applicable to the short stories, and most especially to the late writings among which the Pat Hobby stories take their place.

Legacy One: Fitzgerald had contempt for his short stories—they were "trash," a "poor old debauched form" he had "grown to hate";

writing stories only for the money, he was an "old whore" who got "$4000 a screw . . . because she's mastered the forty positions," as he told Hemingway; he stripped the stories of good prose that he then used for his novels, which he considered the true art form and his real forte; he wrote stories in haste, his repetitive activity and formulaic product both lubricated by drink. All of this was true of some of the stories.

Legacy Two: No matter how cheap the story or its purpose, Fitzgerald brought to it, at a very high price of talent, the extra touch of his commitment and intelligence; he always tried for "something new . . . in substance," as he wrote to his agent, Harold Ober; he took pride in many of his stories and, knowing that they were too good for the mass-circulation outlets that rejected some of the best of them, he wrote them anyhow and sold them for small payment to appreciative magazines; he revised and rerevised even the least of his stories, protesting angrily that you can't write a saleable story—at least not for George Horace Lorimer's *Saturday Evening Post*—on the bottle; he was a veteran who took a true professional's pride in his professionalism. All of this legacy was true, too, and more true than the first.

Some of the Pat Hobby stories belong more to the truth of one legacy, some belong more to the other. Most of them, in very uneven proportion of mix, belong to both, and in this too they are paradigmatic. In his mood swings, all his professional life Fitzgerald further dichotomized art and trash into failure and success, another double complex that has had its effect on all commentators. Essentially, he saw two groups of values and identities. One: commercial success, pandering, trash, the short story, and, most of all, Hollywood bed down together in the exciting palace of contemporary glitz, fame, and quick disintegration. Two: commercial failure, integrity, art, and the novel wander hand in hand in the desert of neglect toward an Elysian oasis of immortal reputation. And, in fact, the statistics generated by Fitzgerald's sales and income over the years support his sense of things, statistics supplied and discussed enough by several scholars that, like Fitzgerald's self-assessments, they need not be repeated and developed here.[21] It is sufficient to assert that like his legacies of self-evaluation, each of his categories of success and failure was more applicable to some of his writings than to others. Some of his fictions *are* trashy. Some are immortal. There are trashy moments and there are fine touches in almost everything he wrote. It's a matter of preponderance.

Preponderantly (despite the fact that it is supposed to be fun to kick scholar-critics), scholar-critics—as distinct from reviewers through the 1940s—generously have sought the fine touches. Consequently, the academic critical commentary on Fitzgerald's short fiction, especially the lesser-known variety, tends to be based on benevolence and appreciation resulting in the assertion that the stories deserve more and better attention than they have received.[22] But the impulse involves more than generosity of critical spirit. It involves tidying up in the house of literary history. All scholars, teachers, editors, and readers who are entranced by the glowing achievement of Fitzgerald's lovely masterpieces wish to solidify Fitzgerald's immortality once and for all and tie up the loose ends. But this just proclivity of scholarship can sometimes lead to an over-redress of balances, an impulse that becomes most noticeable in attempts to justify some of Fitzgerald's early stories that were mostly tinsel, such as "The Offshore Pirate" (1920), and to claim for the Pat Hobby stories (which by and large but not unexceptionably are far superior to Fitzgerald's early fluff) the major coherence of an extended work of fiction.

The deep itch in literary commentators to complete unfinished business by making another Fitzgerald volume, of which *The Pat Hobby Stories* is symptomatic, is one more of Fitzgerald's peculiar legacies. He left a codicil in literary history that what is arguably his richest book, *Tender Is the Night*, be reissued in a new form that revises the shape from a beginning in media res to a straight chronological development of narrative. He left it as a book waiting to be done.[23] But he died too soon and in an impotent relationship with publishers. Furthermore, he left the tantalizingly unfinished chunk of what now can be only the eternal promise of a magnificent novel in the fragment of *The Last Tycoon*, another book waiting to be done. Moreover, in groups of short fictions such as the Pat Hobby stories and the Basil and Josephine stories, he left obvious and tempting material for volumes waiting to be compiled to supplement the four collections of short stories issued in his lifetime. Consequently, makers of posthumous Fitzgerald volumes are psychologically canted to see them as important literary stocktaking, a compensation for neglect and fate, a tying together and summing up that Fitzgerald should have and would have done but was never able to do. Thus, when Malcolm Cowley wrote one of the best summations of the author ever written, his lovely introduction to the 1951 edition of *The Stories of F. Scott Fitzgerald*, lifting the Fitzgerald revival into orbit, the very title suggested a completion. The words "*A Selection*" were reserved for the subtitle, and in his final paragraph Cowley as much as stated that the volume was a summing up. The stories "speak for the author; and taken together they form a sort of journal of his whole career." Then, in 1957, when Arthur Mizener fashioned a volume of Fitzgerald's uncollected stories and essays in *Afternoon of an Author*, he offered the collection as a partial summation because at that time he thought it "probable that a representative selection of the forty-nine stories Fitzgerald wrote between his last collection of stories in 1935 and his death in 1940 will never be made into a book."[74]

When Gingrich published *The Pat Hobby Stories*, he wrote that the "book's seventeen stories, comprising [*sic*] the entire Pat Hobby sequence, bridge the last major gap in the collected writings of F. Scott Fitzgerald," and, "with this volume, . . . the Fitzgerald cast of characters is at last complete." However, in 1965 a last "last major gap in the collected writings of F. Scott Fitzgerald" was filled by John Kuehl, followed by the filling of a last, last "last major gap" by Kuehl and Jackson R. Bryer in 1973. A year later this last, last last was followed by a last, last, last last by Matthew Bruccoli and Scottie Fitzgerald Smith, in which Smith announced that "this is the last book which will ever be published devoted to previously uncollected writings of my parents."

Thereupon, Bruccoli almost immediately published a last, last, last, last last, whose subtitle was *The Last Uncollected Stories of F. Scott Fitzgerald*. In his introduction, Bruccoli accounts for the accumulation of volumes, in which (at last) all but eight of Fitzgerald's 164 published stories appear. Those eight "remain uncollected because Scottie Fitzgerald Smith feels that they are so far below her father's standards that they should be left in oblivion."[25]

Clearly, there are lasts and lasts. In 1982, in his introduction to *The Short Stories of F. Scott Fitzgerald*, Bryer noted that "F. Scott Fitzgerald wrote 178 short stories; 146 of them were published during his lifetime; 18 have been published since his death [accounting for Bruccoli's figure of 164 published stories]; 14 remain unpublished."[26] Bryer's figures suggest that there are still six to go beyond the eight that Mrs. Smith felt "should be left in oblivion." Fitzgerald's daughter is dead, and those remaining fourteen still generate an urge toward the last, last, last, last, last, last, posthumous tidying up and putting in place.

The implications herein for final summations were in part realized by yet another selection when, in 1989, Bruccoli published *The Short Stories of F. Scott Fitzgerald*, whose title, so very much like Cowley's, suggests a final totality. The volume comes full circle in intent to what Cowley began in 1951: the overall summary representation of the best of Fitzgerald's short fiction. Cowley had included two Pat Hobby stories, Bruccoli but one. The production of finalizations and summary overviews indicates that despite Mizener's plaint about the collection of Fitzgerald's last forty-nine short stories, and despite Smith's reservations about eight of her father's stories, one need only hang on long enough before there are the full volumes of *The Complete Stories of F. Scott Fitzgerald*. A remaining question about future volumes of selections is how many Pat Hobby stories each will include.

The placement of the Pat Hobby stories in these legacies of editorial housekeeping and Fitzgerald's shifting, revisions, and evaluations can be approached within the context of the evolution of recognition of the stories. That context and the legacies are the explanatory framework for the reason that the Pat Hobby stories have been written about so sparsely. Some of them are first-rate, but, though good, many are less than distinguished; the "neglect" of commentators has been a reflection of the inexorable judgment of time; though there is something to say about any of them and much to say about some of them, there is the richness of the literary masterpiece in none of them. That context and the legacies are also the explanatory framework for the reason that we come back to them now. As truly good professional writing, the best of them offer model examples of the stylistic modulation in Fitzgerald's prose; as such, they can accommodate more attention than they have received.

Poor Pat, the hack, the rat, one wants to say. What the stories lack in richness and complexity makes it easy to sum up the red-eyed has-been. But poor Fitzgerald, the overburdened genius, both hack and stunning writer—that is another story and one not easy to sum up. Whatever one wants to say on the one hand requires an immediate "BUT" and a complicating opposite on the other. So, too, one wants to say that the Pat Hobby stories are undeveloped BUT that they have force; that many are ephemera BUT some of them most surely will last; that they are not short prose fiction masterpieces BUT that several of them are beautifully wrought successes. If collectively they fall short of greatness, they are the shortfalls of a writer of greatness, and that makes all the difference. The real Pat Hobby might be two-dimensional, but he sticks in the mind. He remains as a bleak yet comic vision of what all of America's most notable Hollywood fiction has conjured up, a specter of the possibility of soulless national culture and identity-destroying vulgarity that the most eminent American literature has brooded upon from the beginning. The balding, pathetic, funny, awful, little gray rat with a "purr" of alcohol on his breath will be around. Although only a few scraps of attention have been thrown to him, he won't go away.

Notes

1. F. Scott Fitzgerald, *The Pat Hobby Stories*. All subsequent page references to the Pat Hobby stories are to this edition and will appear parenthetically in the text.

2. Ray Lewis White, "The Pat Hobby Stories: A File of Reviews," 178-79.

3. Elizabeth M. Varet-Ali, "The Unfortunate Fate of Seventeen Fitzgerald 'Originals': Toward a Reading of *The Pat Hobby Stories* 'On Their Own Merits Completely,'" 87, 98-99, 105, 107-8. The French journal in which this essay appears contains sentences that demand some study and repunctuation before they make clear sense. (I have quietly made a few minor corrections in the material I quote.) Also, the article contains errors in reference and citation. Nevertheless, it is a lively and intelligent attempt to destroy the myth that Fitzgerald was *manqué* and *épuisé* as a writer by the time he wrote the Pat Hobby stories.

4. Matthew J. Bruccoli, ed., *The Short Stories of F. Scott Fitzgerald: A New Collection*; Jackson R. Bryer, ed., *The Short Stories of F. Scott Fitzgerald: New Approaches in Criticism*, 304-7.

5. For reprintings of the Pat Hobby stories through 1982, see Jackson R. Bryer, "The Short Stories of F. Scott Fitzgerald: A Checklist of Criticism," especially part 1 (304-7) and part 7 (348-77). Since 1982, "'Boil Some Water—Lots of It'" has been reprinted in Bruccoli, ed., *Short Stories*.

6. Bryer, ed., *Short Stories of F. Scott Fitzgerald*, 323-47.

7. Bryer lists only Matthew J. Bruccoli, ed., *The Price Was High: The Last Uncollected Stories of F. Scott Fitzgerald*, as receiving more reviews (sixty-seven in 1978-1979) during this period of revival and literary housekeeping. John Kuehl, ed., *The Apprentice Fiction of F. Scott Fitzgerald: 1909-1917*, received twenty-three notices in 1965-1966; and Bryer finds thirty-eight notices for *The Basil and Josephine Stories*, by F. Scott Fitzgerald, in 1973-1974, when *Bits of Paradise: 21 Uncollected Stories by F. Scott and Zelda Fitzgerald* received twenty-seven.

8. Gene D. Phillips, S.J., *Fiction, Film, and F. Scott Fitzgerald*, 146-47; John Kuehl, *F. Scott Fitzgerald: A Study of the Short Fiction*, 117-22; Bryant Mangum, *A Fortune Yet: Money in the Art of F. Scott Fitzgerald's Short Stories*, 163-71; Aaron Latham, *Crazy Sundays: F. Scott Fitzgerald in Hollywood*, 66, 184-85. In addition to the essays on Fitzgerald and the movies in Bryer, ed., *Short Stories of F. Scott Fitzgerald* (especially Robert A. Martin, "Hollywood in Fitzgerald: After Paradise"), see also DeWitt Bodeen, "F. Scott Fitzgerald and Films."

9. F. Scott Fitzgerald, *The Stories of F. Scott Fitzgerald*, xxiv; John O. Rees, "Fitzgerald's Pat Hobby Stories," 555, 556, 558.

10. Walter Wells, *Tycoons and Locusts: A Regional Look at Hollywood Fiction of the 1930s*, 104, 121, and passim.

11. Bruccoli, ed., *Price Was High*, xx.

12. Arnold Gingrich, "Introduction," xv.

13. Gingrich, "Introduction," xi. All dates are furnished by Gingrich.

14. Although neither the manuscripts nor the revised typescripts of the Pat Hobby stories are available, the nine pages of Fitzgerald's notes on them reproduced by Matthew J. Bruccoli, ed., in *F. Scott Fitzgerald: Manuscripts*, Vol. VI, Part 3, 451-59, indicate Fitzgerald's usual plotting, planning, and rethinking.

15. Matthew J. Bruccoli and Margaret M. Duggan, eds., *Correspondence of F. Scott Fitzgerald*, 589-90; Gingrich, "Introduction," xiv, xvi, xvii, xviii.

16. Gingrich, "Introduction," xvii-xviii; Bruccoli and Duggan, eds., *Correspondence*, 593.

17. Bruccoli and Duggan, eds., *Correspondence*, 593, 602-9; Gingrich, "Introduction," xx.

18. Gingrich, "Introduction," ix, x, xi.

19. Gingrich, "Introduction," xv.

20. In addition to the introduction and other essays in this volume, see the introductions to Fitzgerald, *Stories of F. Scott Fitzgerald*; F. Scott Fitzgerald, *Afternoon of an Author: A Selection of Uncollected Stories and Essays*; Fitzgerald, *Pat Hobby*; Fitzgerald, *Basil and Josephine*; Fitzgerald and Fitzgerald, *Bits of Paradise*; Bruccoli, ed., *Price Was High*; Bryer, ed., *Short Stories of F. Scott Fitzgerald*; Bruccoli, ed., *Short Stories*. Kuehl, ed., *Apprentice Fiction*, is devoted to the themes that appear in all of Fitzgerald's fictions, long or short, and does not discuss Fitzgerald's attitudes toward writing short fiction. Four book-length studies of Fitzgerald's short fiction touch on the topic throughout: John A. Higgins's *F. Scott Fitzgerald: A Study of the Stories*, a helpful series of story-by-story statements about the Pat Hobby episodes; Alice Hall Petry, *Fitzgerald's Craft of Short Fiction: The Collected Stories—1920-1935*, a bright study that discusses the four volumes of short stories published during Fitzgerald's lifetime and therefore does not include the Pat Hobby stories; John Kuehl's very useful and informative *Fitzgerald: Study of the Short Fiction*; and Bryant Mangum's thoughtful *A Fortune Yet. Most essays on the short stories* also repeat self-evaluative quotations from Fitzgerald.

21. A study of the categories at work throughout Fitzgerald's short fiction, Kuehl's *Fitzgerald: Study of the Short Fiction* offers a handy summary overview of the facts and figures of Fitzgerald's productivity and of his financial success and failure (3-8 and passim). See also Bryer's introduction to *Short Stories of F. Scott Fitzgerald*, xi-xiv and passim; and Bruccoli's introduction to *Price Was High* (passim). There are also materials on the topic in the various biographies and in specialized periodical studies, especially the *Fitzgerald/Hemingway Annual*. The most productive suppliers of the facts and figures are Bruccoli and Bryer, who have made references readily available for Fitzgerald studies in specialized bibliographies.

22. Bryer's introduction to *Short Stories of F. Scott Fitzgerald* is an angry and eloquent demand on behalf of Fitzgerald's poor ghost. And one of the few essays devoted entirely to the Pat Hobby stories asserts that Fitzgerald's "sardonic picture of a worn-out screen writer deserves to be better known" (John O. Rees, "Fitzgerald's Pat Hobby Stories," 553). The essay is a sane summary and appreciation of the stories.

23. In 1951, Malcolm Cowley prepared a revised version, which generally became available in *Three Novels of F. Scott Fitzgerald*. However, a fully corrected "received" edition of the revised version is yet to be published.

24. Fitzgerald, *Stories of F. Scott Fitzgerald*, xxv; Fitzgerald, *Afternoon of an Author*, 7.

25. Gingrich, "Introduction," ix, xxiii; Kuehl, ed., *Apprentice Fiction*; Fitzgerald, *Basil and Josephine*; Fitzgerald and Fitzgerald, *Bits of Paradise*, 1; Bruccoli, ed., *Price Was High*, xi-xii.

26. Bryer, ed., *Short Stories of F. Scott Fitzgerald*, xi.

Works Cited

Bodeen, DeWitt. "F. Scott Fitzgerald and Films." *Films in Review* 28 (1977): 285-94.

Bruccoli, Matthew J., ed. *F. Scott Fitzgerald: Manuscripts, Vol. VI, Part 3*. New York: Garland, 1991.

_____, ed. *The Price Was High: The Last Uncollected Stories of F. Scott Fitzgerald*. New York: Harcourt Brace Jovanovich, 1979.

_____, ed. *The Short Stories of F. Scott Fitzgerald: A New Collection*. New York: Charles Scribner's Sons, 1989.

_____, and Margaret M. Duggan, eds., with the assistance of Susan Walker. *Correspondence of F. Scott Fitzgerald*. New York: Random House, 1980.

Bryer, Jackson R. "The Short Stories of F. Scott Fitzgerald: A Checklist of Criticism." In *The Short Stories of F. Scott Fitzgerald: New Approaches in Criticism*, ed. Jackson R. Bryer, 303-77. Madison: University of Wisconsin Press, 1982.

_____, ed. *The Short Stories of F. Scott Fitzgerald: New Approaches in Criticism*. Madison: University of Wisconsin Press, 1982.

Fitzgerald, F. Scott. *Afternoon of an Author: A Selection of Uncollected Stories and Essays*. New York: Charles Scribner's Sons, 1957.

_____. *The Basil and Josephine Stories*. Ed. Jackson R. Bryer and John Kuehl. 1971. Reprint. New York: Popular Library, 1976.

_____. *The Pat Hobby Stories*. New York: Charles Scribner's Sons, 1962.

_____. *The Stories of F. Scott Fitzgerald: A Selection of 28 Stories*. New York: Charles Scribner's Sons, 1951.

_____. *Three Novels of F. Scott Fitzgerald*. New York: Charles Scribner's Sons, 1953.

_____, and Zelda Fitzgerald. *Bits of Paradise: 21 Uncollected Stories by F. Scott and Zelda Fitzgerald*. Selected by Matthew J. Bruccoli with the assistance of Scottie Fitzgerald Smith. New York: Charles Scribner's Sons, 1973.

Gingrich, Arnold. "Introduction:" In *The Pat Hobby Stories*, by F. Scott Fitzgerald, ix-xxiii. New York: Charles Scribner's Sons, 1962.

Higgins, John A. *F. Scott Fitzgerald: A Study of the Stories*. Jamaica, N.Y.: St. John's University Press, 1971.

Kuehl, John. *F. Scott Fitzgerald: A Study of the Short Fiction.* Boston: Twayne, 1991.

_____, ed. *The Apprentice Fiction of F. Scott Fitzgerald: 1909-1917.* New Brunswick, N.J.: Rutgers University Press, 1965.

Latham, Aaron. *Crazy Sundays: F. Scott Fitzgerald in Hollywood.* New York: Viking Press, 1971.

Mangum, Bryant. *A Fortune Yet: Money in the Art of F. Scott Fitzgerald's Short Stories.* New York: Garland, 1991.

Petry, Alice Hall. *Fitzgerald's Craft of Short Fiction: The Collected Stories— 1920-1935.* Ann Arbor, Mich.: UMI Research Press, 1989.

Phillips, Gene D., S.J. *Fiction, Film, and F. Scott Fitzgerald.* Chicago: Loyola University Press, 1986.

Rees, John O. "Fitzgerald's Pat Hobby Stories." *Colorado Quarterly* 23 (1975): 553-62.

Varet-Ali, Elizabeth M. "The Unfortunate Fate of Seventeen Fitzgerald 'Originals': Toward a Reading of *The Pat Hobby Stories* 'On Their Own Merits Completely.'" *Journal of the Short Story in English* 14 (spring 1990): 87-110.

Wells, Walter. *Tycoons and Locusts: A Regional Look at Hollywood Fiction of the 1930s.* Carbondale: Southern Illinois University Press, 1973.

White, Ray Lewis. "The Pat Hobby Stories: A File of Reviews." *Fitzgerald/ Hemingway Annual* 11 (1979): 177-80.

F. Scott Fitzgerald_____

Lionel Trilling

"'SO BE IT! I die content and my destiny is fulfilled,' said Racine's Orestes; and there is more in his speech than the insanely bitter irony that appears on the surface. Racine, fully conscious of this tragic grandeur, permits Orestes to taste for a moment before going mad with grief the supreme joy of a hero; to assume his *exemplary* role." The heroic awareness of which André Gide speaks in his essay on Goethe was granted to Scott Fitzgerald for whatever grim joy he might find in it. It is a kind of seal set upon his heroic quality that he was able to utter his vision of his own fate publicly and aloud and in *Esquire* with no lessening of his dignity, even with an enhancement of it. The several essays in which Fitzgerald examined his life in crisis have been gathered together by Edmund Wilson—who is for many reasons the most appropriate editor possible—and published, together with Fitzgerald's notebooks and some letters, as well as certain tributes and memorabilia, in a volume called, after one of the essays, *The Crack-Up*. It is a book filled with the grief of the lost and the might-have-been, with physical illness and torture of mind. Yet the heroic quality is so much here, Fitzgerald's assumption of the "exemplary role" is so proper and right that it occurs to us to say, and not merely as a piety but as the most accurate expression of what we really do feel, that

> Nothing is here for tears, nothing to wail
> Or knock the breast, no weakness, no contempt,
> Dispraise, or blame, nothing but well and fair,
> And what may quiet us in a death so noble.

This isn't what we may fittingly say on all tragic occasions, but the original occasion for these words has a striking aptness to Fitzgerald. Like Milton's Samson, he had the consciousness of having misused the power with which he had been endowed. "I had been only a mediocre caretaker . . . of my talent," he said. And the parallel carries further, to the sojourn among the Philistines and even to the maimed hero exhibited and mocked for the amusement of the crowd—on the afternoon of September 25, 1936, the New York *Evening Post* carried on its front page a feature story in which the triumphant reporter tells how he managed to make his way into the Southern nursing home where the sick and distracted Fitzgerald was being cared for and there "interviewed" him, taking all due note of the contrast between the present humiliation and the past glory. It was a particularly gratuitous horror, and yet in retrospect it serves to augment the moral force of the poise and fortitude which marked Fitzgerald's mind in the few recovered years that were left to him.

The root of Fitzgerald's heroism is to be found, as it sometimes is in tragic heroes, in his power of love. Fitzgerald wrote much about love, he was preoccupied with it as between men and women, but it is not merely where he is being explicit about it that his power appears. It is to be seen where eventually all a writer's qualities have their truest existence, in his style. Even in Fitzgerald's early, cruder books, or even in his commercial stories, and even when the style is careless, there is a tone and pitch to the sentences which suggest his warmth and tenderness, and, what is rare nowadays and not likely to be admired, his gentleness without softness. In the equipment of the moralist and therefore in the equipment of the novelist, aggression plays an important part, and although it is of course sanctioned by the novelist's moral intention and by whatever truth of moral vision he may have, it is often none the less fierce and sometimes even cruel. Fitzgerald was a moralist to the core and his desire to "preach at people in some acceptable form" is the reason he gives for not going the way of Cole Porter and Rodgers and Hart—we must always remember in judging him how many real choices he was free and forced to make—and he was gifted with the satiric eye; yet we feel that in his morality he was more drawn to celebrate the good than to denounce the bad. We feel of him, as we cannot feel of all moralists, that he did not attach himself to the good because this attachment would sanction his fierceness toward the bad—his first impulse was to love the good, and we know this the more surely because we perceive that he loved the good not only with his mind but also with his quick senses and his youthful pride and desire.

He really had but little impulse to blame, which is the more remarkable because our culture peculiarly honors the act of blaming, which it takes as the sign of virtue and intellect. "Forbearance, good word," is one of the jottings in his notebook. When it came to blame, he preferred, it seems, to blame himself. He even did not much want to blame the world. Fitzgerald knew where "the world" was at fault. He knew that it was the condition, the field, of tragedy. He is conscious of "what preyed on Gatsby, what foul dust floated in the wake of his dreams." But he never made out that the world imposes tragedy, either upon the heroes of his novels, whom he called his "brothers," or upon himself. When he speaks of his own fate, he does indeed connect it with the nature of the social world in which he had his early flowering, but he never finally lays it upon that world, even though at the time when he was most aware of his destiny it was fashionable with minds more pretentious than his to lay all personal difficulty whatever at the door of the "social order." It is, he feels, *his* fate—and as much as to anything else in Fitzgerald, we respond to the delicate tension he maintained between his idea of personal free will and his idea of circumstance: we respond to that moral and intellectual energy. "The test of a first-rate intelligence," he said, "is the ability to hold two opposed ideas in the mind, at the same time, and still retain the ability to function."

The power of love in Fitzgerald, then, went hand in hand with a sense of personal responsibility and perhaps created it. But it often happens that the tragic hero can conceive and realize a love that is beyond his own prudence or beyond his powers of dominance or of self-protection, so that he is destroyed by the very thing that gives him his spiritual status and stature. From Proust we learn about a love that is destructive by a kind of corrosiveness, but from Fitzgerald's two mature novels, *The Great Gatsby* and *Tender Is the Night*, we learn about a love—perhaps it is peculiarly American—that is destructive by reason of its very tenderness. It begins in romance, sentiment, even "glamour"—no one, I think, has remarked how innocent of mere "sex," how charged with sentiment is Fitzgerald's description of love in the jazz age—and it takes upon itself reality, and permanence, and duty discharged with an almost masochistic scrupulousness of honor. In the bright dreams begins the responsibility which needs so much prudence and dominance to sustain; and Fitzgerald was anything but a prudent man and he tells us that at a certain point in his college career "some old desire for personal dominance was broken and gone." He connects that loss of desire for dominance with his ability to write; and he set down in his notebook the belief that "to record one must be unwary." Fitzgerald, we may say, seemed to feel that both love and art needed a sort of personal defenselessness.

The phrase from Yeats, the derivation of the "responsibility" from the "dreams," reminds us that we must guard against dismissing, with easy words about its immaturity, Fitzgerald's preoccupation with the bright charm of his youth. Yeats himself, a wiser man and wholly fulfilled in his art, kept to the last of his old age his connection with his youthful vanity. A writer's days must be bound each to each by his sense of his life, and Fitzgerald the undergraduate was father of the best in the man and the novelist

His sojourn among the philistines is always much in the mind of everyone who thinks about Fitzgerald, and indeed it was always much in his own mind. Everyone knows the famous exchange between Fitzgerald and Ernest Hemingway—Hemingway refers to it in his story "The Snows of Kilimanjaro," and Fitzgerald records it in his notebook—in which, to Fitzgerald's remark, "The very rich are different from us," Hemingway replied, "Yes, they have more money." It is usually supposed that Hemingway had the better of the encounter and quite settled the matter. But we ought not be too sure. The novelist of a certain kind, if he is to write about social life, may not brush away the reality of the differences of class, even though to do so may have the momentary appearance of a virtuous social avowal. The novel took its rise and its nature from the radical revision of the class structure in the eighteenth century, and the novelist must still live by his sense of class differences, and must be absorbed by them, as Fitzgerald was, even though he despise them, as Fitzgerald did.

No doubt there was a certain ambiguity in Fitzgerald's attitude toward the "very rich"; no doubt they were for him something more than the mere object of his social observation. They seem to have been the nearest thing to an aristocracy that America could offer him, and we cannot be too simple about what a critic has recently noted, the artist's frequent "taste for aristocracy, his need—often quite open—of a superior social class with which he can make some fraction of common cause—enough, at any rate, to account for his own distinction." Every modern reader is by definition wholly immune from all ignoble social considerations, and, no matter what his own social establishment or desire for it may be, he knows that in literature the interest in social position must never be taken seriously. But not all writers have been so simple and virtuous—what are we to make of those risen gentlemen, Shakespeare and Dickens, or those fabricators of the honorific "de," Voltaire and Balzac? Yet their snobbery—let us call it that—is of a large and generous kind and we are not entirely wrong in connecting their peculiar energies of mind with whatever it was they wanted from gentility or aristocracy. It is a common habit of writers to envision an actuality of personal life which shall have the freedom and the richness of detail and the order of form that they desire in art. Yeats, to mention him again, spoke of the falseness of the belief that the "inherited glory of the rich" really holds richness of life. This, he said, was a mere dream; and yet, he goes on, it is a necessary illusion—

> Yet Homer had not sung
> Had he not found it certain beyond dreams
> That out of life's own self-delight had sprung
> The abounding glittering jet. . . .

And Henry James, at the threshold of his career, allegorized in his story "Benvolio" the interplay that is necessary for some artists between their creative asceticism and the bright, free, gay life of worldliness, noting at the same time the desire of worldliness to destroy the asceticism.[1]

With a man like Goethe the balance between the world and his asceticism is maintained, and so we forgive him his often absurd feelings—but perhaps absurd as well as forgivable only in the light of our present opinion of his assured genius—about aristocracy. Fitzgerald could not always keep the balance true; he was not, as we know, a prudent man. And no doubt he deceived himself a good deal in his youth, but certainly his self-deception was not in the interests of vulgarity, for aristocracy meant to him a kind of disciplined distinction of personal existence which, presumably, he was so humble as not to expect from his art. What was involved in that notion of distinction can be learned from the use which Fitzgerald makes of the word "aristocracy" in one of those serious moments which occur in his most frivolous *Saturday Evening Post* stories: he says of the life of the young man of the story, who during the war was on duty behind the lines, that "it was not so bad—except that when the infantry came limping back from the trenches he wanted to be one of them. The sweat and mud they wore seemed only one of those ineffable symbols of aristocracy that were forever eluding him." Fitzgerald was perhaps the last notable writer to affirm the Romantic fantasy, descended from the Renaissance, of personal ambition and heroism, of life committed to, or thrown away for, some ideal of self. To us it will no doubt come more and more to seem a merely boyish dream; the nature of our society requires the young man to find his distinction through cooperation, subordination, and an expressed piety of social usefulness, and although a few young men have made Fitzgerald into a hero of art, it is likely that even to these admirers the whole nature of his personal fantasy is not comprehensible, for young men find it harder and harder to understand the youthful heroes of Balzac and Stendhal, they increasingly find reason to blame the boy whose generosity is bound up with his will and finds its expression in a large, strict, personal demand upon life.

I am aware that I have involved Fitzgerald with a great many great names and that it might be felt by some that this can do him no service, the disproportion being so large. But the disproportion will seem large only to those who think of Fitzgerald chiefly through his early public legend of heedlessness. Those who have a clear recollection of the mature work or who have read *The Crack-Up* will at least not think of the disproportion as one of kind. Fitzgerald himself did not, and it is by a man's estimate of himself that we must begin to estimate him. For all the engaging self-depreciation which was part of his peculiarly American charm, he put himself, in all modesty, in the line of greatness, he judged himself in a large way. When he writes of his depression, of his "dark night of the soul" where "it is always three o'clock in the morning," he not only derives the phrase from St. John of the Cross but adduces the analogous black despairs of Wordsworth, Keats, and Shelley. A novel with Ernest Hemingway as the model of its hero suggests to him Stendhal portraying the Byronic man, and he defends *The Great Gatsby* from some critical remark of Edmund Wilson's by comparing it with *The Brothers Karamazov*. Or again, here is the stuff of his intellectual pride at the very moment that he speaks of giving it up, as years before he had given up the undergraduate fantasies of valor: "The old dream of being an entire man in the Goethe-Byron-Shaw tradition . . . has been relegated to the junk heap of the shoulder pads worn for one day on the Princeton freshman football field and the overseas cap never worn overseas." And was it, that old dream, unjustified? To take but one great name, the one that on first thought seems the least relevant of all—between Goethe at twenty-four the author of *Werther*, and Fitzgerald, at twenty-four the author of *This Side of Paradise*, there is not really so entire a difference as piety and textbooks might make us think; both the young men so handsome, both winning immediate and notorious success, both rather more interested in life than in art, each the spokesman and symbol of his own restless generation.

It is hard to overestimate the benefit which came to Fitzgerald from his having consciously placed himself in the line of the great. He was a "natural," but he did not have the contemporary American novelist's belief that if he compares himself with the past masters, or if he takes thought—which, for a writer, means really knowing what his predecessors have done—he will endanger the integrity of his natural gifts. To read Fitzgerald's letters to his daughter—they are among the best and most affecting letters I know—and to catch the tone in which he speaks about the literature of the past, or to read the notebooks he faithfully kept, indexing them as Samuel Butler had done, and to perceive how continuously he thought about literature, is to have some clue to the secret of the continuing power of Fitzgerald's work.

The Great Gatsby, for example, after a quarter-century is still as fresh as when it first appeared; it has even gained in weight and relevance, which can be said of very few American books of its time. This, I think, is to be attributed to the specifically intellectual courage with which it was conceived and executed, a courage which implies Fitzgerald's grasp—both in the sense of awareness and of appropriation—of the traditional resources available to him. Thus, *The Great Gatsby* has its interest as a record of contemporary manners, but this might only have served to date it, did not Fitzgerald take the given moment of history as something more than a mere circumstance, did he not, in the manner of the great French novelists of the nineteenth century, seize the given moment as a moral fact. The same boldness of intellectual grasp accounts for the success of the conception of its hero—Gatsby is said by some to be not quite credible, but the question of any literal credibility he may or may not have becomes trivial before the large significance he implies. For Gatsby, divided between power and dream, comes inevitably to stand for America itself. Ours is the only nation that prides itself upon a dream and gives its name to one, "the American dream." We are told that "the truth was that Jay Gatsby of West Egg, Long Island, sprang from his Platonic conception of himself. He was a son of God—a phrase which, if it means anything, means just that—and he must be about His Father's business, the service of a vast, vulgar, and meretricious beauty." Clearly it is Fitzgerald's intention that our mind should turn to the thought of the nation that has sprung from its "Platonic conception" of itself. To the world it is anomalous in America, just as in the novel it is anomalous in Gatsby, that so much raw power should be haunted by envisioned romance. Yet in that anomaly lies, for good or bad, much of the truth of our national life, as, at the present moment, we think about it.

Then, if the book grows in weight of significance with the years, we can be sure that this could not have happened had its form and style not been as right as they are. Its form is ingenious—with the ingenuity, however, not of craft but of intellectual intensity. The form, that is, is not the result of careful "plotting"—the form of a good novel never is—not is rather the result of the necessities of the story's informing idea, which require the sharpness of radical foreshortening. Thus, it will be observed, the characters are not "developed": the wealthy and brutal Tom Buchanan haunted by his "scientific" vision of the doom of civilization, the vaguely guilty, vaguely homosexual Jordan Baker, the dim Wolfsheim, who fixed the World Series of 1919, are treated, we might say, as if they were ideographs, a method of economy that is reinforced by the ideographic use that is made of the Washington Heights flat, the terrible "valley of ashes" seen from the Long Island Railroad, Gatsby's incoherent parties, and the huge sordid eyes of the oculist's advertising sign. (It is a technique which gives the novel an affinity with *The Waste Land*, between whose author and Fitzgerald there existed a reciprocal admiration.) Gatsby himself, once stated, grows only in the understanding of the narrator. He is allowed to say very little in his own person. Indeed, apart from the famous "Her voice is full of money," he says only one memorable thing, but that remark is overwhelming in its intellectual audacity: when he is forced to admit that his lost Daisy did perhaps love her husband, he says, "In any case it was just personal." With that sentence he achieves an insane greatness, convincing us that he really is a Platonic conception of himself, really some sort of Son of God.

What underlies all success in poetry, what is even more important than the shape of the poem or its wit of metaphor, is the poet's voice. It either gives us confidence in what is being said or it tells us that we do not need to listen; and it carries both the modulation and the living form of what is being said. In the novel no less than in the poem, the voice of the author is the decisive factor. We are less consciously aware of it in the novel, and, in speaking of the elements of a novel's art, it cannot properly be exemplified by quotation because it is continuous and cumulative. In Fitzgerald's work the voice of his prose is of the essence of his success. We hear in it at once the tenderness toward human desire that modifies a true firmness of moral judgment. It is, I would venture to say, the normal or ideal voice of the novelist. It is characteristically modest, yet it has in it, without apology or self-consciousness, a largeness, even a stateliness, which derives from Fitzgerald's connection with tradition and with mind, from his sense of what has been done before and the demands which this past accomplishment makes. ". . . I became aware of the old island here that flowered once for Dutch sailors' eyes—a fresh, green breast of the new world. Its vanished trees, the trees that had made way for Gatsby's house, had once pandered in whispers to the last and greatest of all human dreams; for a transitory enchanted moment man must have held his breath in the presence of this continent, compelled into an aesthetic contemplation he neither understood nor desired, face to face for the last time in history with something commensurate to his capacity for wonder." Here, in the well-known passage, the voice is a little dramatic, a little *intentional*, which is not improper to a passage in climax and conclusion, but it will the better suggest in brief compass the habitual music of Fitzgerald's seriousness.

Fitzgerald lacked prudence, as his heroes did, lacked that blind instinct of self-protection which the writer needs and the American writer needs in double measure. But that is all he lacked—and it is the generous fault, even the heroic fault. He said of his Gatsby, "If personality is an unbroken series of successful gestures, there was something gorgeous about him, some heightened sensitivity to the promises of life, as if he were related to one of those intricate machines that register earthquakes ten thousand miles away. This responsiveness had nothing to do with that flabby impressionability which is dignified under the name of 'the creative temperament'—it was an extraordinary gift for hope, a romantic readiness such as I have never found in any other person and which it is not likely I shall ever find again." And it is so that we are drawn to see Fitzgerald himself as he stands in his exemplary role.

From *The Liberal Imagination: Essays on Literature and Society*, pp. 243-254. Copyright © 1950 by Lionel Trilling. Reprinted with permission of The Wylie Agency LLC.

Note

1. George Moore's comment on Æ's having spoken in reproof of Yeats's pride in a quite factitious family line is apposite; "Æ, who is usually quick-witted, should have guessed that Yeats's belief in his lineal descent from the great Duke of Ormonde was part of his poetic equipment."

Fitzgerald:
The Authority of Failure _____

Morris Dickstein

It felt strange indeed in the fall of 1996 to mark the centennial of the birth of F. Scott Fitzgerald, a writer whose work still feels so fresh, who died young and seems perpetually young, like Keats, the poet he most loved. Fitzgerald scholars and enthusiasts met at Princeton to celebrate his life and work, and on his actual birthday I found myself speaking about him at the Great Neck Public Library on Long Island, in the very town where he conceived *The Great Gatsby* and began writing it in 1922 and 1923. Great Neck was then a fashionable new suburb much beloved by show business types like Eddie Cantor. But it was also the place Fitzgerald and his wife threw themselves into the wild, sad, drunken parties portrayed with satiric gusto yet also a tragic edge in *Gatsby*, parties that meant as little to Gatsby as to the guests who sponged off him.

Fitzgerald's Great Neck years were not the happiest time of his life, though he seemed, like Gatsby, to be sitting on top of the world. He had only one writer friend there, Ring Lardner, who drank even more than he did. Fitzgerald himself tended to go off on benders for two or three days in New York. It was there he wrote his only play, a political fantasy called *The Vegetable*, which he hoped would make his fortune, but it died in Atlantic City in November 1923, on its way to a Broadway staging that never took place. This was a taste of failure he never forgot. "I worked hard as hell last winter," he later wrote, "but it was all trash and it nearly broke my heart as well as my iron constitution" (Turnbull 141). He was only twenty-seven years old.

Many people would have been surprised at the sad note of waste and decline that creeps into this comment—partly because his best work was still before him, but also since Fitzgerald and his young wife, Zelda, were just then the very embodiments of youthful energy and style for much of fashionable America. But our continuing sense of

Fitzgerald as a poet of lyrical longing and dreamy aspiration can easily obscure the darker, more somber side of his work. Like his friend Hemingway, Fitzgerald was not simply a writer but a figure, a cultural icon who would always remain linked in the popular mind with the fizz and exuberance of what he himself named the Jazz Age.

A key element of the Fitzgerald myth, especially that sense of his perpetual high spirits, began with his connection to Princeton. Much to his embarrassment, he never graduated, but in a sense he graduated posthumously when the university became the much-visited haven for his voluminous papers. When Fitzgerald arrived in 1913, Princeton was in many ways far from a serious university, though it had become more serious under its most recent president, Woodrow Wilson, who had gone on to become governor of New Jersey and, earlier that year, president of the United States. It was a very white, very male university, hardly expensive by today's standards but accessible mainly to the children of the rich, those from "good" families who had gone to elite boarding schools. While Fitzgerald's friend and classmate Edmund Wilson, later America's leading literary critic, managed to get a splendid education there, for many others the gentleman's C was a way of life, and there was a long tradition behind it. You could get by quite well without cracking a book. Most Ivy League colleges were so frivolous that the more thoughtful undergraduates, Fitzgerald included, later believed they got their education only after they left school.

As a midwestern boy, Fitzgerald felt like an outsider, not one to the manor born. But as an outsider he came to love everything about the school: the dating rituals, the drunken sprees, the football games he never managed to compete in, and the Triangle shows he helped write with his friend Wilson, which became the high points of his college career. A few years later, in the spring of 1920, he published *This Side of Paradise*, a thinly disguised version of his college experiences; to everyone's surprise, it became an overnight sensation. Like Lord Byron in 1812, he awoke and found himself famous. His commercial and literary careers were launched. A few days later, in a grand ceremony in St. Patrick's Cathedral, he married the belle of Montgomery, Alabama, Zelda Sayre, a daffy and beautiful young woman who had once broken off her engagement to him because his financial prospects looked so dim.

With the wild success of the book and the brilliance of their marriage, Scott and Zelda embarked on a decade-long odyssey as the shining young couple whose beauty, charm, and sense of fun embodied the devil-may-care spirit of the new postwar generation. Whether they were living among theater people in Great Neck, swimming with other expatriate Americans along the Riviera, or writing amusing little stories and articles about each other for stylish popular magazines, Scott and Zelda came to personify the new youth culture of the Jazz Age, when life seemed like a drunken lark and a good part of privileged young America went on a big hedonistic spree.

Living in the public eye, always furnishing good copy, Scott and Zelda helped write the script that cast them as legends. This was the beginning of the media age, with its emphasis on personality, novelty, showmanship, and style. The best one can say about Fitzgerald's role as a celebrity was that, unlike Hemingway, he never believed his own clippings, and always kept a good deal of himself in reserve, a sense of being answerable to posterity rather than to the newspapers.

Part of Fitzgerald's problem came later, during the Depression, when his name remained associated with his portraits of the rich; this in turn was mistaken for admiration, approval, and envy of their fashionable lives. But Fitzgerald, though fascinated by the manners and morals of the rich and intrigued by the freedom that came with their money, nourished a burning ambition to be a serious writer, someone whose work would matter to people fifty years later. Among the rich he never forgot that he was an outsider, but Fitzgerald also proved to be a wickedly percipient yet empathetic observer. He took note of how much and yet how little their money could do for them—how much freedom and style it gave them, but how little protection it furnished against disappointment and unhappiness, as he himself would later discover.

Fame is famously fickle. Soon after the Crash, everything from the

1920s seemed like ancient history, a tale of sound, fury, and innocence before the fall; and Fitzgerald's shallow celebrity was no exception. Within a few short years, F. Scott Fitzgerald would become an icon of a different kind: once a byword for youth, elegance, and exuberance, he would become an emblem of failure, a back number. Once again, with a vengeance, the icon would obscure the writer and come close to obliterating him. This remains the lesser-known Fitzgerald, the gifted but chastened Fitzgerald of the 1930s. The legend of his decline, which he helped broadcast—everyone who met him during his last years in Hollywood heard it—continues to haunt his reputation today.

Perhaps the worst moment in this unhappy story comes in the fall of 1936. Fitzgerald is about to turn forty, no easy transition for someone whose life was so identified with the passion and promise of youth. Things had long since begun to sour for him. In 1930, Zelda, increasingly desperate to find herself as a writer, a dancer, or simply someone who had a life in her own right, had suffered a nervous breakdown, and since then she had been in and out of hospitals. Scott himself had had a critical success in 1925 with *The Great Gatsby*, a book admired by writers as different as Edith Wharton and T. S. Eliot, but its sales proved disappointing compared to those of his apprentice novels and widely read short fiction. His effort to storm Broadway had failed. Once he had had an almost golden facility; his prose had a spontaneous poetry all its own, but he had struggled for nine years to finish his next novel, *Tender Is the Night*, which got a mixed reaction from critics and the public when it finally appeared in 1934. Reviewers were puzzled and ambivalent; sales again fell short of expectations. Fitzgerald had become a chronic alcoholic, and the failure of his most ambitious book sent him over the edge. But Fitzgerald did more than abuse his health and break down: in the spring of 1936, in a shocking series of articles for *Esquire*, he wrote about his problems in a harsh, unsparing, confessional vein—something familiar to us today from memoirs and talk shows, in which dysfunction has gone public, but completely unheard-of in those more reticent and buttoned-up times.

In these articles Fitzgerald hardly came clean about either his marital problems or his drinking, but he described in surprising detail his loss of confidence and vitality, his failure to take care of his talent, his waste of energy on simply being a celebrity—on his need to be liked, to be charming and personable, to be all things to everyone he knew. This was not yet a therapeutic culture, though Dale Carnegie was just then making his auspicious debut. Hemingway, his friend and cruel rival, who would spend a lifetime burnishing his own myth, was aghast that he would expose himself in this way. Their mutual editor, the legendary Maxwell Perkins of Scribner's, a man of infinite discretion, was saddened and disapproving. Another friend, John Dos Passos, couldn't imagine how anyone could waste his energy on merely personal problems when the whole world was coming apart. But these poignantly written articles brought Fitzgerald's name before the public again, as it had not been for a long time.

Into this picture came a reporter for the *New York Post*, perhaps not so different then from the Murdoch-driven paper it is today, a reporter with the ominous name of Michel Mok, to interview Scott for his fortieth birthday. There was a scent of blood in the water. Fitzgerald was under a nurse's care at an inn in Asheville, North Carolina, but he was still drinking, and the reporter described in wretched detail how he kept popping up for a thimbleful of gin from the makeshift bar, how his face twitched and hands shook as he described his life and made the usual drunkard's rationalizations.

The front page of the *Post* the next day told the whole story: "The Other Side of Paradise/ F. Scott Fitzgerald, 40,/ Engulfed in Despair/ Broken in Health He Spends Birthday Re-/ gretting That He Has Lost Faith in His Star" (Bruccoli, *Some Sort of Epic Grandeur* 413). What had been eloquent if not wholly frank in Fitzgerald's own articles became pathetic in the tabloid version. *Time* picked up the story and gave it much wider currency. The effect on Fitzgerald was catastrophic. He thought he was ruined and took an overdose of morphine, but luckily vomited it up. He felt that his credibility as a writer and a serious man was gone. The *Post* interview was perhaps the lowest point he reached in the decade, but it fixed his image as a washed-up, self-pitying writer, a miserable caretaker of his talent, the relic of a distant and unlamented era. (Even nine years later, when reviewers like Lionel Trilling wrote about *The Crack-Up*, Edmund Wilson's collection of his late friend's articles and letters, they would still point to the effects of the *Post* story on Fitzgerald's waning reputation.)

In a limited sense this image endures even today. No one, of course, thinks of Fitzgerald as a pathetic drunk—a "rummy," as Hemingway called him. In fact, Fitzgerald's reputation bounced back amazingly after the war, and *The Great Gatsby* is secure as one of the most widely taught of twentieth-century American classics. But most people still think of his life in the 1930s as the melancholy aftermath of his brilliant decade, a period of decline and failure as vividly portrayed by the man himself. There is no doubt how much he really did suffer during this period, when his golden marriage was all but over, when drink and disappointment often made him behave strangely, when his stories were no longer welcome in magazines that had provided most of his income, when even Hollywood could find no real use for his talents. In the popular mind today, he remains the chronicler of the Jazz Age, the flapper era, the frivolous youth culture, and the more flagrant excesses of the American dream.

To the socially minded critics of the Depression years he was simply irrelevant. This view has curiously been resurrected among some scholars today, who have repeatedly drawn attention to neglected black, proletarian, or women writers of the period. It would be an exaggeration to say that an interest in Zora Neale Hurston, Langston Hughes, or the Harlem Renaissance has been purchased at the expense of, say, *The Great Gatsby*, *The Sun Also Rises*, or *As I Lay Dying*. Making space for the rediscovered books of Hurston or Nella Larsen doesn't undercut Faulkner and Fitzgerald: the literary canon isn't a zero-sum game, even if the syllabus may be limited. But to many professors Fitzgerald has simply become one of the dead white males, more a burden than a revelation.

Overall, Fitzgerald's work has weathered the politics of multiculturalism reasonably well. Students today still respond passionately to his books, especially *The Great Gatsby*, even if their teachers have gotten bored with connecting it to the American dream, and perhaps have passed some of this boredom on to their charges. There are scholars today who feel that Fitzgerald deals with much too narrow a class of privileged Americans. This echoes the widespread disapproval of his work that was heard during the Marxist 1930s, when proletarian critics grew tired of reading about the Lost Generation and the emotional entanglements of wealthy expatriates on the Riviera in the 1920s. As the young critic Philip Rahv wrote in the Communist *Daily Worker*, reviewing *Tender Is the Night* when it appeared in 1934, "Dear Mr. Fitzgerald, you can't hide from a hurricane under a beach umbrella" (Bryer, *Fitzgerald: The Critical Reception* 317). The hurricane, of course, was the Depression, which exposed the failure of capitalism and drew attention to the class antagonisms that Americans had usually tried to soften and blur.

To his credit, Rahv understood that Fitzgerald's most complex novel, with its assortment of wealthy and idle characters, was a fierce yet subtle indictment of the rich, not a sycophantic tribute to them. But the interests of readers and critics alike had turned elsewhere; the language of fiction, partly under Hemingway's influence, had grown simpler and more plebeian, and Rahv felt that Fitzgerald's celebrated style obscured his harsh theme, "transforming it into a mere opportunity for endless psychologizing" (Bryer, *Fitzgerald: The Critical Reception* 317). Marxists of the 1930s generally saw psychology as self-indulgence, for it drew attention to personal problems—a bourgeois luxury—rather than the social structures of exploitation and injustice. The *New Masses* reviewer of Henry Roth's *Call It Sleep*, published the same year, had mocked the young protagonist as a "six-year-old Proust" and lamented that "so many young writers drawn from the proletariat can make no better use of their working class experience than as material for introspective and febrile novels" (Rideout 189). The same buzzword, "introspective," appears in Rahv's review of Fitzgerald when he complains about the novel's "delicate introspective wording . . . its tortuous style that varnishes rather than reveals the essential facts" (Bryer, *Fitzgerald: The Critical Reception* 316).

It's certainly no news that Marxist critics of the 1930s were none too fond of introspection or stylistic elaboration. They thought they already knew all "the essential facts" about our society, and they preferred a more hard-boiled manner to lay bare the unvarnished truth as they saw it. Ironically, Fitzgerald's own style did become more spare and direct as his life went downhill after 1929 and 1930. The content of his work changed as well, for he was struck by the eerie parallels between his own change of fortunes and the fate of Americans at large. He had prospered in the 1920s when he was at the peak of his fame, then had broken down just as Zelda had her first nervous breakdown in 1930, and suffered deeply as he himself came apart after the relative failure of *Tender Is the Night*. "My recent experience parallels the wave of despair that swept the nation when the Boom was over," he wrote in the last *Esquire* piece (Wilson, *The Crack-Up* 84). Fitzgerald felt he had experienced the Crash in personal terms.

In short, it was an already wounded man who was mocked in the *Post* in 1936, but, oddly, someone who had become more of a Depression writer than his critics realized, a writer whose own reverses made him more sympathetic to the failure and misery of others. There is irony here: like another great figure from the 1920s, the seemingly mandarin poet Wallace Stevens, he was attacked by the camp which, in his own fashion, he was actually trying to join. Still, as Fitzgerald began to see himself not as the favored child of fortune, the young prince in the fairy tale, but as a representative man, his work became *more* introspective, not less. In the 1930s, taking stock of his own problems, trying to salvage something out of his losses, Fitzgerald virtually invented the confessional mode in American writing. Later works like Mailer's *Advertisements for Myself* or Robert Lowell's *Life Studies* (both published in 1959) would have been impossible or quite different without the much-maligned example of the "Crack-Up" essays. This suggests that it may not be the lyrical, romantic Fitzgerald of the 1920s who most claims our attention today, but the shattered, disillusioned Fitzgerald of the 1930s—not the poet of early success, romantic possibility, and nostalgic regret, but the hard-edged analyst of personal failure and irretrievable loss, the man who redeemed in his work what was slipping away from his life, who achieved a hard-won maturity even as he described himself as a failure, an exhausted man, a spent force.

This is the final irony—that the dark image of Fitzgerald in the 1930s came from Fitzgerald himself, not from the malicious pen of Mr. Mok and the *Post* headline writers. Starting with stories he wrote in 1929 and 1930, long before the "Crack-Up" articles, Fitzgerald gave an unsparing account of what was going wrong in his life. More than that, he made creative use of it to take his work in a daring new direction. As in the 1920s, *he* was the source of the myths that circulated around him, but unlike Hemingway, he saved them for his own work, not simply for the gossip columns. This points to the great difference between a writer who breaks down and cannot work and one who uses his frustrations and disappointments as new material, producing work that shows a quantum leap in human understanding.

In one sense, Fitzgerald's writing after 1929 or 1930 became the opposite of everything that preceded it. He became the poet of failure and decline rather than youthful, romantic inspiration. With each revision of the book that became *Tender Is the Night*, the expatriate life of Gerald and Sara Murphy gave way to the troubled history of Scott and Zelda, including her breakdown and his sense of creative blockage and diminishing promise. Yet in other ways this was a clear development from his earlier writings. In an essay on "Early Success," written in 1937 when such success was long behind him, he recalled how everything seemed to go awry for his young heroes: "All the stories that came into my head had a touch of disaster in them—the lovely young creatures in my novels went to ruins, the diamond mountains of my short stories blew up, my millionaires were as beautiful and damned as

Thomas Hardy's peasants" (Wilson, *The Crack-Up* 87). Fitzgerald came to realize that there was in his fiction always a kernel of tragedy, a dose of melancholy, a backdrop of dark clouds that he had not yet experienced in his own life. But it was all bathed in a romantic glow, a poignant sense of thwarted possibility, loss, and regret.

One of my favorite examples is "Winter Dreams" (1922). Fitzgerald himself said it was an early sketch for *The Great Gatsby*. The very title embodies the story's contradictory moods of hope and frustration, dream and denial. The young hero, with the slightly foolish name of Dexter Green, has invested *his* winter dreams in a young woman with an even more banal name, Judy Jones—a forerunner of Gatsby's great flame, Daisy Buchanan. By the end, after she has toyed with him for years, he finds that Judy Jones has married a man who mistreats her and, worse still, that she has lost her looks, has become commonplace— a shattered dream rather than one that was simply unfulfilled: "The dream was gone. Something had been taken from him." He thinks of

> her mouth damp to his kisses and her eyes plaintive with melancholy and her freshness like new fine linen in the morning. Why, these things were no longer in the world! They had existed and they existed no longer.
>
> For the first time in years the tears were streaming down his face. But they were for himself now. He did not care about mouth and eyes and moving hands. He wanted to care, and he could not care. For he had gone away and he could never go back any more. (*The Short Stories* 235)

No one can fail to be moved by the tender simplicity of these lines, which combine a plangent feeling of loss with a hard-nosed sense of inevitability: these things once seemed possible, but now they are not to be. In his early work Fitzgerald was a dreamer but not someone who believed that dreams could be realized. Already in the 1920s, his work had a tragic and elegiac cast, yet he still valued his heroes, like Gatsby, for their generous illusions, for the glow of possibility that surrounded them. *The Great Gatsby* is a novel about a self-made man, about the grandeur and failure of our dreams, but it is also about all that distinguishes them from reality. Think of Nick Carraway's harsh judgment of Daisy Buchanan and the illusions Gatsby has fabricated around her. But think also of Nick's surprisingly warm farewell to Gatsby himself, to whom he alone remains faithful. With his impetuous faith in people, Gatsby is the kind of creature Emily Dickinson had in mind when she wrote, "I dwell in Possibility—/ A fairer House than Prose."

This poetic glow of possibility was precisely what diminished into prose for Fitzgerald after 1929 or 1930, starting with some harsh stories about the disintegration of a marriage—"The Rough Crossing" (1929) and "One Trip Abroad" (1930)—stories he never reprinted because they were too close to the material he was developing for *Tender Is the Night*. Both stories, like the novel, are about Americans abroad; both use travel and even bad weather as metaphors for what distracts people from each other, wears them out, and shows up the fault lines in their marriages; both make disillusion and disappointment their central theme. While "The Rough Crossing" centers on a single bad trip, "One Trip Abroad" follows a couple through years of aimless wandering as they move from one hollow niche of "Society" to another. Now broken in health, they have finally landed in a sanitarium in Switzerland, "a country where very few things begin, but many things end" (*The Short Stories* 594). There they see another couple and, in a melodramatic flash of lightning, realize that the pair are their younger selves as we saw them at the beginning of the story, not yet tired, ill, decadent, and out of tune with each other. Despite its unusual gothic touches, "One Trip Abroad" is a schematic miniature of *Tender Is the Night*—its heroine is even called Nicole—in much the same way "Winter Dreams" contains the seed of *The Great Gatsby*.

But "One Trip Abroad" also connects directly with Fitzgerald's next important piece of fiction and one of his most resonant and enduring stories, "Babylon Revisited" (1931), probably the only Fitzgerald work as widely taught as *The Great Gatsby*. "Babylon" also has its nonfiction parallel in an oft-quoted essay written around the same time, "Echoes of the Jazz Age." Always a staple for historians writing about the 1920s, the essay debunks the very period with which Fitzgerald's name is associated; by 1931, less than two years after the stock market crashed, the 1920s already felt like ancient history—"Only Yesterday," as Frederick Lewis Allen put it in the title of his famous social history, also published in 1931. Fitzgerald sees the period somewhat nostalgically, with mock horror, as his own and the culture's "wasted youth," a "flimsy structure" built on "borrowed time" that came tumbling down when the players lost all their confidence (Wilson, *The Crack-Up* 21, 22). But whatever elegiac glow could be found in the essay was ruthlessly excised from the story, where there is almost nothing of value to redeem the old way of life.

Charlie Wales returns to Paris, the scene of many a debauch in the 1920s, to reclaim his daughter from the fierce sister-in-law to whom he had been forced to surrender custody. His wife had died under circumstances for which he bore some responsibility, and his own health had broken under the weight of his drinking, but now, like Fitzgerald himself in "The Crack-Up," he has somehow managed to paste it all together. Sober and serious for the first time in years, he wants his daughter back before her childhood has completely passed him by, before she no longer really knows him. Much of the story is taken up with his reflections on his former life: "he suddenly realized the meaning of the word 'dissipate' [a word that had also figured significantly in "One Trip Abroad"]—to dissipate into thin air; to make nothing out of something. . . . He remembered thousand-franc notes given to an orchestra for playing a single number, hundred-franc notes tossed to a doorman for calling a cab" (620). This had once seemed insouciant, carefree, impulsive; but "In retrospect it was a nightmare" (629).

His high-strung sister-in-law blames him unfairly for her sister's death, but much as she dislikes him, she is beginning to relent. She can see that he's a changed man, a man who desperately wants his daughter, his future, restored to him. But into this volatile mix comes a blundering, drunken, intrusive couple from his earlier life—"sudden ghosts out of the past" (622), revenants like the couple in "One Trip Abroad"—the worn remnants of a time when they all lived for pleasure, for the moment. After one particularly jarring intrusion, Charlie's sister-in-law pulls back, refuses even to see him. By reminding everyone of how he used to live, the doppelg nger couple has done him in, ruined him all over again. Once Fitzgerald had focused lovingly on characters who dreamed a life for themselves, imagined an idyllic or romantic future. Now he writes about people who have learned that the past cannot easily be set aside: our actions have consequences, and the ghosts of our earlier selves will continue to haunt us, without a trace of their old romantic gleam.

Elements of Fitzgerald's new hard-edged, almost tragic outlook can be found in virtually every significant piece of writing he did in the 1930s—in stories like "Babylon Revisited" and "Crazy Sunday"; in the essays, letters, and journals collected in Edmund Wilson's landmark edition of *The Crack-Up* (1945), the book that did so much to restore Fitzgerald's reputation after the war; in novels like *Tender Is the Night* and the unfinished *The Last Tycoon*; and even in commercial formula fiction like the seventeen Pat Hobby stories he wrote for *Esquire* in the last year of his life, stories that continued to appear month after month even after Fitzgerald's death in December 1940.

These terse and brutally satiric sketches, written mainly for money, give us Hollywood through the eyes of a hack writer, not Fitzgerald himself but the kind of facile mediocrity who drove him crazy when he was trying to learn screenwriting as a serious craft. As his name suggests, Pat Hobby is the sort of talentless fellow who knows all the little tricks (tricks so old they don't even work anymore), who steals ideas and schemes for screen credit but would hardly dream of reading the books he's supposed to adapt. According to the formula Fitzgerald evolved, Pat Hobby gets his well-deserved comeuppance in every story.

But Fitzgerald could never write about people entirely from the outside, without insinuating something of himself into them, seeking some authentic core of emotion in their character. The mildly despicable Pat Hobby is washed up, an ineffectual remnant of the silent film days, hanging on by a thread. So Fitzgerald invests some of his own sense of failure in Hobby, just as he had invested it, much more subtly, in the inexorable decline of his real alter ego, Dick Diver, in the second half of *Tender Is the Night*. Hobby has always been a hack, even when the little tricks still came off, but Diver was once a serious, promising, brilliant man, a psychiatrist who made an unfortunate marriage to one of his former patients and, though he was acutely aware of the risk of being bought, gradually allowed himself to be taken over by her wealthy family as a private nursemaid. But this is only one of many reasons that his life went awry. Diver's decline has no single, definite cause; it has too many causes. Fitzgerald may have modeled it on the vague disintegration of the ambitious and idealistic young minister in one of his favorite novels, Harold Frederic's *The Damnation of Theron Ware* (1896). Diver's fate rivals the precipitous descent of Hurstwood in *Sister Carrie* as the greatest failure story in American literature. Like the gifted but flawed protagonist of Santayana's 1936 novel *The Last Puritan*, Diver is a man who simply "peters out."

This focus on failure is what makes the last phase of Fitzgerald's career resonate so strongly with the Depression for us in ways that contemporary readers failed to register. The critics who attacked him for still writing about the rich were as misguided as the friends who accused him of wallowing in self-pity. Fitzgerald had always worked not simply by investing himself in his characters but by mythologizing himself, heightening his dreams and disappointments into representative moments, carrying much of the culture on his back. Now, as the world tried to forget him, to relegate him to the past, he turned the miseries of his life into confessional fables, becoming again a symbol of the age, but this time an unwelcome one, a reminder of how much America had lost. Comparing himself as usual to Hemingway, he wrote in his notebooks: "I talk with the authority of failure—Ernest with the authority of success" (Wilson, *The Crack-Up* 181). The operative word here is "authority," not simply "failure": *Something broke in me, but I speak with the force of experience. I am a different animal, someone who has gained a hard-won maturity.* In Whitman's famous words from "Song of Myself," "I am the man, I suffer'd, I was there" (225). He lived it, but rather than buckling under its weight, he also wrote it, transforming it into a story he'd never told before.

Eventually, *Tender Is the Night* grew on readers who had disliked or misunderstood it when it first appeared. Hemingway, though he later came grudgingly to admire the book, at first objected fiercely to the touches of tragedy in it. His own view was more stoical, fatalistic. "We are all bitched from the start," he wrote to Fitzgerald. "You see Bo, you're not a tragic character. Neither am I" (Hemingway, *Selected Letters* 408). A few years later Fitzgerald was determined to write a tragic novel about Hollywood at exactly the moment he was satirizing it in his stories. The source was not self-pity, as Hemingway mistakenly imagined, but something richer, harsher, deeper—a sense of deprivation and loss that alters one's outlook, a distilled clarity that comes through in every line of "The Crack-Up," *Tender Is the Night*, and the unfinished text of *The Last Tycoon*.

My emblem for this last phase of Fitzgerald's work is a little-noted passage in his 1932 essay "My Lost City," one of the greatest tributes ever written to New York. Near the end, Fitzgerald does what many New Yorkers did that year, just as the Depression is approaching its darkest point: he goes up to the top of the Empire State Building, then newly built, and finds that instead of scaling the heavens, as he might have hoped to do, he gets a better perspective on the terrestrial world below:

> Full of vaunting pride the New Yorker had climbed here and seen with dismay what he had never suspected, that the city was not the endless succession of canyons that he had supposed but that *it had limits*—from the tallest structure he saw for the first time that it faded out into the country on all sides, into an expanse of green and blue that alone was limitless.

And with the awful realization that New York was a city after all and not a universe, the whole shining edifice that he had reared in his imagination came crashing to the ground. (Wilson, *The Crack-Up* 32; emphasis in original)

On one level this passage is a little joke on the provinciality of New Yorkers, much like Saul Steinberg's celebrated cartoon of the contracted world west of the Hudson as seen from Manhattan. But something more serious is happening here as well. The "country on all sides," the "expanse of green and blue that alone was limitless," is clearly an allusion to the great climax of *The Great Gatsby* when, before the narrator's very eyes, "the inessential houses began to melt away until gradually I became aware of the old island here that flowered once for Dutch sailors' eyes—a fresh, green breast of the new world." There, in Fitzgerald's grandiose leap of imagination, man had come "face to face for the last time in history with something commensurate to his capacity for wonder" (140). Here, in "My Lost City," that dreamy Utopian capacity for wonder, the whole imagined sense of possibility, crumbles before a new sense of limits.

The *Gatsby* passage, though hedged with subtle qualifications, speaks for the poetic, expansive Fitzgerald of the 1920s; this new version, with its tone of mockery and humility, speaks for the chastened Fitzgerald of the 1930s, a writer who accords far better with our own painfully acquired sense of limits. What was the watchword of social policy and political frustration in post-1960s America if not a sense of dashed hopes and more limited goals? This is the clear-eyed, un-self-pitying mood that underlies every Fitzgerald text of the Depression decade, most patently in "The Crack-Up," which his contemporaries misread and undervalued, though it should have been as congenial to hard times as it is to our own post-utopian era.

This was the mood of the great romantic crisis poems, which formed Fitzgerald's sensibility long before he fully understood them, before he actually experienced their peculiar mixture of elation and regret, loss and renewal, crisis and resolution. This was the disintoxicated mood of the last stanza of Keats's Nightingale Ode, a poem Fitzgerald could never read aloud without tears. On the surface it appears that Fitzgerald goes from being a pie-eyed romantic in the 1920s to a disillusioned realist in the 1930s, except that this very disintoxication is a crucial moment of the romantic imagination. It's the moment of clarity when the dreamer, the visionary, is humanized by loss, by suffering, by fellow feeling, when the mental traveler, no longer adrift in "faery lands forlorn," turns homeward, in Keats's words, in "Ode to a Nightingale," to the "sole self," the self without romantic illusions (371-72).

All these poems proceed from a sense of visionary possibility, through a maelstrom of inner crisis and loss, and finally to a more modest rededication to new beginnings, exactly as Fitzgerald does in the "Crack-Up" essays. This was the thrust of both "Tintern Abbey" and the Intimations Ode, but perhaps Wordsworth put it best in his "Elegiac Stanzas" about Peele Castle written in 1805, after his beloved brother John was lost at sea. He gazes at the turbulent seascape painted by a friend and thinks how he would once have added some calming touch, a romantic glow—in Wordsworth's famous phrase, "the gleam,/ The light that never was, on sea or land." (How much like the way Fitzgerald himself had provided a shimmer of iridescence at every turn in his early stories, even the sad ones.) But Wordsworth tells us he can do this no longer. His whole sense of reality has been altered by his brother's unexpected death. Nature now appears anything but benign:

> So once it would have been,—'tis so no more;
> I have submitted to a new control:
> A power is gone, which nothing can restore;
> A deep distress hath humanised my soul.
>
> (*Selected Poems* 373-74)

These troubled but grimly hopeful lines, stark yet consoling, could serve as a motto for all the neglected writing of F. Scott Fitzgerald's last decade, when the lyrical dreamer gave way to the disillusioned realist with his chastened sense of maturity. This may be the work of Fitzgerald's that makes the deepest claim on us today. Even Hemingway, ever competitive, came around in the end. "Scott's writing got better and better, but no one realized it, not even Scott," he told his son Gregory. "The stuff he was writing at the end was the best of all. Poor bastard!" (Gregory Hemingway 103).

From *F. Scott Fitzgerald in the Twenty-first Century*, edited by Jackson R. Bryer, Ruth Prigozy, and Milton R. Stern, pp. 301-316. Copyright © 2003 by University of Alabama Press. Reprinted with permission of the University of Alabama Press.

Works Cited

Bruccoli, Matthew J. *Some Sort of Epic Grandeur: The Life of F. Scott Fitzgerald.* New York: Harcourt Brace Jovanovich, 1981.

Bryer, Jackson R., ed. *F. Scott Fitzgerald: The Critical Reception.* New York: Burt Franklin, 1978.

Fitzgerald, F. Scott. *The Great Gatsby.* 1925. Ed. Matthew J. Bruccoli. New York: Macmillan/Scribner's, 1992.

_____. *The Short Stories of F. Scott Fitzgerald: A New Collection.* Ed. Matthew J. Bruccoli. New York: Scribner's, 1989.

_____. *Tender Is the Night.* 1934. New York: Scribner's, 1962.

Hemingway, Ernest. *Selected Letters, 1917-1961.* Ed. Carlos Baker. New York: Scribner's, 1981.

Hemingway, Gregory H. *Papa: A Personal Memoir.* Boston: Houghton Mifflin, 1976.

Rideout, Walter B. *The Radical Novel in the United States.* 1956. New York: Hill and Wang, 1966.

Trilling, Lionel. *The Liberal Imagination.* 1950. New York: Harcourt Brace Jovanovich, 1977.

Turnbull, Andrew. *Scott Fitzgerald.* New York: Scribner's, 1962.

Wilson, Edmund, ed. *The Crack-Up.* New York: New Directions, 1945.

Wordsworth, William. *Selected Poems and Prefaces.* Ed. Jack Stillinger. Boston: Houghton Mifflin, 1965.

Remembering Scott_____

Budd Schulberg

I felt a strange sense of unreality—as if I were in a dream—attending the first International F. Scott Fitzgerald Conference in 1992. But mainly it was Scott's dream that I was experiencing fifty-two years after (how vivid it still seems) being with him in his little apartment just off Sunset Boulevard and asking him to inscribe a book for me, a book I loved called *Tender Is the Night*.

Some memories dim, but not the ones I hold of him: talking to him about the work he was involved in then, *The Last Tycoon*, and seeing him in very modest surroundings compared to the glamorous Hollywood everyone read about—the great mansions in Beverly Hills, the stars, the glitter, and the big cars. His was a very modest place just around the corner from Schwab's Drugstore. Feeling the struggle that Scott was enduring, I couldn't help wondering if he'd make it—and what would happen to him if he didn't.

That was the miracle, for me to be standing at the conference delivering an account of my memories of Scott, flashing back, with the young me of my midtwenties standing beside me, leaning over Scott's shoulder to read something he had just written. To me it was miraculous that so many years later, after the kind of despair that Scott had expressed to me, we would gather for what I can only consider a Fitzgerald Festival. God knows, it was well earned—and hard-earned. It was a celebration of the remarkable gift that this man had and that too many overlooked at the time of his death.

This fate seems to be the cross that too many artists have had to carry. Of course Van Gogh comes to mind, but I think also of Melville's *Moby-Dick*. In an anthology of famous American writers published around 1900, there was no mention of Melville. Exactly the same thing happened to Scott. A number of studies of American novelists published in the early 1940s neglected even to mention the name of Scott Fitzgerald.

When you think about his work, even the imperfect works—the successful but somewhat sophomoric *This Side of Paradise*, the strangely prophetically titled *The Beautiful and Damned, Gatsby, Tender Is the Night*, and the unfinished symphony of *The Last Tycoon*—I think we all sense that the special quality that Scott Fitzgerald had was one we talk so much about, and hear a little too much about before every presidential election: the American Dream. We hear a lot of glib things about the American Dream, but in reading Scott Fitzgerald you do get a sense— and maybe that's why he's come back so strong and will survive—that he was the master of the American Dream. I guess he dreamt a lot back home in St. Paul. He dreamt about getting up in the world, dreamt a lot of material dreams. The American Dream was his subject: Where do we want to go in America? The wide open possibilities of life in America. What Gatsby was able to accomplish and the money he was able to accumulate regardless of how he accumulated it. But what does he want to do with it? What does he want it to mean? What does he want to do with that dream? And why does that dream often turn to nightmare, as it did in *Gatsby*, and as it did with Dick Diver in *Tender Is the Night*? And don't think it wasn't going to happen with Monroe, the "Stahr" in *The Last Tycoon*.

The tension between the ideal American Dream and the reality was what haunted Scott. I think it haunted him personally and tore him apart at the same time that it inspired and intensified his body of work. But I leave the analysis to the devoted scholars of his overall plan. As one of the few people left who had the privilege—by odd luck, really— to know him, to work with him, and also, incidentally, to like him, my job is to relate him to you.

I liked Scott enormously almost from the moment that we met, under not the best of circumstances. I was surprised when a mutual friend of ours, our fellow novelist John O'Hara, wrote somewhere that Scott Fitzgerald was not a very likable man. I found him quite the contrary. If you had not known he was a writer, if you had not known that he had written, if you didn't admire those books, I think you still would have found him, as I did, absolutely irresistibly appealing.

Here's exactly how I met him. I was a few years out of Dartmouth College and back in Hollywood where I had been raised. I had written a treatment for a movie based on our Dartmouth Winter Carnival called, with great originality, *Winter Carnival*. My producer was Walter Wanger, the man who had sponsored my going to Dartmouth. He had also gone there, and as Hollywood producers go he was fairly literate and was considered highly sophisticated. Sophisticated or not, he told me when I came into his large office on the Sam Goldwyn Studio lot that he thought my treatment was "lousy."

"Well," I said, "I actually wasn't crazy about the idea either. I didn't see a great story. I didn't see *War and Peace* in *Winter Carnival*. I'm just trying to make a living here."

Walter said, "So I think what we'll do is—"; I thought I was being fired. But instead he said, "What I think I'll do is put another writer on it with you." That was a common practice in those days, to get two writers, often two strangers, to work together as a team. That was more common than anybody writing his own work.

I sighed and said, "Okay, well who?"

"Scott Fitzgerald," he said.

I gulped and thought to myself, "Oh my God!" I had seen him briefly with Dorothy Parker about three years before, and he had looked ghostly white and frail and pale, so I said to Walter Wanger, "Scott Fitzgerald? Didn't he die?"

Walter said, "Scott's in the next room. And he's reading your treatment."

So I went in and there was our hero, there was Scott. There was Scott Fitzgerald indeed reading his way through all of my forty-eight or so pages of *Winter Carnival*. I sat there while he finished reading it. "Well, it's not very good," he said finally.

"I know it," I said. "I know it's not very good."

"Well," he said, "Walter wants us to work together."

I couldn't quite believe it, but I said, "Fine." We talked a little just about the practicalities—how we'd meet and how we'd work.

The next day we met about ten o'clock. I told him that in the honors program in my last year of college I was able to structure my own sociology course. I chose "Sociology and the American Novel." I had read a lot of his novels for the course—almost everything he had written, including the short stories. I told him how much I admired him and what I thought of *The Great Gatsby*, which I still think is one of the most perfect short novels I've ever read. I've read it backwards, forwards, taken it apart, read the holograph, and studied his editing. I still think it's one of the most incredible works of fiction that I've ever read. And there are passages in *Tender Is the Night* that—I said it then and I say it now—are unequaled in American writing. I don't think anyone in American fiction writing has ever matched some of its qualities, especially its feeling.

Anyway, I told him I knew these books and I liked them a lot, putting it mildly. Scott was amazed. He said, "I didn't think anybody your age read any of those books. You know they're practically out of print." I think he said he'd made thirteen bucks in the previous year; he said he had only sold three copies of one and five of the other. He kept saying, "I'm surprised that anybody your age reads me anymore." I said, "I have a lot of friends that do." That was only partly true. Most of my radical, communist-oriented peers looked on him as a relic. He complained that he was having a tough time, all those books out of print. He hadn't been able to make a living in a long time. The short story market had dried up, he had been dropped at MGM, and that's why he had taken this stinking job. He could get quite a lot of money for it. I was getting two hundred a week, and Scott was getting almost two thousand a week. That was an awful lot of money, but it could end very quickly. But I'm getting ahead of my story.

Anyway, we met and met, day after day, and we talked a lot about writers and writing. We compared "his" writers with "my" writers, you might say. We talked about Steinbeck and James T. Farrell. He talked about Hemingway—he seemed fairly obsessed with Hemingway—and we talked about just about everything but *Winter Carnival*. We were having a tough time even thinking about *Winter Carnival*. We would talk for hours, and, as I said, I found him just enormously likable. I was fascinated by him, and he talked very easily and openly. After about four or five days, it reminded me of sitting around a campus dormitory room in one of those bull sessions, talking about all the things we both shared and enjoyed. Every once in a while we would say to each other, "We've got to talk about *Winter Carnival*." But it was more like an afterthought. We'd say yes, and try to get on with it. But it was difficult.

Walter Wanger called us at the end of that week and asked us how we were getting along. Scott looked at me and said, "We're getting along fine. I like Budd. We're getting along. We seem to be very congenial." In Hollywood there's almost a course in the Screenwriters Guild on how to lie to your producer. If he asks you how you're doing, you say, "Oh, great. It's great. We feel very good about it!" But the trouble started when Wanger said, "well, you'd better have an outline by the time you leave. We're going up to the Winter Carnival. We're flying out Monday." Scott said, "Walter, I really don't think that's necessary. Budd's only been out of there two or three years and he certainly knows what a Winter Carnival looks like. And I remember college parties from my Princeton days. I doubt they've changed that much. So I really don't see the need for making that trip." Walter came down on him hard: "Scott, I insist on it. You're going. You have to go." He wouldn't let him out of it. While I felt sorry for Scott, I have to admit that I was looking forward to going back to Dartmouth with Scott Fitzgerald, so I hoped he would give in. And the truth is, since he was only the hired writer and Wanger was the producer, Scott had no choice.

My father was at that time in charge of Paramount Studio. In spite of the fact that Scott had fallen on tough times and felt pretty much unread and neglected, there were still people around with enormous respect for him. My father was one of them. In fact, he was so excited that I was seeing and working with Scott Fitzgerald that when we were ready to take off on what would be an eighteen-hour flight, my father brought two bottles of champagne to the plane by way of celebration.

On the plane we went on talking and talking. Scott was telling me about Dos Passos and Edmund Wilson. And Hemingway. I don't think the whole story of Scott and Hemingway, even with everything that's been written, has ever been fully explored. Anyway, we opened the first bottle of champagne and talked on and on. After the plane stopped to refuel, we opened the second bottle of champagne. Scott was tired but excited. We seemed to stimulate each other, on every subject except the one we were being paid to write, *Winter Carnival*. Finally we landed at the old airport in New York and went to the Warwick Hotel. To this day, whenever I go by the Warwick, at Fifty-third, just off Sixth Avenue—it's amazing how, time is like an accordion; it just moves in and out—I always stop to look up at our room on the tenth floor. It was a funny little suite with a small sitting room, and we each had a small bedroom. It had a little false balcony; you could just barely step out on to it. More than half a century later, I find myself still looking up at that room where we were "incarcerated."

We stayed there into the night, trying to work. Every once in a while we'd say, "We've got to work on this story, we've got to do it!" I would say, "Scott, you've written a hundred short stories, and I've written a few; between the two of us we should be able to knock out a damn outline for this story."

"Yes, we will, we will. Don't worry, pal, we will, we will."

A couple of friends I hadn't seen since I got out of Dartmouth called me. They were just two or three blocks away, they said, and asked if I'd come out just for a short time and see them. I welcomed getting out from under my writing obligations for a while, so I went. I was gone only about an hour and came back to find on my bed a note that I'd give anything to have today. (I have a feeling it may be in one of the cartons in my attic that haven't been opened in a long time.) The note had no punctuation in it. It just said, "Pal you shouldn't have left me Pal because I went down to the bar Pal and then I came back and looked for you Pal and then I went down to the bar again Pal and I'll be waiting for you there Pal when you get back Pal." I rushed down to the King Cole

Bar at the Warwick and asked the bartender for him. I described him—nobody knew his name or anything—and the bartender said, "Oh, yeah, he was here for a while. He was getting pretty smashed. And then he went out somewhere." I asked which way he went and the customers told me east. I ran down that street and stopped in bar after bar after bar. About the third or fourth one down, I stopped at the Monkey Bar. Finally, there was Scott. I realized I had made a bad mistake, leaving him alone for an hour. Scott was pretty far gone.

We went back to the Warwick. We faced a meeting with Wanger early the next morning at nine o'clock at the Waldorf Towers. Back in our little suite in the Warwick, it was time for cold showers and trying to get that damn story together. We worked on it—ridiculous plots and more ridiculous plots. I won't go into them, but each tired plot sounded worse than the others. It's hard to write those kinds of stories, stories you don't believe in and have no interest in, just stories you try to make up—really hard. After a few hours of restless sleep, somehow we got up and went over to see Wanger.

Poor Scott! And I was in almost as bad shape by this time as he was. We'd stayed up all night. We sent down for more liquor. A dapper wide-awake Wanger asked me ever so casually, "Well, how was the trip? How was the flight?"

"Oh, fine," I said.

"Did you see anyone on the flight that you knew?" he asked.

I opened my big mouth and said, "In the back of the plane was someone I knew slightly, Sheilah Graham." She was a movie columnist I knew casually. Walter looked at Scott and said, "Scott, you son of a bitch!" There were a lot of things I didn't know, and one of them was that Sheilah was Scott's girl, and that Sheilah had, without letting Wanger know, come along on the trip.

When we got out of that fairly fruitless story conference, I said, "Scott, I'm really awfully sorry." And Scott, who, as I've said, was always nice, always human and very generous with me, said, "Well Budd, it's not your fault. I really should have told you. I should have told you about Sheilah. Sheilah was coming along on the trip, and she's staying at the Hotel Elysee which is just about a block and a half down."

We had only a few minutes to make the train. There was a Winter Carnival Special in those days, filled with the dates, eager seventeen- and eighteen-year-old children of the late 1930s, the dates of the Dartmouth boys or men panting for them up there in Hanover. There's nothing like it now. It's all past. The entire train was given over to Winter Carnival. Somehow, Scott and I got on the train. Walter wanted Scott and me to walk through the entire train to look at the girls, those beautiful young things, to get the spirit of it. Scott was not too enthusiastic about that.

Knowing a lot of writers, I've had experience with alcoholics, like Charlie Jackson whose novel *The Lost Weekend* describes their agonies and resourcefulness. They are like magicians in their ability to hide and then suddenly produce bottles. I thought about that and decided when I found Scott again that I was not going to let him out of my sight. But, by God, if he didn't have a little bottle of gin with him on the train. It was a half-pint or maybe a pint, a small bottle in his pocket. I don't know where he got it. I just don't have any idea. Maybe the bellboy slipped it to him. Walter Wanger took me aside and said, "Budd, tell me the truth. Has Scott been drinking?"

I swallowed hard and said, "Well, maybe a little bit. Not much."

Wanger said, "God damn it! His agent gave me his word of honor that if I hired Scott on this assignment that he wouldn't touch a drop. Not touch a drop." He went on: "You know Scott is an alcoholic. If he takes a drink, there will be no end to it." Nobody had told me, as they should have, that I was to take care of Scott on the trip; that should have been, I suppose, my main contribution. No one sat me down ahead of time and said, "This could happen, and it's your job to watch him."

We had a fatal weekend in Hanover. We finally made it to the Hanover Inn, which had no room for us. Someone had forgotten to make the reservation for the two of us, and Scott was muttering. (Scott may have sometimes looked as if he were falling-down drunk, but his mind never stopped. I'll never forget how amazed I was that he kept on saying very, very incisive brief things, observing an awful lot.) "We'll take the attic room, because that's where the screenwriters are usually put in Hollywood," he said. "In the system I guess that's where we belong. We'll take the attic room."

So there we were, in the attic in a bare room. It was not really a room for clients of the hotel. The furniture was a metal bed, a double-decker bed, and a small table. I don't remember a chair. We stayed there all the next day because Scott didn't want to go out and I didn't see any reason to.

The Dartmouth professor who had taught the "Sociology and the American Novel" course, Red Merrill, was a wonderful guy and a terrific fan of Scott's, so he couldn't wait to meet him. He also couldn't wait to bring a bottle of liquor along, which we then proceeded to drink. The thing went downhill. As Scott got worse and worse, Wanger was on us more and more.

There was a humorous side to our situation though. Wanger had a second unit director who was full of enthusiasm. He would come in and say, "We're ready. Goddamn it, we're ready! Just tell us where the next setup is and we'll get it for you. We'll knock the hell out of it!" He was like that. We would send him out on fool's errands, saying, "The next scene we have is in front of the Outing Club and we need . . ." "You got it!" he'd say, and out he'd run. We'd laugh, "That'll take care of Lovey"—Otto Lovering was his name—"for the next hour or so." Oddly enough, in *The Last Tycoon*, the unfinished novel Scott was working on when he died, he called him "Robinson." I called him something else, but he was the same character in my novel *The Disenchanted*.

We finally had a showdown. We had a meeting set up with the dean and the English department, with Wanger presenting us, not us, but Scott, wanting to show him off as the literary star telling the story of

Winter Carnival. We tried hard to get out of it. But there was no way we could. We went through this fiasco; it was a disaster since it was pretty obvious not only that Scott was drunk but that we had no story.

That night, in a mood of dismal failure, we went down to the coffee shop; it was humorous in a way because there were all those kids enjoying Winter Carnival, everybody was so *up*, and we were so bedraggled, so down, so worried, in despair. Suddenly, Scott started to improvise a sort of brilliant, surrealist story of an ice carnival. He just went on in a kind of trance. It was fascinating to hear. I wish I had had a tape. So many times with Scott, as I look back, I'd give anything now to have been able to tape all those talks with him. The only substitute for a tape is my memory. I'm playing it back for you now. At the end of this monologue, he was very excited. He said, "Well, what do you think of it, Budd?" It was a fascinating piece. It could have been published somewhere as a prose poem on skiing, on a romantic mysterious meeting on the slopes. But, of course, it wasn't what Wanger was looking for. I said, "Well, you know, Scott, I guess we have to go back upstairs to our room and think some more."

Arm in arm, we staggered around the corner to the front of the inn, and there was Walter Wanger in a top hat. Saturday night it was, the gala Saturday night, and he looked at us and turned colors; I guess Dartmouth green was one of them. I still remember every word he said to us: "I don't know when the next train is out of here, but you two are going to be on it!" And, by God, they put us on the Montrealer that went down to New York. Without our baggage or anything, they put us on that train, and down we went.

Next morning at seven o'clock, we got into the station. We were sleeping in roomettes next to each other. The porter came into my roomette and said, "You'd better come in and try to wake up your friend. I can't get him up, and you've only got about ten or fifteen minutes and then you go into the barn." I jumped up and ran in. Scott was really out, really sick. With the porter's help, I got him up and out on the platform. Somehow we got a cab. We went back to the Warwick. We had no bags, and we had the same clothes on that we had left in. Somehow the days had run together and we hadn't changed.

The desk clerk said, "Oh, we didn't expect you back. Have they made a reservation for you?"

"No, we just came on ahead," I tried to explain.

"Well," he said, "I'm sorry. We don't have a single room."

We got another cab but couldn't get in any hotel. We tried five, six, seven, and the same thing happened every time. Nobody would let us in. No room at the inn. Then Scott finally said to me, "Well, Budd, I know where I can get in, at the Doctor's Hospital." And that's where we went, to the Doctor's Hospital. Finally, I told Sheilah and she took care of him. After about a week or so he was able to leave and go West again.

That's the end of the Winter Carnival story, almost. I got rehired because I was the only one who knew about Winter Carnival, I guess. I worked on it with Maurice Rapf, a Hollywood boyhood friend I had gone to Dartmouth with, and with a real hack writer who knew how to put the damn thing together, and did. It came out, unfortunately, and still shows up on the late-late shows. At Dartmouth now it's become a tradition at the Winter Carnival to show it at midnight on Saturday night. The kids absolutely flip out. I mean, it beats the Marx Brothers for comedy. They scream with laughter and fall out of their seats. I've sat there with them and thought, "Oh, if they only knew. If they only knew."

One of the things that would continue to impress me in the next year and a half that I knew Scott was that he kept sending me notes, ideas for the movie. It's true, it's really true. He sent me one that said, "Don't forget how the student waiters waiting on us were talking with the students they were serving, and asking them about tests or about games and so forth while they were serving them. I think that'll be a nice touch." He would send in little notes like that. I kept seeing him, realizing that he was having a very, very hard time. He was living out in the valley, as the tenant of a very successful film comedian, Edward

Everett Horton. Horton had a big place in Encino and a small guest house over the garage with an outside stairway, which is quite common in Southern California. Scott rented that for about two hundred a month, and I used to go out and see him.

It was May of 1940, and he was struggling to make a living. He was writing those short stories for *Esquire* about a run-down hand-to-mouth screenwriter, the Pat Hobby Stories. I believe he got $250 for each one. I honestly thought, even for those days, they underpaid him. But he got $250, and I think that's how he was paying Horton. He figured if he could write a story in one day, and if he was writing one a month, that was the way he could pay his rent. I found that heartbreaking and endearing about Scott. I remember a number of times sitting down with Sheilah in the back of the Horton place as Scott would come running down the stairs all excited; he'd just finished one of the short stories for *Esquire*, and he would read it out loud to us. They were not top drawer; they were not top-level Scott Fitzgerald. But they were funny and extremely observant, like everything he did. Many of the indignities that he suffered in Hollywood, and that almost every screenwriter except the very, very successful ones suffered and, to some extent, continue to suffer out there, were expressed in those hastily written tongue-in-cheek stories.

He had a quality that to me seemed sophomoric in the best sense. How many people have said of Scott Fitzgerald that he was not a serious thinker, although much of the work, his best work, rebuts that. Somehow he held on to his creative energy, despite all of the beating down that he suffered, trying to support his daughter Scottie and keep her in college and trying to pay for his wife, Zelda, in and out of the sanitarium. He still had this amazing enthusiasm. He was like a good student, a sophomore who had just read something interesting and was eager to learn. He responded to all kinds of ideas. Maybe that doesn't sound like the popular conception of Scott Fitzgerald.

I remember one evening—and I still feel a little uncomfortable about this—I was just about to go out for dinner. It was about six-thirty, and Scott burst in; he hadn't called or anything. He simply ran into my house and said, "Budd, I've just finished reading Spengler's *Decline of the West*, and I've got to talk to you about it."

I still feel guilty about this: I said, "Scott, *Decline of the West*! We'll be here for days, and I'm late for dinner. I've just got to go. I've got to." But he wanted to talk about it. He was so full of *The Decline of the West*. Finally, I walked out. As I look back, I really can't remember where I went to dinner that night or why it was so important, and I still feel bad that I told him I just couldn't stay and talk to him about Spengler and his ideas on the decline of the West. But that's the way he was, with incredible enthusiasm that he was somehow able to maintain in the midst of the enormous struggle to survive.

Another time I went out to see him at Horton's and he was reading another rather unlikely work. Of course, this was 1939 or 1940. The left wing and the Communist Party and the whole Marxist influence were very strong. It seemed like 90 percent of the writers were either members or fellow travelers. Scott was sitting outside and I asked him what he was reading. He held it up: Karl Marx's "The 14th Brumaire." I'll never forget that either. Not only was he reading it, he was, again, all excited about it. He had this kind of adorable naivete about things that you would hardly expect from a man in his early forties. I thought of him as sixty, seventy. Of course, that's the arrogance of youth. Discounting that, he did look much older than forty-two or forty-three, which he was then. And he said, "I have to reexamine the economic relationships and the economic context of all my characters." Having left behind the Jazz Age of the 1920s, he had moved into the Marxist atmosphere of the 1930s. Since he identified me with the Marxist movement, he wanted to talk about it. He was so open, so eager, so curious.

When my daughter was born in May 1940, he had just sold his short story "Babylon Revisited" to an independent film producer, Lester Cowan. He actually sold it for nine hundred dollars and got a job writing the screenplay for five hundred a week, which was a cut in salary from what he had gotten from Wanger and from a few others, but since he barely had a screen credit his screenwriting stock was rather low. As he said at the time, he not only needed the money and felt he could write that screenplay in eight weeks, at least he had the pleasure of working on his own work and not, as he had had to do, adapt the work of other people.

The night my daughter was born he called me at the Cedars of Lebanon Hospital. When I told him she had just been born and that her name would be Victoria, he said, "Well then, in my screenplay 'Babylon Revisited' in her honor, I'm going to change the name from Honoria to Victoria." And so indeed in the "Babylon Revisited" screenplay, which I arranged to have published in 1993, the child is called Victoria. In my introduction I explain the circumstances of the screenplay; they were so typical of Scott's career in Hollywood. Cowan had paid Scott $5,000 for it. Then Cowan sold it to Metro-Goldwyn-Mayer for $100,000. They made the film and decided to change the title to "The Last Time I Saw Paris." Although that came after his premature death, once again I felt Scott had been cheated out of both money and any sort of artistic satisfaction in Hollywood.

A lot of eastern writers, famous novelists, went to Hollywood hoping to pick up the money—one can't blame them—and go back and do their own work. But Scott was different from them. I could see it, having been raised in Hollywood and having watched the many famous writers on my father's Paramount payroll at that time. Aside from the coveted paychecks, Scott had a truly serious interest in film. He went to films all the time and kept a card file of the plots. He'd go back and write out the plot of every film that he saw. He was seriously interested in the process of the motion picture and even in the art of the motion picture. He had moments when he thought it might even replace the novel as an art form.

Scott and I reacted to the *Winter Carnival* ordeal in different ways. I was fed up with Hollywood. I wanted to go away, away from screenwriting, so I went back to Dartmouth and started working on a novel, *What Makes Sammy Run?* As it turned out, Scott went to work on a novel also. In the course of our friendship, he had shown a very keen, extremely curious interest in Hollywood. He wanted to know how I grew up there, how I felt there, what it was like to be the son of a very prominent studio head, and how my father worked. He met my father, B.P., who admired him enormously.

At the end of November 1940, I went to see Scott at that little flat he had just rented—it was more convenient for him—on Laurel just off Sunset, and right around the corner from Sheilah's. Scott was in bed writing when I saw him the last time. I asked him about what he was working on, and, somewhat to my surprise, he showed me an opening chapter. I read it slowly, standing by the bed. I guess he noticed the look on my face. When I read the opening paragraph, although it was written more gracefully than I would have been able to write it, it said very much what I had said to Scott: being raised in Hollywood, you could never look at it as a glamorous town. It may look glamorous from the outside, but if you're from the inside, it's really just like any other factory town. It's very much a company town. The only difference is, instead of turning out steel or tires, you're turning out cans of film. The story of *The Last Tycoon* is narrated by a film executive's daughter, Cecelia, who goes to Bennington, which was at the time the women's equivalent of Dartmouth.

At that moment I was wondering, did Scott really like me as much as I thought he liked me, or was I just a convenient source, the son of a Hollywood mogul, you might say. B.P. and producer Irving Thalberg were often compared as Hollywood "intellectuals" and it hurt my feelings a little bit.

Scott saw the look on my face and said, "In Cecelia, I guess I did combine my daughter Scottie and you, and I hope you don't mind." Of everything I remember about him, this feeling of having been used may be the most negative, but I realize that's what all writers do. They can't help themselves. The only material they have is the material they draw from other people and the experiences they go through.

I was leaving to go East again to put the finishing touches on *Sammy* and would be back in a few months. He told me that when I came back he would show me more of the chapters that he had written.

Scott died a few weeks after that. Exactly twenty days later, Sheilah Graham called John O'Hara and me together and said that there was some thought from Scribner's we might go over the outline and try to finish the book, which was not quite half finished and still a very rough draft. Well, John and I kicked it around for a few nights and decided that we'd be crazy to do it—that it could be worse than any tilting of any windmill by Don Quixote. Having read what Scott had written even in the first draft and having read the outline of where he planned to go with it, we felt that there was a tone and a voice that no one else could possibly capture. A perfectionist, Scott would have written it over and over again, as we know from his other work. O'Hara and I admired him too much. He was a hell of a writer. Nobody could touch what he was able to do at his best. *The Last Tycoon* had to stay the way it was. It was a tragedy that he couldn't finish that book. I admired him so much because for someone with failing health to mount that kind of creative energy, to put into it the remarkable work he did at the time of his heart attack, was an incredible act of heroism.

Finally, I want to turn my attention to Ernest Hemingway and his relationship to Scott. I'm sorry to say that Ernest was really mean-spirited toward Scott, putting him down at every opportunity. I wish I could have taped some examples of Scott's ambivalence toward Hemingway. It's been remarked over and over again how Scott could be inside of a subject and outside of it at the same time, able to observe it and somehow still be in the middle of it, writing basically about himself but somehow managing to shift from the subjective to the objective, and to observe so clearly what he was actually, personally suffering. I know that was very true of his attitude toward Hemingway. In some ways he was like a starstruck child looking up to a living legend. He idolized Hemingway. He was in awe of him. He was almost afraid of Hemingway. He wondered what Hemingway was going to think about this and think about that. Scott was obsessed with Hemingway, and at the same time Hemingway did not have the grace to return the favor.

Scott Fitzgerald showed great generosity toward me and Nathanael West but also toward Hemingway. When he first found Hemingway in Paris in the twenties, Hemingway was poor and unknown. He was writing those great early short stories but was not able to get them published. It should be better known that Scott was helping to support him with a check for a hundred dollars a month, pretty good money for France in those days. Scott also fought for him. When Hemingway wrote to ask him if "you can get me away from my Jew publishers" (Covici-Friede), Scott actually got him to Scribner's. He helped him in every possible way. He became his sponsor, a rare and generous act for someone who might be considered a rival. When you read Hemingway's memoirs, like *A Moveable Feast*, you realize how Hemingway reciprocated that generosity by giving Scott the back of his hand, page after page of gratuitous put-downs. It was a heartless, mean-spirited, malicious thing that Ernest did to Scott. Scott didn't deserve it. Hemingway should have been bigger than that, although I know from many other experiences, my own as well as those of friends like the late Irwin Shaw, that it just wasn't in Ernest to be generous with people he considered his rivals or potential rivals.

I recall receiving an unexpected phone call from Scott about *For Whom the Bell Tolls*. *The Bell* was another big one for Ernest, a big moneymaker, a big critic-grabber, appearing in 1940 (when Hemingway had a large dollar sign on his forehead, an S for Success, while Scott bore the brand of Failure). Scott said, "You know, Budd, it's strange, but after all these years, from the time I first met him, Ernest hasn't learned a thing about women. He knows about me and he knows about those tests he's so crazy about, those tests of courage. But when it comes to women he still writes like a schoolboy. He's known interesting women, complicated women, but the way he writes women in *The Bell* is sophomoric. It made me uncomfortable to read it. He's really a child, a gifted child!"

His intelligence knew and understood his friend and rival's weaknesses and strengths, but his emotions left him to the very end the victim of Hemingway's emotions. He never stopped worrying what Hemingway would think of him. It was pathetic really, for Hemingway had had the gall to write to him that *Tender Is the Night* was not really a novel, since all the characters in the book were transparently Gerald and Sara Murphy and the famous people around them at Cap d'Antibes. As if readers in the know had not been able to fill in just as easily the real names for the characters Hemingway had limned in *The Sun Also Rises*!

But when Scott died, he left a lot of friends: Dorothy Parker, Donald Ogden Stewart, John O'Hara, Edmund Wilson. He had a lot of literary friends. To our consternation, the obituaries ran from condescending to downright vicious. They dismissed him as a spokesman for an age, the Jazz Age, an age that was dead, as if his own work and his own literary reputation had died with the trumpets and the saxophones of the twenties, almost like "good riddance!" To Westbrook Pegler, he was "just one of those crazy kids." It was mean and nasty. So a group of us, O'Hara and all, urged the *New Republic* to publish a special memorial issue dedicated to Scott Fitzgerald, not only in his memory but to his future. I wrote: "Despite the twin ironies that the best book that Scott wrote in the twenties had nothing to do with flaming youth, and his most profound if not most perfect work, *Tender Is the Night*, appeared toward the middle of the thirties, my generation thought of F. Scott Fitzgerald as an 'age,' not as a writer. And when the economic stroke of '29 began to turn 'sheiks' and 'flappers' into unemployed boys and underpaid girls, we consciously and a little belligerently turned our backs on Fitzgerald. We turned our backs on many things."

I'm talking now of "we" as a generation, my generation, but not of my own feeling for Scott. For in that memorial issue I'm quoting from, I noted, "Three weeks later I was up at Dartmouth, actually leaning, oddly enough, against an outside wall of the Hanover Inn where we had struggled together, when I heard that Scott was gone. The 'draft' he had promised to let me see when I returned was *The Last Tycoon*, which even in its sadly unfinished state reaffirmed Scott's high place as 'our best novelist.' 'He was writing a page a day now,' I had reported from his bedside. But it was a good page. Scott's comeback novel for the 40's was on its way."

From the final tribute in that memorial issue, I'd like to close with these words of Stephen Vincent Benét: "You can take off your hats now, Gentlemen. And I think perhaps you had better. This is not a legend. This is a reputation. Now seen in perspective, it may well be one of the most secure reputations of our century." That's the way a small group of us felt then, and that's the way I'm delighted to see that we all feel now.

From *F. Scott Fitzgerald: New Perspectives*, edited by Jackson R. Bryer, Alan Margolies, and Ruth Prigozy, pp. 3-17. Copyright © 2000 by The University of Georgia Press. Reprinted with permission of The University of Georgia Press.

RESOURCES

1896	Francis Scott Key Fitzgerald is born in St. Paul, Minnesota, on September 24 to Edward Fitzgerald and Mollie McQuillan.
1898-1908	After the failure of his furniture business, Edward Fitzgerald takes a job as a salesman at Procter & Gamble, and the family moves to Buffalo, then Syracuse, New York.
1908	Edward Fitzgerald loses his job. The Fitzgeralds move back to St. Paul.
1911	Fitzgerald attends a Catholic boarding school in Hackensack, New Jersey. He writes his first play, *The Girl from Lazy J*, which is produced in St. Paul.
1913	Fitzgerald enters Princeton University and works on productions for the university's amateur theatrical company, The Triangle Club.
1917	Fitzgerald leaves Princeton without receiving a degree. He joins the U.S. Army as a second lieutenant and begins writing a novel titled "The Romantic Egotist."
1918	While stationed at Camp Sheridan, near Montgomery, Alabama, Fitzgerald meets Zelda Sayre at a dance. "The Romantic Egotist" is rejected by Scribner's.
1919	After being discharged from the Army, Fitzgerald is hired by an advertising firm in New York. He and Zelda become engaged, but later that year Zelda breaks off the engagement. He returns to St. Paul to rewrite "The Romantic Egotist" under a new title, *This Side of Paradise*.
1920	*This Side of Paradise* is published after being accepted by Maxwell Perkins at Scribner's. Zelda and Scott are married on April 3. His short-story collection *Flappers and Philosophers* is published.
1921	Fitzgerald's daughter, Frances "Scottie" Fitzgerald, is born.

1922	*The Beautiful and Damned* is published by Scribner's. *Tales of the Jazz Age*, a collection of stories, is published.
1925	*The Great Gatsby* is published; it receives good reviews but does not sell well.
1926	A third collection of stories, *All the Sad Young Men*, is published. The Fitzgeralds travel to the Riviera.
1927	Zelda begins taking ballet lessons; Fitzgerald spends two months in Hollywood writing scripts.
1930	Both the Fitzgeralds are drinking heavily; Zelda suffers her first nervous breakdown while they are traveling in Europe.
1931	"Babylon Revisited" is published in the *Saturday Evening Post*.
1932	Zelda suffers a second breakdown after the death of her father. She is admitted to a psychiatric clinic in Baltimore and is later discharged. That same year, her novel *Save Me the Waltz* is published.
1934	Zelda suffers her third breakdown. Fitzgerald falls into deeper despair, finding himself in dire financial straits. *Tender Is the Night* is published, but sales are disappointing.
1935	*Taps at Reveille*, a short-story collection, is published. Fitzgerald's physical health declines, owing to his heavy drinking. He recuperates in Asheville, North Carolina.
1936	While living in North Carolina, Fitzgerald writes "The Crack-Up," a series of three essays published in *Esquire*. Zelda enters a sanatorium in Asheville, where she will remain, intermittently, for the rest of her life.
1937	Fitzgerald moves to Hollywood to work as a scriptwriter for Metro-Goldwyn-Mayer. He begins a relationship with gossip/movie columnist Sheilah Graham.
1939	Fitzgerald begins writing *The Last Tycoon*.

1940	The "Pat Hobby" stories are published in *Esquire*. Fitzgerald suffers a fatal heart attack on December 21.
1941	The unfinished manuscript and notes for *The Last Tycoon* are published.
1945	*The Crack-Up*, edited by Edmund Wilson, is published by New Directions. Dorothy Parker compiles *The Portable F. Scott Fitzgerald*.
1948	Zelda Fitzgerald dies in a fire at the sanatorium in Asheville; she is buried beside Scott in Rockville, Maryland.

Works by F. Scott Fitzgerald

Long Fiction

This Side of Paradise, 1920
The Beautiful and Damned, 1922
The Great Gatsby, 1925
Tender Is the Night, 1934
The Last Tycoon, 1941

Short Fiction

Flappers and Philosophers, 1920
Tales of the Jazz Age, 1922
All the Sad Young Men, 1926
Taps at Reveille, 1935
The Stories of F. Scott Fitzgerald, 1951
Babylon Revisited, and Other Stories, 1960
The Pat Hobby Stories, 1962
The Apprentice Fiction of F. Scott Fitzgerald, 1909-1917, 1965 (John Kuehl, editor)
The Basil and Josephine Stories, 1973 (Jackson R. Bryer and John Kuehl, editors)
Bits of Paradise: Twenty-one Uncollected Stories by F. Scott and Zelda Fitzgerald
    1973 (Matthew J. Bruccoli, editor)
The Price Was High: The Last Uncollected Stories of F. Scott Fitzgerald, 1979 (Matthew J. Bruccoli, editor)
Before Gatsby: The First Twenty-six Stories, 2001 (Matthew J. Bruccoli, editor)

Drama

The Vegetable: Or, From President to Postman, pb. 1923

Nonfiction

The Crack-Up, 1945 (Edmund Wilson, editor)
The Letters of F. Scott Fitzgerald, 1963 (Andrew Turnbull, editor)
Thoughtbook of Francis Scott Key Fitzgerald, 1965
Letters to His Daughter, 1965 (Andrew Turnbull, editor)
Dear Scott/Dear Max: The Fitzgerald-Perkins Correspondence, 1971 (John Kuehl and Jackson R. Bryer, editors)
As Ever, Scott Fitzgerald, 1972 (Matthew J. Bruccoli, editor)
F. Scott Fitzgerald's Ledger, 1972 (Matthew J. Bruccoli, editor)
The Notebooks of F. Scott Fitzgerald, 1978 (Matthew J. Bruccoli, editor)

A Life in Letters, 1994 (Matthew J. Bruccoli, editor)

F. Scott Fitzgerald on Authorship, 1996 (Matthew J. Bruccoli, editor)

Dear Scott, Dearest Zelda: The Love Letters of F. Scott and Zelda Fitzgerald, 2002 (Jackson R. Bryer and Cathy W. Barks, editors)

Conversations with F. Scott Fitzgerald, 2004 (Matthew J. Bruccoli and Judith S. Baughman, editors)

Miscellaneous

Afternoon of an Author: A Selection of Uncollected Stories and Essays, 1958 (Arthur Mizener, editor)

F. Scott Fitzgerald: The Princeton Years, Selected Writings, 1914-1920, 1996 (Chip Deffaa, editor)

Bibliography

Allen, Joan M. *Candles and Carnival Lights: The Catholic Sensibility of F. Scott Fitzgerald*. New York: New York University Press, 1978.

Berman, Ronald. *Fitzgerald, Hemingway, and the Twenties*. Tuscaloosa: University of Alabama Press, 2001.

_____. *"The Great Gatsby" and Fitzgerald's World of Ideas*. Tuscaloosa: University of Alabama Press, 1997.

_____. *"The Great Gatsby" and Modern Times*. Urbana: University of Illinois Press, 1994.

_____. *Modernity and Progress: Fitzgerald, Hemingway, Orwell*. Tuscaloosa: University of Alabama Press, 2005.

_____. *Translating Modernism: Fitzgerald and Hemingway*. Tuscaloosa: University of Alabama Press, 2009.

Bloom, Harold, ed. *F. Scott Fitzgerald*. New York: Chelsea House, 1985.

_____, ed. *F. Scott Fitzgerald: "The Great Gatsby."* New Haven, CT: Chelsea House, 1986.

Bruccoli, Matthew J. *The Composition of "Tender Is the Night": A Study of the Manuscripts*. Pittsburgh: University of Pittsburgh Press, 1963.

_____. *F. Scott Fitzgerald: A Descriptive Bibliography*. Pittsburgh: University of Pittsburgh Press, 1972.

_____. *Fitzgerald and Hemingway: A Dangerous Friendship*. New York: Carroll & Graf, 1994.

_____ (with Judith S. Baughman). *Reader's Companion to F. Scott Fitzgerald's "Tender Is the Night."* Columbia: University of South Carolina Press, 1996.

_____. *Some Sort of Epic Grandeur: The Life of F. Scott Fitzgerald*. 2d rev. ed. Columbia: University of South Carolina Press, 2002.

_____, ed. *New Essays on "The Great Gatsby."* New York: Cambridge University Press, 1985.

Bruccoli, Matthew J., and Jackson R. Bryer, eds. *F. Scott Fitzgerald in His Own Time: A Miscellany*. Kent, OH: Kent State University Press, 1971.

Bruccoli, Matthew J., Scottie Fitzgerald Smith, and Joan P. Kerr, eds. *The Romantic Egoists: A Pictorial Autobiography from the Scrapbooks and Albums of F. Scott and Zelda Fitzgerald*. New York: Charles Scribner's Sons, 1974.

Bryer, Jackson R. *The Critical Reputation of F. Scott Fitzgerald*. Hamden, CT: Archon Books, 1967.

_____, ed. *F. Scott Fitzgerald: The Critical Reception*. New York: Burt Franklin, 1978.

_____, ed. *New Essays on F. Scott Fitzgerald's Neglected Stories*. Columbia: University of Missouri Press, 1996.

_____, ed. *The Short Stories of F. Scott Fitzgerald: New Approaches in Criticism*. Madison: University of Wisconsin Press, 1982.

Bryer, Jackson R., Alan Margolies, and Ruth Prigozy, eds. *F. Scott Fitzgerald: New Perspectives*. Athens: University of Georgia Press, 2000.

Bryer, Jackson R., Ruth Prigozy, and Milton R. Stern, eds. *F. Scott Fitzgerald in the Twenty-first Century*. Tuscaloosa: University of Alabama Press, 2003.

Canterbery, E. Ray, and Thomas Birch. *F. Scott Fitzgerald: Under the Influence*. St. Paul, MN: Paragon House, 2006.

Conroy, Frank. "Great Scott." *Gentlemen's Quarterly* 66 (Dec. 1996): 240-45.

Cowley, Malcolm. "The Fitzgerald Revival: 1941-53." *Fitzgerald/Hemingway Annual* (1974): 11-13.

_____. *A Second Flowering: Works and Days of the Lost Generation*. New York: Viking Press, 1973.

Crosland, Andrew T. *A Concordance to F. Scott Fitzgerald's "The Great Gatsby."* Detroit: Bruccoli Clark/Gale, 1975.

Cross, K. G. W. *F. Scott Fitzgerald*. New York: Grove Press, 1964.

Curnutt, Kirk. *The Cambridge Introduction to F. Scott Fitzgerald*. New York: Cambridge University Press, 2007.

_____, ed. *A Historical Guide to F. Scott Fitzgerald*. New York: Oxford University Press, 2004.

Dixon, Wheeler Winston. *The Cinematic Vision of F. Scott Fitzgerald*. Ann Arbor, MI: UMI Research Press, 1986.

Donaldson, Scott. *Fitzgerald and Hemingway: Works and Days*. New York: Columbia University Press, 2009.

_____. *Fool for Love: F. Scott Fitzgerald*. New York: Congdon & Weed, 1983.

_____. *Hemingway vs. Fitzgerald: The Rise and Fall of a Literary Friendship*. New York: Overlook Press, 1999.

_____. "Possessions in *The Great Gatsby*." *Southern Review* 30 (2001): 187-210.

_____, ed. *Critical Essays on F. Scott Fitzgerald's "The Great Gatsby."* Boston: G. K. Hall, 1984.

Eble, Kenneth. *F. Scott Fitzgerald*. Rev. ed. Boston: Twayne, 1977.

_____, ed. *F. Scott Fitzgerald: A Collection of Criticism*. New York: McGraw-Hill, 1973.

Fitzgerald, F. Scott. *The Apprentice Fiction of F. Scott Fitzgerald: 1909-1917*. Ed. John Kuehl. New Brunswick, NJ: Rutgers University Press, 1965.

_____. *As Ever, Scott Fitzgerald*. Ed. Matthew J. Bruccoli, with Jennifer McCabe Atkinson. Philadelphia: J. B. Lippincott, 1972.

_____. *Correspondence of F. Scott Fitzgerald*. Ed. Matthew J. Bruccoli and Margaret M. Duggan, with Susan Walker. New York: Random House, 1980.

_____. *The Notebooks of F. Scott Fitzgerald*. Ed. Matthew J. Bruccoli. New York: Harcourt Brace Jovanovich/Bruccoli Clark, 1978.

Fitzgerald, F. Scott, and Maxwell Perkins. *Dear Scott/Dear Max: The Fitzgerald-Perkins Correspondence*. Ed. John Kuehl and Jackson R. Bryer. New York: Charles Scribner's Sons, 1971.

Fryer, Sarah Beebe. *Fitzgerald's New Women: Harbingers of Change*. Ann Arbor, MI: UMI Research Press, 1988.

Gale, Robert L. *An F. Scott Fitzgerald Encyclopedia*. Westport, CT: Greenwood Press, 1998.

Goldhurst, William. *F. Scott Fitzgerald and His Contemporaries*. Cleveland: World, 1963.

Gross, Dalton, and MaryJean Gross. *Understanding "The Great Gatsby": A Student Casebook to Issues, Sources, and Historical Documents*. Westport, CT: Greenwood Press, 1998.

Higgins, John A. *F. Scott Fitzgerald: A Study of the Stories*. Jamaica, NY: St. John's University Press, 1971.

Hindus, Milton. *F. Scott Fitzgerald: An Introduction and Interpretation*. New York: Holt, Rinehart and Winston, 1968.

_____. "F. Scott Fitzgerald and Literary Anti-Semitism." *Commentary* 3 (1947): 508-16.

Hook, Andrew. *F. Scott Fitzgerald: A Literary Life*. New York: St. Martin's Press, 2002.

Kazin, Alfred, ed. *F. Scott Fitzgerald: The Man and His Work*. New York: Collier, 1967.

Kuehl, John. *F. Scott Fitzgerald: A Study of the Short Fiction*. Boston: Twayne, 1991.

Latham, Aaron. *Crazy Sundays: F. Scott Fitzgerald in Hollywood*. New York: Viking Press, 1971.

Lee, A. Robert, ed. *Scott Fitzgerald: The Promises of Life*. New York: St. Martin's Press, 1989.

Lehan, Richard D. "F. Scott Fitzgerald and Romantic Destiny." *Twentieth Century Literature* 26 (1980): 137-56.

_____. *F. Scott Fitzgerald and the Craft of Fiction*. Carbondale: Southern Illinois University Press, 1966.

_____. *"The Great Gatsby": The Limits of Wonder*. Boston: Twayne, 1990.

Le Vot, André. *F. Scott Fitzgerald*. Garden City, NY: Doubleday, 1983.

Mangum, Bryant. *A Fortune Yet: Money in the Art of F. Scott Fitzgerald's Short Stories*. New York: Garland, 1991.

Mellow, James R. *Invented Lives: F. Scott and Zelda Fitzgerald*. Boston: Houghton Mifflin, 1984.

Meyers, Jeffrey. *Scott Fitzgerald: A Biography*. New York: HarperCollins, 1994.

Milford, Nancy. *Zelda*. New York: Harper & Row, 1970.

Miller, James E., Jr. *F. Scott Fitzgerald: His Art and His Technique*. New York: New York University Press, 1964.

Mizener, Arthur. *The Far Side of Paradise: A Biography of F. Scott Fitzgerald*. Rev. ed. Boston: Houghton Mifflin, 1965.

_____, ed. *F. Scott Fitzgerald: Twentieth Century Views*. Englewood Cliffs, NJ: Prentice-Hall, 1963.

Moers, Ellen. "F. Scott Fitzgerald: Reveille at Taps." *Commentary* 34 (1962): 526-30.

Monk, Craig. "The Political F. Scott Fitzgerald: Liberal Illusion and Disillusion in *This Side of Paradise* and *The Beautiful and Damned*." *American Studies International* 33 (1995): 60-70.

Monk, Donald. "Fitzgerald: The Tissue of Style." *Journal of American Studies* 17 (1983): 77-94.

Ornstein, Robert. "Scott Fitzgerald's Fable of East and West." *College English* 18 (1956): 139-43.

Oxford, Edward. "F. Scott Fitzgerald." *American History* 31 (Nov.-Dec. 1996): 44-49, 63.

Parker, Dorothy. "Professional Youth." *Saturday Evening Post* 28 Apr. 1923: 14, 156-57.

Petry, Alice Hall. *Fitzgerald's Craft of Short Fiction*. Ann Arbor, MI: UMI Research Press, 1989.

Phillips, Gene D. *Fiction, Film, and F. Scott Fitzgerald*. Chicago: Loyola University Press, 1986.

Piper, Henry Dan. *F. Scott Fitzgerald: A Critical Portrait*. New York: Holt, Rinehart and Winston, 1965.

Prigozy, Ruth. "From Griffith's Girls to *Daddy's Girl*: The Masks of Innocence in *Tender Is the Night*." *Twentieth Century Literature* 26 (Summer 1980): 189-221.

_____. "Gatsby's Guest List and Fitzgerald's Technique of Naming." *Fitzgerald/ Hemingway Annual* 4 (1972): 99-112.

_____. "A Matter of Measurement: The Tangled Relationship Between Fitzgerald and Hemingway." *Commonweal* 29 Oct. 1971: 103-109.

_____. "The Unpublished Stories: Fitzgerald in His Final Stage." *Twentieth Century Literature* 20 (1974): 69-90.

_____, ed. *The Cambridge Companion to F. Scott Fitzgerald*. New York: Cambridge University Press, 2002.

Rees, John O. "Fitzgerald's Pat Hobby Stories." *Colorado Quarterly* 23 (1975): 553-62.

Ring, Frances Knoll. *Against the Current: As I Remember F. Scott Fitzgerald*. Berkeley, CA: Creative Arts, 1985.

Roulston, Robert. "Whistling 'Dixie' in Encino: *The Last Tycoon* and F. Scott Fitzgerald's Two Souths." *South Atlantic Quarterly* 79 (1980): 355-63.

Roulston, Robert, and Helen H. Roulston. *The Winding Road to West Egg: The Artistic Development of F. Scott Fitzgerald*. Lewisburg, PA: Bucknell University Press, 1995.

Scharnhorst, Gary. "'Scribbling Upward': Fitzgerald's Debt of Honor to Horatio Alger, Jr." *Fitzgerald/Hemingway Annual* 10 (1978): 161-69.

Sklar, Robert. *F. Scott Fitzgerald: The Last Laocoön.* New York: Oxford University Press, 1967.

Slater, Peter. "Ethnicity in *The Great Gatsby.*" *Twentieth Century Literature* 19 (1973): 53-62.

Stern, Milton R. *The Golden Moment: The Novels of F. Scott Fitzgerald.* Urbana: University of Illinois Press, 1970.

_____. "On Editing Dead Modern Authors: Fitzgerald and Trimalchio." *F. Scott Fitzgerald Society Newsletter* 10 (2000): 9-18.

_____. *"Tender Is the Night": The Broken Universe.* New York: Twayne, 1994.

_____, ed. *Critical Essays on F. Scott Fitzgerald's "Tender Is the Night."* Boston: G. K. Hall, 1986.

Stone, Edward. "More About Gatsby's Guest List." *Fitzgerald/Hemingway Annual* 4 (1972): 315-16.

Tamke, Alexander R. "Abe North as Abe Lincoln in *Tender Is the Night.*" *The Fitzgerald Newsletter*, no. 36 (1967): 6-7.

_____. "Basil Duke Lee: The Confederate F. Scott Fitzgerald." *Mississippi Quarterly* 20 (1967): 231-33.

Tate, Mary Jo. *F. Scott Fitzgerald A to Z: The Essential Reference to His Life and Work.* New York: Facts On File, 1998.

Taylor, Kendall. *Sometimes Madness Is Wisdom: Zelda and Scott Fitzgerald, a Marriage.* New York: Ballantine, 2001.

Turnbull, Andrew. *Scott Fitzgerald.* New York: Charles Scribner's Sons, 1962.

Way, Brian. *F. Scott Fitzgerald and the Art of Social Fiction.* London: Edward Arnold, 1980.

West, James L. W., III. "Fitzgerald Explodes His Heroine." *Princeton University Library Chronicle* 49 (1988): 159-65.

_____. *The Making of "This Side of Paradise."* Philadelphia: University of Pennsylvania Press, 1983.

Wilson, Edmund. *The Shores of Light: A Literary Chronicle of the Twenties and Thirties.* 1952. Boston: Northeastern University Press, 1985.

Yates, Donald A. "The Road to 'Paradise': Fitzgerald's Literary Apprenticeship." *Modern Fiction Studies* 7 (1961): 19-31.

CRITICAL INSIGHTS

About the Editor

Don Noble has been the host of the Emmy-nominated Alabama Public Television literary interview show *Bookmark* since 1988. Since 2002 his weekly reviews of fiction and nonfiction, mainly southern, have been broadcast on Alabama Public Radio. His most recent edited books include Salem Press's Critical Insights volumes on *To Kill a Mockingbird*, by Harper Lee (2010), and on John Steinbeck (2011); *A State of Laughter: Comic Fiction from Alabama* (2008); *Climbing Mt. Cheaha: Emerging Alabama Writers* (2004); and *Zelda and Scott/Scott and Zelda: New Writings on Their Works, Lives, and Times* (2005). He is also the editor of *Hemingway: A Revaluation* (1983), *The Steinbeck Question: New Essays in Criticism* (1993), *The Rising South* (with Joab L. Thomas; 1976), and *A Century Hence*, by George Tucker (1977). His reviews, essays, and interviews have appeared in numerous periodicals over the past forty years, and he has written introductions to several books, most recently a reissue of William Cobb's *Coming of Age at the Y* (2008). He serves on the board of directors of the Alabama Humanities Foundation and is an honorary lifetime member of the Alabama Writers' Forum. He holds a B.A. and an M.A. from the State University of New York-Albany. After receiving a Ph.D. from the University of North Carolina, Chapel Hill, Noble joined the English Department at the University of Alabama in 1969 and is now Professor Emeritus of English. He has been a Senior Fulbright Lecturer in the former Yugoslavia (1983-1984) and Romania (1991-1992) and has been a faculty member and director of the Alabama in Oxford Program and director of the Alabama in Ireland Program. He has been inducted into the international scholars' society Phi Beta Delta. In 2000, Noble received the Eugene Current-Garcia Award for Alabama's Distinguished Literary Scholar. With Brent Davis, he received a regional Emmy in 1996 for Excellence in Screenwriting for the documentary *I'm in the Truth Business: William Bradford Huie*.

About *The Paris Review*

The Paris Review is America's preeminent literary quarterly, dedicated to discovering and publishing the best new voices in fiction, nonfiction, and poetry. The magazine was founded in Paris in 1953 by the young American writers Peter Matthiessen and Doc Humes, and edited there and in New York for its first fifty years by George Plimpton. Over the decades, the *Review* has introduced readers to the earliest writings of Jack Kerouac, Philip Roth, T. C. Boyle, V. S. Naipaul, Ha Jin, Ann Patchett, Jay McInerney, Mona Simpson, and Edward P. Jones, and published numerous now classic works, including Roth's *Goodbye, Columbus*, Donald Barthelme's *Alice*, Jim Carroll's

Basketball Diaries, and selections from Samuel Beckett's *Molloy* (his first publication in English). The first chapter of Jeffrey Eugenides's *The Virgin Suicides* appeared in the *Review*'s pages, as well as stories by Rick Moody, David Foster Wallace, Denis Johnson, Jim Crace, Lorrie Moore, and Jeanette Winterson.

The Paris Review's renowned Writers at Work series of interviews, whose early installments include legendary conversations with E. M. Forster, William Faulkner, and Ernest Hemingway, is one of the landmarks of world literature. The interviews received a George Polk Award and were nominated for a Pulitzer Prize. Among the more than three hundred interviewees are Robert Frost, Marianne Moore, W. H. Auden, Elizabeth Bishop, Susan Sontag, and Toni Morrison. Recent issues feature conversations with Salman Rushdie, Joan Didion, Norman Mailer, Kazuo Ishiguro, Marilynne Robinson, Umberto Eco, Annie Proulx, and Gay Talese. In November 2009, Picador published the final volume of a four-volume series of anthologies of *Paris Review* interviews. *The New York Times* called the Writers at Work series "the most remarkable and extensive interviewing project we possess."

The Paris Review is edited by Philip Gourevitch, who was named to the post in 2005, following the death of George Plimpton two years earlier. A new editorial team has published fiction by André Aciman, Colum McCann, Damon Galgut, Mohsin Hamid, Uzodinma Iweala, Gish Jen, Stephen King, James Lasdun, Padgett Powell, Richard Price, and Sam Shepard. Poetry editors Charles Simic, Meghan O'Rourke, and Dan Chiasson have selected works by John Ashbery, Kay Ryan, Billy Collins, Tomaž Šalamun, Mary Jo Bang, Sharon Olds, Charles Wright, and Mary Karr. Writing published in the magazine has been anthologized in *Best American Short Stories* (2006, 2007, and 2008), *Best American Poetry*, *Best Creative Non-Fiction*, the Pushcart Prize anthology, and *O. Henry Prize Stories*.

The magazine presents two annual awards. The Hadada Award for lifelong contribution to literature has recently been given to Joan Didion, Norman Mailer, Peter Matthiessen, and in 2009, John Ashbery. The Plimpton Prize for Fiction, awarded to a debut or emerging writer brought to national attention in the pages of *The Paris Review*, was presented in 2007 to Benjamin Percy, to Jesse Ball in 2008, and to Alistair Morgan in 2009.

The Paris Review was a finalist for the 2008 and 2009 National Magazine Awards in fiction, and it won the 2007 National Magazine Award in photojournalism. The *Los Angeles Times* recently called *The Paris Review* "an American treasure with true international reach."

Since 1999 *The Paris Review* has been published by The Paris Review Foundation, Inc., a not-for-profit 501(c)(3) organization.

The Paris Review is available in digital form to libraries worldwide in selected academic databases exclusively from EBSCO Publishing. Libraries can contact EBSCO at 1-800-653-2726 for details. For more information on *The Paris Review* or to subscribe, please visit: www.theparisreview.org.

Don Noble has been the host of the Emmy-nominated Alabama Public Television literary interview show *Bookmark* since 1988. His most recent edited books are *A State of Laughter: Comic Fiction from Alabama* (2008), *Climbing Mt. Cheaha: Emerging Alabama Writers* (2004), and *Zelda and Scott/Scott and Zelda: New Writings on Their Works, Lives, and Times* (2005). He is also the editor of *Hemingway: A Revaluation* (1983), *The Steinbeck Question: New Essays in Criticism* (1993), *The Rising South* (with Joab L. Thomas; 1976), and *A Century Hence*, by George Tucker (1977).

Jill B. Gidmark was Morse-Alumni Distinguished Professor of Literature and Writing at the University of Minnesota.

Elizabeth Gumport is an MFA candidate at Johns Hopkins University. Her writing has appeared or is forthcoming in *Canteen*, the *New York Observer*, *n+1*, and *The Believer.*

Jennifer Banach is a writer and independent scholar from Connecticut. She has served as the Contributing Editor of *Bloom's Guides: Heart of Darkness* (2009) and *Bloom's Guides: The Glass Menagerie* (2007) and is the author of *Bloom's How to Write About Tennessee Williams* (2009) and *Understanding Norman Mailer* (2010). She has also composed teaching guides to international literature for Random House's Academic Resources division and has contributed to numerous literary reference books for academic publishers such as Facts On File, Inc., and Oxford University Press on topics ranging from Romanticism to contemporary literature. Her work has appeared in academic and popular venues alike; her fiction and nonfiction have appeared under the *Esquire* banner. She is a member of the Association of Literary Scholars and Critics.

Suzanne del Gizzo is Assistant Professor of English at Chestnut Hill College, where she teaches courses in American literature and culture, gender studies, and film. She has published articles and reviews in journals such as *Modern Fiction Studies*, *The F. Scott Fitzgerald Review*, *The Hemingway Review*, and the *Journal of the History of Sexuality.* She also serves as a Trustee of the Hemingway Foundation and Society.

Cathy W. Barks is Associate Director of the Honors College at the University of Maryland, where she teaches American literature. She is coeditor, with Jackson R. Bryer, of *Dear Scott, Dearest Zelda: The Love Letters of F. Scott and Zelda Fitzgerald* (2002) and compiles the annual F. Scott Fitzgerald bibliography for *The F. Scott Fitzgerald Review.* She serves on the board of the F. Scott Fitzgerald Society.

Matthew J. Bolton is Professor of English at Loyola School in New York City, where he also serves as the Dean of Students. He received his doctor of philosophy degree in English from the Graduate Center of the City University of New York (CUNY) in 2005. His dissertation at the university was titled "Transcending the Self in Robert Browning and T. S. Eliot." Prior to attaining his Ph.D. at CUNY, he also earned a master of philosophy degree in English (2004) and a master of science degree in English education (2001). He did his undergraduate work at the State University of New York at Binghamton, where he studied English literature.

Kirk Curnutt is Chair of the English Department at Troy University in Alabama, where he teaches nineteenth- and twentieth-century American literature. He has published many volumes of literary criticism and fiction. *Breathing Out the Ghost* (2008), his first novel, has earned him several honors, including the bronze IPPY. He is also the recipient of a 2007-2008 Alabama State Arts Council literary fellowship.

Ruth Prigozy is Professor of English at Hofstra University and Executive Director of the F. Scott Fitzgerald Society. Her publications include *F. Scott Fitzgerald: An Illustrated Life* (2004). She has also served as editor for *The Cambridge Companion to F. Scott Fitzgerald* (2002), *F. Scott Fitzgerald: New Perspectives* (2000), and the Oxford University Press edition of *The Great Gatsby* (1998), and as coeditor for *F. Scott Fitzgerald in the Twenty-first Century* (2003). Her critical essays have appeared in *The Hemingway Review, Twentieth Century Literature*, and *Literature Film Quarterly*.

Scott Donaldson is Emeritus Professor of English at the College of William and Mary, where he taught for more than twenty-five years. A leading literary biographer of twentieth-century American authors, he has published *John Cheever: A Biography* (1988), *Fool for Love: F. Scott Fitzgerald* (1983), and *By Force of Will: The Life and Art of Ernest Hemingway* (1977). He has served on the board of the Hemingway Foundation/Society and also as the organization's president from 2000 to 2002. His most recent work is *Fitzgerald and Hemingway: Works and Days* (2009).

Edwin S. Fussell was Emeritus Professor of Literature at the University of California, San Diego. His teaching and writings centered on nineteenth-century literature, particularly the American novel and American poetry. He is the author of *The Catholic Side of Henry James* (1994), *Lucifer in Harness: American Meter, Metaphor, and Diction* (1973), and *Frontier: American Literature and the American West* (1966).

Michael K. Glenday is Honorary Research Affiliate in the Department of Literature at the Open University, United Kingdom. He is a founding coeditor of *The F. Scott Fitzgerald Review* and has authored and edited many books, including *F. Scott Fitzgerald* (2009), *American Mythologies: Essays on Contemporary Literature* (2005), *Norman Mailer* (1995), and *Saul Bellow and the Decline of Humanism* (1990).

James H. Meredith is a former Lieutenant Colonel and Professor of English at the United States Air Force Academy. His writings center on such literary figures as Joseph Heller, F. Scott Fitzgerald, Ernest Hemingway, and Stephen Crane. He has served on the boards of several literary societies and is the author of *Understanding the Literature of World War II* (1999).

Michael Reynolds was Professor of English at North Carolina State University in Raleigh. As founder and president of the Hemingway Foundation and Society, he was most noted for his five-volume biography of Ernest Hemingway. His books include *Hemingway's Reading, 1910-1940* (1981) and *Hemingway's First War: The Making of "A Farewell to Arms"* (1976).

Milton R. Stern was Dean Emeritus of University Extension at the University of California, Berkeley, for twenty years. He also served as a visiting fellow of the Institute of Studies and as a faculty associate of the Center for Studies in Higher Education at Berkeley. An advocate for the theory of continuing education, he coined the term "sixty-year curriculum" to stress the importance of constant learning. His efforts have been recognized with honorary degrees from three universities and various awards.

Lionel Trilling was Professor of English at Columbia University and a renowned American literary writer and critic. As a member of the New York Intellectuals and frequent contributor to the *Partisan Review*, he published many collections of literary essays, such as *Speaking of Literature and Society* (1980), *A Gathering of Fugitives* (1956), *The Opposing Self: Nine Essays in Criticism* (1955), and *E. M. Forster: A Study* (1943).

Morris Dickstein is Distinguished Professor of English at the Graduate Center of the City University of New York and senior fellow and the founder of the Center for the Humanities. His publications include *A Mirror in the Roadway: Literature and the Real World* (2005) and *Leopards in the Temple: The Transformation of American Fiction, 1945-1970* (2002). His most recent book is *Dancing in the Dark: A Cultural History of the Great Depression* (2009). He served as president of the Association of Literary Scholars and Critics in 2006-2007.

Budd Schulberg was an American screenwriter, novelist, and television producer. He is recognized for his Academy Award-winning screenplay of *On the Waterfront* and his screenplay for *A Face in the Crowd*. His novels include *The Disenchanted* (1950) and *What Makes Sammy Run?* (1941), and he was a sportswriter and correspondent for *Sports Illustrated*.

Acknowledgments _____

"F. Scott Fitzgerald" by Jill B. Gidmark. From *Cyclopedia of World Authors, Fourth Revised Edition*, pp. 1032-1034. Copyright © 2004 by Salem Press, Inc. Reprinted with permission of Salem Press.

"The *Paris Review* Perspective" by Elizabeth Gumport. Copyright © 2011 by Elizabeth Gumport. Special appreciation goes to Christopher Cox, Nathaniel Rich, and David Wallace-Wells, editors at *The Paris Review*.

"Youth Culture and the Spectacle of Waste: *This Side of Paradise* and *The Beautiful and Damned*" by Kirk Curnutt. From *F. Scott Fitzgerald in the Twenty-first Century*, edited by Jackson R. Bryer, Ruth Prigozy, and Milton R. Stern, pp. 79-103. Copyright © 2003 by University of Alabama Press. Reprinted with permission of the University of Alabama Press.

"F. Scott and Zelda Fitzgerald in American Popular Culture" by Ruth Prigozy. From *Zelda and Scott/Scott and Zelda: New Writings on Their Works, Lives, and Times*, edited by Donald R. Noble, pp. 63-91. Copyright © 2005 by Whitston Publishing. Reprinted with permission of Whitston Publishing.

"Scott Fitzgerald's Romance with the South" by Scott Donaldson. From *The Southern Literary Journal* 5 (1973): 3-18. Copyright © 1973 by the Department of English and Comparative Literature of the University of North Carolina at Chapel Hill. Published by the University of North Carolina Press. Used by permission of the publisher. www.uncpress.unc.edu

"Fitzgerald's Brave New World" by Edwin S. Fussell. From *ELH, Journal of English Literary History* 19.4 (1952): 291-306. Copyright © 1952 by The Johns Hopkins University Press. Reprinted with permission of The Johns Hopkins University Press.

"American Riviera: Style and Expatriation in *Tender Is the Night*" by Michael K. Glenday. From *Twenty-first Century Readings of "Tender Is the Night,"* edited by William Blazek and Laura Rattray, pp. 143-159. Copyright ©2007 by Liverpool University Press. Reprinted with permission of Liverpool University Press.

"*Tender Is the Night* and the Calculus of Modern War" by James H. Meredith. From *Twenty-first Century Readings of "Tender Is the Night,"* edited by William Blazek and Laura Rattray, pp. 192-203. Copyright © 2007 by Liverpool University Press. Reprinted with permission of Liverpool University Press.

"A Stricken Field: Hemingway, Fitzgerald, and Medievalism During the Thirties" by Michael Reynolds. From *Zelda and Scott/Scott and Zelda: New Writings on Their Works, Lives, and Times*, edited by Donald R. Noble, pp. 131-145. Copyright © 2005 by Whitston Publishing. Reprinted with permission of Whitston Publishing.

"Will the Real Pat Hobby Please Stand Up?" by Milton R. Stern. From *New Essays on F. Scott Fitzgerald's Neglected Stories*, edited by Jackson R. Bryer, pp. 305-337.

Index